careers around the world

Companies are becoming more global and international, and commerce and information flow seamlessly across national borders. In addition, modernization, rapid technological change, an increasingly (shared) global culture, and shifting socio-demographic values have created conditions in which career stability is more threatened, while the importance of managing the career well is paramount. But what do we know about careers in different contexts and how those career experiences vary in different regions and countries of the world?

The goal of this book is to develop new understandings of career from the vantage point of those who live in diverse cultures and who belong to different generations.

Careers Around the World explores the very meaning of: What is a career for individuals in different countries, cultures, professions, and age groups? What does career success mean for people around the world? What are key career transitions, and how are they best managed in different cultures? As those questions have not yet been investigated in the literature of careers across cultures and generations, the authors have taken an approach that led to hearing the answers directly from working people around the globe. This book presents the answers to these questions from each of the seven major cultural regions of the world and the practical implications of these differences for those who manage human resources in organizations that cross national boundaries, as well as those who advise on careers.

Jon P. Briscoe is Associate Professor of Management at Northern Illinois University. Jon is a Co-Founder and the Director of the Cross-Cultural Collaboration on Contemporary Careers (The "5C Group") whose research forms the basis for this book. A graduate of Boston University's Graduate School of Management, Jon has served as Chair of the Careers Division of the Academy of Management. In addition to careers in different cultures, Jon's research focuses on self-directed career management, management and leadership development, and value-expression in the workplace. He has published several scholarly journal articles and book chapters, and regularly presents his work internationally.

Douglas T. (Tim) Hall is Morton H. and Charlotte Friedman Professor in Management in the Organizational Behavior Department of the Boston University School of Business.

His areas of research interest are career development, leadership development, executive succession planning, and work–life integration. He is the author of the books *Career Management and Work–Life Integration* (with Brad Harrington, Sage, 2007), *Careers In and Out of Organizations* (Sage, 2002) and *The Career Is Dead—Long Live the Career: A Relational Approach to Careers* (Jossey-Bass, 1996).

Wolfgang Mayrhofer is Professor of Organisational Behaviour and Management at Vienna University of Economics and Business, Austria. He has authored, co-authored or co-edited over 21 books, including *European Human Resource Management: Evidence of Convergence?* (with Chris Brewster and Michael Morley, Heinemann, 2003) and *Managing Human Resources in Europe* (Routledge, 2006). In addition, he has contributed over 100 book chapters and articles in peer-reviewed journals. His research focuses on comparative perspectives in human resource management and leadership, careers, and social systems theory and management.

careers around the world

individual and contextual perspectives

editors

jon p. briscoe
douglas t. hall
wolfgang mayrhofer

Routledge
Taylor & Francis Group

NEW YORK AND LONDON

First published 2012
by Routledge
711 Third Avenue, New York, NY 10017

by Routledge
2 Park Square, Milton Park, Abingdon, Oxon OX14 4RN

Routledge is an imprint of the Taylor & Francis Group, an informa business

© 2012 Taylor & Francis

Library of Congress Cataloging in Publication Data
Careers around the world / Jon P. Briscoe, Douglas T. Hall, Wolfgang Mayrhofer, editors.
   p. cm.
   1. Occupations. 2. Vocational guidance. I. Briscoe, Jon P.
II. Hall, Douglas T., 1940–
III. Mayrhofer, Wolfgang.
HF5381.C267 2011
331.702—dc22
2011003234

ISBN: 978–0–415–87141–9 (hbk)
ISBN: 978–0–415–87142–6 (pbk)
ISBN: 978–0–203–86642–9 (ebk)

Typeset in Minion
by Swales & Willis Ltd, Exeter, Devon

Printed and bound in the United States of America on acid-free paper by Edwards Brothers

SUSTAINABLE FORESTRY INITIATIVE
Certified Fiber Sourcing
www.sfiprogram.org

Contents

Figures

Tables

Contributors

Jon P. Briscoe is Associate Professor of Management at Northern Illinois University. He received his doctorate in business administration from Boston University and has been a Visiting Professor at the University of Utah. His primary research interests involve self-directed careers and how people and organizations in different countries understand and manage careers. He also has active research, teaching and consulting interests in leadership and leadership development. He is former Chair of the Careers Division of the Academy of Management. Email: jpbriscoe@aol.com

Katharina Chudzikowski works as Assistant Professor for the Interdisciplinary Group for Management and Organizational Behavior at the Vienna University of Economics and Business (WU), Vienna, Austria. Her current research interests include career research from various perspectives. She is particularly interested in careers over time, career transitions, and careers in different cultural and organizational contexts. Her work on careers in different settings has appeared in book chapters and journals (e.g. *Journal of Occupational and Organizational Psychology*). Email: katharina.chudzikowski@wu.ac.at

Ociel Colorado is Professor at the International Business Department of Tecnológicode Monterrey in Monterrey, Mexico. He is currently pursuing his doctoral studies at Grenoble Ecole de Management in Grenoble, France. His research interests are focused on the cross-cultural aspects of doing business in emerging economies. He has co-authored several articles for arbitrated congresses and is the author of a master's thesis focused on the conception of career success among Mexican employees. E-mail: ociel.colorado@itesm.mx

Barbara Demel earned her doctoral degree in organizational behavior and is a Research Associate and Lecturer at the Institute of Management and Organizational Behavior at the Vienna University of Economics and Business (WU), Vienna, Austria. Since August 2010 she has worked as a consultant in talent management for Deloitte Human Capital. In her time as a researcher she received several scholarships and awards, e.g. Best International Paper Award by the Careers Division at the Academy of Management Conference 2009. Her main research interests include careers and career success of expatriates and flexpatriates. Email: barbara.demel@gmx.net

Michael Dickmann is Professor for International Human Resource Management (HRM) and the Director of Cranfield University's executive master's program in international HRM. His research focuses on human resource strategies, structures and processes of multinational organizations, global mobility and careers. He has published in key academic and professional journals, and is the lead author of two recent Routledge books on international HRM and global careers. He has worked as a consultant for the United Nations, governments, humanitarian agencies and multinational corporations. Email: m.dickmann@cranfield.ac.uk

Douglas T. (Tim) Hall is the Morton H. and Charlotte Friedman Professor of Management in the School of Management at Boston University and Faculty Director of the MBA program. He was recently a Visiting Professor at IESE Business School in Barcelona. His research deals with careers, work–life dynamics and leadership development. Email: dthall@bu.edu

Afam Ituma is a Senior Lecturer at Bournemouth Business School, Bournemouth University. His research interests include career dynamics and career benefits of the MBA in different national contexts. His work is characterized by a strong theoretical emphasis on the importance of societal institutions in shaping career dynamics. His work has been published in journals such as *Human Relations, International HRM Journal, Personnel Review, International Journal of Management Education, Journal of Management Development* and *Career Development International*. Email: afamituma@googlemail.com

Svetlana N. Khapova is Associate Professor of Career Studies and Director of Doctoral Education at VU University Amsterdam, The Netherlands. She also holds a Visiting Professor position at ESMT—European School of Management and Technology in Berlin, Germany. She is Chair-Elect of the Careers Division of the Academy of Management. Her research interests center on the career behaviors of contemporary employees and their implications for organizations and society at large. Her work has been published in numerous journals and edited volumes. Email: skhapova@feweb.vu.nl

Mireia Las Heras is a Professor at IESE Business School, University of Navarra, Spain. She is an industrial engineer by training, and holds an MBA from IESE Business School and a doctorate in business administration from Boston University. She has published and researched on work/family issues around the world, on women's leadership and on career development. She is a consultant and a personal coach. Email: mlasheras@iese.edu

Wolfgang Mayrhofer is Professor of Business Administration and holds a Chair for Management and Organizational Behavior at the Vienna University of Economics and Business (WU), Vienna, Austria. Previously, he held teaching and research positions at German universities. His research interests focus on international comparative research in human resource management, leadership and careers. He has co-edited, authored and co-authored 25 books and more than 150 book chapters and peer-reviewed articles. He regularly conducts training for both public and private organizations, especially in the area of outdoor training (www.championships.at). Email: wolfgang.mayrhofer@wu.ac.at

Biljana Bogićević Milikić is Professor of Organizational Design and Behavior and Human Resource Management at the Faculty of Economics, University of Belgrade, Serbia. Her research interests focus on comparative research in human resource management and cross-cultural management. Biljana has authored and co-authored three books and more than 90 book chapters and peer-reviewed articles. She regularly conducts training for both public and private organizations and is involved in a number of reform projects led by international organizations in Serbia. Email: bbiljana@eunet.rs

Jorge-Vinicio Murillo is a Professor of Management at EARTH University and a Senior Researcher at INCAE Business School in Costa Rica. His research work includes studies of corporative social responsibility, competitiveness, alliances among small enterprises and strategies of the agribusiness sector in Latin America. He holds an MBA degree with a subfield in sustainable development from INCAE Business School. Email: jorge.murillo@incae.edu

Enrique Ogliastri (Ph.D., Northwestern) teaches at INCAE and IE Business Schools (Costa Rica and Spain). He taught at Universidad de los Andes (Bogotá) for 25 years and has been visiting faculty at Harvard (1980–84), Ajiken (Tokyo, 1990) and France (ESC Toulouse, Nancy University, 1997, 1999). He had a leading role in two major international collaborative research projects (GLOBE and SEKN). His current research focuses on intercultural negotiations, careers and the management of non-profits in Latin America. He has published 18 books.

Emma Parry is Principal Research Fellow in Human Resource Management at Cranfield School of Management, UK. She has conducted research across the whole spectrum of HRM, but her particular research interests are in age and generational diversity, international comparative HRM, e-HRM and HRM in the voluntary sector. She is the Co-ordinator of Cranet, a network of academics worldwide that conducts research into comparative HRM. She has authored numerous publications and is a regular speaker at academic conferences. Email: emma.parry@cranfield.ac.uk

Asya Pazy is Professor of Management at the Leon Recanati Graduate School of Business Administration, Tel Aviv University, Israel. Her research interests include human resource management and career development, negotiation and social exchange processes in organizations. Her publications have appeared in journals such as *Personnel Psychology, Journal of Personality and Social Psychology, Organizational Behavior and Human Decision Processes, Human Relations, Applied Psychology—An International Review, Journal of Organizational Behavior* and *Journal of Management.* Email: asyap@tau.ac.il

Astrid Reichel works as an Assistant Professor in the Department of Management at the Vienna University of Economics and Business (WU), Vienna, Austria. She received her master's and doctoral degrees in business and social sciences from the University of Vienna. Her research focuses on international and comparative human resource management, status and power of HRM and careers. Her work is published in international peer-reviewed journals such as the *International Journal of Human Resource Management, Human Resource Management Review* and *Gender in Management.* Email: astrid.reichel@wu.ac.at

Dana Shefer earned her BA degree in psychology and business management from Tel Aviv University, and an M.Ed. in special education from Bar Ilan University. She is involved in the 5C project as a research assistant, and also works with special needs children. Email: danashefer@gmail.com

Yan Shen is currently a Postdoctoral Associate at the Human Resources Policy Institute of the School of Management, Boston University. She will be an Assistant Professor in the Faculty of Business of the University of Victoria from July 2011. Previously, she held teaching and research positions at Chinese universities. Her research interests center on careers, expatriation and repatriation, and developmental relationships across different cultures. She has co-authored one book and several peer-reviewed articles. Email: shenyan@bu.edu

Mami Taniguchi is a Professor of International Business at the Graduate School of Commerce, Waseda University and Waseda Business School, Japan. For the past 18 years, she has been investigating the relationship between leadership development processes and organizational characteristics. She is also interested in the development of global leaders in Japanese corporations and the development of local leaders in Japanese MNCs. Her book *Diversity Management*, the first book in Japanese on this topic, appeared in 2005. Email: mami@waseda.jp

Julie Unite is currently completing her Ph.D. in industrial and organizational psychology at Northern Illinois University. Prior to starting her Ph.D. she was a practicing psychologist in both Australia and the United Kingdom, where she completed her master's degree in occupational psychology. Her work and research interests include career/executive coaching, emotion and emotional intelligence in the workplace and managing career change and transitions. Email: julieunite@hotmail.com

Burger van Lill received an MA (Psychology) from the University of Stellenbosch, South Africa and D.Litt. et Phil. (Psychology) and Master of Business Leadership degrees from the University of South Africa (UNISA). He has been lecturing and doing research at a number of South African universities. His fields of interest and expertise are philosophy of science, research methodology, measurement and aspects of human resource management such as career management, recruitment, selection and talent management. He also acts as consultant to private and public institutions. Email: 21913579@nwu.ac.za

Jelena Zikic is an Associate Professor at York University in Toronto. She developed her research program and expertise in career transitions, stress and coping and career development theory. Previously, she worked internationally and held a faculty position at the IE Business School in Madrid. She has presented at numerous national and international conferences, and her work has appeared in journals such as *Journal of Organizational Behavior*, *Journal of Vocational Behavior*, *Journal of Managerial Psychology* and *Journal of Occupational and Organizational Psychology*. Email: jelena.zikic@atkinson.yorku.ca

Preface

This book is a manifestation of goodwill from many people. The research group responsible for this book, the Cross-Cultural Collaboration on Contemporary Careers (5C Group), started with a few people who shared an interest in careers and culture, but who also trusted one another and were willing to set aside personal agendas for a larger goal. Within the 5C Group, "strangers" became colleagues and friends, as they accepted invitations and took risks. Talkative and knowledgeable group members reserved their thoughts at times, inviting quieter or less knowledgeable members to bring their voices to the table. Participating in the various layers of conversation, on and off topic, in perfect or less than perfect English, was an act of goodwill. Doctoral students with distracting and pressing dissertations dedicated reservoirs of goodwill and energy to the project and gave it legs when it needed them. Administrators trusted our vision of this work even if it was not going to be a "quick hit." Perhaps most importantly, the interesting and diverse people we interviewed around the world expressed their goodwill as they shared their experiences, feelings, values and thoughts regarding their careers. We invite the reader of this book to approach it with goodwill and to transform criticism into better research and ideas into action that can help others live and work better.

Acknowledgements

We would like to acknowledge the material and financial support of the Northern Illinois University College of Business and Department of Management, Boston University's Graduate School of Management and Department of Organizational Behavior, and WU (Vienna University of Economics and Business). These and other university units of the authors of this book helped provide the means to hold essential meetings and defray travel costs. We are grateful for the vision of Routledge to explore creating a "hybrid" book rather than the standard textbook or handbook. We thank John Szilagyi, our editor at Routledge, for his steady encouragement and patience. We thank and acknowledge Julie Unite, our co-author and colleague, who served various "behind the scenes" roles in the creation and production of this book and was extremely reliable and helpful in that process.

Part I

Introduction

1

Careers Around the World

Jon P. Briscoe, Douglas T. Hall and Wolfgang Mayrhofer

A laborer in South Africa leaves his job on a work crew to work for another work crew. When asked about his definition of career success, he gives a surprised stare and says "feeding my family." A businesswoman in the U.S.A. targets achievement after achievement (succeeding) until, late in her career, she realizes she is not fulfilled or learning, and changes course. A young nurse in Malaysia follows her family's wishes to enter the field, but her heart lies elsewhere. A young businessman in Mexico is able to connect his vocational aspirations to the spiritual resonance he feels toward his family responsibilities.

These very brief vignettes paint a picture of careers that vary based upon cultural contexts, personalities, family dynamics, social class and myriad other factors. They immediately attest to the fact that "one size does not fit all" when it comes to careers. Yet in terms of theory and to a lesser degree research, we have not had a good idea of how careers vary across cultures. This matters. It matters deeply, because the career is the nexus of so many relevant contexts representing many different levels of analysis.

It is through the career that one provides immediate and basic sustenance to support self and family well-being. But it is also true that the career is a primary way of discovering and expressing one's identity (Katz & Kahn, 1978). Likewise, the career is a space where family and work lives merge (Friedman & Greenhaus, 2000; Hall & Associates, 1996). From an organizational point of view it is critical both to supply motivators to fuel the career and to extract temporal, mental and physical resources from that career. On social (Sennett, 1998) and economic levels (Cappelli, 1999, 2002; McClelland, 1967), ways of life and national well-being can depend upon the degree to which the right preparation and a given execution of careers are realized. Thus, we submit that careers' significance represents far more than might initially meet the eye of the casual observer.

Appreciating the special significance of careers, it is essential to better understand how careers play out *across* various cultures. This is what this book, and as its basis the research of 5C (the Cross-Cultural Collaboration on Contemporary Careers), is all about. As with other realms of study (especially management), much of the available theory has been created in the United States or other Western contexts. While we hardly discount this type of research, we recognize that the world is a much bigger place than one country. To do justice to the existing variety of the (career) world, it must be better understood on a local and global level for us to be effective as scholars and practitioners.

We present this book as a sort of hybrid between traditional textbooks that at times serve as high-end glossaries, and the much more academic treatise that is valuable to our academic peers but not known or accessible to others. In doing so, we offer our findings and insights to a variety of users—to professors and students, yes, but also to individuals managing their own careers; to managers, organizations and consultants trying to understand individuals and groups that they strive to serve; and to anyone who desires to better understand the strivings of people as they attempt to make sense of and optimize their working lives across time.

While the book contributors mostly work in schools of management, we believe that the findings we present and the questions we pose will be relevant to a number of fields: education, health care, vocational training, government and non-profit studies, sociology, psychology, anthropology and many others.

In the rest of this chapter we will explore briefly some major historical and contemporary understandings of the "career" as a starting-off point. Then we will explore existing international studies focused on careers as well as other important topics such as human resources. As we explore these, we will make a case for why more cross-cultural research is needed in order to fully understand how careers vary across cultures including from a theoretical and practical standpoint. Finally, as we close the chapter, we will outline the remainder of the book.

The Study of Careers: Past, Present and Future

Both careers in general and managerial careers in particular have been subject to extensive and multi-disciplinary research (Arthur, Hall & Lawrence, 1989a: 10), including views from, among others, psychology, sociology, anthropology, economics, political science, history and geography (Bird, Gunz & Arthur, 2002: 1, 9). Within this broad stream of research, typical schools of thought can be identified (Collin, 1998: 413), for example work that focuses on career choice, education and counseling (e.g. Baker & Taylor, 1998; Dagley & Salter, 2005; Fouad & Byars-Winston, 2005; Osipow, 1983) or on the link between organization and individuals (see, for example, Brousseau, Driver, Eneroth & Larsson, 1996; Hall, 1976, 2002; Schein, 1978). Basically, career research tries to understand at different analytic levels what happens when individuals travel through their professional lives. Over the past decades, there have been a number of informative overviews about career studies (see, for example, Arnold, 1997; Arthur, Hall & Lawrence, 1989b; Baruch, 2004; Becker & Strauss, 1956; Dalton, 1972; Glaser, 1968; Hall, 1987; Holland, 1973; Hughes, 1951; Ornstein & Isabella, 1993; Schein, 1980; Slocum, 1974; Super, 1957; Van Maanen, 1977).

More recently, two major benchmark books have provided a good opportunity to get an overall perspective on the field of career studies, and to determine what has been and what has not been studied.

Greenhaus and Callanan (2006) not only try to give a concise overview about key concepts and issues in career studies, but also look at cultural and international perspectives of careers. In particular they focus upon international careers and various forms of expatriation, the significance of culture and globalization for careers, and the role of multinational organizations. Gunz and Peiperl (2007) structure the field around three major themes—the individual, the context and the institution. Again, careers across cultures and global careers do play a major role. In addition to these more explicitly career-related studies, the whole field of expatriation with its link to human resource management (HRM) addresses numerous career issues, for example career aspirations, career patterns or career outcomes.

The works mentioned do address conceptual as well as methodological issues in the study of careers across national and cultural borders. In addition, there is a considerable body of research, in particular about international careers and expatriation, looking at drivers and effects of such individual careers (see, for example, Harrison, Shaffer & Bhaskar-Shrinivas, 2004; Mendenhall, Kühlmann, Stahl & Osland, 2002). Yet a closer look at these works also reveals a clear deficiency in two areas. First, there is a significant dearth of systematic *comparative* studies across different nation states and culture clusters looking at how core concepts of career studies play out in different parts of the world; in particular, what does career actually mean for individuals and how is career success conceptualized? Second, there is little if any systematic reflection of the issue of an ethnocentric and universalistic bias in career research.

Regarding the former, this lack of systematic empirical research beyond the notorious two- or three-country comparison (see, for example, the overview by Thomas & Inkson, 2007) is surprising. Cross-cultural and comparative research in general and areas closely related to career in particular such as comparative HRM or international business have a considerable history. Yet we lack sufficient insight into how country- and culture-related factors such as cultural norms, societal fabric or legal regulations shape individual career behavior and organizational career systems. Such an understanding is crucial—few would dispute that action at the individual and organizational level is strongly shaped by such factors. Existing calls for a more systematic inclusion of culture into various aspects of career research and practice (see, for example, Young, Marshall & Valach, 2007) remain largely unheard. Especially in industries or segments of the population heavily affected by globalization or doing business across national and/or cultural borders (as well as in world regions which are culturally and institutionally highly differentiated such as Europe; see Mayrhofer & Schneidhofer, 2009), more insight is needed into issues such as: conceptualizations of different aspects of careers in various countries and cultures; interplay between various contextual factors and consequences for career outcomes; and implications for HRM following from similarities and differences with regard to career.

Regarding a potential ethnocentric bias in career research, much current research seems firmly rooted in a universalist paradigm (in more detail see Brewster & Mayrhofer, 2011). In brief, it assumes that individuals and organizations ultimately are identical across the world and that there is one best way to manage them. Conversely, we argue that organizations and individuals are socially embedded in their external environment and affected by respective forces that require them to adapt their structures and behaviors to deal with their respective contexts. Context in this sense goes beyond the internal organizational context (e.g. organizational size) and includes the cultural (national culture and values) as well as the institutional (e.g. legal regulations or the respective industry) environment(s). Our view is more in line with the contextual position of HRM which searches for an overall understanding of what is contextually unique and why it is different. It is focused on understanding what is distinctive between and within HRM in various contexts, and what the antecedents of those differences are. The policies and practices of "leading-edge" companies, often the focus of universalist HRM research, are of less interest than identifying ways that labor markets work and examining what the more typical organizations are doing. As a result, researchers increasingly acknowledge that HRM is one of the management subjects in which organizations are most likely to maintain a national flavor and have a strong contextual interface. This switches the focus from best practice to best fit, especially related to different contexts. For example, for Europe, arguably a continent with a high density of different cultural and institutional contexts, many studies reveal substantive differences between various aspects of HRM in European countries (e.g. Brewster, Mayrhofer & Morley, 2004; Morley, 2009).

Applied to career studies, this type of thinking challenges much of career research. Implicitly, most career studies do assume some universalist quality of what a career "is," do regard the distinction between objective and subjective career success as a given and are on the lookout for universally applicable factors responsible for the development of careers and for career outcomes. Yet there is no convincing empirical or theoretical evidence that such implicit assumptions are conceptually sound or empirically robust.

Thus, a large part of our motivation in conducting our study was to find out for ourselves how careers are perceived both within and across varying national contexts, through the eyes of local career actors. In this way we could discover where generalizations are appropriate and where the local context(s) must be understood in order to adequately make sense of career understanding and behavior. Beyond our personal interest, this type of research strengthens the contextual perspective within career research and contributes to comparative career research, a line of inquiry very much in its infancy compared to other areas of research such as comparative HRM. Specifically, we pursue six questions in the book.

First, what is the role of culture for understanding careers? When considering contextual influences on careers, be it individual career behavior or organizational career decision making, culture is a primary candidate as the source for differences and peculiarities. Research on the role of culture for the behavior of individuals and organizations abounds (see, for example, Smith, Peterson & Thomas, 2008). Yet for careers there are, to the best of our knowledge, no systematic accounts that address how individuals in different cultures across the globe view basic issues such as, for example, what constitutes careers and career success.

This leads to a second question: What is the relative importance of culture vis-à-vis other contextual forces? This, of course, is a big issue and goes well beyond the scope of a book like this and a limited research effort. Yet we were curious to see what role culture plays and how other contextual factors come into the picture. We chose culture as the point of departure because of the rich research tradition and the face value. Yet we were aware that other factors would play a role, too. For example, lessons from comparative HRM tell us that the institutional environment will play a role. Factors such as legal regulations or the political and economic system influence organizational policies and individual decisions related to the work life. In addition, research from several areas of social science points towards the importance of generational issues. Looking at the demographic situation, world regions clearly differ in terms of their populations' age distributions. In addition, there is a growing debate about the development of a global youth culture, influenced and socialized along similar lines because of YouTube, Facebook, globally available TV series, films and music. This raises, among others, also the issue whether young people entering the labor market differ systematically and worldwide from their parent generation.

A third question focuses on careers themselves: Are different facets of careers influenced by contextual influencing factors in a similar way? It is one thing to argue, as we do as a starting point, that contextual factors, in a particular culture, make a difference in terms of how careers play out across the globe. It is another thing to strive for more detailed analyses regarding how the various facets of careers are influenced. We decided to take a closer look at career success and career transitions. Both are essential themes in career research history for a number of reasons. Career success represents the heart of much individual aspiration, assigns status in the world of work and also in society, and potentially incorporates a great variety of individual and collective meanings. Career transitions specifically are essential to understand careers in general; after all, careers are made of a series of career transitions. In addition, they typically involve individual decisions as well as decisions by actors from the focal context such as supervisors, organizations, spouses or children. This makes them a good test-bed for research, looking at the interplay between various contextual factors and individual as well as organizational decisions.

A fourth question targets core elements of research: Assuming a contextualized position, what is required from adequate theories, methods and methodologies that help in researching major career issues in culturally mixed settings? As argued above, much of career research implicitly assumes a universalist position. Yet research from other areas shows that applying existing theories, methods and methodologies in culturally different settings without adequate adaptation is highly questionable. In particular, cross-cultural and comparative research has generated a rich debate about this. In terms of methods and methodology, there is probably little that career research can genuinely contribute. The study of careers is one among myriad other research topics and, in terms of methods and methodology, has to rely on the existing set of methods and methodological positions that the respective literatures provide (see, for example, Matsumoto & van de Vijver, 2011; Schaeffer & Riordan, 2003). To be sure, even in this area the issue of using existing scales to measure core career constructs in a variety of cultural settings emerges. Yet existing literature from other areas offers some advice here (Leung, 2008). In terms of theories, this is different. Here, career research has to strongly rely on its own work. Yet theoretical approaches that explicitly take this into account are rare. Of course, there are some theoretical streams such as institutionalist theory (e.g. Djelic & Quack, 2003; Meyer & Rowan, 1977; Scott, 2001) or cross-cultural psychology (e.g. Berry, Poortinga, Segall & Dasen, 2002; Goldstein, 2008; Shiraev & Levy, 2010) that can help as a starting point. Yet it remains the task of career researchers to make use of these concepts and apply them to career issues.

A fifth question points at the use of our insight: What is the practical relevance of the insight gained by looking at core career issues across the globe? Of course, we want our results to contribute to the career discourse in academia in order to develop this further. Yet we are convinced that, ideally, career research also has some relevance beyond this. In particular, individuals interested in dealing with their own careers, counselors helping others to cope with their careers, and managers taking adequate responsibility for the careers of their subordinates should be able to profit from research efforts. This is even more necessary in a culturally mixed setting where misunderstandings, inadequate assumptions and parochial tendencies tend to flourish.

A sixth and final question relates to the way we research careers: How do we organize the process of researching career issues across cultures? We are convinced that doing career research across national borders requires a team of researchers representing the respective countries and cultures. Most importantly, they provide access to the local environment and have specific expertise about the local environment. Both are absolutely essential in the process of data gathering and data interpretation. To avoid a safari-research type of endeavor where researchers without adequate local knowledge misinterpret their findings by applying universalist categories of thinking, an international collaboration is essential (Peterson, 2001). This raises a number of issues, for example how to bring together such a group of researchers; what qualities these researchers ideally and at the minimum have to bring in; how one manages the collaboration on such a topic over time; how the issue of language is handled not only in research terms (such as how to relate to your respondents) but also in terms of the lingua franca of the team, or how the varying life and work conditions of the members of the research team influence the collaboration.

These six questions not only guided the research efforts of 5C, but also are the underlying themes of this book. Not all of them will be addressed in the same depth and length. Likewise, the structure of the book does not totally match these questions. Yet contributions to answering these questions can be found throughout the book.

Plan of the Book

While we feel that this book has implications for those who work *across* cultures, it is not our intention to cover expatriate careers or international management per se, but rather the contrasting perceptions and experience of the career *within* respective cultures. We hope that the findings will be useful to those who want to better understand any of the covered cultures individually, as well as to those who want to make comparisons and conclusions across cultures, for academic or practical reasons. As we stated earlier, the book is intended for scholars as well as students, managers, career practitioners and all others who wish to understand careers from both a local and a global perspective.

Part I: Introduction

Chapter 2, "Careers in Cross-Cultural Perspective," reviews major global theories of culture and discusses their implications for career theory and research. It serves as an overview for those wishing to begin a study of worldwide cultures and allows us to establish a framework upon which we explain our own research foundations.

Chapter 3, "The 5C Project: Our Story and Our Research," discusses the history of the 5C project and our research design. The values and assumptions we held as individuals and as a group informed the formation of the group, the way we organized ourselves across the project, and the methods we decided to utilize. We explain why we ultimately used Schwartz's theory of cultural values to select our country sample, how we selected samples within countries, our decision to use qualitative methods, and various other methodological issues that emerged across the project. As will be seen, separating the research team from the research method was neither possible nor desirable.

Part II: The Research Findings

Chapter 4, "Career Success Around the World: Its Meaning and Perceived Influences in 11 Countries," explores how research participants across 11 countries, three occupations and early and late career stages subjectively define career success. In addition, Chapter 4 examines the factors people perceive to *influence* their career success. Of course, beyond career success, these findings have substantial implications for motivation, leadership, development and so on. The chapter ends with a brief case study to help the reader reflect upon and apply the chapter findings.

Chapter 5, "Career Transitions: Windows Into the Career Experience in 11 Country Contexts," looks at how people experience significant changes in their careers (as self-defined). In doing so, it offers an opportunity to look at the "triggers" that drive career changes (internal and external), the factors that influence them, their outcomes, and the contexts in which they play out (including of course cultural ones). A case study is provided at the end of the chapter for those interested in applying the findings.

In Chapter 6, "Careers and Age: Career Success for Older and Younger Workers," we look more deeply at age or generational differences regarding career success, because the world in which careers play out has changed so much in just a few decades. While the exact reason older and younger workers differ both within and across cultures cannot be ascertained with certainty, we document in this chapter that indeed such differences exist. We explore the degree to which these differences are idiosyncratic or global in nature. Again, a case study is offered to allow exploration and application of the chapter data.

Part III: Analysis

Chapter 7, "Culture and Context: Understanding Their Influence Upon Careers," takes a deeper analytical look at the research findings in terms of cultural and institutional contexts. Looking across the previous chapters, this chapter explores the degree to which the research reflects cultural and institutional theories in a way that looks back and ahead in terms of research implications.

While practical implications of the research were explored in Chapters 4–6 respectively, Chapter 8, "Implications for the Management of People and Organizations," is devoted to discussing these issues in greater depth. We discuss implications for individual career development, for leadership development, for occupations, for HRM and for multinationals.

Chapter 9, "The 5C Project: Harvesting Lessons for Future Career Research," is the chapter in which we look back at the collective findings and reflect upon lessons for the pursuit of cross-cultural research as well as the implications for what sort of career research might be fruitfully carried out. In particular, we look at implications at the theoretical level, identifying research themes emerging from our results as well as analyzing their consequences for current and future career theories; we discuss consequences for methods and methodology arising from our study; and, finally, we reflect on how (career) research can and should be done in a culturally mixed setting, in terms of both the research team and the focus.

Part IV: Country Chapters

A paradox of this book is that one cannot understand the parts and the whole at the same time when looking at careers across cultures. In the first nine chapters we present our findings in a comprehensive way. In order to explore the 5C country samples in more detail, the 11 chapters in this section serve as "spotlights" upon individual country cultures and contexts.[1] Each chapter looks at country characteristics relevant to careers before taking a more detailed look at career success and career transitions in the national context. These chapters will be better understood if the earlier parts of the book are read, but they may be fruitfully consulted independently as well.

Country Chapters

Austria
China
Costa Rica
Israel
Japan
Mexico
Serbia
South Africa
Spain
United Kingdom
United States of America

Note

1 Malaysia is the only original 5C country for which a close-up chapter is not available in this volume. While the United Kingdom was not part of the original 5C data analyzed for the findings

chapters, the chapter authors followed our method and have repeated our research in their own country. We are happy to offer their findings here as an additional source of careers insight.

References

Arnold, J. 1997. *Managing Careers into the 21st Century.* London: Paul Chapman Publishing.

Arthur, M. B., Hall, D. T. & Lawrence, B. S. 1989a. Generating new directions in career theory: The case for a transdisciplinary approach. In M. B. Arthur, D. T. Hall & B. S. Lawrence (Eds.), *Handbook of Career Theory:* 7–25. Cambridge, U.K.: Cambridge University Press.

Arthur, M. B., Hall, D. T. & Lawrence, B. S. (Eds.). 1989b. *Handbook of Career Theory.* Cambridge, U.K.: Cambridge University Press.

Baker, S. B. & Taylor, J. G. 1998. Effects of career education interventions: A meta-analysis. *The Career Development Quarterly*, 46(4): 376–386.

Baruch, Y. 2004. *Managing Careers: Theory and Practice.* Harlow, U.K.: Pearson Education.

Becker, H. S. & Strauss, A. L. 1956. Careers, personality, and adult socialization. *American Journal of Sociology*, 62(Nov.): 254–263.

Berry, J. W., Poortinga, Y. H., Segall, M. H. & Dasen, P. A. 2002. *Cross-Cultural Psychology: Research and Applications* (2nd ed.). Cambridge, U.K.: Cambridge University Press.

Bird, A., Gunz, H. P. & Arthur, M. B. 2002. Careers in a complex world: The search for new perspectives from the "new science." *M@n@gement,* 5(1): 1–14.

Brewster, C. & Mayrhofer, W. 2011. Comparative human resource management. In A.-W. Harzing & A. Pinnington (Eds.), *International Human Resource Management* (3rd ed.): 47–78. London: Sage.

Brewster, C., Mayrhofer, W. & Morley, M. (Eds.). 2004. *Human Resource Management in Europe: Evidence of Convergence?* Oxford, U.K.: Elsevier/Butterworth-Heinemann.

Brousseau, K. R., Driver, M. J., Eneroth, K. & Larsson, R. 1996. Career pandemoniums: Realigning organizations and individuals. *Academy of Management Executive*, 10(4): 52–66.

Cappelli, P. 1999. *The New Deal at Work: Managing the Market-Driven Workforce.* Boston, MA: Harvard Business School Press.

Cappelli, P. 2002. The path to the top: The changing model of career advancement. Paper presented at the Harvard Business School Conference on Career Evolution, London, June 13–15.

Collin, A. 1998. New challenges in the study of career. *Personnel Review*, 27(5): 412–425.

Dagley, J. C. & Salter, S. K. 2005. Practice and research in career counseling and development. *Career Development Quarterly*, 53(2): 98–157.

Dalton, G. W. 1972. A review of concepts and research on careers. In J. W. Lorsch & L. B. Barnes (Eds.), *Managers and Their Careers*: S.59–84. Homewood, IL, Georgetown, OH: Irwin, Dorsey.

Djelic, M.-L. & Quack, S. (Eds.). 2003. *Globalization and Institutions: Redefining the Rules of the Economic Game.* Cheltenham, U.K.: Edward Elgar.

Fouad, N. A. & Byars-Winston, A. M. 2005. Cultural context of career choice: Meta-analysis of race/ethnicity differences. *The Career Development Quarterly*, 53(3): 223–234.

Friedman, S. D. & Greenhaus, J. H. 2000. *Work and Family—Allies or Enemies?* New York: Oxford University Press.

Glaser, B. (Ed.). 1968. *Organizational Careers: A Sourcebook for Theory.* Chicago, IL: Aldine.

Goldstein, S. 2008. *Cross-Cultural Explorations: Activities in Culture and Psychology* (2nd ed.). Boston, MA: Pearson/Allyn & Bacon.

Greenhaus, J. & Callanan, G. A. (Eds.). 2006. *Encyclopedia of Career Development.* Thousand Oaks, CA: Sage.

Gunz, H. & Peiperl, M. (Eds.). 2007. *Handbook of Career Studies.* Los Angeles, CA: Sage.

Hall, D. T. 1976. *Careers in Organizations.* Santa Monica, CA: Goodyear.

Hall, D. T. 1987. Careers and socialization. *Journal of Management*, 13(2): 301–321.

Hall, D. T. 2002. *Careers In and Out of Organizations.* London: Sage.

Hall, D. T. & Associates. 1996. *The Career Is Dead—Long Live the Career.* San Francisco, CA: Jossey-Bass.

Harrison, D. A., Shaffer, M. A. & Bhaskar-Shrinivas, P. 2004. Going places: Roads more and less traveled in research on expatriate experiences. *Research in Personnel and Human Resource Management,* 23: 199–247.

Holland, J. L. 1973. *Making Vocational Choices.* Englewood Cliffs, NJ: Prentice-Hall.

Hughes, E. C. 1951. Ambition, mobility and sponsorship. In R. Dubin (Ed.), *Human Relations in Administration:* S.240–243. New York: Prentice-Hall.

Katz, D. & Kahn, R. L. 1978. *The Social Psychology of Organizations* (2nd ed.). New York: Wiley.

Leung, K. 2008. Methods and measurement in cross-cultural management. In P. B. Smith, M. F. Peterson & D. C. Thomas (Eds.), *The Handbook of Cross-Cultural Management Research:* 59–76. Los Angeles, CA: Sage.

Matsumoto, D. & van de Vijver, F. J. R. (Eds.). 2011. *Cross-Cultural Research Methods in Psychology.* Cambridge, U.K.: Cambridge University Press.

Mayrhofer, W. & Schneidhofer, T. 2009. The lay of the land: European career research and its future. *Journal of Occupational and Organizational Psychology,* 82: 721–737.

McClelland, D. 1967. *The Achieving Society.* New York: Free Press.

Mendenhall, M. E., Kühlmann, T. M., Stahl, G. K. & Osland, J. 2002. Employee development and expatriate assignments. In M. J. Gannon & K. L. Newman (Eds.), *Handbook of Cross-Cultural Management:* 155–183. Oxford, U.K.: Blackwell.

Meyer, J. W. & Rowan, B. 1977. Institutionalized organizations: Formal structure as myth and ceremony. *American Journal of Sociology,* 83(2): 340–363.

Morley, M. (Ed.). 2009. *Managing Human Resources in Central and Eastern Europe.* London: Routledge.

Ornstein, S. & Isabella, L. A. 1993. Making sense of careers: A review 1989–1992. *Journal of Management,* 19(2): 243–267.

Osipow, S. H. 1983. *Theories of Career Development* (3rd ed.). Englewood Cliffs, NJ: Prentice-Hall.

Peterson, M. F. 2001. International collaboration in organizational behavior research. *Journal of Organizational Behavior,* 22: 59–81.

Schaeffer, B. S. & Riordan, C. M. 2003. A review of cross-cultural methodologies for organizational research: A best-practices approach. *Organizational Research Methods,* 6: 169–215.

Schein, E. H. 1978. *Career Dynamics: Matching Individual and Organizational Needs.* Reading, MA: Addison-Wesley.

Schein, E. H. 1980. Career theory and research: Some issues for the future. In C. B. Derr (Ed.), *Work, Family, and the Career:* S.357–365. New York: Praeger.

Scott, W. R. 2001. *Institutions and Organizations* (2nd ed.). Thousand Oaks, CA: Sage.

Sennett, R. 1998. *The Corrosion of Character: The Personal Consequences of Work in the New Capitalism.* New York: W.W. Norton.

Shiraev, E. & Levy, D. 2010. *Cross-Cultural Psychology: Critical Thinking and Contemporary Applications* (4th ed.). Boston, MA: Allyn & Bacon.

Slocum, W. L. 1974. *Occupational Careers* (2nd ed.). Chicago, IL: Aldine.

Smith, P. B., Peterson, M. F. & Thomas, D. C. (Eds.). 2008. *The Handbook of Cross-Cultural Management Research.* Los Angeles, CA: Sage.

Super, D. E. 1957. *The Psychology of Careers.* New York: Harper & Row.

Thomas, D. C. & Inkson, K. 2007. Careers across cultures. In H. P. Gunz & M. A. Peiperl (Eds.), *Handbook of Career Studies:* 451–471. Thousand Oaks, CA: Sage.

Van Maanen, J. 1977. Summary: Toward a theory of career. In J. Van Maanen (Ed.), *Organizational Careers: Some New Perspectives:* 161–181. London: Wiley.

Young, R. A., Marshall, S. K. & Valach, L. 2007. Making career theories more culturally sensitive: Implications for counselling. *Career Development Quarterly,* 56(1): 4–18.

2

Careers in Cross-Cultural Perspective

Svetlana N. Khapova, Jon P. Briscoe and Michael Dickmann

Introduction

Careers unfold over social space. For years, career researchers focused on the social space of careers in single organizational settings (Van Maanen & Schein, 1977). While some people's careers still play out in a traditional setting, for others today the social space of careers has gone global.

The contextual influences on careers can be separated into at least two broad categories: (a) the macro-level and (b) the micro-level influences. On the macro-level, we can think of the social and economic influences shaping national cultural arenas in which careers unfold. Let us take an example of the past decade. Owing to the world economic crisis, organizations have been experiencing restructurings and cost cuts. How have those organizational actions affected employees' careers? In the United States, cost cuts have been translated into mass layoffs. Although not an employee-oriented practice, laying off employees in times of hardship is a common practice across the U.S.A. At the same time, in the Netherlands, a strong social system and legislation that protects people's employment made it very difficult to downsize organizations. The Dutch managers had been forced to search for other remedies to downsize personnel. For example, a lucrative employee buyout has been frequently used. In Japan, layoffs or any other practices of dismissing people had not even been considered. They are considered to lead to the loss of public reputation for an organization. They would also put business and future hiring opportunities at risk. Thus, instead of dismissing employees, Japanese managers had been transferring redundant employees to other parts of the organization or to subsidiaries (Steers & Sanchez-Runde, 2010).

On the micro-level, the cultural context is affecting employees' careers through their everyday activities in office. Let us imagine a situation in an international bank in which a multicultural team of people work on a project. On this collaborative project each person will not experience personal career success. Some of the team members will be overlooked for a promotion, simply based on their communication style inherited from their culture. (For more information on cultural differences in communication see Edward T. Hall's 1976 theory of "high and low context cultures.") Consider a quote of one manager of Mexican origin, who was working on a credit and underwriting team for a bank:

> In Mexican culture, you are always supposed to be humble. So whether you understand something or not, you're supposed to put it in the form of a question. You have to keep it open-ended, out of respect. I think that actually worked against me, because the Americans thought I really didn't know what I was talking about.
>
> (Brett, Behfar & Kern, 2006)

Either through the macro-level influences represented in national legislation or practices used by organizations or through the micro-level behaviors of individuals, cultures influence and shape employees' careers. So what is culture? What are its dimensions? And what are the key theories that explain cultural differences at work? Finally, what are culture's consequences for careers? Let us now turn to answering these questions.

What Is Culture?

The word *culture* comes from the Latin verb *colere*—tend, guard, cultivate, till (Wagner, 1981). This concept is a human construct rather than a product of nature. In English, the word culture was first used in 1510 in the sense of "cultivation through education." Later, in 1805 it was used to mean "the intellectual side of civilization," and consequently "collective customs and achievements of people" in 1867.

There are hundreds of different definitions of culture in modern literature. They all represent the different disciplinary assumptions of authors about culture. However, all authors agree that culture consists of language, ideas, beliefs, customs, taboos, codes, institutions, tools, techniques, works of art, rituals, ceremonies and symbols. It has played a crucial role in human evolution, allowing human beings to adapt the environment to their own purposes rather than depend solely on natural selection to achieve adaptive success. Every human society has its own particular culture or socio-cultural system.

Hofstede (1991) posited that *culture* is like an onion that can be peeled, layer by layer, to reveal the content. At the core of the onion are *values* or, in other words, how people believe things "ought to be," what they hold dear to them. This level is invisible and is manifested through the three other layers: symbols, rituals and icons.

Trompenaars and Hampden-Turner (1997) further proposed that, next to values, cultures differ based on *norms*. These are expectations of how people should behave in different situations. They are the "right" and "wrong" of culture, and are often represented in the written law. Finally, on the outer layer of the onion there are "artifacts." These are things or material culture that reflect the culture's values and norms but are tangible and manufactured by humans.

Many culture theories have resulted from the "onion" conceptualization of culture. Among them are Hofstede's (1991) five-dimensional model of culture, and Trompenaars and Hampden-Turner's (1997) seven-dimensional model of culture. However, there are also other theories that are helpful in explaining differences among cultures, such as, for example, the GLOBE's nine-dimensional model of culture (House, Javidan & Dorfman, 2001) and Schwartz's (2006) values approach to culture.

Hofstede's Five-Dimensional Model of Culture

Hofstede (2001: 9) defines national culture as "the collective programming of the mind that distinguishes the members of one group or category of people from another." He suggests that culture is to a human collectivity what personality is to an individual. It determines the uniqueness of a human group in the same way personality determines the uniqueness of an individual. Hofstede proposes that five dimensions explain differences among cultures:

- *Power distance* refers to the extent to which the less powerful members of organizations and institutions accept and expect that power is distributed unequally. The basic problem involved is the degree of human inequality that underlies the functioning of each particular society.
- *Individualism–collectivism* describes the relationships individuals have in each culture. In individualistic societies, individuals look after themselves and their immediate family only, whereas in collectivistic cultures individuals belong to groups that look after them in exchange for loyalty.

- *Masculinity–femininity* refers to the distribution of emotional roles between the genders. Masculinity stands for a society in which social gender roles are dearly distinct: men are supposed to be more modest, tender and concerned with the quality of life. Femininity stands for a society where gender roles overlap: both men and women are supposed to be modest, tender and concerned with the quality of life.
- *Uncertainty avoidance* refers to "the extent to which people feel threatened by uncertainty and ambiguity and try to avoid these situations" (Hofstede, 1991: 113). This dimension deals with the need for well-defined rules for prescribed behavior.
- *Long-term orientation* "stands for the fostering of virtues oriented towards future rewards, in particular perseverance and thrift" (Hofstede, 2001: 359). A late addition to the initial four (Bond, 1988), this dimension represents a range of Confucian-like values and was termed Confucian dynamism. Hofstede (1991) later proposed the long- versus short-term designation as more appropriate for this dimension.

Hofstede's five-dimensional model of culture has been widely used in research by scholars representing various disciplines and is described as "probably the dominant explanation of behavioral differences between nations" (Williamson, 2002). It is noted to provide "the beginnings of the foundation that could help scientific theory building in cross-cultural research" (Sekaran, 1983: 69). At the moment of writing this chapter, a search for citations of Hofstede's original book, published in 1984, returned 14,588 citations. The later edition, published in 2001, has been cited 5,173 times.

The model, however, has not been without criticism (e.g. Signorini, Wiesemes & Murphy, 2009). Some scholars argued that Hofstede's methodology is not valid. For example, Ailon (2008) found several inconsistencies at the level of both theory and methodology. Other scholars noted that findings resulting from a survey on a company level should not be generalized to a national level. Smith (2002) has also warned against the implications of the quantitative, normative nature of Hofstede's research. He pointed out that, "if we compare culture A and culture B on some attribute, the mean scores that we achieve will tell us nothing about variability within each nation, nor will it tell us whether the particular individuals whom we sampled are typical or atypical of that culture" (Smith, 2002: 122–123). Hofstede himself (2001) cautions against ideographic interpretations, admitting that his research describes entire populations, rather than individuals. Nevertheless, thus far

Hofstede's model has been one of the most influential theories explaining differences among cultures.

Trompenaars and Hampden-Turner's Seven-Dimensional Model of Culture

Trompenaars and Hampden-Turner's seven-dimensional model of culture is another model that has been inspired by the "onion" concept of culture. The authors propose that culture is "the way in which a group of people solves problems and reconciles dilemmas" (Trompenaars & Hampden-Turner, 1997: 6). The authors suggest that problems can be separated into three categories:

- those which arise from our relationships with other people;
- those which come from the passage of time; and
- those which relate to the environment.

Based on the solutions different cultures propose to these problems, the authors developed seven fundamental dimensions of culture (five of which belong to the first category):

- *Universalism–particularism* refers to the degree of importance a culture assigns to either the law or personal relationships. In a universalistic culture, people share the belief that general rules, codes, values and standards take precedence over the needs and claims of friends and other relationships. In a pluralistic culture, people see culture in terms of human friendship and intimate relationships.
- *Individualism–communitarianism* refers to the degree to which people see themselves function more as a community or more as individuals. In a principally individualistic culture, people place the individual before the community. This means that individual happiness, fulfillment and welfare prevail and people take their own initiative and take care of themselves. In a principally communitarian culture, people place the community before the individual.
- *Specific–diffuse* refers to the degree to which responsibility is specifically assigned or is diffusely accepted. In a specific culture, people first analyze the elements individually and then put them together. Specific individuals concentrate on hard facts, standards and contracts. A diffusely oriented culture starts with the whole and sees individual elements from the perspective of the total.

- *Affectivity–neutrality* refers to the degree to which individuals display their emotions. In an affective culture, people display their emotions and it is not deemed necessary to hide feelings. However, in a neutral culture, people are taught not to display their feelings overtly.
- *Achievement–ascription* refers to the degree to which individuals must prove themselves to receive status versus status being simply given to them. In a culture with achieved status, people derive their status from what they have accomplished. In a culture with ascribed status, people derive their status from birth, age, gender or wealth.
- *Sequential–synchronic* refers to the degree to which individuals do things one at a time versus several things at once. Time orientation has two aspects: the relative importance cultures assign to the past, present and future, and their approach to structuring time. In a sequential culture, people structure time sequentially and do things one at a time. In a synchronic time culture, people do several things at once, believing time is flexible and intangible.
- *Inner directed–outer directed* refers to the degree to which individuals believe the environment can be controlled versus believing that the environment controls them. In an inner-directed culture, people have a mechanistic view of nature; nature is complex but can be controlled with the right expertise. In an outer-directed culture, people have an organic view of nature. Humankind is viewed as one of nature's forces and should therefore live in harmony with the environment.

Although popular among business practitioners, Trompenaars and Hampden-Turner's (1997) seven-dimensional model of culture has been criticized by researchers (e.g. Chanchani & Theivanathampillai, 2001). In particular, the dimensions were found to lack quite considerably in both precision and clarity. The theory around dimensions is mainly supported by anecdotal evidence rather than scholarly insights into theory, or any rigorous empirical research.

The GLOBE's Nine-Dimensional Model of Culture

Another influential model of culture is of the Global Leadership and Organizational Behavior Effectiveness (GLOBE) project. The GLOBE study (House, Javidan & Dorfman, 2001) defines culture as shared motives, values, beliefs, identities, and interpretations or meanings of significant events that result from common experiences of members of collectives that are transmitted across generations (House, Hanges, Javidan, Dorfman & Gupta, 2004). GLOBE follows Schein's (1992) view of culture as a product of a collective's attempts to address two sets of group issues: internal integration and external adaptation. According to GLOBE, culture evolves as a collective adapts to ongoing challenges, surviving in the face of external threats and opportunities and managing relations among its members (Javidan, House, Dorfman, Hanges & Luque, 2006). GLOBE proposes that culture consists of nine dimensions (House et al., 2001, 2004):

- *Uncertainty avoidance* refers to the extent to which members of an organization or society strive to avoid uncertainty by reliance on social norms, rituals and bureaucratic practices to alleviate the unpredictability of future events.
- *Power distance* refers to "the degree to which members of an organization or society expect and agree that power should be stratified and concentrated at higher levels of an organization or government" (House et al., 2004: 12).
- *Collectivism I: societal collectivism* reflects the degree to which organizational and societal institutional practices encourage and reward collective distribution of resources and collective action.
- *Collectivism II: in-group collectivism* reflects the degree to which individuals express pride, loyalty and cohesiveness in their organizations or families.
- *Gender egalitarianism* is the extent to which an organization or a society minimizes gender role differences and gender discrimination.
- *Assertiveness* is the degree to which individuals in organizations or societies are assertive, confrontational and aggressive in social relationships.
- *Future orientation* is the degree to which individuals in organizations or societies engage in future-oriented behaviors such as planning, investing in the future, and delaying gratification.
- *Performance orientation* refers to the extent to which an organization or society encourages and rewards group members for performance improvement. This dimension includes the future-oriented component of the dimension called Confucian dynamism by Hofstede and Bond (1988).
- *Humane orientation* is the degree to which individuals in organizations or societies encourage and reward individuals for being fair, altruistic, friendly, generous, caring and kind to others.

Despite the significance of the study, the GLOBE project has also been criticized on numerous points. Among them is the criticism that GLOBE is a very U.S.-centered study, that its measurement of national culture separates between values and practices, and that items used in the measurement are too abstract and far removed from the respondents' daily concerns. An informative debate between Hofstede and the GLOBE team discussing these and related criticism has been published in the *Journal of International Business Studies* (Javidan et al., 2006).

Schwartz's Theory of Cultural Values

Amongst reputable and robust models of culture is Schwartz's theory of cultural values (2006). His approach assumes that culture is a "rich complex of meanings, beliefs, practices, symbols, norms and values prevalent among people in a society," further suggesting that "prevailing values emphases in a society may be the most central feature of culture. . . . Cultural value emphases shape and justify individual and group beliefs, actions, and goals" (2006: 3).

Based upon an earlier study of individual values from 54 countries and 44,000 respondents (detailed in Schwartz, 1997), Schwartz (1994; Schwartz & Ros, 1995) developed a different conceptual framework for classifying *collective* "value types" at the *cultural* level derived from the same data used to deduce the individual values framework. The six cultural level values in this framework are presented as three bipolar dimensions: autonomy versus embeddedness, hierarchy versus egalitarianism, and mastery versus harmony.

In Schwartz's approach, *autonomy* (further delineated as *intellectual* and *affective* autonomy) emphasizes freedom to pursue one's own ideas, independence and affectively positive experience. In contrast, *embeddedness* describes a value set centered upon framing life in a collective context and identifies with the group and a shared way of life. According to Schwartz, this value type emphasizes the status quo and opposes action that would disrupt the traditional order (Schwartz, 2004). *Hierarchy* corresponds with ascribed roles and obligations; this is distinguishable from *egalitarianism*, which views people as being on equal footing and cooperation as based on a voluntary basis and less on a sense of conformity or duty as with hierarchy. In the final dichotomy, *mastery* cultural values are characterized by assertive attempts to change the environment when such action is seen as contributing to positive individual or group outcomes. In contrast, *harmony* cultures emphasize fitting into the world as it is, rather than trying to change it.

Several features differentiate Schwartz's approach to cultural dimensions from other approaches (Schwartz, 2004: 73):

> (a) It derived the cultural orientations from a priori theorizing rather than post hoc examination of data; (b) It designated a priori the value items that serve as markers for each orientation; (c) It used as measures only items tested for cross-cultural equivalence of meaning; (d) It included a set of items demonstrated to cover the range of values recognized cross-culturally, a step toward ensuring relative comprehensiveness of cultural value dimensions; (e) It specified how the cultural orientations are organized into a coherent system of related dimensions and verified this organization, rather than assuming that orthogonal dimensions best capture cultural reality; (f) It brought empirical evidence that the order of national cultures on each of the orientations is robust across different types of samples from each of a large number of nations around the world [and using different instruments].

These distinctive features suggest the great promise of this approach for studying differences among cultures.

What Are Culture's Consequences for Careers?

We began this chapter by suggesting that cultures affect careers. After showing in the previous section that cultures differ and that there are many approaches which can be used to explain differences among cultures, let us turn to discussing the consequences that cultural differences bear for careers.

We suggest that cultures affect careers through multiple sets of influences. One set of influences is embedded in the individual values towards work and career. Another key set of influences is reflected in organizational values embedded in the organizational human resource management (HRM) practices. While multiple organizational "frames" exist (Bolman & Deal, 2003) with which we can analyze careers, HRM is especially applicable to the management of careers.

Both sets of influences (individual values and HRM) have received a considerable amount of attention from researchers. Below, we offer a brief overview of ideas corresponding to each set.

Cultural Differences in Individual Work Values

Differences in individual values toward work and partly careers across cultures have been studied by a large international team as part of the World Values Survey (Inglehart, 2008). The study focuses on cross-national and cross-time comparisons of values and norms on a wide range of topics. Data concerning work and career values has been unfortunately limited. However, analysis of the available data from four waves of data, 1981–84, 1990–93, 1995–97 and 1999–2004, collected in 23 countries offer important observations with regard to the differences in work values among employees representing different cultures (Warr, 2008). The study has analyzed individual values regarding two aspects of work. One aspect was concerned with the perceived centrality of work and was indexed in terms of "how important it is in your life." Another aspect was concerned with particular job characteristics endorsed as "important in a job."

Available data concern only three cultural zones of the "global cultural map" (Inglehart and Baker, 2000): "historically catholic," "historically communist" and "historically protestant" countries. Inglehart and Baker (2000) have developed their map based on countries' distribution along two value dimensions (1) traditional/secular-rational and (2) survival/self-expression: the traditional/secular-rational values dimension reflects the contrast between societies in which religion is very important and those in which it is not. The survival and self-expression values dimension reflects the contrast between societies regarding the transition from industrial society to post-industrial societies.

In the data of work values, the historically catholic countries were represented by Austria, Belgium, France, Ireland, Italy, Portugal and Spain. The historically communist countries were represented by Bulgaria, Belarus, East Germany, Estonia, Latvia, Lithuania, Romania, the Russian Federation and Ukraine. And the historically protestant countries were represented by Denmark, Finland, Iceland, the Netherlands, Sweden, the U.K. and West Germany.

The results of the study have shown that, with respect to the work role centrality, respondents from all countries scored relatively high, with significantly more positive evaluations made by men than by women. However, gender difference in the perceived importance of work was only significant among part-time employees and among all workers between 25 and 44—the age range in which women's part-time employment is relatively high. Education level was found to be unrelated to these findings. At the same time, respondents in historically communist countries rated work as significantly more important than those in historically protestant countries.

With respect to more specific work values, examined in terms of the perceived importance of 15 job characteristics (good pay, pleasant people to work with, a job that is interesting, good job security, a job that meets one's abilities, that you can achieve something, an opportunity to use initiative, good hours, meeting people, a responsible job, a respected job, a useful job for society, good chances of promotion, not too much pressure, generous holidays), the following findings were attained:

- Significantly more women than men endorsed as important pleasant colleagues, the opportunity to meet people, and convenient working hours.
- Older workers tended overall to endorse job features as important less frequently than did younger ones.
- Older workers would less frequently endorse good pay, social interaction, and promotion prospects.

Further, it was found that workers in historically protestant countries most often made positive evaluations of intrinsic job features. On the other hand, workers in historically communist countries least often rated as important intrinsic aspects of a job. Table 2.1 depicts the summary of the results.

In sum, although importance or centrality of work was rated high by all respondents, its scores were significantly higher for full-time employed male respondents. Concerning the variation in the countries' responses, ex-communist countries, where paid employment may be most

Table 2.1 Rated importance of job features: percentage of positive responses as a function of a country's cultural heritage

Job feature: object of evaluation	Proportion describing the feature as important in a job		
	Historically catholic countries	Historically communist countries	Historically protestant countries
Good pay	78	90	74
Pleasant people to work with	72	65	81
A job that is interesting	64	69	73
Good job security	63	66	56
A job that meets one's abilities	61	59	56
That you can achieve something	58	50	61
An opportunity to use initiative	53	41	57
Good hours	51	50	48
Meeting people	52	45	51
A responsible job	48	32	47
A respected job	44	44	36
Useful job for society	44	34	31
Good chances of promotion	37	36	32
Not too much pressure	34	25	29
Generous holidays	32	31	24

Adapted from Warr (2008).

essential to meet basic needs, scored higher on almost all work-related values. This may be explained by a country's national wealth.

Cultural Differences in Organizational HRM Practices

The World Values Survey shows that individual work values result from a country's religious, political, economic and social backgrounds, which also form culture. These cultural backgrounds also shape organizational values, and consequently are embedded in organizational HRM practices (Aumann and Ostroff, 2006). HRM practices are based on norms transmission and beliefs about how people should be managed. Kats, van Emmerik, Blenkinsopp and Khapova (2010) refer to these norms as "norms regarding HRM practices" or, in other words, organizational norms about how employees should be managed. A recent study of associations between the cultural environment and internal work culture and HR on a sample of 1,954 employees from business organizations in ten countries showed that specific patterns are associating culture with techniques such as job enrichment, empowering supervision, and performance management (Aycan, Kanungo, Mendonca, Yu, Deller, Stahl & Kurshid, 2000). For instance, managers who perceived high power distance in their national culture assumed employee reactivity, and did not provide job enrichment and empowerment.

Kats et al. (2010) suggest that HRM practices that are likely to be sensitive to cultural influences include:

- employment security;
- reduction of status distinctions;
- selective hiring;
- training and development;
- performance appraisal;
- career planning and advancement.

Employment security and reduction of status distinctions can be characterized as maintenance-oriented HRM because they protect employees' well-being. Employment security may induce employees to stay in their job. Selective hiring, training and development are aimed at developing an organizational talent pool. Performance appraisal and career planning and advancement motivate employees to produce (Kats et al., 2010).

Drawing on Hofstede's (2001) five-dimensional model of culture and through reviewing existing evidence regarding HRM practices, Kats

Table 2.2 Cultural dimensions and norms regarding HRM practices

Cultural dimension	Norms regarding HRM practices	HRM practices
Power distance	Empowerment	Reduction of status distinctions
Uncertainty avoidance	Stability and security	Employment security
Individualism versus collectivism	Rewarding individual performance	Performance appraisal
Femininity versus masculinity	Gender equality	Selective hiring
Long-term orientation	Deferred gratification: taking a long view on the value of skills and career development	Career planning and advancement

Adapted from Kats et al. (2010).

et al. (2010) proposed a framework of how cultural dimensions lead to specific norms regarding HRM, which in turn influence HRM practices (Table 2.2). For example, in a strong collectivist culture one organization may emphasize the rewarding of individual performance, while another may emphasize the rewarding of team performance. In both cases, these more specific organizational HRM practices of reward management can be consistent with the higher-order culturally based collectivism.

In sum, cultural norms are often exhibited in the organizational norms regarding HRM and consequently in HRM practices. The HRM practices are facilitators of career development. They can enable a person's objective career success and they can also disable one's career opportunities. Let us now turn to considering empirical evidence of how different cultural dimensions shape a person's subjective and objective career outcomes.

Differences in Career Patterns Across Cultures

In the previous sections, we showed that, on the one hand, cultures predict the values people ascribe to their work and, on the other hand, cultures predict organizational practices shaping individual careers. But how do the cultural differences shape employees' career preferences? A review of existing comparative studies shows that there are many differences in career preferences among cultures as well. Let us turn to presenting some of the observations from our research. Considering that the majority of available previous empirical studies have used Hofstede's (2001) five-dimensional model of culture, we have organized our findings along his five culture dimensions: individualism–collectivism, masculinity–femininity, power distance, uncertainty avoidance and long-term orientation. Table 2.3 presents scores of a selected number of cultures on the five dimensions. Table 2.4, in turn, presents an overview of our findings.

Table 2.3 Extract of index scores for countries from Hofstede's IBM study

Country	Individualism	Masculinity	Power distance	Uncertainty avoidance	Long-/short-term orientation
Argentina	46	56	49	86	
Australia	90	61	36	51	31
Austria	55	79	11	70	31
Belgium	75	54	65	94	38
Brazil	38	49	69	76	65
Canada	80	52	39	48	23
Colombia	13	64	67	80	
Costa Rica	15	21	35	86	
Denmark	74	16	18	23	46
Eastern Africa	27	41	64	52	25
Ecuador	8	63	78	67	
Finland	63	26	33	59	41
France	71	43	68	86	39
Germany	67	66	35	65	31
Great Britain	89	66	35	35	25
Greece	35	57	60	112	
India	48	56	77	40	61
Iran	41	43	58	59	
Ireland	70	68	28	35	43
Israel	54	47	13	81	
Italy	76	70	50	75	34
Japan	46	95	54	92	80
Malaysia	26	50	104	36	
Mexico	30	69	81	82	
Netherlands	80	14	38	53	44
New Zealand	79	58	22	49	30
Pakistan	14	50	55	70	0
Portugal	27	31	63	104	30
Russia	42	37	90	70	
Singapore	20	48	74	8	48
South Africa	65	63	49	49	
Spain	51	42	57	86	
Switzerland	68	70	34	58	40
Thailand	20	34	64	64	56
Turkey	37	45	66	85	
United States	91	62	40	46	29
Uruguay	36	38	61	100	
West Africa	20	46	77	54	16

Based on Hofstede (2001).

Table 2.4 Culture effects on subjective and objective career along Hofstede's culture dimensions

Dimensions	Subjective careers	Objective careers
Individualism vs. collectivism	In individualistic cultures the following are important: Pay and status (Agarwala, 2008). Career advancement (Agarwala, 2008; Lee, Aaker & Gardner, 2000). Less networking (Claes & Ruiz-Quintanilla, 1998). A high need for social recognition and a low need for abasement (Hui, Triandis & Yee, 1991). Motivation through competition (Pearson & Stephan, 1998). In collectivistic cultures the following are important: "Choice" and "love of career" (Agarwala, 2008). Less autonomy (Hui et al., 1991).	In individualistic cultures: Employees are less interested in tenure (Ramamoorthy, Kulkarni, Gupta & Flood, 2007). Employees report less normative and affective commitment (Ramamoorthy et al., 2007). Organizations offer equitable reward systems, formal appraisal systems, job-based hiring and merit-based promotions (Ramamoorthy et al., 2007). In collectivistic cultures: Employees score higher on commitment (Parkes, Bochner & Schneider, 2001). Organizations use fewer selection tests and formal appraisal practices (Ramamoorthy & Carroll, 1998). Employees do not demand promotions based on merit (Ramamoorthy & Carroll, 1998). Team-based reward systems are expected (Kirkman & Shapiro, 2001). Organizations offer equality-based rewards and informal appraisals, hire on the basis of person organization fit, and offer seniority-based promotions that may value loyalty to the organization (Ramamoorthy et al., 2007).
Femininity vs. masculinity	In masculine cultures: Monetary rewards are important (Chiang & Birtch, 2005). Company interference in personal lives is more accepted (Poelmans, 2005). Possession and the financial value of stocks have an important psychological effect (Alves, Lovelace, Manz,	In masculine cultures: There are greater value differences between men and women in the same jobs, resulting in gender segregation (Poelmans, 2005). CEOs get higher levels of pay (Tosi & Greckhamer, 2004). There is less networking (Claes & Ruiz-Quintanilla, 1998).

Table 2.4 *Continued*

	Matsypura, Toyasaki & Ke, 2006). In feminine cultures: Social relations and non-rational processes motivate employees (Alves et al., 2006). Managers focus on building close relationships and avoiding conflicting situations with their subordinates (Pellegrini & Scandura, 2006).	In feminine cultures: Women are promoted into management positions more often (Hofstede, 2001). More women hold high positions in politics (Skjelsbæk & Smith, 2001). There more equal opportunities policies for women and less gender segregation at the higher hierarchical levels (Hofstede, 2001).
Power distance	In high power distance cultures: There is more guidance and acceptance of guidance by hierarchically higher superiors (Aycan, 2005). There is higher importance of the symbolic value of tasks and corresponding covert processes (Alves et al., 2006). In low power distance cultures: Employees in lower power positions expect to have more voice in decision processes (Alves et al., 2006). Leadership styles that promote flexibility, innovation, job mobility and general rather than specialized skills are preferred (Dickson, Den Hartog & Mitchelson, 2003).	In high power distance cultures: Lower-status employees are addressed by their first names, whereas for higher-status people different prefixes are added before their first names (Pellegrini & Scandura, 2006). Proactive career behavior is less common (Claes & Ruiz-Quintanilla, 1998). In low power distance cultures: Wage differentials between men and women are smaller (Hofstede, 2001). Organizations are likely to use non-performance-based reward systems (Chiang, 2005).
Uncertainty avoidance	In uncertainty avoiding cultures: Employees may prefer to be told exactly what to do (Pellegrini & Scandura, 2006). Employees will seek involvement in relationships with mentors, which reduces uncertainty regarding the organizational environment (Bozionelos, 2006). Employees would prefer non-rational, intuition-based thought processes (Alves et al., 2006). Employees also prefer leadership styles that promote planning, career stability, formal rules and the development of expertise (Dickson et al., 2003).	In uncertainty avoiding cultures: Employment contracts should specify details of the job description (Leat & El-Kot, 2007). Employees prefer longer job tenure (Chang & Lu, 2007). Employees who work in hierarchical and rule-oriented companies report lower levels of stress (Joiner, 2001). There is more employment law strictness (Mentzer, 2007). There is less networking (Claes & Ruiz-Quintanilla, 1998).

Future orientation	In long-term-oriented societies: Development of skills over time is likely to be more important than short-term rewards (Zhang, Song, Hackett & Bycio, 2006). Immediate results are less motivating (Alves et al., 2006).	In long-term-oriented cultures people take better account of retirement.

Individualism–Collectivism

The main difference with regard to work between individualistic and collectivistic cultures lies in employees' definitions of satisfaction (Di Cesare and Sadri, 2003). In individualistic countries, employees are driven by improving themselves and their own positions in life. Thus, on the objective side of careers, employees from individualistic countries are more likely to compete at work to achieve their personal goals (Probst, Carnevale & Triandis, 1999), focus on promotion (Kirkman, Lowe & Gibson, 2006), work independently (Jaw, Ling, Wang & Chang, 2007) and change jobs frequently (Albrecht, 2001). For example, a higher level of individualism among Indian students was found to be significantly correlated with extrinsic factors (money, status, etc.), suggesting that these students placed a greater value on material benefits, such as money, social prestige and career advancement. Because it is more usual in individualistic societies to differentiate employees based on their performance, there is also more acceptance of large differences in reward between individuals compared to collectivistic cultures (Beer & Katz, 1998).

In collectivistic countries, employees are motivated by the success of the group as a whole. They prefer reward systems that are non-competitive in nature (Chiang, 2005), and have an expectation that organizations will take care of employees beyond the obligations prescribed under the formal contracts (Ramamoorthy, Kulkarni, Gupta & Flood, 2007). They also expect more in-house training and development, as they have no intention of moving to any other organization (Gannon & Newman, 2002). They appreciate group feedback as an important motivational factor (Earley, 1999). In the same study of Indian students, students who had a collectivistic orientation emphasized "free choice" and "love of career" as important influences on their career choice (Agarwala, 2008). Students who were high on collectivism were influenced by their father in their career choice decision.

Femininity–Masculinity

According to Hofstede (1984), the symbolic meaning of a career is greater in masculine than in feminine countries. So the cultural dimension femininity influences the cultural context within which careers occur. In highly feminine cultures social relations and non-rational processes motivate people to work (Alves, Lovelace, Manz, Matsypura, Toyasaki & Ke, 2006). Individuals in highly feminine cultures try harder to build close relationships between colleagues and subordinates. They also want to avoid conflicting situations with their subordinates (Pellegrini & Scandura, 2006). Feminine societies put more weight on subjective, intuition-oriented conditions at work such as care, nurturing and relationships (Alves et al., 2006). There is also less gender segregation (Hofstede, 2001), leading to a higher percentage of women in high positions in politics and management (Skjelsbæk & Smith, 2001).

In masculine cultures individuals place greater value on monetary rewards than in feminine countries (Chiang & Birtch, 2005). Therefore CEOs in masculine countries get higher levels of pay (Tosi & Greckhamer, 2004). They also appreciate the possession and the financial value of equity stocks (Alves et al., 2006). In masculine cultures people prefer more salary to shorter working hours (Poelmans, 2005), and reward systems that link monetary reward to results and personal achievement (Beer & Katz, 1998). Furthermore, in masculine cultures there is a greater difference between men and women in the same jobs (Poelmans, 2005). Research shows that in highly masculine cultures the society and business tend to promote fewer women into management positions (Hofstede, 2001).

Power Distance

Power distance concerns the degree to which the less powerful members of a social group (e.g. a family or an organization) accept that power is distributed unequally (Hofstede, 2001). Thus high power distance cultures tend to view inequality as normal and natural. Differences between bosses and subordinates are clear: both groups sit separately in dining areas, do not socialize together and use different vehicles. The lower-status people are addressed by their first names, whereas for higher-status people different prefixes are added before their first names (Pellegrini & Scandura, 2006). People in high power distance cultures accept more guidance from superiors; this extra attention makes high-status employees more enthusiastic in their work. Claes and Ruiz-Quintanilla (1998) found that proactive career behavior (i.e. initiatives and interventions to shape future careers) in career management was less common in high power distance cultures (Lockwood, 2008). In combination with high uncertainty avoidance, high power distance led to senior people (like supervisors, older colleagues and parents) taking active roles in young adults' early careers. In these countries, it might not be expected of young adults to take the initiative.

In cultures with low uncertainty avoidance and low power distance, people are encouraged to take the initiative for themselves (Claes & Ruiz-Quintanilla, 1998). It is very exceptional in lower power distance cultures for the pay gap between men and women to be smaller (Hofstede, 2001). Moreover, HR planning in low power distance cultures often includes input from managers at many levels. There is evidence that in high power distance cultures employees often look for guidance to their superiors, whom they assume know what is best for their career development (Aycan & Fikret-Pasa, 2003). In low power distance cultures leadership styles that promote flexibility, innovation, job mobility and general rather than specialized skills are preferred (Dickson, Den Hartog & Mitchelson, 2003).

Uncertainty Avoidance

A theoretical assumption behind this dimension is that individuals from a high uncertainty avoidance culture will be more anxious about exploring new things in life. So they will have a longer mean tenure than individuals from a low uncertainty avoidance culture (Chang & Lu, 2007). People in uncertainty avoidance cultures will prefer to be told exactly what to do, instead of getting some independence (Pellegrini & Scandura, 2006). This also relates to the specifics of a job contract. Employees in high uncertainty avoidance cultures will be motivated by certainty and security (Chiang, 2005; Raghuram, London & Larsen, 2001). They will also prefer contracts that specify details of the job description (Leat & El-Kot, 2007), and reward systems that do not orient on performance (Chiang, 2005). Consequently, they will be more attracted to secure, governmental jobs (Chhokar, Brodbeck & House, 2007), and will be more motivated by leadership styles that promote planning, career stability, formal rules and the development of expertise (Dickson et al., 2003).

In turn, employees in countries which score low on uncertainty avoidance prefer independence in their work, responsibility and possibilities for creativity (Pellegrini & Scandura, 2006). They prefer leadership that allows for individual leadership in one's work, and they prefer proactive job crafting and entrepreneurship. Work designs in such cultures are open and less defined. Thus, in these countries, employees are likely to experience higher degree of stress at work (Joiner, 2001).

Long-Term Orientation

There is a conceptual link between the long-term orientation dimension of culture and careers. Careers can be seen as an exercise in deferred gratification (Stinchcombe, 1983; Wilensky, 1960). Thus reward for present job performance is expected to come in the future through career development (Schein, 1971). However, thus far research into this link between long-term orientation and careers has been scarce. From what is available we see that lifetime employment is coupled with promotion by seniority practices, as can be observed in collectivistic cultures (Rhodes, Lowe, Litchfield & Walsh-Samp, 2008), and is often related to long-term orientation. A short-term orientation can be viewed as leading to changing jobs or altering career visions.

In long-term-oriented cultures people are not motivated by immediate results, although this would motivate people in short-term-oriented cultures (Alves et al., 2006). The importance of career and skills development over time is likely to be greater in long-term-oriented cultures than short-term rewards (Zhang, Song, Hackett & Bycio, 2006), so it is probable that people from long-term-oriented cultures will stay longer in jobs they do not really like.

Discussion and Conclusions

From the previous discussion, it is clear that culture has various significant sorts of influence on careers. While all of the studies were not career-specific, we were able to use them to infer ideas about culture and career relationships. The individualistic dimension of culture is especially interesting, as some have wondered if an individualistic youth culture has begun to prevail. Individualism would seem to echo the refrains of the new self-directed careers more (e.g. protean [Hall, 1996] and boundaryless [Arthur & Rousseau, 1996]), but it is undoubtable that the pressures of the new career have hit people in all cultures, collectivistic, individualistic and everything in between. How are people in different types of cultures responding?

We strongly feel that, where existing data and theory are inadequate, a more exploratory spirit and research method are called for. It was with such a spirit that we started our research in earnest, the methodological details of which form the next chapter.

However, while we organized the past research in this chapter in terms of Hofstede's model, we chose to base our country-level sampling on Schwartz's theory of cultural values. We did so in part because of the methodological rigor of his studies and partly because of the utility his cultural "mapping" offered in trying to approach nations on a global scale. We discuss these decisions, their rationale and their ramifications in Chapter 3.

References

Agarwala, T. 2008. Factors influencing career choice of management students in India. *Career Development International*, 13(4): 362–376.

Ailon, G. 2008. Mirror, mirror on the wall: Culture's consequences in a value test of its own design. *Academy of Management Review*, 33(4): 885–904.

Albrecht, M. H. 2001. *International HRM: Managing Diversity in the Workplace*. Oxford, U.K.: Wiley-Blackwell.

Alves, J. C., Lovelace, K. J., Manz, C. C., Matsypura, D., Toyasaki, F. & Ke, G. 2006. Cross-cultural perspective of self-leadership. *Journal of Managerial Psychology*, 21(4): 338–359.

Arthur, M. B. & Rousseau, D. M. (Eds.). 1996. *The Boundaryless Career. A New Employment Principle for a New Organizational Era*. New York: Oxford University Press.

Aumann, K. A. & Ostroff, C. 2006. Multi-level fit: An integrative framework for understanding HRM practices in cross-cultural contexts. In F. J. Yammarino & F. Dansereau (Eds.), *Multi-Level Issues in Social Systems*, Vol. 5: 13–79. Bradford, U.K.: Emerald.

Aycan, Z. 2005. A cross-cultural approach to work–family conflict. International Conference on Work and Family, Barcelona, Spain.

Aycan, Z. & Fikret-Pasa, S. 2003. Career choices, job selection criteria, and leadership preferences in a transitional nation: The case of Turkey. *Journal of Career Development*, 30(2): 129–144.

Aycan, Z., Kanungo, R., Mendonca, M., Yu, K., Deller, J., Stahl, G. & Kurshid, A. 2000. Impact of culture on human resource management practices: A 10-country comparison. *Applied Psychology: An International Review*, 49(1): 192–221.

Beer, M. & Katz, N. 1998. *Do Incentives Work? The Perceptions of Senior Executives From Thirty Countries*. Boston, MA: Harvard Business School.

Bolman, L. G. & Deal, T. E., II. 2003. *Reframing Organizations: Artistry, Choice, and Leadership*. San Francisco, CA: Jossey-Bass.

Bond, M. H. 1988. Finding dimensions of individual variation in multicultural studies of values: The Rokeach and Chinese value surveys. *Journal of Personality and Social Psychology*, 55(6): 1009–1115.

Bozionelos, N. 2006. Mentoring and expressive network resources: Their relationship with career success and emotional exhaustion among Hellenes employees involved in emotion work. *International Journal of Human Resource Management*, 17(2): 362–378.

Brett, J., Behfar, K. & Kern, M. C. 2006. Managing multicultural teams. *Harvard Business Review*, Nov.

Chanchani, S. & Theivanathampillai, P. 2001. Typologies of culture. Working paper, Department of Accountancy and Business Law, University of Otago, New Zealand.

Chang, K. & Lu, L. 2007. Characteristics of organizational culture, stressors and wellbeing: The case of Taiwanese organizations. *Journal of Managerial Psychology*, 22(6): 549–598.

Chhokar, J. S., Brodbeck, F. C. & House, R. J. 2007. *Culture and Leadership Across the World: The GLOBE Book of In-Depth Studies of 25 Societies*, Mahwah, NJ: Lawrence Erlbaum Associates.

Chiang, F. 2005. A critical examination of Hofstede's chapter and its application to international reward management. *International Journal of Human Resource Management*, 16(9): 1545–1563.

Chiang, F. F. T. & Birtch, T. A. 2005. A taxonomy of reward preference: Examining country differences. *Journal of International Management*, 11: 357–375.

Claes, R. & Ruiz-Quintanilla, S. A. 1998. Influences of early career experiences, occupational group, and national culture on proactive career behavior. *Journal of Vocational Behavior*, 52(3): 357–378.

Di Cesare, J. & Sadri, G. 2003. Do all carrots look the same? Examining the impact of culture on employee motivation. *Management Research News*, 26(1): 29–40.

Dickson, M. W., Den Hartog, D. N. & Mitchelson, J. K. 2003. Research on leadership in a cross-cultural context: Making progress, and raising new questions. *Leadership Quarterly*, 14(14): 729–768.

Earley, P. C. 1999. Playing follow the leader: Status-determining traits in relation to collective efficacy across cultures. *Organizational Behavior and Human Decision Processes*, 80(3): 192–212.

Gannon, M. J. & Newman, K. L. 2002. *The Blackwell Handbook of Cross-Cultural Management*. Oxford, U.K.: Wiley-Blackwell.

Hall, D. T. 1996. Protean careers of the 21st century. *Academy of Management Executive*, 10(4): 8–16.

Hall, E. T. 1976. *Beyond Culture*. New York: Doubleday.

Hofstede, G. 1984. Cultural dimensions in management and planning. *Asia Pacific Journal of Management*, 1(2): 81–99.

Hofstede, G. 1991. *Cultures and Organizations: Software of the Mind*. London: McGraw-Hill.

Hofstede, G. 2001. *Culture's Consequences: Comparing Values, Behaviors, Institutions, and Organizations Across Nations*. Thousand Oaks, CA: Sage.

Hofstede, G. & Bond, M. H. 1988. The Confucius connection: From cultural roots to economic growth. *Organizational Dynamics*, 16: 4–21.

House, R., Javidan, M. & Dorfman, P. 2001. Project GLOBE: An introduction. *Applied Psychology: An International Review*, 50(4): 489–505.

House, R. J., Hanges, P. J., Javidan, M., Dorfman, P. W. & Gupta, V. 2004. *Societal Culture and Industrial Sector Influences on Organizational Culture*. London: Sage.

Hui, C. H., Triandis, H. C. & Yee, C. 1991. Cultural differences in reward allocation: Is collectivism the explanation? *British Journal of Social Psychology*, 30(2): 145–157.

Inglehart, R. 2008. Changing values among Western publics from 1970 to 2006. *West European Politics*, 31: 130–146.

Inglehart, R. & Baker, W. E. 2000. Modernization, cultural change, and the persistence of traditional values. *American Sociological Review*, 65(1): 19–51.

Javidan, M., House, R. J., Dorfman, P. W., Hanges, P. J. & Luque, M. S. D. 2006. Conceptualizing and measuring cultures and their consequences: A comparative review of GLOBE's and Hofstede's approaches. *Journal of International Business Studies*, 37: 897–914.

Jaw, B. S., Ling, Y. H., Wang, C. Y. P. & Chang, W. C. 2007. The impact of culture on Chinese employees' work values. *Personnel Review*, 36(5): 763–780.

Joiner, T. A. 2001. The influence of national culture and organizational culture alignment on job stress and performance: Evidence from Greece. *Journal of Managerial Psychology*, 16: 229–243.

Kats, M. S., van Emmerik, I. J. H., Blenkinsopp, J. & Khapova, S. 2010. Exploring the associations of culture with careers and the mediating role of HR practices: A conceptual model. *Career Development International*, 15(4): 401–418.

Kirkman, B. L. & Shapiro, D. L. 2001. The impact of cultural values on job satisfaction and organizational commitment in self-managing work teams: The mediating role of employee resistance. *Academy of Management Journal*, 44: 557–569.

Kirkman, B. L., Lowe, K. B. & Gibson, C. B. 2006. A quarter century of *Culture's Consequences*: A review of empirical research incorporating Hofstede's cultural values framework. *Journal of International Business Studies*, 37: 285–320.

Leat, M. & El-Kot, G. 2007. HRM practices in Egypt: The influence of national context? *International Journal of Human Resource Management*, 18(1): 147–158.

Lee, A. Y., Aaker, J. L. & Gardner, W. L. 2000. The pleasures and pains of distinct self-construals: The role of interdependence in regulatory focus. *Journal of Personality and Social Psychology*, 78(6): 1122–1134.

Lockwood, N. R. 2008. *Selected Cross-Cultural Factors in Human Resource Management*. Alexandria, VA: Society for Human Resource Management.

Mentzer, M. S. 2007. A quantitative approach to national culture and employment law. *Employee Responsibilities and Rights Journal*, 19: 263–277.

Parkes, L. P., Bochner, S. & Schneider, S. K. 2001. Person–organization fit across cultures: An empirical investigation of individualism and collectivism. *Applied Psychology: An International Review*, 50(1): 81–108.

Pearson, V. M. S. & Stephan, W. G. 1998. Preferences for styles of negotiation: A comparison of Brazil and the U.S. *International Journal of Intercultural Relations*, 22: 67–83.

Pellegrini, E. K. & Scandura, T. A. 2006. Leader–member exchange (LMX), paternalism, and delegation in the Turkish business culture: An empirical investigation. *Journal of International Business Studies*, 37: 264–279.

Poelmans, S. A. Y. 2005. *Work and Family: An International Research Perspective*. London: Routledge.

Probst, T. M., Carnevale, P. J. & Triandis, H. C. 1999. Cultural values in intergroup and single group social dilemmas. *Organizational Behavior and Human Decision Processes*, 77: 171–191.

Raghuram, S., London, M. & Larsen, H. H. 2001. Flexible employment practices in Europe: Country versus culture. *International Journal of Human Resource Management*, 12: 738–753.

Ramamoorthy, N. & Carroll, S. J. 1998. Individualism/collectivism orientations and reactions toward alternative human resource management practices. *Human Relations*, 51(5): 571–588.

Ramamoorthy, N., Kulkarni, S. P., Gupta, A. & Flood, P. C. 2007. Individualism–collectivism orientation and employee attitudes: A comparison of employees from the high-technology sector in India and Ireland. *Journal of International Management*, 13: 187–203.

Rhodes, J., Lowe, S. R., Litchfield, L. & Walsh-Samp, K. 2008. The role of gender in youth mentoring relationship formation and duration. *Journal of Vocational Behavior*, 72: 183–192.

Schein, E. H. 1971. The individual, the organization and the career: A conceptual scheme. *Journal of Applied Behavioral Science*, 7: 401–426.

Schein, E. H. 1992. *Organizational Culture and Leadership: A Dynamic View* (2nd ed.). San Francisco, CA: Jossey-Bass.

Schwartz, S. H. 1994. Beyond individualism/collectivism: New cultural dimensions of values. In U. Kim, H. C. Triandis, C. Kagitcibasi, S.-C. Choi and G. Yoon (Eds.), *Individualism and Collectivism: Theory, Methods and Applications*: 85–119. London: Sage.

Schwartz, S. H. 1997. Values and culture. In D. Munro, S. Carr & J. Schumaker (Eds.), *Motivation and Culture*: 69–84. New York: Routledge.

Schwartz, S. H. 2004. Mapping and interpreting cultural differences around the world. In H. Vinken, J. Soeters and P. Ester (Eds.), *Comparing Cultures: Dimensions of Culture in a Comparative Perspective*: 43–73. Leiden, The Netherlands: Brill.

Schwartz, S. H. 2006. Basic human values: Theory, measurement, and applications. *Revue Française de Sociologie*, 47: 249–288.

Schwartz, S. H. and Ros, M. 1995. Values in the West: A theoretical and empirical challenge to the individualism–collectivism cultural dimension. *World Psychology*, 1: 99–122.

Sekaran, U. 1983. Methodological and theoretical issues and advancements in cross-cultural research. *Journal of International Business Studies*, 14(2): 61–73.

Signorini, P., Wiesemes, R. & Murphy, R. 2009. Developing alternative frameworks for exploring intercultural learning: A critique of Hofstede's cultural difference model. *Teaching in Higher Education*, 14(3): 253–264.

Skjelsbæk, I. & Smith, D. 2001. *Gender, Peace and Conflict*. London: Sage.

Smith, P. B. 2002. Culture's consequences: Something old and something new. *Human Relations*, 55(1): 119–135.

Steers, R. M. & Sanchez-Runde, C. 2010. Discovering what makes your employees tick. *IESE Insight*, 5, ART-1786-E.

Stinchcombe, A. E. 1983. *Economic Sociology*. New York: Academic Press.

Tosi, H. L. & Greckhamer, T. 2004. Culture and CEO compensation. *Organization Science*, 15: 657–670.

Trompenaars, F. & Hampden-Turner, C. 1997. *Riding the Waves of Culture: Understanding Cultural Diversity in Business* (2nd ed.). London: Nicholas Brealey.

Van Maanen, J. & Schein, E. H. 1977. *Improving the Quality of Work Life: Career Development*. Santa Monica, CA: Goodyear.

Wagner, R. 1981. *The Invention of Culture*. Chicago, IL: University of Chicago Press.

Warr, P. 2008. Work values: Some demographic and cultural correlates. *Journal of Occupational and Organizational Psychology*, 81: 751–775.

Wilensky, H. L. 1960. Work, careers, and social integration. *International Social Science Journal*, 12: 543–560.

Williamson, D. 2002. Forward from a critique of Hofstede's model of national culture. *Human Relations*, 55(11): 1373–1383.

Zhang, K., Song, L. J., Hackett, R. D. & Bycio, P. 2006. Cultural boundary of expectancy theory-based performance management: A commentary on DeNisi and Pritchard's performance improvement model. *Management and Organization Review*, 2(2): 279–294.

3

The 5C Project: Our Story and Our Research

Jon P. Briscoe, Katharina Chudzikowski,
Barbara Demel, Wolfgang Mayrhofer and Julie Unite

The Collaboration for the Cross-Cultural Study of Contemporary Careers, or "5C" project, began with ambitious goals (which remain) but has reshaped itself from time to time to meet the demands and opportunities of the research. Why we did the research, who we are and how we did the research are part of a closely intertwined story. In this chapter we will tell the story of the 5C group and project as well as our methodological design and decision making. For other researchers and international project teams, we feel that the informal information about our group process is as important as our formal decisions and outcomes.

Forming a Research Group: The Early Stages of 5C

Originally one of us (Jon P. Briscoe) became interested in exploring the "protean career" across cultures. The protean career is the brainchild of Douglas T. (Tim) Hall, who coined the term in a 1976 book, *Careers in Organizations*. Born in an era in the United States in which the corporate management of careers was just being challenged, it depicted a career not directed by the organization but by the individual's own values and behaviors. While it in some ways is an orientation witnessed across cultures, it was clearly a U.S. creation by reflecting the "rugged individualism" of U.S. culture (Inkson, 2006).

Briscoe approached Hall, who had been his professor and dissertation chair at Boston University, and Wolfgang Mayrhofer (from WU—Vienna University of Economics and Business) about the possibilities of starting a project to explore the "new" career across cultures. Both were receptive, and Hall went as far as to coin the acronym and abbreviation for the 5C group (the Cross-Cultural Collaboration on Contemporary Careers). Briscoe led the group in nominal ways as well as in formal ways (to a degree), but key decisions were made by the tripartite consensus of him, Hall and Mayrhofer throughout the project.[1] Briscoe had met Mayrhofer at an annual conference of the European Group for Organizational Studies (EGOS). This conference has a unique format compared to other major conferences in management. Across multiple subgroups it encourages heavy involvement and familiarity with a relatively small (about 30 people) group of researchers. They read one another's papers and meet in a confined space to discuss the papers over two days. The contacts and relationships formed at this conference would be a key to starting a critical mass of researchers.

It was determined to begin to identify like-minded researchers from other countries, and in 2004 a handful of us met at the EGOS meeting in Ljubljana, Slovenia to scope out the project, with follow-up by those in attendance at the Academy of Management meetings that same year in New Orleans. We had received good advice from others to select partners for research reasons and not just because of the convenience of acquaintance. With this in mind and with a growing interest in Schwartz's theory of cultural values (see Chapter 2), we began to target potential country collaborators who represented the distinct regions within Schwartz's framework. In the first very informal meeting at Ljubljana, Jelena Zikic, a Serbian careers researcher who had studied at the University of Toronto and then worked in Spain at the Instituto de Empresa (she is now at York University in Canada), was also present. We outlined our broad interests as a group to explore new careers across cultures (an evolving and general shift from the more peculiar question of testing the protean career across cultures) and begin to brainstorm about other group members. Later Zikic would be instrumental in bringing Enrique Ogliastre (INCAE, Costa Rica and Instituto de Empresa in Madrid) and Biljana Bogićević Milikić (University of Belgrade) into the 5C fold.

Further members, most of whom remain with the group today, were added based upon contacts and networking with group members already mentioned. A group of young researchers in their Ph.D. phase provided ample energy and enthusiasm for the project: Barbara Demel and Katharina Chudzikowski from WU (Vienna University of Economics and Business), Mireia Las Heras and Yan Shen from Boston University, and Julie Unite from Northern Illinois University. In some countries or regions where contact could not be made, we identified potential partners through reviewing their profiles on the internet. We prepared summaries of the project and wrote them with invitations. This proved to be a fruitful strategy for data gathering, although some of these invited members have not remained as long into later stages of the project. We had hoped to have two research teams to represent each of Schwartz's (then seven, now eight) cultural regions. This proved to be a little ambitious, in part because (as will be detailed shortly) we chose a very interactive method versus the more usual and more passive survey research.

For practical reasons it was critical that collaborators spoke English. When possible we targeted colleagues from prominent universities within given countries. This was an attempt to try to ensure well-trained researchers, but also we recognized that such schools would be more likely to have the financial resources to fund research and travel for their professors and students. It is possible that we missed some unique perspectives from being so selective; however, this was a practical trade-off for us.

Values were an important criterion for group membership, at first informally and then more and more explicitly. We were looking for people who were not overly instrumental about the benefits their membership would accrue for them personally. We strived to create a climate of trust and mutual well-being. Further, we wanted people with good interpersonal and conflict resolution skills. Finally we wanted the group members to truly value careers research, as such a priority would be manifest in their enthusiasm and expertise. We chose collaborators who seemed to have a learning rather than performance orientation toward the research (Button, Mathieu & Zajac, 1996), i.e. who were open-minded and not committed to one particular theoretical position but rather had a strong curiosity and willingness to explore and learn.

This profile we sought may have "cost" us some points of view and talented people but again seemed to be a reasonable and practical trade-off that was also appealing on a social and professional level.

In 2005 we had gathered enough of a "critical mass" that we felt ready to jump in with both feet and get about the research we had long discussed. We had a group meeting in Hawaii at the setting of the annual Academy of Management meeting.[2] At this stage we were ready to develop our research to a more refined degree.

The Research Questions

All of our decisions regarding methodology were dependent upon the research questions. At an earlier point, we developed an interest in doing more exploratory and less hypothesis-testing research. Recall that the original motivation of our initial research team was to test, not develop, career theory. As mentioned, a few of the group's founders were interested in testing the efficacy of the "protean" career theory (Hall, 1976, 2002) across cultures. The protean career theory has a cultural context to be sure. It was born in an era in the U.S.A. in which corporate management of careers was just being challenged. It depicted a career not directed by the organization but by the individual's own values and behaviors. In this sense it reflects the "rugged individualism" of U.S. culture and, while it in some ways is an orientation witnessed across cultures, it was clearly a U.S. creation (Inkson, 2006).

We realized that if we were to simply test Hall's theory we would not discover anything independently about how careers are conceptualized and managed in other cultures, in other ways. The writing of Brett and his colleagues was influential to us at this time (Brett, Tinsley, Janssens, Barsness & Lytle, 1997). What they characterized as a "one-way" approach could describe our original design of hypothesis testing—a valid comparison of how cultures exhibit a particular construct. However, they captured our imagination when they discussed an "N-Way" approach. In this approach, a multinational team of researchers with knowledge of a given concept would meet to define the relevant research question, such as "How does individual career management impact career transitions?" Then each cultural "representative" would take the lead in a collaborative effort to develop a local model of the research question. This N-Way approach shaped our formation and research process.

With these assumptions in mind, we defined more open-ended questions to guide our research: (1) How do people define "career success"? (2) How do people experience and manage changes in their careers? Implicit in the first question is the question of how people understand "career" and how they understand "success." We felt that the sharing of personal values (Rokeach, 1973) or standards (Carver & Scheier, 1981) regarding one's retrospective assessment and/or aspirational view of "success" would provide valuable insight into whether such evaluations would be impacted by cultural differences as well as other factors.

Our assumption with the second question was that focusing upon recent and significant changes in people's careers would allow us to understand how contemporary changes in the modern career environment, cultural differences, and micro, macro and meso influences impacted how people interpreted and managed career episodes. This line of inquiry eventually evolved into a closer focus upon career *transitions*.

Methodology

Our choice of taking an exploratory approach to careers across cultures was also inspired by a grounded theory approach (Glaser and Strauss, 1967). This tactic relies not upon testing specific hypotheses so much as using established or assumed theoretical categories to target sampling criteria that would assumedly cause the phenomena under focus to vary or change in important (theoretically and/or practical) ways. With this in mind, we of course were interested in the variation cultural differences might imply in career understanding and behavior, but we also focused upon occupational categories, age and gender as theoretical categories that would likely impact careers.

Sampling

Country-Level Sampling

In Chapter 2 we reviewed several theories of national culture. As briefly discussed earlier, we decided to base our country-level sampling on Schwartz's theory of cultural values for several reasons, including perceived methodological superiority as well as the fact that its data is more recent. However, the chief advantage from a sampling perspective is that Schwartz organized his value polarities into a dimensional arrangement which allowed him to group countries according to distinct world regions. Hofstede grouped countries on several two-by-two grids (e.g. uncertainty avoidance/individualism) but not into completely discrete regions beyond the separate grids. Schwartz (2004, 2006) was able to designate seven distinct cultural regions[3] based upon their combined variance in each of the seven (three bipolar) dimensions reviewed in Chapter 2 (affective autonomy/intellectual autonomy versus embeddedness, hierarchy versus egalitarianism, and mastery versus harmony). His mapping of the countries in his data set is presented in Figure 3.1 (see Schwartz, 2006 for an interpretation of the figure). Schwartz generated the following transnational cultural regions in his country mapping: Africa and the Middle East, Confucian Asia, Eastern Europe, English speaking, Latin America, South Asia and Western Europe.[4]

In Table 3.1, we display the countries in our sample that represented the various transnational cultural regions, as well as the research teams and affiliated institutions associated with the assorted countries.

Table 3.2 profiles the countries and their relative emphases upon different values dimensions both in Schwartz's understanding and in key dimensions from Hofstede's theory (for comparison's sake).

In selecting cultures we took a broad approach and did not specify ahead of time how cultural variations would impact careers. However, by using Schwartz's cultural regions we strategized that we could

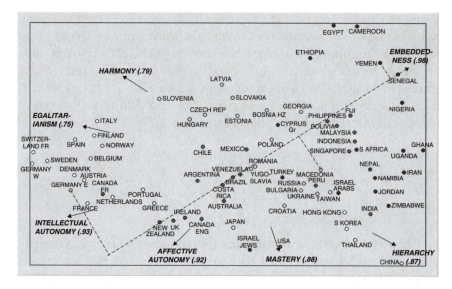

Figure 3.1   Co-plot map of 76 national groups on seven cultural orientations

Note: Coefficient alienation .11.
From Schwartz (2006). Used by permission.

capture and compare a great range of possible variation amongst cultural variables.

Occupations

Great thought went into which occupations to include in the study. Occupations appeal to different values in people, and they shape how careers progress, how easily they can be pursued and how flexibly they can be changed. In the end we settled on three occupations: nursing, business and blue-collar.

Nurses' careers are highly structured in many countries. Medical care is regulated by licensure, and often hospitals and other care-giving facilities have structured hierarchies in which career promotion is stratified and controlled. In addition, while it is not universally true, we assumed that many nurses were motivated by a sense of service or duty. This could be a cause in variability for career motivation.

Businesspeople have a stereotypical "free agent" career more than nurses. Their opportunities are limited in highly specialized areas (public accounting, for example) but are highly flexible in broader enterprise. Switching activities is easier, and performance is less subject to external

Table 3.1 Profile of cultural regions and associated countries, country teams and affiliations

Cultural regions	Countries	Country teams (each team's members are listed in alphabetical order, and country natives are italicized)	Affiliations
Africa and Middle East	South Africa	Jon P. Briscoe	Northern Illinois University
		Julie Unite	Northern Illinois University
		Jacobus Van Lill	North West University
Confucian Asia	China	*Yan Shen*	Boston University
		Zhangfeng Fei	Donghua University
Confucian Asia	Japan	*Mami Taniguchi*	Waseda University
Eastern Europe	Serbia	*Biljana Bogićević Milikić*	University of Belgrade
		Jelena Zikic	York University
English speaking	United States	*Jon P. Briscoe*	Northern Illinois University
		Douglas T. (Tim) Hall	Boston University
		Mireia Las Heras	IESE, University of Navarra
		Julie Unite	Northern Illinois University
English speaking	United Kingdom	Michael Dickmann	Cranfield School of Management
		Emma Parry	Cranfield School of Management
Latin America	Costa Rica	*Enrique Ogliastri*	INCAE, Instituto de Empresa
Latin America	Mexico	*Ociel Colorado*	ITESM, University of Grenoble
South Asia	Malaysia	*Rohayu Abdul-Ghani*	Universiti Kebangsaan, Malaysia
		Jon P. Briscoe	Northern Illinois University
		Eric Jones	Northern Illinois University
		June Poon	Universiti Kebangsaan, Malaysia
Western Europe	Austria	*Katharina Chudzikowski*	WU Vienna
		Barbara Demel	WU Vienna
		Wolfgang Mayrhofer	WU Vienna
		Astrid Reichel	WU Vienna
Western Europe	Spain	*Mireia Las Heras*	IESE, University of Navarra
Israel	Israel	*Asya Pazy*	Tel Aviv University
		Dana Shefer	Tel Aviv University

Table 3.2 Key cultural dimensions of sample countries

Countries/ categories	Austria	China	Costa Rica	Israel	Japan	Malaysia	Mexico	Serbia	South Africa	Spain	U.S.A.
Schwartz's cultural values:											
Master/harmony	Harmony	Mastery	In between	Mastery	Mastery	In between	Leans toward harmony	In between	Leans toward harmony	Harmony	Mastery
Egalitarianism/hierarchy	Egalitarian	Hierarchy	In between	Hierarchy	Hierarchy	Leans towards hierarchy	In between	In between	Hierarchy	Egalitarian	Medium hierarchy
Autonomy/embeddedness	Autonomy	Embedded	Leans toward autonomy	Autonomy	Leans toward autonomy	Embedded	Leans toward autonomy	In between	Embedded	Autonomy	Autonomy
Hofstede's culture dimensions (select):											
Collectivism/individualism	Leans toward individualism	Collectivism	Collectivism	Slight individualism	Leans toward collectivism	Collectivism	Collectivism	Collectivism	Individualism	Leans toward individualism	Individualism
Power distance	Small	High	Small	Low	Medium high	High	High	High	Slightly high	High	Medium
Uncertainty avoidance	Low	Medium high	Strong	Low	In between	High	High	High	Medium high	Medium high	Medium

validation in many cases. Also, our informal observation was that many businesspeople did not have the same intrinsic motivation toward their careers as did nurses, especially in the early career. There was frequently a more instrumental orientation toward what the career could produce in other realms of life (e.g. lifestyle).

Finally, blue-collar workers relied upon different career preparation. While some countries (e.g. Austria) have highly specialized and structured career paths for blue-collar work, many countries do not require specialized licensure or oversight in many such career paths. Blue-collar workers' motivations may vary from an intrinsic interest in a craft or skill, to a more instrumental approach to providing for costs of living and so on. Also, in order to find new work, blue-collar workers often need to utilize networks in ways that may vary from those of nursing, business and other occupations.

While other occupations were surely compelling, we felt that the three we chose offered a good opportunity to compare people in similar occupational contexts as they varied across cultures. Operationalizing the constructs was simple with nurses, as they faced similar professional requirements and hurdles. For businesspeople, we elected to select business school graduates where possible in order to standardize the sample. This was easier with younger people, and in some countries older generations of business school graduates were either not available or very impractical to target. With blue-collar workers we looked for manual laborers. We learned as the research progressed that this was harder to standardize from country to country, but similarities were found in the cross-country samples.

Gender and Age

Gender would seem to have a significant impact upon both career success and career management, owing to how men and women are socialized into playing life and career roles in varying ways. Some of this is due to culture, and genetic differences surely play a role as well. Gender balance was not difficult to obtain in proportionate numbers for the overall sample. However, across the nurse sample women were much more prolific, and the blue-collar sample was much more likely to be made up of men.

Age was an important consideration for many reasons. People of different career stages represent different generations and are in different life stages (Erikson, 1980; Super, Savickas & Super, 1996). Age is probably the biggest window we have into how different eras shape career behavior (Bennis & Thomas, 2002). A lot of speculation has centered upon how youth may be becoming more individualistic or similar in other ways on a global scale (Triandis, 1995). Comparing similar age groups across cultures and to their counterparts from other age groups *within* the same culture could provide valuable contrasts. We chose to focus upon early and late generations in the working world. Our reasoning was that this would provide the maximum contrast in exploring how the world of work had shifted owing to economic, societal or other changes. Thus we targeted individuals who had been working at least two years but were in roughly the first ten years of their careers, and correspondingly those who were within about ten years of retirement.

To achieve the sampling goals in each country, research teams used convenience samples and approached occupational groups through institutional or personal contacts. We strived to get at least three people per age group in each occupation, for comparison purposes. Effort was made to include people in rural and urban areas in most countries. That said, it is difficult to argue that our samples were representative of whole countries, but they did vary within and between countries in significant ways that allowed us to juxtapose differences, make generalizations and suggest theoretical and research directions. Table 3.3 profiles the total global sample.[5] A total of 226 people were included, and the average age of the overall younger generation was 27.5 years and 57 years for the older generation.

Data Gathering Through Interviews

Qualitative methods are ideal for generating new theory, and as McGrath (1982) recommends they should be used early in a research cycle to identify dimensions, which can be later measured quantitatively. Interviews were conducted in person (or by telephone in a few cases where introductions had been previously made in person). Semi-structured interviews were used to give us optimal flexibility while still focusing upon the questions of interest (Patton, 1990). In constructing the interview guide the 5C group met to discuss the applicability of certain concepts and jargon to their own culture. Based upon this, ambiguous language was removed where identified in the interview guide. Interviewees were queried regarding their views of career success and recent career transitions, perceived influences on the same, and their observations of generational differences. Following Patton's (1990) guidance, we focused first upon memories of the events themselves and then on feelings and interpretations. The interview guide can be found in Figure 3.2.

Table 3.3 Total sample profile

Cluster	Confucian Asia		Eastern Europe	English speaking	Israel	Latin America		South Asia	Sub-Saharan Africa	Western Europe	
Countries	China	Japan	Serbia	U.S.A.	Israel	Costa Rica	Mexico	Malaysia	South Africa	Austria	Spain
Sample size (N=226)	28	20	21	20	19	19	18	18	24	18	21
Female/male	15/13	7/13	14/7	11/9	8/11	11/8	6/12	8/10	16/8	8/10	17/4
Older/younger age group	16/12	10/10	10/11	9/11	10/9	10/9	9/9	9/9	14/10	9/9	8/13
Business/nurses/blue-collar	8/6/14	8/6/6	7/8/6	8/6/6	6/6/7	6/6/7	5/6/7	6/6/6	9/7/8	6/6/6	6/6/9

1. [Brief description of research, assurance of confidentiality.]
2. Could you please complete a "timeline" on this piece of paper showing major milestones and transitions in your career (or "work history") so far?

[Provide interviewee with paper(s)—more detail on this will follow soon.]

3. Considering what you have said so far: if you could create an ideal career for yourself, what characteristics would your ideal career have?
4. Are you satisfied with your career to this point? Why or why not?
5. Can you tell us about the last career-related change you experienced? [Career transition.]

Example (if they need): job change, vocation change, unemployment, going to half-time, etc.

a. What happened? [Focus upon memory of events and their sequence.]
    i. What led to the transition? [Self-initiated, externally initiated.]
    ii. Please describe how you tried to manage the transition.
    iii. How were you feeling during this time?
    iv. What was the outcome of the transition? In your mind what turned out well? What turned out differently than you thought it would?
b. Interpretation/explanation of the transition
    i. What is there about you (personality, approach to problems, etc.) that made this transition easier and/or less difficult?
    ii. What other factors that made this transition more or less difficult have we not addressed yet?
    —People
    —Organization(s)
    iii. Please tell us anything you think you may have learned from this event.
    —About yourself.
    —About managing career transitions.
    —Etc.
    iv. What would you do the same, differently, now?
    v. Can you tell us which areas of your (work and private) life have been impacted by this transition?
    vi. [If not answered already] Was the transition smooth, like a constant stream? Or did it have interruptions, etc?
6. Career success
    a. Looking back at your experience and your career [may be helpful to refer to timeline] thus far: What does "career success" mean for you?
    b. Considering your career, what do you see as the crucial factors for career success?
Probe areas:
—Self-dimensions: personality, etc.
—Family background.
—Education.
—Social relationships.
—Organizational resources (career development, training, etc.).
7. Generational comparisons
    a. For the "young generation": If you compare your situation with that of a senior person (e.g. roughly 60-plus years old) in your profession, what is similar and what is different?
    —In terms of your career characteristics.
    —In terms of how your different generations define "career success."
    b. For the "older generation": If you compare your situation with that of a young person (say roughly 25–30 years old) in your profession, what is similar, what is different and how do you evaluate this?
Concluding questions
8. Is your career or are your career opportunities turning out any differently than you thought they might earlier in your career? Please explain. [If necessary, "Why do you think this is true?"]
9. We've asked you a lot of questions today and we have found your perspective very helpful! Do you have any questions for us as we finish the interview?

Thank you so much for your willingness to participate in this project.

Figure 3.2 5C interview guide

Data Analysis

This was clearly the most complex part of our research journey. While the goal of developing a cross-culturally derived framework or frameworks was one worthy of our best efforts, the reality of doing so proved to be anything but simple. There was the logistical and intellectual complication of coordinating different country findings, all while honoring differences and identifying commonalties. Then there were linguistic and social complexities as well. The entire research process was interactive and non-linear and required intuitive skills on many levels in addition to rationality and logic. Certainly there were limitations resulting from this imperfect "dance," but the data reflects a richness and comprehensiveness that could not be obtained with a process where control was completely predictable and in hand up front. After all of these considerations we still believe our efforts were rewarded with empirical and theoretical progress which advances the field of career studies and hopefully the effective management of careers.

Data analysis proceeded in a multi-stage process. All but a few interviews were recorded and transcribed. Notes were taken on the other interviews, and these interviews were also analyzed, except in a few cases where they seemed inadequate to capture the interviewee's response.

Phase 1: Generation of Core Categories

This first phase was completed at a country level with a shared standardized process (Briscoe, 2006; Demel, Chudzikowski & Mayrhofer, 2006) coding guide. We utilized a form of critical discourse analysis (Mayring, 2008) in which the base interview material was paraphrased, organized into theme areas and eventually developed into coding units. This was combined with a constant comparative method (Strauss & Corbin, 1990) and the use of matrices and coding strategies (Miles and Huberman, 1994) to compare core categories across subgroups. The analysis was structured by looking at emerging patterns, observing contrasts, making comparisons, clustering similar elements and counting the frequency of specific aspects. Conclusions and steps towards formulating a framework were guided by following up on surprises, triangulating insights with other sources of information from the original text and independent sources, making "if-then tests" and checking out rival explanations. This was done at each country level with two or more coders using the original language and resulted in sets of independently generated categories representing career success, career transitions and other variables of interest. These generated categories were translated into English in order for the larger 5C team to compare results.

Phase 2: Integration of Core Categories

In the form of the N-Way approach, members of the 5C team from each participating country except two met for several days in order to explore and discuss differences and similarities in the different sets of core categories. This phase was organized but spontaneous as well. Desirous of avoiding a dominant perspective, or group-think, this process was organized early on to give equal voice and opportunity to each country team both to present their data and to ask questions. This needed to be emphasized at times not just because of cultural differences but because of personality differences and group size. During this stage, agreement was made upon areas of focus, including career success and career transitions. From here sub-teams met to construct a single focused and integrated set of core categories (on career success, career transitions and generational differences) that was representative of each country's own category set(s). These integrated sets of core categories were sent to absent team members for inspection and feedback. In our view, the complexity of this phase required a degree of interaction and clarification that could only be achieved in person.

Phase 3: Finalization of Global Coding Book

Subsequent to Phase 2, a guide we titled the Global Coding Book (GCB) was generated (in English) that represented integrated coding guidelines and core categories to be used in *recoding* the original data across all participating countries. Great care was taken in this process to ensure that final categories adequately represented more discrete themes as found in the separate country sets of core categories. As iterations were developed, they were shared with the larger team and modified as necessary. Also, where obvious and/or reasonable, we used existing theoretical categories if they adequately matched our emergent categories (for example, "openness to experience" or "internal locus of control").

Phase 4: Recoding of Data Using the Integrated Global Coding Book

Each country team recoded their data using the GCB. Six of the participating countries used NVivo version 7 to code and organize their data.

The remaining countries used the exact same themes but used MS Excel to label and store their coded data. If new categories emerged during recoding that were not part of the coding scheme in the GCB, they were added as "free nodes" and integrated in a second step into the coding scheme for future analysis.

Phase 5: Extrapolation of Findings

Finally, with the recoded data in hand various team members were able to focus upon a more collective-level analysis of the data. Some of these analyses were presented in published peer-reviewed journal and conference articles (see Briscoe, Chudzikowski, Mayrhofer, Unite, Las Heras, Didi, Fei, Gasteiger, Abdul-Ghani, Hall, Jones, Noordin, Ogliastri, Pazy, Poon, Shen, Taniguchi, Van Lill & Zikic, 2007; Briscoe, Unite, Chudzikowski, Colorado, Demel, Hall, Las Heras, Mayrhofer, Milikic, Ogliastri, Taniguchi, Yan & Zikic, 2009; Chudzikowski, Demel, Mayrhofer, Briscoe, Unite, Bogicevic Milikic, Hall, Las Heras and Zikic, 2009; Demel, Shen, Hall, Mayrhofer, Chudzikowski, Unite, Briscoe, Abdul-Ghani, Bogicevic Milikic, Colorado, Fei, Las Heras, Ogliastri, Pazy, Poon, Shefer, Taniguchi and Zikic, 2009), but several of our original findings are offered primarily in this book.

Conclusion

We discuss what we learned regarding the issues of methods, methodology, and management of culturally mixed research teams in Chapter 9. Of course, all of our research decisions had various options, and in some cases we probably could have chosen others to our benefit. Still, we would argue that the route we took was adequate when looking at the mix of research questions, local context, members of the research group, timeline and restrictions in terms of resources. In addition, we trust the reader has a better understanding of the terrific array of decisions and alternatives that go into such a project as this.

In the next three chapters, we will share our general findings with you on career success, career transitions and generations. We hope that some of our findings demonstrate to the reader the richness and diversity our methods were designed to uncover.

Notes

1 Leadership of the group is further discussed in Chapter 9. In reality, most decisions were discussed by the group. At times decisions needed quick action or were sensitive in nature (e.g. new members, conflict resolution) and were made by Briscoe, Hall and Mayrhofer.

2 As the reader might imagine, the space for these meetings was a research cost. Where possible we met with local universities that were cooperative. However, most meetings required a rented meeting room, and these costs had to be calculated into the research.

3 In Schwartz (2008) he modified the regional framework we used into 8 regions (dividing Eastern Europe into "East Central and Baltic European" and "Orthodox East European").

4 Schwartz views Israel as unique and not corresponding to any of the seven cultural regions.

5 The U.K., which is profiled in a country focus chapter in Chapter 19, is not included in this overall sample profile, as its data was not part of the theory-generation stage of the research.

References

Bennis, W. G. & Thomas, R. 2002. *Geeks and Geezers*. Boston, MA: Harvard University Press.

Brett, J. M., Tinsley, C. H., Janssens, M., Barsness, Z. I. & Lytle, A. L. 1997. New approaches to the study of culture in industrial/organizational psychology. In P. C. Earley & M. Erez (Eds.), *New Perspectives on International Industrial/Organizational Psychology*: 75–129. San Francisco, CA: New Lexington Press.

Briscoe, J. P. 2006. Theory generation: Using the constant comparative method to generate theory. In 5C Coding and Theory Generation Guide, Unpublished technical report, Wien University, Vienna.

Briscoe, J. P., Chudzikowski, K., Mayrhofer, W., Unite, J., Las Heras, M., Didi, M., Fei, Z., Gasteiger, R., Abdul-Ghani, R., Hall, D. T., Jones, E., Noordin, F., Ogliastri, E., Pazy, A., Poon, J. M. L., Shen, Y., Taniguchi, M., Van Lill, B. & Zikic, J. 2007. Career success across cultures: Dancing to the beat of their own drummers. Paper presented at the annual conference of the European Group for Organization Studies, Vienna, Austria, July 5.

Briscoe, J. P., Unite, J., Chudzikowski, K., Colorado, O., Demel, B., Hall, D. T., Las Heras, M., Mayrhofer, W., Milikic, B. B., Ogliastri, E., Taniguchi, M., Yan, S. & Zikic, J. 2009. Orientations to career transitions: A cross-cultural framework for understanding their impact. Paper presented at the annual conference of the European Group for Organization Studies, Barcelona, Spain, July 2–4.

Button, S. B., Mathieu, J. E. & Zajac, D. M. 1996. Goal orientation in organizational research: A conceptual and empirical approach. *Organizational Behavior and Human Decision Processes*, 67: 26–48.

Carver, C. S. & Scheier, M. F. 1981. *Attention and Self-Regulation: A Control Theory Approach*. New York: Springer-Verlag.

Chudzikowski, K., Demel, B., Mayrhofer, W., Briscoe, J. P., Unite, J., Bogicevic Milikic, B., Hall, D. T. T., Las Heras, M. & Zikic, J. 2009. Career transitions and their causes: A country-comparative perspective. *Journal of Occupational and Organizational Psychology*, 82: 825–849.

Demel, B., Chudzikowski, K. & Mayrhofer, W. 2006. 5C Qualitative content analysis and interpretation guide, Unpublished technical report, Vienna University of Economics and Business, Vienna.

Demel, B., Shen, Y., Hall, D. T., Mayrhofer, W., Chudzikowski, K., Unite, J., Briscoe, J. P., Abdul-Ghani, R., Bogicevic Milikic, B., Colorado, O., Fei, Z., Las Heras, M., Ogliastri, E., Pazy, A., Poon, J. M. L., Shefer, D., Taniguchi, M. & Zikic, J. 2009. Cracking the fortune cookies: Influencing factors in career success across 11 countries. Presentation at the Academy of Management annual meeting, Chicago, IL, Aug. 10.

Erikson, E. H. 1980. *Identity and the Life Cycle*. New York: Norton.

Glaser, B. G. & Strauss, A. L. 1967. *The Discovery of Grounded Theory*. New York: Aldine de Gruyter.

Hall, D. T. 1976. *Careers in Organizations*. Santa Monica, CA: Goodyear.

Hall, D. T. 2002. *Careers In and Out of Organizations*. Thousand Oaks, CA: Sage.

Inkson, K. 2006. Protean and boundaryless careers as metaphors. *Journal of Vocational Behavior*, 69: 48–63.

Mayring, P. (2008). *Qualitative Inhaltsanalyse: Grundlagen und Techniken* (10th ed.). Weinheim: Beltz Verlag.

McGrath, J. E. 1982. Dilemmatics: The study of research choices and dilemmas. In J. E. McGrath, J. Martin & R. A. Kulka (Eds.), *Judgment Calls in Research*. Newbury Park, CA: Sage.

Miles, M. B. & Huberman, A. M. 1994. *Qualitative Data Analysis: An Expanded Sourcebook* (2nd ed.). Newbury Park, CA: Sage.

Patton, M. Q. 1990. *Qualitative Evaluation and Research Methods* (2nd ed.). Newbury Park, CA: Sage.

Rokeach, M. 1973. *The Nature of Human Values*. New York: Free Press.

Schwartz, S. H. 2004. Mapping and interpreting cultural differences around the world. In H. Vinken, J. Soeters & P. Ester (Eds.), *Comparing Cultures: Dimensions of Culture in a Comparative Perspective*: 43–73. Leiden, The Netherlands: Brill.

Schwartz, S. H. 2006. A theory of cultural value orientations: Explication and applications. *Comparative Sociology*, 5: 136–182.

Strauss, A. & Corbin, J. 1990. *Basics of Qualitative Research: Techniques and Procedures for Developing Grounded Theory*. London: Sage.

Super, D. E., Savickas, M. L. & Super, C. M. 1996. The life-span, life-space approach to careers. In D. Brown, L. Brooks & Associates (Eds.), *Career Choice and Development* (3rd ed.): 121–178. San Francisco, CA: Jossey-Bass.

Triandis, H. C. 1995. *Individualism and Collectivism*. Boulder, CO: Westview.

Part II

The Research Findings

4

Career Success Around the World: Its Meaning and Perceived Influences in 11 Countries

Barbara Demel, Yan Shen, Mireia Las Heras, Douglas T. (Tim) Hall and Julie Unite

> From nurse, to head nurse, to the director of the whole nursing department, which is the highest position to me, I think this is a successful career.
>
> (Younger female Chinese nurse)

> In my success . . . children are already included. It is your life, and you only have one life. Because if professionally you get where you wanted to, and you accomplish your dream, and you are divorced, and your children hate you, and you are an alcoholic . . . what's the deal!? My plan accounts for the different elements in my life; it delineates how I want my life to be in the future, not only my work.
>
> (Younger Spanish businesswoman)

> Completing different kinds of additional education also means career success to me.
>
> (Older female Austrian nurse)

> I don't know there's a perfect career as much as if you're satisfied with what you're doing.
>
> (Younger male American blue-collar)

Introduction

"I know what time is," said Saint Augustine, "but if someone asks me I cannot tell him." The historian and economist David Landes, specialist in cultural, technological and manufacturing aspects of measuring time, adds, "No one knows what time is; certainly no one knows how to define and explain it to the general satisfaction. But we sure know how to measure it" (Landes, 2000: 202). From the academic perspective one can say the same about career success. People have a sense of what career success is, and researchers have long measured it; however, there is a gap in the career literature regarding the elements that define individuals' career success across cultures. So the question is: What exactly is career success?

Research and theory on career success are closely connected with literature on career per se and revert to its definitions (Arthur, Khapova & Wilderom, 2005). Careers have been regarded as an "evolving sequence of work experience over time" (Arthur, Hall & Lawrence, 1989a: 8) or a "sequence of positions occupied by a person during the course of a lifetime" (Super, 1980: 282). The two definitions show a duality between two perspectives on careers, a subjective and an objective one (Hughes, 1937, 1951). Similarly, career success, often defined as "the positive psychological or work-related outcomes or achievements one has accumulated as a result of one's work experiences" (Judge, Cable, Boudreau & Bretz, 1995: 486; see also London & Stumpf, 1982), covers a dichotomy of objective and subjective elements (Hughes, 1937, 1951). Objective career success denotes components of career success such as income or hierarchical advancement that are visible and "objectively" measurable (e.g. Gattiker & Larwood, 1988; Judge & Bretz, 1994). On the other hand, subjective career success heavily depends on individuals' (re)construction of their career according to subjective and individualized patterns. Subjective career success is mostly operationalized as career or job satisfaction (e.g. Aryee, Chay & Tan, 1994; Judge et al., 1995; Judge, Higgins, Thoresen & Barrick, 1999), since it is often defined as "individuals' feelings of accomplishment and satisfaction with their careers" (Judge et al., 1995: 2).

This chapter presents results from an inductive, qualitative study across 11 countries, and seeks to understand what elements are related to career success, how people in different cultures and occupations perceive and define career success, and whether these meanings are similar or different across countries and cultures. The culture-comparative angle in careers research has not been well developed yet (e.g. Spokane, Fouad & Swanson, 2003), and there has been a growing quest for multidisciplinary research across cultural boundaries on careers and career outcomes (e.g. Arthur, Hall & Lawrence, 1989b). As Arthur et al. (2005: 196) note in their review of literature of the decade 1992–2002, qualitative research is asked for in particular to gain a fuller understanding of what career success actually means:

> not one of the 68 articles we examined involved listening directly to the research subjects, or even allowing them to elaborate on their own criteria for career success. . . . How can subjective careers be adequately researched when the subjective interpretations of the career actors themselves—apart from their non-verbal responses to a limited set of questionnaire items—are not allowed expression?

Based on our multicultural analysis, we first show the most important meanings of career success of our global sample (i.e. the 226 interviewees in 11 countries as a whole). Furthermore, we highlight commonalities and differences as well as a certain universalism of meanings of career success across different countries and culture clusters. To be more specific, we will address the following questions:

1 What are the three most important meanings of career success identified from our global sample of 226 interviewees?
2 What are the most important meanings of career success within each of the 11 countries?
3 What are the elements of career success commonly valued across the 11 countries? In other words, to what extent do the meanings of career success demonstrate universalisms?

Before looking at the results of this qualitative study we give an overview of the prior studies on career success, focusing upon objective and subjective career success.

Literature Review

Objective Career Success

The bulk of research on career success has focused on antecedents of objective career attainment in terms of salary and hierarchical position (e.g. Gattiker & Larwood, 1988). Such a career success definition enables relatively easy comparison across nations and occupations. The variables considered to measure objective success include salary, rate of salary growth, number of promotions, rate of promotion, hierarchical level, and proximity to CEO (Arnold & Cohen, 2008). These rewards might be granted to the individual by societal agents (rewards such as recognition and fame), the company (e.g. money and promotions), other associates or one's own family (e.g. respect and praise).

Despite the interest of the studies on objective success, and the advantages that those studies present, the focus on objective aspects also presents major issues because scholars studying the predictors and moderators of career success base most of their studies on four implicit assumptions. The first assumption is that people have similar definitions of success. The second is that the definition of success is static throughout the individual's life. The third is that the opportunity cost of career outcomes plays no role in one's career success. The fourth is that career decisions are always made to maximize extrinsic rewards and that objective career success is the single most desirable outcome of one's career (Las Heras, 2009).

Hence it is necessary to consider both objective and subjective aspects of career success, because "only through conceiving both sides could the researcher grasp the social processes that lie behind careers and career success" (Arthur et al., 2005: 180).

Subjective Career Success

The other dimension present in studies of career success is subjective career success (e.g. Hughes, 1937). Some researchers describe subjective career success as individuals' evaluations of their own careers, defined as "individuals' feelings of accomplishment and satisfaction with their careers" (Judge et al., 1995: 2). Other researchers refer to subjective career success as "the success that comes from fulfilling one's needs by engaging in the work" (Betz, Fitzgerald & Hill, 1989). To achieve this type of success people should, for instance, learn, develop skills or enhance a facet of their personality. They could also engage in a meaningful relationship with a peer. Others define subjective career success as outcomes that the job yields by itself, that remain in the individual, and hence cannot be distributed or split (Ferreiro & Alcázar, 2002).

The most widely used scale to measure subjective success focuses on how people feel about their objective career achievements (Greenhaus, Parasuraman & Wormley, 1990). In their five-item scale, Greenhaus et al. (1990) ask participants to report their satisfaction in terms of overall success, progress toward career goals such as income, advancement, and development of new skills. Thus the scale is basically concentrating on how people feel about their external achievements. However, an important aspect is missing, i.e. their overall career experiences that involve much more than mere accomplishments (Las Heras, 2009).

Scholars have long assumed that objective measures capture what most individuals would recognize as success. For instance, Kirchmeyer (1998: 673) says that "success is equated with progression within a corporation, and assessed in terms of personal income, hierarchical level, and promotions." However, there is also some evidence that objective success does not necessarily lead to the feeling of pride and satisfaction (Bartolomé & Evans, 1980) or "psychological success" in which goals are only meaningful to the individual rather than those set by parents, peers, organizations or society (Hall, 1996). Examples of these goals are family happiness or inner peace. As Hall and Chandler (2005: 158) describe, "[a] sense of psychological success would likely be achieved when the person independently sets and exerts effort toward a challenging, personally meaningful goal and then goes on to succeed in attaining that goal."

Over the past decade, the consideration of both objective and subjective aspects as well as their interrelatedness has become increasingly important (e.g. Arthur et al., 2005; Nicholson & de Waal-Andrews, 2005), particularly in line with the discussion about the "new careers" (e.g. Arthur, Inkson & Pringle, 1999; Hall, 1996) where individuals' motivations, values, own initiative and independence are emphasized and advocated.

Sources of Career Success

In order to gain a deeper understanding of how people perceive and define career success, particularly considering different cultural roots, it is important also to look at the perceptual factors that influence career success. Many studies have investigated predictors of careers and career success (e.g. Judge & Bretz, 1994; Judge et al., 1995; Mayrhofer, Meyer & Steyrer, 2007; Ng, Eby, Sorensen & Feldman, 2005). Crucial factors that have been identified in empirical studies include human capital, demographic characteristics, personality and socio-demographic status, as well as organizational, industrial and regional developments (Ballout, 2007; Judge et al., 1995; Mayrhofer et al., 2005; Ng et al., 2005). In addition, work–life balance and organizational sponsorship are also considered as important factors influencing career success (e.g. Aryee et al., 1994; Eddleston, Baldridge & Veiga, 2004; Ng et al., 2005).

A possible way of structuring these influencing factors is shown in Figure 4.1. Beyond individual predictors such as dispositional individual differences, various layers of external factors influence career success as well. These include the context of work, the context of origin, the context of society and culture and the even broader global context.

Findings

This section includes major findings on meanings of career success. It is important to note that our results present what our interviewees report when they are talking about their own career success and how they connect such success with influencing factors. We first highlight the main categories of career success identified from the global sample. Second, we report the most important meanings of career success across

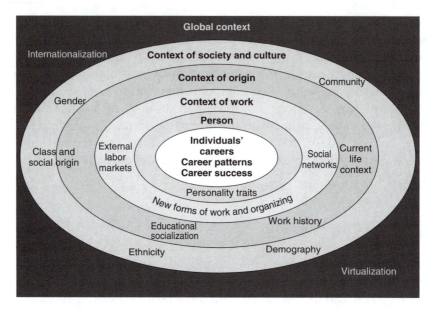

Figure 4.1 Contextual factors influencing careers and career success

Source: Mayrhofer, Meyer & Steyrer (2005: 16, 2007: 217).

the global sample (i.e. 226 interviewees in the 11 countries). Third, we present commonalities across countries and culture clusters as well as categories unique to specific countries. Fourth, we examine the extent of universalism regarding meanings of career success, which is indicated by categories that are mentioned by at least two people in each occupation in each country. Fifth, we use stories that somehow summarize the actual interviews in a country (Spain, China and Austria) to exemplify some unique patterns identified in those countries. Finally, we give a short overview of the perceived influencing factors of career success across the 11 countries.

Where Career Success Resides

Before presenting actual results it is important to introduce the major categories of the meanings of career success identified through content analysis of our interviews (Figure 4.2) and integrated into the 5C Global Coding Book (see Chapter 3 on our research methods). Concluding, we find that there are three main places where career success "lives" in the mind of the worker, which are labeled as follows: *person, job* and *interaction with the environment.*

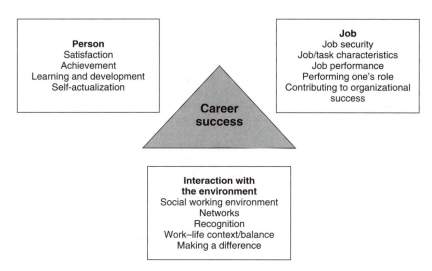

Figure 4.2 Where success "lives": the three main categories of career success

Source: Developed from the 5C Global Coding Book.

Each of the four categories includes several sub-categories. With regard to the person, career success is linked to satisfaction, achievement, learning and development, and self-actualization. As regards the job, the elements that are perceived to be important are job security, job/task characteristics (e.g. responsibility, autonomy and participation or scope and variety of tasks), job performance, performing one's role and contributing to organizational success. The third dimension is interaction with the environment. It includes social working environment, networks, recognition from others, work–life interaction (particularly work–life context/balance) and making a difference for others/for society.

Conceptualizations of Career Success of the Global Sample

With regard to major findings, we first present the results for the overall global sample, i.e. all of the individuals in our sample, without dividing into countries or occupational or generational groups. The three most important meanings of career success, worldwide, are shown in Table 4.1.

The dominance of achievement (e.g. financial achievement and promotion) and satisfaction (e.g. work/job satisfaction) across the global sample (Table 4.1) echoes the career literature that career success

Table 4.1 Top three perceived meanings of career success and influencing factors

	Meaning of career success	*Quotes*
1	Achievement (objective career success) *Financial achievement* *Promotion/advancement* *Person*	"Progression from one job to another and moving from one company to a better one which offers you better pay and more benefits" (Younger Malaysian businesswoman). "Thinking in the long run, maybe having an own business" (Younger male Austrian blue-collar).
2	Satisfaction (subjective career success) *Satisfaction with work/job* *Enjoyment and fun* *Person*	"I think that a successful person is the one who finds the job that really pleases him or her" (Older male Mexican blue-collar). "I say that for me it is being satisfied with my job and not so much hierarchical advancement" (Younger female Austrian businesswoman).
3	Job/task characteristics (objective and subjective career success) *Responsibility (objective)* *Challenge (subjective)* *Job*	"I want to manage a profit and loss account, because now I only have an internal client, and I want to have an external one that allows me to measure myself against others in the market" (Younger Spanish businessman). "Challenge, that's probably the only thing that keeps you really liking a job. If you go in there every day and it is the same old thing, you know, you have to have a whole different mindset, which I never had. I had no patience with—I had no patience with doing the same old thing over and over and over and over" (Older male American blue-collar).

Notes:
Global sample, n = 226.
The three major categories included in this table are all mentioned by over half of the total 226 interviewees; the sub-categories (italic) show the most important themes under these major categories.

includes both objective and subjective dimensions. In addition, the relative salience of job/task characteristics that include objective and subjective sub-categories indicates that actually engaging in the types of work one desires (e.g. job featuring challenges or varieties) *is* perceived as "career success" as well. It seems interesting that the two first meanings (i.e. achievement and satisfaction) belong to the "person" category, while the third belongs to the "job" category. This reflects a rather actor-centered perspective on career success, pointing to a central component of what is referred to as protean careers (e.g. Hall, 1996), where focus is put on independent selves with individual values, needs and actions.

Perceived meanings of career success are further investigated within and across 11 countries to get a deeper understanding of career success. In addition, we will look at dimensions that tend to be universal across occupations and countries.

Most Important Perceived Meanings of Career Success Within and Across Countries

In order to identify certain commonalities and differences across countries and cultures, we present the most important categories mentioned within each country (Table 4.2). Further details about sub-level categories are explained in the text.[1]

Table 4.2 shows that achievement is among the top three categories concerning the meaning of career success in almost all the 11 countries except in Spain, where it is ranked the fourth (Table 4.2). It is particularly predominant in Serbia (20 interviewees out of 21) and China (24 out of 28). The sub-category most stressed under achievement is financial achievement, ranked high in eight countries and particularly emphasized in China and Mexico.

> For me career success is when you can earn good money, sufficient for the existence of the family, holidays and normal life, but within a limited number of working hours to provide for private life.
>
> (Younger male Serbian blue-collar)

> It is important to succeed in both the social and the economic aspects to consider it as a real success.
>
> (Younger Mexican businessman)

The salience of achievement, particularly financial achievement, across the ten countries indicates that it is a global dimension of career success regardless of the country and culture contexts. Achievement may be instrumental in fulfilling one's need for mastery (Deci, Connell & Ryan, 1989), which refers to the sensation that one is effective and capable in one's behavior rather than ineffective and inept (Sheldon & Elliot, 1999). This effect might also possibly be influenced by the turbulent economic and social environment with a shifting psychological contract that often results in shorter-term employment, feeling of insecurity and lower organizational commitment (Rousseau, 1995). Therefore it is reasonable to expect the pursuit of achievement as a way to demonstrate one's success on objectively observable measures (Nicholson & de Waal-Andrews, 2005).

Moreover, its predominance in Serbia and China may reflect the dramatic economic and social changes in these two countries during

Table 4.2 Ranking within countries of perceived meanings of career success

Cluster	Confucian Asia		Eastern Europe	English speaking	Latin America		Southeast Asia	Sub-Saharan Africa/Middle East	Western Europe			Sum of countries mentioning the category (within the threshold below)
Countries/categories	China	Japan	Serbia	U.S.A.	Costa Rica	Mexico	Malaysia	South Africa	Austria	Spain	Israel	
Achievement	1	3	2	1	1	1	1	1	1	4	3	**10**
Job/task characteristics	2	1	2	2	2	3			3	2	1	**9**
Satisfaction	4		1	3	1	2	4	2	1	1	2	**8**
Learning and development	2		3	3	3		3		2			6
Making a difference				2			2	2				3
Recognition		2	3	2								3
Work–life context/balance			1									2
Social working environment (including network)	3		2							3		2
Job performance			3	2								2
Self-actualization			3									1
Job security	3											1

Note:

Categories listed in this table are mentioned by at least 30 percent of the interviewees in each country. The three most important ones within this threshold are listed in this table. There are more than three most important categories in some countries because some categories rank the same. The numbers indicate the internal ranking of categories within one country. The same number means the same level of importance. If there is no third ranking it is due to the threshold of 30 percent. The first three categories and respective figures are in bold to show that the most important categories are the same ones as in Table 4.1.

the past two decades. The external, visible achievements (e.g. having a decent salary, owning a car and a house and occupying a good job position, as shown in the following quote from an older Chinese blue-collar) have become very important criteria of assessing one's career success in China.

> Career success means a relatively high income, a car, a house, a good position and promising developmental opportunities.
>
> (Older male Chinese blue-collar)

Another category important in nine countries is job/task characteristics. The most important sub-categories are more heterogeneous than those under achievement or satisfaction. For instance, they include challenges at work, responsibility, solving problems, scope and variety of tasks or the possibility to work with others. Job/task characteristics is ranked the first in Japan, with the need for responsibility and challenges as the two most important sub-dimensions, and Israel, where challenges and working with others are particularly important.

> In the future I see myself in our company. It's an ideal environment for me. I'm free to do and develop whatever I want. I maintain existing things and develop other fields—that's ideal. It's a challenge, an international environment, and I'm at the front.
>
> (Younger Israeli businessman)

> Career success for me is when I am assigned many tasks and have more responsibility.
>
> (Younger female Japanese nurse)

Satisfaction is another dominant category in eight countries, except in Japan, China and Malaysia, in which it is not included among the top three dimensions (further details are discussed with country specifics). Satisfaction is ranked the first in four countries: Austria, Spain, Serbia and Costa Rica. The most important sub-category is satisfaction with one's work or job, ranked high in seven countries.

> Only people who are satisfied with their jobs may be successful.
>
> (Older female Serbian nurse)

Learning and development is a salient dimension in six countries. While the U.S.A. and Costa Rica put special emphasis on informal learning, Austria and China emphasize formal learning. In Serbia and Malaysia both informal and formal learning are important.

> It's a job or a position where it allows you to grow as a whole person. It allows you to grow in your personal skills, and working with other people. So it's not

just you as a wonderful person, but there's the team synergy that you're growing and improving them as well.

(Younger American businesswoman)

Career success? To me, of course, finishing this education means success.

(Younger female Austrian nurse)

What is quite surprising is that none of the country pairs within the
same culture clusters show an identical picture regarding the top three
categories. The most similar country pair is Costa Rica and Mexico
(Latin American cluster) (Table 4.2). Moreover, although Austria and
Israel belong to different clusters, they demonstrate a similar picture to
the Latin American cluster too.

By contrast, the two country pairs China and Japan, in the Confucian
Asian cluster, and Spain and Austria, in the Western European cluster,
present quite a different pattern regarding the meanings of career success. A closer examination of Table 4.2 shows that China and Austria are
more homogeneous regarding the top four categories. These findings
pose an important question for further exploration, i.e. to what extent
does the culture influence individuals' conceptualization of career success? In other words, the overall institutional environment (i.e. the economic, social, cultural, political and historical contexts) may play a joint
role in shaping individuals' perception of career success.

Take China and Austria, for example. The two countries are surprisingly similar, particularly regarding the objective indicators of career
success. Schwartz asserts that the pursuit of power and wealth is more
salient in cultures embracing hierarchy and mastery values (Schwartz,
1999). But this applies only in China, not in Austria, which is low in hierarchy and mastery yet shows strong desire for achievement. One possible
explanation is that both China and Austria share recent histories of strong
autocratic rule, in which individual freedom had been suppressed. Both
countries suffered great economic hardship during World War II and had
long periods of rebuilding. This shows the importance of institutional
factors other than culture. Thus, because of these historical factors, individuals are socialized to assume that they must strive strongly to achieve
upward mobility and power through financial and other tangible success
in these two countries. These explanations are tentative. More research is
needed here to explore the underlying reasons for this phenomenon.

Occupational Differences Around the World

People in different occupations around the world seem to see the
meaning of success in somewhat different ways. The group that appears

most distinct, in relation to the others, is the one of nurses. Worldwide, nurses tend to see their work as a calling. They seem to define their success in terms of making a difference in the world. More specifically, they value helping others and, of the three occupational groups, they have the lowest percentage of people who define success in terms of material rewards. Listen to the words of two nurses in Austria and China:

> I thought about it less like a job—it sounds a little bit tacky—but more like a calling.
>
> (Older female Austrian nurse)
>
> Success means seeing my patients leave the hospital healthily—this gives me a sense of fulfillment.
>
> (Younger female Chinese nurse)

Nurses also attach great importance to recognition. Feedback is important. Undoubtedly, much of this recognition comes directly from patients, who spend much more time with their nurses than with their doctors. But this feedback is also important for nurses to receive from supervisors, peers and society at large. In terms of human resource management, this suggests that, even though material rewards may not be too critical for nurses, the organization should find ways to provide formal recognition, such as through public acknowledgement of exemplary service, awards, and celebrations of personal events such as birthdays, weddings and family milestones. It is important to take good care of the care providers!

For the blue-collar workers, financial and material rewards are important. As many of them may be operating near the subsistence level, security is important. They are not necessarily interested in promotion or advancement, perhaps because they do not see upward mobility as very likely to be available to them. Having a job is important. In a similar vein, learning and development and self-actualization are not major elements in how they define success. However, making money is seen as an indicator of achievement, and it is important for them to derive satisfaction from their work.

> The most important is to be able to earn a better salary. . . . Of course, everyone wants to be successful. To me, that means being able to earn more money.
>
> (Younger male Malaysian blue-collar)

People in business roles, interestingly, fall somewhere between the blue-collar workers and the nurses. While achievement and material rewards are also important for them, making a difference is a considerable element of success for over a third of the businesspeople. One of the most striking differences between the businesspeople and the other two groups is that the businesspeople are much more likely to define success in terms of the balance they can attain between the demands of their professional lives and their personal and family lives. This may be because their jobs are so demanding and spill over into their private lives so much, so that it is more difficult for them to have this balance, and that may be why it is so important to them.

> And for my career success I adapt my vacations to job requirements. If there is an important business audit I wouldn't go on holiday in that week but, if possible, I try to arrange audits according to school holidays so that I can still go abroad with my son.
>
> (Older female Austrian businesswoman)

> Career success for me, again, is being able to take care of my parents, and being able to afford to come home and see my parents. That's career success to me, because success to me is what's important to me, and within my career to be able to facilitate that.
>
> (Younger female American businesswoman)

But, for all of these groups, basic experiences such as achievement and satisfaction are critical elements in the definition of success. As the psychologist David McClelland (1987) found many decades ago, these are fundamental human needs, and they are represented across all of our occupational groups.

Universalisms

Universalism means that a category is important regardless of the culture or country. The way we have operationalized for it in this study is considering that a category is universalistic when it is mentioned by at least two people in each occupation and in each country. Based on this restrictive criterion, there are no universal categories in terms of the perceived meaning of career success across the 11 countries (Table 4.3).

"Achievement" is close to being "universal," since it is salient in nine countries except in Japan and Spain, followed by job/task characteristics (important in eight countries except Japan, Malaysia and South Africa) and satisfaction (present in seven countries except the U.S.A., China, Japan and Malaysia).

Table 4.3 Universalisms: perceived meanings of career success across occupations and countries

Cluster	Confucian Asia		Eastern Europe	English speaking	Latin America		Southeast Asia	Sub-Saharan Africa/Middle East	Western Europe			Sum of countries mentioning the category (within the threshold below)
Countries/categories	China	Japan	Serbia	U.S.A.	Costa Rica	Mexico	Malaysia	South Africa	Austria	Spain	Israel	
Achievement	x		x	x	x	x	x	x	x		x	9
Job/task characteristics	x		x	x	x	x			x	x	x	8
Satisfaction			x		x	x		x	x	x	x	7
Learning and development	x		x	x		x			x		x	6
Social working environment												
Performing one's role/job (including network)	x		x			x			x		x	5
performance			x	x					x		x	4
Recognition			x						x		x	3
Self-actualization	x		x								x	3
Work–life context/balance			x									1
Financial security			x									1
Financially supporting family			x									1
Affording material goods			x									1

Note: Categories marked with crosses in this table are mentioned by at least two persons in each occupational group in each country. The numbers in the last column indicate how universal the categories are (in how many countries they are mentioned by at least two people in each occupational group and country).

The three different analytical approaches, considering our global sample (Table 4.1), specific findings within each country (Table 4.2) and the universalism pattern (Table 4.3), reveal the same top three categories. This result highlights the importance of achievement, satisfaction and certain job/task characteristics as the crucial career success dimensions in most countries.

Japan demonstrates a unique pattern here, i.e. no categories were mentioned by at least two people in each occupation. This indicates that the three occupations in Japan seem to conceptualize career success quite differently. Malaysia reveals a similar though less extreme pattern, with only "achievement" as the common dimension for all of the three occupations. By sharp contrast, the three occupations in Serbia, Israel and Austria perceive career success from a much more common perspective. These findings indicate that the occupational differences regarding the conceptualization of career success vary significantly across countries. This result has important implications for organizations in terms of employee motivation and talent development.

In Focus: Country Specifics

In this section we discuss country specifics in more detail, with quotes and stories. Four countries, China, Spain, South Africa and Austria, are selected to show some particularities as compared with other countries. For example, China focuses more on objective career success, whereas Spain and South Africa emphasize subjective career success more. Austria is chosen owing to the relatively balanced subjective and objective aspects of career success. We also include some quotes to illustrate country specifics in other countries.

The China data demonstrate two patterns that deserve more detailed illustration: (1) the emphasis upon career achievement (e.g. financial achievement and promotion and advancement) across both generations and the three occupations, and (2) the salience of job security, particularly in the blue-collar workers across the two generations (see the following quote from an older blue-collar and the story about a younger blue-collar in China).

> Now I am old, without strong educational background and competences, I only want a stable job, with a certain amount of money and a secured peaceful life till my formal retirement at the age of 60.
>
> (Older male Chinese blue-collar)

Jun was in his early 30s. He has been working for more than ten years since he graduated from a polytechnic school. At that time, which company he would go to was still subject to school arrangement. He was assigned to a state-owned enterprise (SOE) in Shanghai as a maintenance staff worker. He considered his work at this factory dull and the rewarding system ineffective to motivate the employees.

This factory was acquired by another SOE several years later owing to its poor performance. His friends and former classmates all tried to persuade him to leave the company, but he decided to stay with the newly merged company because of his needs for stability, the family influence and his good relationship with his current supervisor. His salary was increased afterwards, but he thought it was still lower than that of the original employees of the new company and the growth range was much smaller than that of the managers. He hoped that his salary could be doubled in the future.

He has felt the need for a career change in the near future. Such a thought never crossed his mind in his earlier years. At that time, "stability" and "a decent income" were all that he wanted. Jun's parents were also blue-collars. They wanted him to have a stable job before, but they changed their minds after seeing Jun's difficulty in finding a girlfriend because of his lower salary. In addition, his friends and former classmates earned more than he did, which made him feel the necessity to reconsider his career plans.

> My family does not have high expectations for me. In the past, [my parents] always told me to be obedient and not to go against the fate. However, what I learned from my relatives and friends is that people need to take the initiative and be creative. . . . I have a friend who was laid off by his former company and had to find a new job. He is a hard-working person. Now he is a department manager, with a quite decent salary and much improved life quality. The bigger gap between him and me really pushed me to think more about my job.

Jun thought promotion in SOEs was based more on "relationships with the management" than on individual competencies, which further strengthened his decision to seek another job elsewhere. He was pursuing further studies in a three-year diploma program in the hope that better education could help him become more competitive in the job market. His conceptualization of career success is mainly based upon objective criteria such as salary and external recognition (see the quote below).

> Successful career means an income of at least RMB 3,000, purchasing an apartment on my own, a sense of fulfillment at work, and a good job performance that is recognized by my colleagues. . . . The key to success depends on several aspects: first is education, second is being innovative, and third is the working environment and good relationships with my colleagues.

Jun's story shows several important themes concerning the results identified in the China sample. First, financial achievement and promotion are important indicators of career success and underlying reasons for one's career change. Second, one's need for job stability/security is challenged by one's own desire for more income, the social comparison with one's peers, and the turbulent environment. Third, family and friends play an important role in one's career development. The former influence one's basic values, whereas the latter trigger one to reexamine one's career path.

Our data also show that not only friends and family but also one's social working environment, e.g. relationships with superiors and peers, is perceived as an important element of career success in China as well as in Serbia.

> For me, the working environment should be harmonious, with no factions and a cohesive team.
>
> (Younger female Chinese nurse)

In general the results from China show a very objective perspective on career success across the sample. A similar pattern is observed for Japan. Both countries together with Malaysia are the only ones where satisfaction is not included among the top three categories. In Japan this dimension was mentioned by only three out of 20 interviewees. One important category in Japan is recognition, particularly receiving positive feedback. The U.S.A. is another country where recognition is ranked high.

> Um, I think what I am doing right now I would consider career success. I preceptor new orientees. I feel that my thoughts and my contributions are useful and I feel that people respect my practice and my, um, and my information that I have to share and I think that is probably, um, the feeling that I have that my coworkers respect my work and my patients appreciate what I am doing. I feel that the families that I work with appreciate my support and what I do for them, and to me that is success.
>
> (Older female American nurse)

One additional category that is emphasized most in the U.S.A. is job performance.

> I think that that's a question that I probably would answer differently if I pondered it for a day or two. My immediate reaction to it is that I felt pleased by the financial performance of my companies. When they were successful, then that was a reflection on me.
>
> (Older American businessman)

As indicated above, our sample also includes countries showing a strong emphasis on subjective career success. The following two stories give more detailed information about Spain and South Africa, where subjective aspects of career success prevail. One theme worth mentioning here is work–life context/balance, since it is quite prevalent in career success literature (see, for example, Chompookum & Derr, 2004; Derr & Laurent, 1989; Schein, 1996); surprisingly, however, it is only perceived as a salient career success aspect in two (i.e. Spain and Serbia) out of the 11 countries. For instance, a younger Spanish businessman says:

> For me to succeed would be to achieve what I thought I would love to do when I graduated from my MBA: to create a company where I would give jobs to other people, serve my family and achieve my dream. That would be success for me. My dream includes my family, because my life is one, and my dream includes my career, my family and everything I want for the future.

This comment captures the balance of factors that make up success in Spain. Professional achievement and job rewards (intrinsic and extrinsic) are certainly important, but it is clear that the family is part of the dream. Job attainments for this interviewee cannot come at the expense of time with his family or at the cost of working and living in a place far away from his family. In many other cultures, such as the U.S., success is weighted far more toward the work and job side of the equation, and these rewards often come at the expense of work–life balance. If someone wants to see how work and life can be brought into harmony, they should go to Spain!

The following story of Tony, an older Spanish businessman, covers the theme of work–life interaction too. Altogether this story is a good example of how careers have developed in Spain for people who are currently in their 50s and 60s. People in this age group have had rather stable careers with very few job changes. For them, satisfaction and identification with their company are very important, as well as respect from peers and a good work–life balance. Surprisingly enough, careers of people in younger generations are not substantially different.

Tony studied business in Barcelona, which is the city where he was born. He had been working as an accountant in a rather small company two years after graduating, when his friends insisted that he take an exam for a position at a bank. As he describes his decision:

> I was working in a small firm and my colleagues and friends convinced me to take an exam to be eligible to work at a caja.[2] There were seven of them and all of them were planning to take the exam except me. However, I ended up taking it with them. I took it and I passed it and I was the only one! Ever since then I've been working at a caja.

After accepting a position from a caja, Tony never thought about changing jobs. As he explains it, he has enjoyed the opportunities the job has offered and the relationships he has developed. He reflects on how he has been able to adapt his job to his preferences over time. While he is in his 50s, what he enjoys the most is to share and transfer his knowledge to younger employees:

> I love passing on my experience to younger people who are eager to learn but have no experience. Since I am older, I am not that eager to learn, but I do have a lot of experience. Thus, to combine their youth with my experience feels really satisfying.

At the caja Tony was working at, the only opportunities for promotion were if one worked at the bank's headquarters. At some point in his career, Tony deliberately made the decision not to accept any offers from headquarters because he saw promotions as a conflict with his family life. As he explains it:

> I think that you need to know where you want to be and, once you are there, you need to say "Enough! I made it!" I got to a point at which I did not want more because that would have conflicted with my family life, which for me is very important. I love my wife and my children, and I love my friends. But I came to the point where, in order to be promoted at the caja, I would have needed to work even longer hours, and I was already working very long hours. There my success is to work well, to be motivated and to work well with my peers and my subordinates. Those things are rewarding.

A strong focus on subjective success is also observed in South Africa. The South African interviewees place particular emphasis on making a difference; career success to them has a lot to do with helping others, as can be seen in the two following short stories.

Peter is an older white businessman who has worked in a number of different business settings during his professional career. After many years of climbing the corporate ladder, Peter now chooses to run his own small business, where he has the autonomy to direct projects and be his own boss. He lives in a community where the poverty disparity between the main racial groups (black, "colored" and white) is great, much of it a result of the apartheid era. Part of his current career is helping other, more disadvantaged individuals in this office and the surrounding community:

> What's becoming more and more apparent for me is that career success is actually being able to make a very pleasant environment for my colleagues at work. I've got a program going, which started with all the black employees' children having their school fees paid by us and to get the black kids out of township schools into better schools. We also try to have a youngster in each office and we try and build him, educate him, train him, expecting him to leave and go on, but we try to make it a sort of introduction into business, which will train him to further his business interests somewhere else.

Chris is a very accomplished and educated older black businessman who overcame many of the barriers associated with apartheid South Africa. He gained an excellent education despite his color, traveled abroad to work and study at well-known universities, and eventually came back to his country to teach and work in organizations that required his unique skills set.

Reflecting on his career he talks about the different sectors he has worked in and the different types of projects he has been involved with. Some of them have been in large multinational corporations where the results of his work are often not tangible or significant to others. Similarly, he has worked in consulting positions where his knowledge has not been put to appropriate use. He now chooses to work in roles where he can see a direct result of his actions, together with the potential benefits to others:

> I think career success is the ability to—whether you're selling something to somebody, either a commodity or a service, the person appreciates it. I think, for me, that's the finest career. Money is important, but I don't think it can buy that.

Making a difference is also ranked high in the U.S.A., where—similarly to South Africa—the focus is put on helping others, whereas in Malaysia having a positive impact on society is stressed.

> And I feel that what I learned is that you achieve what you want. If you think that money is important then find a career that gives you that, you know. In my life it was always, you know, people. How can I help to make it easier or better? That's why even the case writers' workshops meetings are always held here, because if I can do something to help out something or somebody, you know, I do it. So, to me, I think I am successful, not in monetary terms but in other ways.
>
> (Older Malaysian businesswoman)

In contrast to Japan, China, Spain and South Africa, Austria is one of the countries where both objective and subjective elements of career success are stressed in the same way. We present three short stories, one representing each occupational group, that show the importance of a balance between, for example, satisfaction or happiness and financial or hierarchical achievements.

Iris is a young business graduate in Vienna. After finishing her studies at WU Vienna she also started working there as a research and teaching assistant. After about a year she was not happy there anymore. It was the atmosphere at work, the job itself, as well as her colleagues, that did not make her feel satisfied and successful anymore, either with her job or with herself. Hence she changed job and started at a private company. To Iris career success covers a couple of themes. It is not only about hierarchies but also about satisfaction; however, a certain objective development is also something she is striving for:

> At the moment I am very satisfied and really enthusiastic about my job, also about the opportunities it offers. I say that success to me is to be satisfied with one's tasks and that the scope of tasks is expanding over the years. But of course you also want to get ahead and get more responsibility.

In a comparable way Karl, a younger Austrian blue-collar employee working in a pharmaceutical laboratory, is fully satisfied with his career and job: "I actually can't think of anything I am not satisfied with in my job right now."

However, thinking in the longer run, he indicates that he needs development and change to stay satisfied; success to him also means to "open my own business one day; I definitely don't want to be in the same position for the next 40 years or so."

A very similar pattern is presented by Claudia, an Austrian nurse at the age of 55. After giving birth to four children and after having worked in a nursing home for two years she changed to an outpatient clinic of a public hospital. Of course it was a big change and a challenge to adapt to the new system; after all she had not been working in a hospital for a really long time. As tough as it was, Claudia felt really satisfied about herself pretty much from the beginning on: "Well, to me personally, I felt successful. Actually I felt proud in some way . . . because only after a very short time I was integrated, within three weeks actually I was fully integrated." And, although others almost intimidated her with their warnings about competitive nurses in this clinic, she managed to also develop professionally quite fast; hence "as career success I would probably define my leading position, my managerial responsibility and apart from that also the pay increase."

These three short stories show how important the simultaneous consideration of both subjective and objective success factors, as well as their interrelation, is. This is observed across all occupational and generational groups.

Additional Findings: Influencing Factors in Career Success

In order to grasp a fuller understanding of what people in different countries mean when they talk about career success, it is also important to consider the sources of career success, i.e. the perceived influencing factors. An analysis of our global sample of 226 interviews (Table 4.4) shows the four most important influencing factors in career success ("motives" and "traits" ranked the same).

The most important source of career success is the context of work, with particular emphasis on the company, superiors, peers and work networks. All the categories are external to a person. Second ranks personal history, including educational history, job history and family background. These categories are internal factors, since they describe one's own internalized experiences. Third come traits (e.g. persistence and diligence, positive attitude and work ethic) and motives (e.g. goal-related drivers such as efforts and emotional drivers such as enthusiasm), both internal to a person.

Table 4.4 Top three perceived influencing factors (global sample)

	Influencing factors in career success	Quotes
1	Context of work (work) *Company* *Superiors* *Peers* *Work networks*	"My problem along the years was the lack of support of the medical doctors who looked down on us and our contribution" (Older female Costa Rican nurse). "Well, and a meeting with colleagues, we have a meeting once a month, for a couple of years now, also in former times, at least every now and then, you could talk to colleagues about problems. This is really important, and in these meetings everybody presents certain problems and we talk about all sorts of issues and try to find solutions" (Older Austrian businesswoman).
2	Personal history (person) *Educational history* *Job history* *Family background*	"I would say that I am successful today because of my basic education from the primary school. Without that, I wouldn't be who I am now. I mean, that is the base: the education I got when I was at SM Agama Persekutuan Kajang. What I got there gave me the knowledge and faith that I have now" (Younger Malaysian businessman). "I was raised by driven parents. I have got two grannies who are like huge in the community. My granny organizes the old people to get food and organizes fundraisings. Yeah, I have to think it has a lot to do with upbringing and the type of people that have influenced my life" (Younger South African businesswoman).
3	Traits (person) *Persistence/diligence* *Positive attitude* *Work ethic*	"I think the key factor influencing one's career success is whether you are willing to work hard or not" (Older male Chinese blue-collar). "You have to create the good in all you do. Not always what you plan comes true but, even if not, you have to make the best out of it. That is easy for me to do. I am a very optimistic person. I have a good basis" (Older female Israeli nurse).
3	Motives (person) *Goal-related drivers* *Emotional drivers*	"My mom said, 'If you want to be a good lawyer, what you need to do is to work with your father, to join his office, and to get ready to inherit it in the future.' Well, I thought it made sense, and so I did" (Younger Spanish businessman). "Well, decisive for your success is definitely your personal interest in the job itself; plus, you have to make sacrifices, you need ambition that drives you and make you need to be resilient" (Younger Austrian businessman).

The three major categories included in this table are all mentioned by over half of the total 226 interviewees; the sub-categories (italic) show the most important themes under these major categories.

It seems that across the globe both individual experiences and good relationships with superiors and peers, as well as support from the organization, are vital for individuals' career success. Previous studies have attached a lot of attention to individual differences as the determining factors of career success (Judge et al., 1999). Our study, however, identified even greater emphasis on supportive relations within the context of work, thus highlighting the necessity to take a relational perspective when examining individuals' career success (Fletcher, 1999; Hall & Associates, 1996; Kram & Hall, 1996).

Practical Implications

When one considers the commonalties and differences observed in the meaning of career success across the 11 countries in our sample, it becomes clear that multinational companies will have to have career development practices that appeal to a diverse set of employee needs, and also that there are common needs across countries and generations.

A first step is simply to be aware of those needs and pay equal attention to both the similarities (e.g. financial achievement and hierarchical advancement) and the differences. Managers need to balance imposing rules with listening, and disseminating the corporate culture with accommodating new ways of doing things. Depending upon the culture (for example, if they prefer an egalitarian or hierarchical approach), active organizational learning can be accommodated to capture the career goals and aspirations of varied corporate employees, and to try to reflect that diversity in emerging training, socialization and policy. For example, while visible opportunity is very important in China, work–life flexibility is more salient to workers in Spain and Serbia. While the opportunity to demonstrate competence and achieve goals is paramount in Austria, family and community relations are more salient in Malaysia and Spain. The balancing act is learning how to develop career and performance systems that have integrity yet meet local needs.

One way to meet the needs of a diverse set of global employees is to focus on creating an integrated set of basic developmental management practices that promote career development. For example, Lips-Wiersma and Hall (2007) found in a New Zealand public agency that employee satisfaction was enhanced when a pattern of career-enhancing management practices was present: developing talent; strategic assignment of talent; focus on employability; diversity; developmental culture; and communication transparency. It also appears that all of these practices are self-reinforcing, that is, they tend to work together to create a cluster of forces that drive employee career development. Further, they apply equally well to all different types of employees, regardless of what their career needs or definitions of success are. Thus these general career-enhancing management practices have potential for applicability in a range of cultures.

Case Study

We now provide a short case to illustrate how the key findings and themes discussed in this chapter might be used to provide some meaningful variations in the international human resource management practices from country to country.

Bob Smith is the global HR vice president in Segwy, a U.S.-based manufacturing company with operations across the world. He is responsible for the annual talent review and needs to prepare a detailed report to the top management team by the end of this month about how to develop high-potential, middle-level managers into effective top-level leaders.

Before Bob joined this company in 2004, he was an HR director in another American company and was assigned to work in China for about three years. This international assignment enabled him to appreciate the cultural differences between China and the U.S.A. and, in particular, the difficulties and challenges in managing the culturally diversified workforce.

Bob understands that a standardized, U.S.-based career development approach would not work across different country contexts. Therefore, after he became the vice president in 2009, he spent a lot of time meeting HR directors and managers from different foreign subsidiaries, and put the annual talent review as one of the top priorities in his agenda.

This year's review is particularly concentrated upon four countries, i.e. China, Austria, Spain and South Africa, since the high-potential employees on the final list are from these four countries. The key issues Bob has to consider in the report include:

- How does the company create a motivating environment for these high-potential candidates in various country contexts?
- What kind of career development plan would be most appropriate?
- How does the company design their jobs?
- What type of leadership training program is necessary and effective?

Notes

1 Table 4.2 shows relative rankings of perceived meanings of career success within countries. To see data regarding the reporting levels of *all* perceived career success categories within countries, consult Table 4.5.

Table 4.5 Percentages within countries of research participants reporting perceived meanings of career success

Cluster	Confucian Asia		Eastern Europe	English speaking	Latin America		Southeast Asia	Sub-Saharan Africa/Middle East	Western Europe		
Countries/categories	China	Japan	Serbia	U.S.A.	Costa Rica	Mexico	Malaysia	South Africa	Austria	Spain	Israel
Achievement	**86%**	35%	95%	40%	95%	**89%**	56%	**50%**	89%	33%	84%
Job/task characteristics	36%	55%	95%	35%	63%	78%	11%	13%	61%	57%	95%
Satisfaction	29%	15%	100%	30%	95%	83%	28%	33%	89%	67%	89%
Learning and development	36%	25%	90%	30%	53%	56%	33%	29%	67%	33%	68%
Making a difference	14%	15%	48%	35%	16%	33%	39%	33%	17%	14%	47%
Recognition	21%	**40%**	90%	35%	21%	50%	6%	13%	**56%**	19%	53%
Work–life context/balance	7%	20%	100%	20%	32%	22%	22%	29%	22%	38%	47%
Social working environment (including network)	32%	15%	95%	10%	37%	50%	0%	25%	50%	24%	79%
Job performance	7%	0%	90%	35%	16%	17%	6%	13%	33%	14%	47%
Self-actualization	29%	20%	90%	20%	42%	39%	17%	29%	28%	14%	63%
Job security	32%	0%	33%	0%	0%	6%	11%	0%	6%	14%	26%

Note: The numbers listed in this table show how many people within one country mention the respective categories. The percentages are based on the total number of interviewees within the respective countries. Categories listed in bold are mentioned by at least 30 percent of the interviewees in each country.

2 "Cajas" are a special type of bank that operates in Spain. In order to work at a caja, an applicant must pass a specialized exam. Once an applicant accepts an offer from a caja, it is quite difficult to be laid off or discharged.

References

Arnold, J. & Cohen, A. 2008. The psychology of careers in industrial and organizational settings: A critical but appreciative analysis. *International Review of Industrial and Organizational Psychology*, 23: 1–43.

Arthur, M. B., Hall, D. T. & Lawrence, B. S. 1989a. Generating new directions in career theory: The case for a transdisciplinary approach. In M. B. Arthur, D. T. Hall & B. S. Lawrence (Eds.), *Handbook of Career Theory*: 7–25. Cambridge, U.K.: Cambridge University Press.

Arthur, M. B., Hall, D. T. & Lawrence, B. S. (Eds.). 1989b. *Handbook of Career Theory*. Cambridge, U.K.: Cambridge University Press.

Arthur, M. B., Inkson, K. & Pringle, J. K. 1999. *The New Careers: Individual Action and Economic Change*. London: Sage.

Arthur, M. B., Khapova, S. N. & Wilderom, C. P. M. 2005. Career success in a boundaryless career world. *Journal of Organizational Behavior*, 26(2): 177–202.

Aryee, S., Chay, Y. W. & Tan, H. H. 1994. An examination of the antecedents of subjective career success among a managerial sample in Singapore. *Human Relations*, 47(5): 487.

Ballout, H. I. 2007. Career success: The effects of human capital, person–environment fit and organizational support. *Journal of Managerial Psychology*, 22(8): 741.

Bartolomé, F. & Evans, P. A. L. 1980. Must success cost that much? *Harvard Business Review*, 58(2): 137–148.

Betz, N. E., Fitzgerald, L. F. & Hill, R. E. 1989. Trait-factor theories: Traditional cornerstone of career theory. In M. Arthur, D. T. Hall & B. S. Lawrence (Eds.), *Handbook of Career Theory*: 26–37. Cambridge, U.K.: Cambridge University Press.

Chompookum, D. & Derr, C. B. 2004. The effects of internal career orientations on organizational citizenship behavior in Thailand. *Career Development International*, 9(4/5): 406–423.

Deci, E. L., Connell, J. P. & Ryan, R. M. 1989. Self-determination in a work organization. *Journal of Applied Psychology*, 74(4): 580.

Derr, C. B. & Laurent, A. 1989. The internal and external career: A theoretical and cross-cultural perspective. In M. Arthur, D. T. Hall & B. S. Lawrence (Eds.), *Handbook of Career Theory*: 454–471. Cambridge, U.K.: Cambridge University Press.

Eddleston, K. A., Baldridge, D. C. & Veiga, J. F. 2004. Toward modeling the predictors of managerial career success: Does gender matter? *Journal of Managerial Psychology*, 19(4): 360.

Ferreiro, P. & Alcázar, M. 2002. *Gobierno de Personas en la Empresa*. Barcelona: Ariel.

Fletcher, J. K. 1999. *Disappearing Acts: Gender, Power, and Relational Practice at Work*. Cambridge, MA: MIT Press.

Gattiker, U. E. & Larwood, L. 1988. Predictors for managers' career mobility, success and satisfaction. *Human Relations*, 41: 569–591.

Greenhaus, J. H., Parasuraman, S. & Wormley, W. M. 1990. Effects of race on organizational experiences, job performance evaluations, and career outcomes. *Academy of Management Journal*, 33(1): 64–86.

Hall, D. T. 1996. Protean careers of the 21st century. *Academy of Management Executive*, 10(4): 8–16.

Hall, D. T. & Chandler, D. E. 2005. Psychological success: When the career is a calling. *Journal of Organizational Behavior*, 26(2): 155–176.

Hall, D. T. & Associates (Eds.). 1996. *The Career Is Dead—Long Live the Career: A Relational Approach to Careers*. San Francisco, CA: Jossey-Bass.

Hughes, E. C. 1937. Institutional office and the person, *Men and Their Work*: 57–67. Glencoe, IL: Free Press.

Hughes, E. C. 1951. Ambition, mobility and sponsorship. In R. Dubin (Ed.), *Human Relations in Administration*: 240–243. New York: Prentice-Hall.

Judge, T. A. & Bretz, R. D. 1994. Political influence behavior and career success. *Journal of Management*, 20(1): 43–65.

Judge, T. A., Cable, D. M., Boudreau, J. W. & Bretz, R. D. J. 1995. An empirical investigation of the predictors of executive career success. *Personnel Psychology*, 48(3): 485–519.

Judge, T. A., Higgins, C. A., Thoresen, C. J. & Barrick, M. R. 1999. The big five personality traits, general mental ability, and career success across the life span. *Personnel Psychology*, 52(3): 621.

Kirchmeyer, C. 1998. Determinants of managerial career success: Evidence and explanation of male/female differences. *Journal of Management*, 24(6): 673–692.

Kram, K. E. & Hall, D. T. 1996. Mentoring in a context of diversity and turbulence. In E. E. Kossek & S. A. Lobel (Eds.), *Managing Diversity: Human Resource Strategies for Transforming the Workplace*: 108–136. Cambridge, MA: Blackwell Business.

Landes, D. S. 2000. *Revolution in Time: Clocks and the Making of the Modern World*, rev. ed. Cambridge, MA: Belknap Press.

Las Heras, M. 2009. Psychological career success, preferred success set and its dynamism. Unpublished doctoral dissertation, Boston University, Boston, MA.

Lips-Wiersma, M. & Hall, D. T. 2007. Organizational career development is not dead: A case study on managing the new career during organizational change. *Journal of Organizational Behavior*, 28(6): 771–792.

London, M. & Stumpf, S. 1982. *Managing Careers*. Reading, MA: Addison-Wesley.

Mayrhofer, W., Meyer, M. & Steyrer, J. (Eds.). 2005. *Macht? Erfolg? Reich? Glücklich? Einflussfaktoren auf Karrieren*. Wien: Linde.

Mayrhofer, W., Meyer, M. & Steyrer, J. 2007. Contextual issues in the study of careers. In H. P. Gunz & M. A. Peiperl (Eds.), *Handbook of Career Studies*: 215–240. Thousand Oaks, CA: Sage.

McClelland, D. C. 1987. *Human Motivation*. Cambridge, U.K.: Cambridge University Press.

Ng, T. W. H., Eby, L. T., Sorensen, K. L. & Feldman, D. C. 2005. Predictors of objective and subjective career success: A meta-analysis. *Personnel Psychology*, 58(2): 367–408.

Nicholson, N. & de Waal-Andrews, W. 2005. Playing to win: Biological imperatives, self-regulation, and trade-offs in the game of career success. *Journal of Organizational Behavior*, 26(2): 137.

Rousseau, D. M. 1995. *Psychological Contracts in Organizations*. Thousand Oaks, CA: Sage.

Schein, E. H. 1996. Career anchors revisited: Implications for career development in the 21st century. *Academy of Management Executive*, 10(4): 80–88.

Schwartz, S. H. 1999. A theory of cultural values and some implications for work. *Applied Psychology: An International Review*, 48(1): 23–47.

Sheldon, K. M. & Elliot, A. J. 1999. Goal striving, need satisfaction, and longitudinal well-being: The self-concordance model. *Journal of Personality and Social Psychology*, 76(3): 482–497.

Spokane, A. R., Fouad, N. A. & Swanson, J. L. 2003. Culture-centered career intervention. *Journal of Vocational Behavior*, 62(3): 453–458.

Super, D. E. 1980. A life-span life-space approach to career development. *Journal of Vocational Behavior*, 16: 282–298.

5

Career Transitions: Windows Into the Career Experience in 11 Country Contexts

Jon P. Briscoe, Katharina Chudzikowski and Julie Unite

Sofi was a young ethnic Malay graduate in health studies in Kuala Lumpur, Malaysia. Watching her aunt's career (and with a strong interest in athletics), she desired to be an athletics instructor or a physical therapist specializing in sports medicine. However, her mother and father strongly felt she should become a nurse, because she could maintain a set schedule more easily and make good money for the family.

Sasha had great aspirations to apply his education in business to the emerging corporate sector in Serbia. At first his new job at an exporting company allowed him to learn a lot. However, he found that over time, as his job became more secure and new opportunities scarce, his desire for new learning waned. He was "plateaued" at a relatively young age, but he did not seem to mind.

Angela was experiencing success at the "Big 5" accounting firm for which she had worked for the last five years in Boston. After obtaining a coveted internship as an accounting major, she assumed she had her dream job. She sought out visible and developmental assignments—and received them. She was told she was on the "fast track" to make partner one day. Still, she did not feel like a success. She now felt bored and unfulfilled. She wondered if she should have gone into teaching as she had originally wanted to before deciding that the money was not good enough. Abruptly, she quit her job and took jobs substitute-teaching while she figured out her next move.

Each of the above examples illustrates various dimensions of a career "transition." Simply put, a career transition occurs when people have a significant change in their career. It could be within the same role (greater scope, for example), a new role in the same organization, a new or similar role in another organization—or a move to reduced or modified activity such as self-employment or retirement.

Career transitions are important for many academic as well as practical reasons. From an academic perspective, career transitions represent a point or segment in time at which the confluence of many factors comes to bear. There are the individual's values, health, identity, livelihood, personality, motivation, interests, skills and so on. Then there are the interests of employers in maintaining the employee's vitality, motivation, job performance, etc. The employee's loved ones including family and/or friends have a vested interest in the career transition. Their physical, temporal, financial and even emotional well-being may be on the line, depending upon the choices their loved one makes. To complicate all of this, market forces, political dynamics, cultural dynamics and other "macro" factors guarantee that the path and outcomes of contemporary career changes can never be taken for granted. While there may have been stable employment in the past, that is not the norm for many people today.

Amidst this ambiguous soup of interrelated and sometimes conflicting forces and considerations, a career actor tries to navigate the decision (if it is a "free" decision and not a default or mandated career move) of whether and how to pursue a career transition, how to adapt to the new realities and when and how it is time to move on yet again. Yet, important as the confluence of interests and the career actor's decisions are, many people proceed through career transitions as though they were driving down a street in a strange neighborhood, hoping and assuming everything will turn out well but without a good map or driving skills. And often those who impact career actors' transitions are not aware of the negative and positive impact they might have on those transitions.

Besides career success, career transitions are also important for understanding careers and represent turning points in each career path. Thus we explore career transitions across individuals, groups and countries. We define causes of career transitions by how individuals conceptualize the reason for starting a new job or phase in their careers. We will briefly review the established literature on career transitions. Then we will look at the 5C research into what causes and influences career transitions in different countries, occupations and generations and amongst men and women. We will examine the role culture may play in all this, as well as other contextual factors. Finally we will explore attitudes and learning approaches that seem to encourage more productive transitions.

Career Transitions in the Literature

Career transitions form a crucial part of one's personal identity and potentially have consequences for all areas of life (Driver, 1980;

Schlossberg, 1981). Thus career transitions are an integral part of career research and practice. Careers evolve over time and have different phases. Career transitions can be conceptualized as a phase of change bridging two jobs or professional careers or significant changes in role or responsibility within the same job or employment setting.

Since the career is defined as the sequence of work experiences over a person's life (Arthur, Hall & Lawrence, 1989), we are interested in the stories of work experiences over the life span. This is consistent with a large body of research that employs narratives or life stories as a way of capturing a person's career experiences and construction of careers (see, for example, Cohen, 2006; Young & Collin, 2004).

This chapter utilizes the insight generated in transition research. This includes work based on role theory (Allen & Van de Vliert, 1984), status passage (Glaser & Strauss, 1971), a transition cycle concept (Nicholson, 1990, 1996; Nicholson & West, 1988) or a model of transition process (Bridges, 1986; Nortier, 1995). A great deal of research also focuses on the *management* of career transitions, especially coping strategies (Bridges, 1986; Broscio & Scherer, 2003; Franzinger, 2001; Ibarra, 2004; Leibowitz & Schlossberg, 1982; Louis, 1982; Nortier, 1995; Sargent & Schlossberg, 1988; Schlossberg, 1981, 1984; Schlossberg, Troll & Leibowitz, 1978; Sullivan, 2003).

Conceptually, the chapter refers to a simple time-based framework of transitions (see Figure 5.1). This framework builds on the work of Nicholson and West (1989) and assumes that transitions have identifiable causes and lead to specific outcomes. Causes consist of individual factors closely linked to the individual ("internal") and situational factors from the environment ("external"). The way individuals identify causes for novel, sometimes threatening, events like career transitions helps in dealing with similar situations in the future, and produces causal attributions that build a cognitive framework (Silvester, Anderson & Patterson, 1999). Such attributional factors make a difference in the course of how transitions are interpreted. Nicholson and West (1988) identify this as a high desire for control—meaning perceived internal factors causing career transitions—as a predictor for role innovation. This process is seen as a mode of adjustment and therefore changing the way individuals cope with transitions. Outcomes of transitions can be classified as desired outcomes and actual outcomes. The former are outcomes for an aspired future career condition, and the latter are the actual results of the process that unfolds in attaining this. Desired and actual outcomes can, but need not, be related.

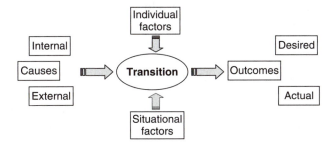

Figure 5.1 Framework of career transitions

Based on Nicholson & West (1989).

Career Transitions: Across Cultures, Occupations, Genders and Generations

We shall now consider patterns of career transitions on a *collective* scale. We will also take a closer look at generations and transitions as well as the influence of major cultural variables. Of course, when discussing "average" patterns within any one group—be it a nation, an occupation, an age group, etc.—we of necessity eliminate the unique detail that makes any one person's story meaningful. We will attempt to compensate for this by highlighting a few individual and country examples throughout the chapter, but we also recognize the value in understanding broad patterns across groups.

We evaluated patterns based primarily upon the percentage of research participants who were coded as being represented within a certain category. In general we highlight groups when at least 30 percent of them were coded as reflecting a certain category. This is an arbitrary cutoff, and lesser percentages of response rates can also have meaning and will be discussed where useful.

As part of the interview protocol research participants were asked to describe recent "career-related change(s)" including (beyond the basic details of the transition) their subjective feelings, their interpretation of influencing factors, and a report of outcomes (see Chapter 3 for more details on the interview). Frequently the participants' own reports drove all of the coding. However, in some cases inference was made (in assigning codes) where deemed appropriate for factors that seemed clear to the researcher but perhaps less visible to the focal person. For example, extreme poverty or extreme privilege may include constraints or enabling factors that are clear from an external comparative perspective but not as closely appreciated from the perspective of the "insider."

Transition "Triggers": What Drives Career or Job Change?

We describe transition "triggers" as those events and causes which lead to a career or job change. We left "change" to the subjective definition of the interviewee—in other words we let them define a significant change for themselves. We subdivided transition triggers into: those which were driven by the person, based upon his or her own initiative (such as a desire for something new, a desire for more development, etc.); those in which the perceived transition driver was from outside but the transition was initiated and pursued by the individual's efforts (described as "own initiative: external source"); and, finally, those triggers that are primarily attributed to external sources such as organizational change, economic factors and even luck/contingencies.

Tables 5.1 and 5.2 (respectively) profile the transition triggers for countries and for occupations, gender and generations. Categories where over 30 percent of the research participants were coded are marked in bold.

In Table 5.1 the first thing that is striking is that in most countries well over half of those interviewed indicated at least one transition that was driven by their own initiative. The dominant reasons varied from seeking development, to seeking balance, to looking for higher pay. Table 5.2 demonstrates that, when looking at occupations, gender and generations, all groups report over 50 percent believing their own initiative primarily drove their career transition. This overwhelming trend of self-perceived personal influence on career change strongly supports the notion of a protean career (Briscoe & Hall, 2006; Hall, 1976, 2002) which the person drives by him- or herself.

Internal triggers to career transitions certainly do not tell the entire story. Table 5.1 demonstrates that in seven of the 11 countries over 30 percent of the participants also reported that the primary trigger for their career transition(s) was organizationally driven. This was also true for each occupational, gender and age category, as seen in Table 5.2. This seems to indicate that, even if the organizational career does not dominate as much as it might have traditionally, it still has a partial hold upon our careers. While not as prevalent, family role(s) and macro factors (e.g. the political-legal environment) amongst other factors were seen as driving career transitions (as shown in Table 5.1).

Table 5.1 Career transitions by country

Coding categories	Sample countries										
	Austria	China	Costa Rica	Israel	Japan	Malaysia	Mexico	Serbia	South Africa	Spain	U.S.A.
Transition driven by own initiative (internal)	**0.67**	**0.54**	**0.89**	**0.84**	0.25	**0.68**	**0.67**	**0.81**	**0.54**	**0.81**	**0.60**
External transition sources:											
Organizationally driven	**0.33**	**0.89**	**0.37**	**0.42**	**0.65**	0.16	**0.44**	**0.57**	0.25	0.19	0.20
Family role	**0.33**	0.29	**0.37**	0.16	0	0.16	0.06	0.29	0.21	0.29	0.10
Macro factors	**0.33**	**0.61**	0.26	0.11	0.05	0.11	0	**0.67**	0.13	0.24	0.15
Individuals' management of career transitions:											
Planning/setting goals and priorities	**0.33**	0.11	NA	**0.32**	0	NA	**0.56**	**0.38**	0	0	**0.30**
Formal education, training, short courses	0.28	**0.39**	NA	**0.58**	0.05	NA	0.11	0.19	0.17	0.14	**0.60**
Influencing factors upon transitions:											
Boss/superior	**0.61**	**0.57**	NA	**0.63**	**0.55**	0.26	0.22	**0.62**	0.21	0	**0.40**
Peers	**0.39**	0.18	NA	**0.63**	**0.35**	0.26	0	**0.71**	0.25	0.14	**0.60**
Family	**0.61**	**0.43**	NA	**0.53**	0.10	**0.37**	0.17	**0.76**	**0.54**	0.19	**0.65**
Friends	**0.44**	**0.46**	NA	**0.37**	0.05	0.21	0.17	0.29	0	0.05	0.25
Organization	**0.39**	**0.50**	NA	**0.68**	**0.40**	0.21	**0.39**	1.0	0.21	0.10	**0.55**
Network	**0.50**	**0.36**	NA	**0.53**	0.10	0.16	**0.56**	**0.86**	0.17	0.19	0.25
Education and training	**0.50**	**0.50**	NA	**0.37**	0.15	0.11	**0.44**	**0.48**	0.25	0.14	**0.45**
Role of luck and contingencies	**0.39**	0.04	NA	0.16	0.10	0	0	0.29	0.04	0	0

Over 30 percent marked in bold.

Table 5.2 Career transitions by occupation, gender and age

Coding categories	Sample subgroups						
	Nurses	Blue-collar	Business	Female	Male	Younger	Older
Transition driven by own initiative (internal)	**0.58**	**0.62**	**0.77**	**0.63**	**0.64**	**0.72**	**0.56**
External transition sources: Organizationally driven	**0.48**	**0.37**	**0.44**	**0.43**	**0.43**	**0.34**	**0.52**
Family role	0.23	0.27	0.12	0.27	0.11	0.13	0.26
Macro factors	0.26	0.29	0.21	0.25	0.27	0.16	**0.36**
Individuals' management of career transitions: Planning/setting goals and priorities	**0.32**	0.25	0.27	0.22	**0.3**	0.28	0.14
Formal education, training, short courses	**0.32**	**0.33**	**0.35**	**0.31**	**0.40**	**0.37**	0.19
Influencing factors upon transitions: Boss/superior	**0.40**	**0.39**	**0.45**	**0.42**	**0.40**	**0.46**	**0.37**
Peers	**0.49**	0.29	0.28	**0.42**	0.27	**0.37**	**0.33**
Family	**0.49**	**0.37**	**0.46**	**0.49**	**0.39**	**0.48**	**0.40**
Friends	0.22	0.28	0.19	0.20	0.27	0.27	0.19
Organization	**0.57**	**0.33**	**0.45**	**0.50**	**0.39**	**0.45**	**0.44**
Network	**0.38**	**0.33**	**0.38**	**0.38**	**0.35**	**0.36**	**0.37**
Education and training	**0.35**	0.23	**0.46**	**0.37**	**0.32**	**0.39**	**0.30**
Role of luck and contingencies	0.05	0.16	0.07	0.07	0.12	0.09	0.11

Over 30 percent marked in bold.

Individual Management of Career Transitions

We categorized efforts to cope with or influence a career change as "managing" the transition. We listed and coded the behaviors in this area that corresponded to this transition management.[1] In half of the countries for which we have data, 30 percent or more of the participants were coded as setting goals and planning as a part of their transition management. Nurses set goals and planned more than business and blue-collar interviewees; men did so more than women; and younger people did so more than older research participants. What is perhaps more striking

Country Close-Up: Career Transitions in Malaysia

(Contributed by Rohayu Abdul-Ghani)

Apart from the findings that higher pay is a driving force that influenced career change decisions of Malaysians in the study, our data also demonstrate that two internal transition triggers should be examined in more detail. More specifically, these triggers are the individual's *desire to seek new opportunity* and also the *desire to seek development*. This is illustrated in the following description of one Malaysian's career transition experience.

Lily is a 50-something Malaysian-Chinese woman, with strong interests in caring for and nurturing others. Her passion got her to start her working life teaching at a secondary school in her hometown (U.S. high school equivalent). But that was a very short stint for Lily, as she felt she really had to pursue her stronger interest, which was a career as a nurse. This led her to take up a nursing degree, and she subsequently spent over 20 years of her life in the public nursing service in Malaysia. During her nursing years, Lily took up other responsibilities beyond patient care, such as taking on administration tasks. At the time, she felt she would benefit from the experience and probably even gain leverage for her career progression.

However, although nursing satisfied her need to nurture and the occasional administration tasks allowed her to have some variety in the job, Lily eventually felt that nursing wasn't really giving her the career satisfaction she was looking for. Having spent quite some years in the profession, Lily realized she had reached a point where her nursing duties didn't really present much challenge to her and her tasks were becoming rudimentary. As a result, Lily decided to move away from her routine nursing duties and ventured back into teaching. This change wasn't that difficult for Lily, because she had had some early career experience, albeit a short one, in teaching at a secondary school. To a degree, this helped Lily ease herself into the change. In addition, Lily's positive view towards her career change was a factor that helped her manage the transition.

> I've been doing the same thing and I've been working in pediatrics. Most of my career I've been in a pediatrics unit, so it seems like quite routine to me. So I decided to change back to education, more to train the future nurses. . . . Maybe at first we feel it's quite difficult because everything is new and everything you have to learn. . . . We have to give and take in that sense—flexibility.

Lily worked hard at being a good educator and made sure that she was always knowledgeable about her subject area. For this, she read a lot so that she was able to impart her knowledge to the nurses she trained. This helped in her move into teaching. Lily's drive for self-development is further underscored by her decision to take up a master's degree. She made the decision to take up her second degree whilst continuing to work full time. Lily did not do so simply to propel her career forward, but more because she wanted to challenge and fulfill her own desire to be better.

> [I took up the master's degree] to satisfy myself, not just to change or whatever it is. It's more to satisfy myself to take the master's. . . . With a master's I thought maybe I can impart more to my students what I've learned or be better.

is that goal setting and planning were apparently not employed *more*. Such actions seem rational and/or like a coping response that could be driven by less rational motives such as anxiety about one's security or self-fulfillment.

The next most frequently turned to method for managing career transitions consisted of formal education and informal training. These were reported over the 30 percent level only in China, Israel and the United States. Interestingly, of the countries in the study, China, Israel and the U.S.A. are highest in terms of Schwartz's (2006) mastery dimension (as opposed to harmony), suggesting a belief that the environment and events can be manipulated. When looking at formal education, every occupational group, males and females, and younger workers (but not older) reported at least a 30 percent level of activity.

Country Close-Up: Managing Career Transitions in Mexico
(Contributed by Ociel Colorado)

A considerable majority of the Mexican interviewees reported managing their career transitions in a more self-driven way. One example is Rosa, an older female blue-collar who currently works in the cleaning department of one university and whose husband has never allowed her to work before:

> My husband didn't allow me to work; he just wanted me to take care
> of our kids.

With her two children grown and soon to be enrolled at the university, Rosa realized that more money would be needed to fulfill their needs:

> When one of my kids was almost 15, I decided to talk to my husband
> and have him understand that we would need more financial resources
> to succeed; I told him that I really wanted to work and thus contribute
> to our family expenses.

That is how Rosa contacted her sister, who was working as secretary in the university and who offered her the employment Rosa had at the time of the interview.

In addition, some of the young Mexican interviewees showed entrepreneurial characteristics to plan and set their career priorities. Let's talk about Pablo, a younger Mexican businessman who started his own business while still employed by a separate company:

> I used to work until very late every day because I liked my job very
> much, so I decided to better invest this extra time in starting to create
> my own graphic design company.

That is how Pablo started to look for support and found it quickly:

> I joined a business incubator, which enormously helped me to start
> developing a business plan for my own company.

Thus, one day Pablo decided to quit his job to be 100 percent dedicated to his own business:

> When I realized that one of my projects as [a] freelancer was too big
> and would need my full-time attention, I decided to resign my contract
> in the company and to formally found my own business.

Today Pablo is a successful self-employed person with his own small but fruitful graphic design business.

These examples refer to the self-driven way many of the Mexican interviewees used planning and goal setting when managing their career transitions.

External Influences Upon Career Transitions

When we coded responses to the question regarding factors "that made the transition easier or more difficult," we learned a lot. Participants in six of the ten reporting countries had 40 percent or more of their participants reporting their boss as a significant influence upon their career transitions, and this influence mostly reported as positive. About 40 percent or more of people in each occupation, males and females, younger and older workers, reported the boss as a significant (and typically positive) influence. This is interesting, since a lot of blame seems to be laid at the boss's door in popular perception (whereas in terms of career transitions only Israeli participants reported this).

In terms of peer support four of the ten countries had a 30 percent or higher level of interviewees saying that peers were an influential group, and each reported the influence as positive. Nurses and females were the only of their respective (occupational and gender) groups to report peers as a (positive) influence at the 30 percent level, while both younger and older participants reported peer support at the same 30 percent and above level.

Seven of the countries and all occupations, gender and age groups had at least 30 percent of the participants reporting family as a significant influence and almost always in a positive way. While Austria reported the positive influence of family, it is the only country to report a negative influence at the level of 30 percent. It is very interesting to note that two of the countries where family was *not* reported as a key influence at high levels (Mexico and Spain) are deeply family oriented. We suspect that this ironically made either research participants or even the research teams less likely to perceive family influence as remarkable.

Country Close-Up: The Role of the Social Context in Israel

(Contributed by Asya Pazy and Dana Shefer)

Career transitions are viewed by the Israeli interviewees as self-initiated, driven mostly by a desire for new experiences and self-development or arising from unsought opportunities and organizational changes. Across these categories, the social context plays a crucial role in enabling these transitions. Two examples illustrate these two points.

In her mid-20s, Iris, a business graduate specializing in finance, co-founded a small start-up company that managed bank investments. Two years later, dissatisfied with the insufficient growth of the company, Iris was ready for a change.

> Even though I knew I wanted something else I wouldn't have initiated it without an external trigger.

An opportunity arose when she was approached by a manager from another company who was connected to people she knew and worked with. Though it was difficult for her to leave her "own baby," having been part of the founding team, she accepted the offer. It was the challenge rather than higher pay that tipped the scales:

> I wanted to be a part of a bigger company with visibility and budgets, to be open to more opportunities.

The transition was smooth, primarily because of her good personal relations with people both in the previous and in the current company, and these relationships helped her succeed in her new job. She strongly believes that "friendly relations with the right people in the professional context are most crucial; without them, for example, the person who recommended me wouldn't have remembered me."

In retrospect, Iris points to an important trend among young Israeli businessmen and women, which in her view is less typical among older ones:

> The difference is that they [the older generation] would have stayed for years in the same position, in the same company. . . . Today we always look for change; we are always ready to leave and move on.

Iris's story illustrates the drive for growth and achievement and points to the role of networking in enabling the realization of such a need and overcoming the difficulties involved.

The story of Nurit, a geriatrics nurse in her mid-60s, illustrates an additional aspect of the social context, that of the family, which is particularly salient in women's careers. Early on she specialized in rehabilitation, but her priorities shifted when she became a mother. She quit professional work for 11 years, and then came back part time for two years, "so that I would have enough free time and could still take care of my children." She refused to return to her previous job because of a much disliked supervisor, who was still working in the same department after all those years.

By chance she happened to hear that the geriatrics department was seeking to create a new team, and she applied and was accepted.

> At the beginning it was very difficult, the transition to something so different from rehabilitation, and much harder, treating old people in a nursing home, near death . . . [but] I felt I was very effective. The old people showed me how they liked and needed me.

Though the pay has always been quite low, for her the work is a calling. Unlike what she sees among young nurses, pay and advancement do not appeal to her.

Together, these two stories highlight the importance of the social context for careers in Israel, be it in the form of weighing priorities of family versus work, drawing social support from relationships with peers and colleagues or using the social network to open up new opportunities.

Six of ten countries and all occupations, both genders and both age groups reported the organization as an influence (almost always in a positive light) upon the career transition (at the 30 percent level or above). The positive tone expressed regarding organizations is a little surprising, since along with "the boss" organizations are often given the blame for so many career problems. Yet in the case of career transitions bosses and organizations are perceived to perform positive functions to a great degree.

Network connections—work, personal or professional—played a large role in transitions for half of the countries and all of the other categories. Simply put, people rely upon others to embrace or survive transition, to find new work, to learn the ropes and to cope with career change. This seems to support at least some of the rhetoric of the boundaryless career (Arthur & Rousseau, 1996) and the advice to turn to relevant others to facilitate career change (Arthur, Claman, DeFillippi & Adams, 1995).

Close-Up on Generations

In taking a closer look at younger and older workers in specific countries, some differences in career transitions are revealed.

First, in some countries (Austria, Serbia, Israel, South Africa, the U.S.A. and Mexico) more of the younger interviewees tend to mention internal sources as the most important causes of career transition (e.g. identifying new opportunities or seeking development). This is contrary to older age groups in the same countries, especially Austria and Serbia. One explanation offered by the career literature is that today's careers are more individualized. The so-called "new career" (e.g. Arthur, 1994; DeFillippi & Arthur, 1994; Hall, 1996) seems to be reflected here. Although organizational and structural issues also do play a role as causes of career transitions, the individual level is emphasized to a much greater extent by younger workers in the respective countries. This is in line with Hall's statement (1996: 8) that "the career of the twenty-first century will be protean, a career that is driven by the person, not the organization, and that will be reinvented by the person from time to time." Individuals are taking an increased amount of responsibility for the course of their careers. Thus emphasis is put on their own initiative and proactivity. Countries where we identified generational differences are also those that are undergoing significant change, with the exception of Austria. Given the Western flavor of our sample and the counterpoint that the data from Serbia present, it is premature to claim that the new independent career is universal.

Second, concerning external sources, mainly older workers in Austria, Serbia, Mexico and the U.S.A. emphasize organizationally driven causes for their career transitions. China and Japan—both countries belonging to the Confucian cluster—show similar results regarding their perceived causes of career transitions. Research participants there mentioned organizational forces, especially "organizational restructuring." While in Japan only organizations play a major role, in Serbia macro factors (e.g. economic pressure, governmental policies, etc.) are also recognized by both generations. Particularly in Serbia, there are different working conditions for both generations reflected in our interviews. In China, for most interviewees belonging to the older generation, career paths were structured by government policies. In contrast, the younger generation highlight their "own initiative" more, indicating that they have been allowed to take responsibility for their own career transition. A similar picture is shown in Serbia, where the causes of the career transitions of younger interviewees are expressed by drawing attention to internal change "triggers." In China and Austria macro factors (e.g. economic pressure, governmental policies, etc.) are also mentioned as an external source for causes of career transitions, but only by the older age group. While China is a country going through major transitions, Austria can be characterized by rather stable economic conditions.

This builds on some assumptions of institutional and cultural change. Previous research states that dynamic economic change causes a shift in cultural values. In particular, it increases the support for individualism and decreases hierarchical values (Allen, Ng, Ikeda, Jawan, Sufi, Wilson & Yang, 2007: 261). This can be seen especially in China (Wong & Slater, 2002), but also in Austria. Particularly in transitioning countries, generational differences should be taken into account, since they may show variations in values within the country. Thus we assumed that a high degree of economic development and social change widens generational differences concerning perceived causes of career transitions.

It is notable that networks are not more pronounced in the U.S.A., since it is the home country of the boundaryless and protean career theories. Is this conundrum similar to the finding discussed earlier where family support is not as recognized in Mexico and Spain? Could networking be so dominant a factor in the U.S.A. that it is not recognized by "the natives"?

Six of ten countries and all other categories except blue-collar workers reported that education and training constituted an important influence upon their career transition. Typically such activity is turned to in either proactive (usually early career) or reactive fashion to equip one with the tools needed to succeed in anticipated or forced career change. Thus formal education is a key avenue to consider both for employees and for those who would shape their careers.

Stepping Back: Considering Cultural Dimensions' Influence Upon Career Transitions

A key interest in our research was better understanding the influence of culture upon what people value in their careers and how they manage their careers. Beyond culture there are other unique factors that impact careers, such as the impact of economic dynamics, boundaries surrounding immigration, war and peace, and myriad other possible influences. But we can approximate the impact of culture broadly through looking at how certain known culture dimensions "play out" with career transitions.

Our main analytical tool, for reasons explained in earlier chapters, has been the cultural values survey of Shalom Schwartz (2004, 2006). However, owing to its long-standing dominance in the literature, we also consider how Hofstede's (1980) framework impacts careers. Table 5.3 profiles how the countries in our sample vary according to Schwartz's main categories and some of Hofstede's categories that seem especially relevant to career transitions.

Taking an even closer look at some of the dimensions illuminates the data. Using Schwartz's cultural values dimensions (see Chapters 2 and 3 for more detail on Schwartz's framework), Figures 5.2 and 5.3 profile mastery (versus harmony) and autonomy (versus embeddedness) respectively and their potential impact upon key dimensions of career transitions. The nature of our data gathering is qualitative, of course, and thus all of these figures should be considered suggestive of patterns but not statistically adequate. Nonetheless they indicate interesting possibilities about how broad cultural dimensions may modify the way career changes are managed.

In Figure 5.2 it is interesting to note that the countries characterized by harmony and not mastery report a greater proportion of their

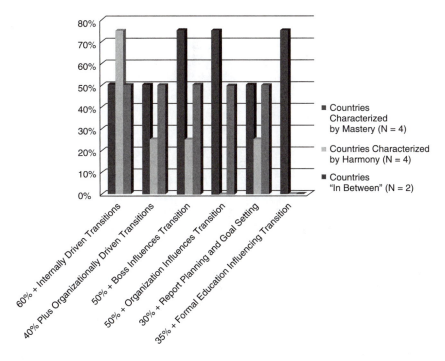

Figure 5.2 Mastery/harmony cultural values and career transitions

Table 5.3 Key culture dimensions and career transitions

Countries/ categories	U.S.A.	Austria	Spain	Serbia	China	Costa Rica	Japan	Malaysia	South Africa	Mexico	Israel
Schwartz's cultural values:											
Mastery/ harmony	Mastery	Harmony	Harmony	In between	Mastery	In between	Mastery	In between	Leans toward harmony	Leans toward harmony	Mastery
Egalitarianism/ hierarchy	Medium hierarchy	Egalitarian	Egalitarian	In between	Hierarchy	In between	Hierarchy	Leans toward hierarchy	Hierarchy	In between	Hierarchy
Autonomy/ embeddedness	Autonomy	Autonomy	Autonomy	In between	Embedded	Leans toward autonomy	Leans toward autonomy	Embedded	Embedded	Leans toward autonomy	Autonomy
Hofstede's culture dimensions (select):											
Collectivism/ individualism	Individualism	Leans toward individualism	Leans toward individualism	Collectivism	Collectivism	Collectivism	Leans toward collectivism	Collectivism	Individualism	Collectivism	Slight individualism
Power distance	Medium	Small	High	High	High	Small	Medium high	High	Slightly high	High	Low
Uncertainty avoidance	Medium	Low	Medium high	High	Medium high	Strong	In between	High	Medium high	High	Low
Internally driven over 60 percent	X	X	X	X		X		X		X	X
Organizationally driven 40 percent plus				X	X		X			X	X
Boss influences transition						NA					
50 percent plus	X	X		X	X	NA	X				X
Organization influences						NA					
50 percent plus	X	X	X	X		NA				X	
Setting goals/planning 30 percent plus	X	X	X	X		NA				X	X
Formal education over 35 percent	X				X	NA					X

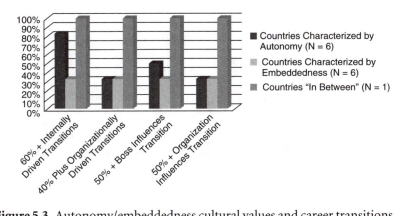

Figure 5.3 Autonomy/embeddedness cultural values and career transitions

research participants as internally driving their career transitions and a great proportion of countries categorized as mastery-driven countries are more likely to have participants report organizationally driven career transitions. Why this is so is not clear and seems counterintuitive. In the case of the mastery-driven countries perhaps the organization is seen as expressing the mastery value more than the individual, or at least equally so.

In countries characterized by mastery values, there are greater levels of interviewees reporting both boss and organizational influence on career transitions. Could this reflect the notion of bosses and organizations operating under the assumption that they can (and should) orchestrate their employees' careers? Furthermore, mastery country interviewees were more likely to report both planning/goal setting and formal education strategies in managing their career transitions. This seems to reflect mastery and the idea of being able to change one's circumstances through direct action.

In reaction to Figure 5.3 it is telling that more people we interviewed in countries driven by autonomy (which is in many ways similar to Hofstede's notion of individualism) view their career transitions as internally driven than those in countries driven by embeddedness. The other dimensions of career transitions are relatively similar between the two polar dimensions. Thus it seems reasonable to postulate that, when it comes to inferring causality, participants in autonomy-driven countries see their career transitions as self-driven but, when it comes to organizational causes and other influences upon career transitions, autonomy-driven and embedded cultures see things in a more similar fashion.

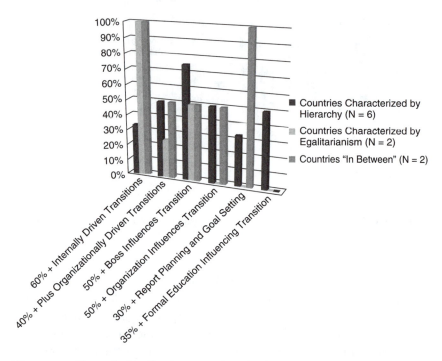

Figure 5.4 Hierarchy/egalitarianism cultural values and career transitions

Figure 5.4 concerns cultures driven by hierarchy and egalitarianism. Research participants in egalitarian cultures clearly were more likely to ascribe the causality of their career transitions to themselves. In contrast, those from hierarchy-driven cultures were more likely to see their boss and organizations as influencing their transitions.

Finally, we take a closer look at Hofstede's dimension of uncertainty avoidance in Figure 5.5. Countries exhibiting low uncertainty avoidance had a great proportion of interviewees prone to view their career transition as internally driven. It could be that a willingness to tolerate uncertainty *drives* more independent career behavior, or perhaps it merely frames how one interprets career transition causality. The same group of research participants (tolerant of uncertainty) are likely to see their boss as influencing their transitions, but their counterparts (who prefer to avoid uncertainty) are more likely to consider the organization as having an influencing factor.

While we cannot be conclusive about the relationships between the Schwartz and Hofstede cultural dimensions and career transitions, the collective findings reviewed here indicate many avenues that can inform management practice and future research.

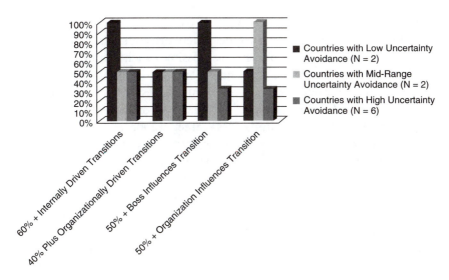

Figure 5.5 Uncertainty avoidance and career transitions

Discussion: The Power of Context and the Power of the Individual

We would like to step back from a detailed look at the data and finish our discussions of transitions through evaluating two very powerful forces upon career transitions: the "context" and the individual. By context we refer to social and organizational contexts—but also beyond those to sometimes invisible cultural/institutional contexts (discussed in more detail in Chapter 8) that might seem inaccessible to some but which we realized wield great power over careers.

On the other hand, we discovered that seemingly small differences in individuals could result in enormous changes to one's career and even life. We will end the chapter by discussing how individuals might be able to better manage their transitions, but we will start by exploring the tremendous power of context.

Career transitions do *not* occur in a vacuum and, in spite of our driving assumptions undergirding the 5C project that culture and other contexts influence career transitions, we were ourselves surprised at the enormous degree of that influence when we stepped back to have a look. It was only fully evident as we compared circumstances and opportunities both within and across cultures, both in "the moment" of our interviewees' careers and across their career histories.

The key point is that, seen or unseen, appreciated or not, context makes an enormous difference. For every Barack Obama who overcame the disadvantages of his childhood and rose to fame, there are millions for whom their context, circumstances, networks or skills were not adequate to achieve (or even perceive as possible) such a transformation. In that sense, we reject the idea that people can fully be "free agents" or truly have "boundaryless" careers. Boundaries very much exist and perhaps, as Kerr Inkson asserts, a "boundary crossing career" might be a more apt phrase than a "boundaryless career" (2006).

Context becomes especially clear in countries where older and younger generations face vastly different circumstances, such as China, Malaysia, Serbia and South Africa. In China many in the older generation were simply assigned careers and jobs, while many of the younger generation, at least in urban areas, have choices their parents could only imagine. In South Africa, only post-apartheid could many coloreds and blacks have access to basic (let alone higher) education. These were boundaries that placed a severe restriction on career possibilities. The story below relates one man's interpretation of career context in Serbia.

Country Close-Up: A Story of Career and Context in Serbia

(Contributed by Jelena Zikic and Biljana Bogićević Milikić)

Ivan is 60 years old with grown-up children and a wife who is not working. He finished high school and a course for machine operators, and worked mainly on construction machines. He was personally very satisfied with this career, since he worked in a job he liked and was very respected as an operator and as a person.

Ivan's career transition came completely unexpectedly when, after 39 years working at his company, he got laid off. He feels that the company picked him and not somebody else because he had sold all of the company shares he got in 1993 during the process of state-owned companies becoming private again.

His sudden job loss was extremely difficult. He feels very bitter, as he had spent his whole life working for the company. The job layoff happened during a period of general downsizing that took place in many other similar companies in Serbia as part of the transitional measures in the country's economy from 2000 on. Ivan does not think that there was a reason why the company would have let him go other than the fact that he was forced to sell his shares in order to survive the difficult economic situation in Serbia. However, many other workers also got laid off from the same company at the same time.

Ivan does not see anything good in this transition. He was completely shocked by the situation, as he had quite different expectations. He had been an operator for 39 years in his company, and people respected him; he had been hoping to keep his job despite the difficult economic situation. He had believed that he would be able to leave his job on his own initiative and that he would in turn obtain a desired pension and proceed to retirement.

Ivan sees the reasons for his layoff in the wider societal context:

> We live in a society where corruption became widespread and a normal, "small" person can expect just about anything. That is why people like myself must fight. I am in a situation now that in my old age my children must support me; that is a shame. I don't think I had anything to learn from this transition. Who is going to employ me now? All I have to hope for is to reach the age for a deserved pension. And in my life I only wanted to work and be able to have a normal, modest life for my family, without starving and hardship. I expected my hard work to be appreciated much more. And now look what happened to me!

Ivan's story presents an example of a sudden, externally triggered transition. It is interesting to note, however, the interplay of subjective and objective factors in how Ivan understood the transition. On the one hand he cannot comprehend how this has happened to him and he has no way of explaining why someone who is so hard-working and respected could be let go. On the other hand, he talks about the broader cultural and political context, such as the forces of corruption in the society that he sees as partly responsible for his situation, and he feels he is a victim of this who needs to "fight."

However, instead of being proactive during this major transition, Ivan is experiencing some real career barriers, such as nearing retirement age as well as his inability to find a similar job. Being an example from Serbia, a country in transition itself, Ivan illustrates the kinds of coping and struggle that some Serbs have to undergo while living in transitional times.

In addition to the countries where the power of context is palpable, it is also fascinating to consider context in countries where its influence is less obvious. For example, we noticed that U.S. research participants seemed less likely to notice the influence of context upon career transitions. And it is remarkable that countries such as Austria, Japan, Spain and others have had as much continuity between eras as they have. When such stable conditions and assumptions are prevalent, it may make context that much stronger and that much harder to detect, especially for insiders. That can be a challenge to career "actors" themselves as well as the organizations and career practitioners who try to help them.

What are the contextual factors that impact career transitions? We have analyzed and discussed such factors at the social and organizational level earlier in the chapter. While we were not equipped to directly *assess* macro contextual variables in most cases, we identify such factors below (besides culture, which has been heavily covered earlier in the chapter) that impact careers and career transitions based upon inference across contexts.

Macro Contextual Factors Impacting Career Transitions

Occupational and professional structures and systems shape how transitions *can* be pursued and managed. For example, nursing in many countries has a structured progression system, while blue-collar in many countries does not.

Legal, political and government factors have a huge impact on how career transitions play out. Groups can be legally (if not morally) prevented from attaining certain jobs based upon race or other status. Government regulations can greatly control employment options.

Education (formal and informal) also had a disproportionately large impact on transitions. Formal education, which is often restricted by socio-economic or political status, created options and entire careers for many of our interviewees. Informal education, provided by families and mentors, enabled people to take a reflective posture that made proactive and learning orientations toward career transitions much more likely.

Class and socio-economic status very much influence career transitions. Individuals from poor and otherwise disadvantaged groups lacked the education and means to pursue more than the most basic opportunities. They also lacked role models at times who would help them see a different path. Some poor interviewees lacked such a basic level of even informal education that they exhibited no ability to set goals beyond the very short-term horizon. On the other hand, advantaged groups have many opportunities and options. While this generally enables an active learning orientation to career transitions, it can also lead to a "scripted" career in which one does not need to think too much in order to enjoy the status quo and/or progress.

Gender and race do not inherently inhibit or enable career transitions except to the degree to which their meaning is assigned abstractly, socially, culturally and politically. For example, one colored woman we interviewed in South Africa was the first in her company to be allowed to speak to a white customer. Such boundaries are technically abstract but are very real to the focal person. Gender and race can serve to one's advantage as well through preferential treatment or access to informal networks, among other things.

As regards *age and generation*, as profiled earlier in this chapter younger workers in most cultures were more likely to be independent in managing their careers than older workers. Chapter 6 also documents how generational differences do impact perceptions of career success. It is impossible to say if this is based upon age, stage or era, and so on.

Managing Career Transitions: The Power of the Individual

Context is indeed powerful and at times seems overwhelming. Often it appeared to be the prevailing factor explaining our research participants' careers. However, the way individuals manage their transition can be a very powerful factor in challenging and improving their experience. The actions that a person takes to be mindful of and manage a transition turn out to be very important and vary from person to person and culture to culture.

Personality traits, attitudes, skills and emotions all play a role in how individuals frame and manage transitions. These factors were observed and sometimes reported across our samples. Of course, these observations are clinical and inferential, as with most qualitative research. Personality has been found to be somewhat consistent across culture (McCrae & Costa, 1997), and we can assume that traits such as a learning orientation are freely distributed predispositions as well.

We were curious about what made a transition more successful—in terms of meeting career goals, finding satisfaction and providing ongoing capacity to meet future challenges (adaptability). So, starting with South Africa and the United States, we looked more closely at those interviewees who seemed—by their own admission or our inference—to be successful in the terms outlined above. What we found is that mindfulness, attitudes and learning skills were very important and typically taken for granted.

We identified that people undergoing career transitions may take either a *performance* or a *learning* orientation toward the transition.

A performance orientation is concerned primarily with executing the demands of the new role to greater or lesser standards. On the other hand a learning orientation *may* include performance goals, but the main emphasis is upon learning and mastery of the task, the role or even one's identity. Other authors have carefully explored learning orientation (Button, Mathieu & Zajac, 1996) and experimenting with identity and role (Ibarra, 1999, 2000). Some advantages of a learning orientation toward the role transition are that it enables one to harvest the lessons transitions provide regardless of ultimate performance or practical outcomes, and it produces great adaptability and transformation for future transitions and roles.

In addition to performance/learning skills and approaches we noticed that people seem to exhibit a *reactive* or *proactive* approach toward career transitions. In a proactive approach, people seek the initiative at various stages of the transition to influence the career shift to desired ends based primarily upon their own values and goals. In a reactive approach, people may be "active" but more in response to an event or standards that are primarily outside of their control. So, for example, a reactive person's response may be to fit in and please the employer, whereas a proactive approach involves reflection, goal setting and behaviors that project a desired consequence driven by the career actor independently of outside expectations. A proactive approach has the advantage of keeping at least some outcomes of the transition within a person's control and design, thus optimizing the chance to personally gain from the experience.

One late career state businessman from South Africa, Lesedi, was especially striking in his ability to be mindful about his career experiences before, during and after his career transitions. As a South African black, he was one of the few who "broke" out before apartheid ended and obtained a graduate education in the United States. Post-apartheid he found himself with many opportunities back in his home country owing to the changed political landscape and his burgeoning skill set. He had mastered basic management well, but wanted to focus his skills on finance and team building, because he had certain career goals he felt required these competencies in order to be fulfilled. We interviewed Lesedi a short while into his tenure of a new management team. He was very attentive to the functional skills he was trying to gain, his own efficacy and learning needs as a teammate, and the abilities he hoped to gain in finance (in order to fulfill later career stages in non-governmental organization service roles). He was mindful, with a strong focus not only upon how he wanted to improve, but why.

Note that the advantages of being proactive and having a learning orientation seemed to pay dividends at different stages of a transition—entering a new career phase, during the middle or stable portion of a career segment—and ending a career transition as one looks toward the next one.

At the point of writing, analysis and verification of these patterns observed are ongoing across the wide 5C sample. However, the early results suggest that indeed these approaches to career transitions make a difference—moderated, of course, by the unique country context.

It is interesting to note that these approaches mirror much (but not all) of the advice found in modern career templates such as protean (Briscoe & Hall, 2006; Hall, 1976, 2002) and boundaryless (Arthur, 1994; Arthur & Rousseau, 1996) perspectives. Such attitudes and career approaches have been observed in English speaking, Germanic, Italian and Latin American cultures (Briscoe, Hall & DeMuth, 2006; Gasteiger & Briscoe, 2007; Lo Presti, Nonnis & Briscoe, 2010; Veloso, 2009). Combined, these perspectives advocate reflection, awareness of self and others and a learning orientation (Button, Mathieu & Zajac, 1996). They do so, however, at times with less reverence to context than we think is appropriate based upon our findings.

In our samples, only a small minority (perhaps 10 percent) of our research participants demonstrate proactive and learning orientations within the course of their career transitions. Even rarer are the people who maintain such orientations as they approach, pass through and even segue from one transition to another. Why might this be? It seems that the normal human reaction to change is reaction and adaptation, representing something perhaps as primal as survival. Reflection and mindful learning are seemingly rare. However, they might be less so.

We found that, almost invariably, interviewees identified people in their lives who helped them learn to question their "scripts." Sometimes it was as simple as challenging someone to think out of the box. Sometimes it was a deep and personal challenge from a loved one to question one's purpose. Often, the "intervention" was casual, innocent and unintended. However, we see a significant role for those in professional or personal, formal or informal, roles to make a real difference by simply helping others to think differently and to question more deeply.

This has tremendous implications for research, management and career development. How can research and theory help us move toward a better understanding of how to inculcate mindful career skills in self and others? Can managers learn to optimize learning alongside performance? How can people learn or be taught to more proactively manage their own careers? How do culture and context inform such approaches?

Case Study and Application: Susan Euhus at University Hospital, Chicago

Susan Euhus was not like most of the other nurses who had been assigned to be a floor supervisor before. Typical floor supervisors are not only ready for the job, but they have been pursuing it (and the higher pay and status that come with it) for months if not years. Beyond the normal skills required of a registered nurse, a floor supervisor has to be a problem solver, a trainer, a coach, a friend and sometimes a disciplinarian. Susan was comfortable with the friend part; it was the other stuff she had a problem with.

Just a year away from retirement, Susan had expected and hoped to stay on the second floor, making her assigned rounds. She had a lot of friends there amongst the staff, and the patients in long-term care appreciated her friendly smile. Susan was good at being friendly and not making waves. She did not think she had the will or the personality to stand up to people when she needed to. She liked to keep to herself.

But Stacie, the chief of nursing, informed Susan that, owing to two unexpected retirements, they needed Susan to be floor supervisor on the fifth floor, where cardiovascular care was delivered. The hospital was simply not willing to hire an outsider who did not know the ropes, and nobody else had the wealth of experience Susan had. As Susan sat in Stacie's office and heard this she felt sick and afraid. She wanted to say "no," but she realized there was nobody else who was ready or could be spared.

Susan was a single mother and a grandmother. She had married and started her career at a very young age. Some of her distaste for dealing with conflict stemmed from her divorce several years later, when her three children stayed with her. These children, now grown, tried to encourage their mother that "she could do it"! Besides, they reminded her, this would give her a bigger retirement pension. Susan would gladly have traded that for the friendly confines of the second floor.

Susan made it through the first week on the fifth floor. She actually surprised herself by what she knew. She had not had a rotation in cardiovascular care before, but her other experience served her well. She got along with the doctors and the senior nursing staff. However, she felt that the young "hot shot" nurses who already had specialty degrees did not really respect her. She worried what would happen if "push came to shove" with them.

The weekend was better. Susan's grandchildren helped her forget about work for a few days as they helped her plant her vegetable garden, an annual ritual she had started shortly after becoming single again. Then Monday came. When she asked one of the newer nurses what the procedure code was for incoming "life flight" patients, she was met with a stunned look and a rude "You mean you don't know?" Susan dreaded this moment; she did not enjoy fighting for respect and felt she had already proven anything she had to years ago.

Stacie saw Susan staring out the window at lunch. She knew Susan well enough to know that her body posture communicated discouragement. She wondered what she could do to help ease the transition.

What sort of emotions do you think Susan is experiencing? Who could help her? How? With what processes and resources should Stacie, or the hospital itself, provide new supervisors to help them best adapt to their new role? What should Susan herself do to make this transition successful?

Note

1 Note that for management of career transitions (Tables 5.1 and 5.2) data for Costa Rica is not available and percentages are produced based upon a different total.

References

Allen, M. W., Ng, S. H., Ikeda, K., Jawan, J. A., Sufi, A. H., Wilson, M. & Yang, K.-S. 2007. Two decades of change in cultural values and economic development in eight East Asian and Pacific Island nations. *Journal of Cross-Cultural Psychology*, 38(3): 247–269.

Allen, V. L. & Van de Vliert, E. (Eds.). 1984. *Role Transitions*. New York: Plenum.

Arthur, M. 1994. The boundaryless career: A new perspective for organizational inquiry. *Journal of Organizational Behavior*, 15(4): 295–306.

Arthur, M. B. & Rousseau, D. M. (Eds.). 1996. *The Boundaryless Career: A New Employment Principle for a New Organizational Era*. New York: Oxford University Press.

Arthur, M. B., Hall, D. T. & Lawrence, B. S. (Eds.). 1989. *Handbook of Career Theory*. Cambridge, U.K.: Cambridge University Press.

Arthur, M. B., Claman, P. H., DeFillippi, R. J. & Adams, J. 1995. Intelligent enterprise, intelligent careers. *Academy of Management Executive*, 9(4): 7–20.

Bridges, W. 1986. Managing organizational transitions. *Organizational Dynamics*, 15: 24–33.

Briscoe, J. P. & Hall, D. T. 2006. Special section on boundaryless and protean careers: Next steps in conceptualizing and measuring boundaryless and protean careers. *Journal of Vocational Behavior*, 69(1): 1–3.

Briscoe, J. P., Hall, D. T. & DeMuth, R. L. F. 2006. Protean and boundaryless careers: An empirical exploration. *Journal of Vocational Behavior*, 69(1): 30–47.

Broscio, M. & Scherer, J. 2003. Managing job transitions: Thirteen questions for a successful search. *Journal of Healthcare Management*, 48(5): 287.

Button, S. B., Mathieu, J. E. & Zajac, D. M. 1996. Goal orientation in organizational research: A conceptual and empirical approach. *Organizational Behavior and Human Decision Processes*, 67: 26–48.

Cohen, L. 2006. Remembrance of things past: Cultural process and practice in the analysis of career stories. *Journal of Vocational Behavior*, 69(2): 189–201.

DeFillippi, R. J. & Arthur, M. 1994. The boundaryless career: A competency-based perspective. *Journal of Organizational Behavior*, 15(4): 307–324.

Driver, M. J. 1980. Career concepts and organizational change. In C. B. Derr (Ed.), *Work, Family, and Career: New Frontiers in Theory and Research*. New York: Praeger.

Franzinger, K. 2001. Mentors and seminars ease career transitions. *Machine Design*, 73(23): 148.

Gasteiger, R. M. & Briscoe, J. P. 2007. What kind of organizations do protean people prefer? The case of Germany and the United States. In George T. Solomon (Ed.), *Proceedings of the Sixty-Seventh Annual Meeting of the Academy of Management* (CD), ISSN 1543-8643.

Glaser, B. G. & Strauss, A. L. 1971. *Status Passage*. Chicago, IL: Aldine.

Hall, D. T. 1976. *Careers in Organizations*. Santa Monica, CA: Goodyear.

Hall, D. T. 1996. Protean careers of the 21st century. *Academy of Management Executive*, 10(4): 8–16.

Hall, D. T. 2002. *Careers In and Out of Organizations*. Thousand Oaks, CA: Sage.

Hofstede, G. 1980. *Culture's Consequences: International Differences in Work-Related Values*. Beverly Hills, CA: Sage.

Ibarra, H. 1999. Provisional selves: Experimenting with image and identity in professional adaptation. *Administrative Science Quarterly*, 44(4): 764.

Ibarra, H. 2000. Making partner: A mentor's guide to the psychological journey. *Harvard Business Review*, 78(2): 146.

Ibarra, H. 2004. Men and women of the corporation and the change masters: Practical theories for changing times. *Academy of Management Executive*, 18(2): 108.

Inkson, K. 2006. Protean and boundaryless careers as metaphors. *Journal of Vocational Behavior*, 69: 48–63.

Leibowitz, Z. B. & Schlossberg, N. K. 1982. Critical career transitions: A model for designing career services. *Training and Development Journal*, 36(2): 12.

Lo Presti, A., Nonnis, M. & Briscoe, J. 2010. The protean and boundaryless career in Italy: Game on? In G. Tanucci, M. Cortini & E. Morin (Eds.), *Boundaryless Careers and Occupational Wellbeing: An Interdisciplinary Approach*. London: Palgrave Macmillan.

Louis, M. R. 1982. Managing career transition: A missing link in career development. *Organizational Dynamics*, 10(4): 68.

McCrae, R. R. & Costa, P. T., Jr. 1997. Personality trait structure as a human universal. *American Psychologist*, 52: 509–516.

Nicholson, N. 1990. The transition cycle: A conceptual framework for the analysis of change and human resource management. In G. R. Ferris & K. M. Rowland (Eds.), *Career and Human Resource Development*. Greenwich, CT: JAI Press.

Nicholson, N. 1996. Career systems in crisis: Change and opportunity in the information age. *Academy of Management Executive*, 10(4): 40.

Nicholson, N. & West, M. 1988. *Managerial Job Change: Men and Women in Transition*. Cambridge, U.K.: Cambridge University Press.

Nicholson, N. & West, M. 1989. Transitions, work histories, and careers. In M. Arthur, D. T. Hall & B. S. Lawrence (Eds.), *Handbook of Career Theory*: 181–201. Cambridge, U.K.: Cambridge University Press.

Nortier, F. 1995. A new angle on coping with change: Managing transition!, *Journal of Management Development*, 14: 32–46.

Sargent, A. G. & Schlossberg, N. K. 1988. Managing adult transitions. *Training and Development Journal*, 42(12): 58.

Schlossberg, N. K. 1981. A model for analyzing human adaptation to transition. *Counseling Psychologist*, 9(2): 2–18.

Schlossberg, N. K. 1984. *Counseling Adults in Transition: Linking Practice With Theory*. New York: Springer.

Schlossberg, N. K., Troll, L. E. & Leibowitz, Z. B. 1978. *Perspectives on Counseling Adults: Issues and Skills*. Pacific Grove, CA: Brooks/Cole.

Schwartz, S. H. 2004. Mapping and interpreting cultural differences around the world. In H. Vinken, J. Soeters & P. Ester (Eds.), *Comparing Cultures: Dimensions of Culture in a Comparative Perspective*. Leiden, The Netherlands: Brill.

Schwartz, S. H. 2006. A theory of cultural value orientations: Explication and applications. *Comparative Sociology*, 5(2–3): 136–182.

Silvester, J., Anderson, N. R. & Patterson, F. 1999. Organizational culture change: An inter-group attributional analysis. *Journal of Occupational and Organizational Psychology*, 72: 1–23.

Sullivan, S. E. 2003. Working identity: Unconventional strategies for reinventing your career. *Academy of Management Executive*, 17(3): 154–155.

Veloso, E. 2009. Boundaryless careers in the personal management of professional transition: A study of former employees of an organization with state-owned enterprise-like characteristics. Unpublished doctoral dissertation, University of Sao Paulo, Brazil.

Wong, A. L. Y. & Slater, J. R. 2002. Executive development in China: Is there any in a Western sense? *International Journal of Human Resource Management*, 13(2): 338–360.

Young, R. A. & Collin, A. 2004. Introduction: Constructivism and social constructionism in the career field. *Journal of Vocational Behavior*, 64(3): 373–388.

6

Careers and Age: Career Success for Older and Younger Workers

Julie Unite, Emma Parry, Jon P. Briscoe and Katharina Chudzikowski

I'm not looking for security out of my job. I'm looking for fulfillment. And I can say to my parents, "I am tired of this job. I want to do something else." But my parents would like stick to one thing. And then my aunties, they have been nurses forever. They don't like it. But they're too scared to move because then they're too scared to find out what will happen beyond this next step. So I think, for them, they measure success more on stability. Whereas I don't want to take eight years to increase my salary by 200K. I need it to happen as soon as possible. And I don't mind jumping around to do that.

(Younger South African businesswoman)

I think that people of the older generation are actually pretty satisfied with what they have achieved, and I believe that younger people are striving for a little bit more.

(Younger male Austrian blue-collar)

There is lots of differences (between older and younger nurses). Older nurses can be happy to still have a job. They give more importance to family. They want to work less. They have a different value system, different priorities. They have more experience, but we are more accepted. But I think this can't be generalized.

(Younger female Israeli nurse)

Introduction

The chapters so far in this book have described the general perspectives of individuals around the world and how they experience career success and career transitions. The focus so far has therefore been on the impact of culture and national context on individuals' career experiences. We will now shift our focus to the impact of age and/or generation on people's conceptions of career success. This chapter takes a closer look at the specific experiences of two age groups, compares these two groups and looks at how they differ across the globe. As the quotes above suggest, the experiences of these individuals vary greatly depending on the country and group to which they belong.

Anyone taking a quick glance at the current popular and academic literature will see a growing interest in the concept of "generations" and continued emphasis on age diversity in the workforce. Age has become an important issue for employers and individuals owing to the dynamic demographics of the workforce (e.g. a greater proportion of older people in the U.S. and Western European workforces, with a greater proportion of younger people in the Mexican economy), extended life expectancy and the existence of four different generations of employees in the workforce. Consequently, employers have to examine and address potential differences in the needs and preferences of these employees according to their age.

While the research on age differences at work has grown over recent years, there is still little known about how different age groups, or generations, experience their careers. We address this need and add to the body of literature on both age diversity and careers by providing unique insights and stories from older and younger individuals regarding their perceptions of career success. We also combine this with information on cultural differences in career experiences to examine how national context plays a role in shaping these perceptions. With an increasingly age-diverse workforce, fewer global organizational boundaries and a never-ending quest to attract, retain and motivate talented staff, it is more important than ever to understand how individuals experience their careers at all ages and how this differs across countries. Before discussing this, we will explore what the current literature tells us about these issues.

The Literature to Date

The potential impact of age on careers can be understood using three research perspectives: age or maturation effects, career or life stage theories and generational cohort effects. Perspectives emphasizing maturation effects recognize that people's needs change as they get older owing to the physiological and psychological changes they experience. Career or life stage theories propose that people have different needs as they reach different stages in their careers or lives. Finally, generational effects are studied through an emphasis on eras, where people in different age cohorts have unique preferences or attitudes owing to experiences during their formative years. Generational differences are believed to be stable, so don't change as people age, whereas maturation or career/life stage effects do (Rhodes, 1983). Each of these will be discussed briefly, with a particular emphasis on how they relate to careers and more specifically people's notion of career success.

Age or Maturation Differences

A number of researchers have suggested that the drivers that motivate people for work change as they age. For example, Sterns and Miklos (1995) suggested that factors such as health, outside interests and other responsibilities might have a greater and more diverse effect on individuals' motivation in later years. They also suggested that normative biological or environmental factors, including individual health and stress-inducing events, can affect behavioral change in older individuals. Similarly, survival needs in older individuals are likely to be less urgent. Sturges (1999) suggested that material criteria for success become less important with age and are replaced by an emphasis on influence and autonomy. She proposed that aspects of employment such as innate meaning, quality of relationships, inclusion, stimulation and continuing opportunity to contribute may become particularly important in the later years of an individual's career. Similarly, Loretto, Vickerstaff and White (2005) noted that, while primary motivators such as pay, promotion and associated status may be important for younger workers, older workers may not be motivated by the same factors.

Career and Life Stage Differences

Levinson's (1978) life stage model and Super's (1957) career stage model suggest that people have different preferences according to which age or career stage they are in. Accordingly, what constitutes career success may be different as individuals move through different age or career stages (Baruch, 2006; Hall & Mirvis, 1996; Levinson, 1978; Schein, 1978; Super, 1957). For instance, success at the exploration stage (Super, 1957) may be related to overcoming uncertainties and successfully finding a career niche (Ornstein, Cron & Slocum, 1989), while people at the advancement stages may be more concerned about their professional identity or working hard for future promotion and growth (Hall, 2002).

Generational Differences

Age can also be treated as a categorical variable as opposed to a continuous variable through the use of age cohorts or, more specifically, generations. Kupperschmidt (2000: 66) defined a generation as "an identifiable group that shares birth years, location and significant life events at critical development stages." Mannheim (1952) suggested that individuals in a generation share the same year of birth and so have a common historical social location through their limited range of potential experience. Members of a generation therefore share common experiences which have shaped their preferences, attitudes and values.

It is generally accepted that, within the Western world at least, there are currently four generations within the workforce. These are Veterans (born 1925–42), Baby Boomers (born 1943–60), Generation X (born 1961–81) and Generation Y/GenMe/Millennials (born after 1982) (Strauss & Howe, 1991; Twenge, 2010). These four generations are hypothesized to be different in their preferences and attitudes. For example, Generation X are thought to have a boundaryless attitude towards careers and believe that each job is temporary, as they saw their parents made redundant and suffer from a lack of job security (Filipczak, 1994). Alternatively, Veterans believe in hard work and being loyal to employers in return for job security, as they grew up during the Great Depression.

Twenge (2010) recently reviewed the empirical literature on generational differences in work values from time-lag studies in predominantly Western cultures. Her findings showed that Generation X and Generation Y rate work as less central to their lives, value leisure more and express a weaker work ethic than their older counterparts. Extrinsic work values such as salary are more important for Generation Y and Generation X, and there are no generational differences in altruistic values (i.e. helping others). Generation X and especially Generation Y are consistently higher in individualistic traits. Overall the author concludes that generational differences are important where they appear. Parry and Urwin (forthcoming), however, provide a detailed examination of the theory and evidence behind the notion of generational differences and found a number of difficulties inherent in the work surrounding this phenomenon. Parry and Urwin suggested that, while the idea of generations has a sound theoretical basis in sociology (Mannheim, 1952), the empirical evidence base is actually mixed and problematic owing to the general reliance on cross-sectional research designs and a failure to operationalize "generations" in accordance with the theory. It is therefore necessary to view the idea of generational differences with some caution, at least until a more solid empirical base has been established.

Generational Differences and Culture

Many of the studies on generational differences have been conducted in Western (mostly U.S.) contexts, and there has been a tendency in practitioner circles to discuss the American definitions of generations as though they are globally applicable. However, the early theoretical basis (Mannheim, 1952) and some current studies (Bennis & Thomas, 2002) about generations emphasized the need for individuals to experience historical events in the same way in order to constitute a generation. This suggests that generations should be conceptualized as being within a particular national context. If this is true, then, we might assume that generational structures within different countries will not follow the Western model.

Some research has examined generational characteristics in non-Western countries. Ralston, Egri, Stewart, Terpstra and Kaicheng (1999) found clear differences in individualism, collectivism and Confucianism across generational groups in China, using generational cohorts based upon Chinese history. Egri and Ralston (2004) found clear differences between U.S. and Chinese generational structures. Outside of Asia, Whiteoak, Crawford and Mapstone (2006) found differences in values between older and younger U.A.E. nationals. This evidence provides some support for the proposition that there are different generational characteristics in different national contexts.

Edmunds and Turner (2005) argued against the idea of national differences in generations through their suggestion that globally experienced traumatic events such as the 2001 attacks in New York may facilitate the development of global generations, rather than nationally bounded generational categories. Indeed, Hui-Chun and Miller (2003) found that, in Taiwan, Baby Boomers and Generation X displayed similar characteristics to those of Western societies. Other than this, research comparing generational differences across countries is sparse, so it is difficult to conclude whether Edmunds and Turner's (2005) notion of global generations can be empirically supported. If global generations do exist, then we might expect generational differences to be similar across countries. We might also suggest that globalization would have a greater effect on younger individuals, because they have grown up with prevalent international communication and media. As a result there might be larger differences between countries for older age groups, while younger age groups would show fewer differences.

Current Research

As previous literature suggests, age and/or generation plays an important role in an individual's career and how the individual perceives what a successful career might be. Conceivably, differences between age groups could be related to one or all of the three effects described above, and national context or culture is likely to play an important role. For instance, we might expect older age groups to place more emphasis on health and workload because of the physiological issues associated with age. They may also be less concerned with career progression or financial issues and more concerned with intrinsic benefits owing to their career stage. Alternatively, they may place more emphasis on formal recognition and authority as Baby Boomers, compared to Generation X-ers. These perceptions of career success may be consistent across cultures, particularly if they are related to an individual's career stage or maturation. However, they may be very inconsistent across cultures, as each age group experiences different contexts, including political and economic turmoil and changing social roles.

In this chapter we explore some of the above ideas a little further, with a particular emphasis on how people perceive career success in two broad age groups: younger individuals (M=27.5 years) and older individuals (M=57.0 years) across ten countries (see Table 6.1 for sample details). As specified in Chapter 3, our aim was to have samples that stood in strong relief to one another, and we believed the contrast of early and late career interviewees would serve that purpose. Beyond sampling age, this design inevitably samples generational experience and other peculiarities as well. We were able to explore generations and career transitions somewhat in Chapter 5; however, space did not allow an adequate exploration of generations in Chapter 4. In this chapter we specifically ask the following questions:

1 How do younger and older individuals define career success globally? What are the most important meanings of career success for each age group?
2 What do the career stories from these different individuals around the globe tell us?
3 What implications for practice can we draw from the research in terms of managing a multicultural and multigenerational workforce?

Findings

Table 6.1 provides a profile of the overall sample used in this research. For more information regarding the sample, please refer to Chapter 3 and individual country chapters.

Table 6.2 shows the percentage values for each career success category according to country and generational group. Following that, Table 6.3 shows the top three career success categories mentioned by each age group for each country. From these results we can make a number of interesting observations.

Most Important Meanings of Career Success for Older and Younger Individuals

Across both age groups the most prominent career success categories mentioned are achievement, satisfaction and job/task characteristics. If there are "universal" meanings of career success across groups, these would be the closest. That said, we emphasize that, within and between cultures, substantial variation exists that must be explored and acknowledged. First we will look at some of the more common success factors.

Achievement for the younger group is the most important meaning in all countries except for Spain, Japan and Mexico (see Table 6.2) and appears in the top three most mentioned categories for all the younger individuals in all countries except Japan (see Table 6.3). Therefore it appears that achievement in most cases is a universal element in career success for younger people around the world.

For the older group the profile is a little more varied. While achievement is still one of the most prominent perceived meanings of career success (especially for Austria, China and Mexico), it is not seen in the top three categories for Israel, Serbia, South Africa, Spain and the U.S.A.

There are some possible reasons why achievement is not as strong an element of career success for the older generation in these countries. In the first three cases one could argue that the older workers had less chance or opportunity for achievement-related goals owing to turbulent contextual factors (these will be talked about in more detail later in the chapter). In Spain, achievement was not mentioned at all by any of the older interviewees, and this could be related to their heavy emphasis upon work–life balance. In the U.S.A., perhaps the way success was achieved by older U.S. employees is *through* an organizational context rather than via more self-directed career management (Hall, 2002) as younger U.S. employees exhibit. Achievement, then, appears to have a

Table 6.1 Overview of country samples

Cluster	Sub-Saharan Africa	Confucian Asia		English speaking	Western Europe		Eastern Europe	Southeast Asia	Latin America	Israel
Countries	South Africa	China	Japan	U.S.A.	Austria	Spain	Serbia	Malaysia	Mexico	Israel
Sample size (N=207)	24	28	20	20	18	21	21	18	18	19
Older/younger age group	14/10	16/12	10/10	9/11	9/9	8/13	10/11	9/9	9/9	10/9

Table 6.2 Perceived career success categories across age group and country

Cluster	Sub-Saharan Africa		English speaking		Western Europe				Eastern Europe		Confucian Asia				Southeast Asia		Latin America		Israel	
Countries/categories	South Africa		U.S.A.		Austria		Spain		Serbia		China		Japan		Malaysia		Mexico		Israel	
Age group	Y	O	Y	O	Y	O	Y	O	Y	O	Y	O	Y	O	Y	O	Y	O	Y	O
Achievement Job/task characteristics	80%	29%	46%	33%	77%	100%	53%	0%	100%	90%	92%	81%	30%	40%	78%	33%	78%	100%	100%	70%
Satisfaction	0%	21%	18%	56%	67%	56%	61%	50%	100%	90%	67%	13%	50%	60%	11%	11%	89%	67%	100%	90%
Learning and development	20%	43%	36%	38%	77%	100%	69%	63%	100%	100%	50%	13%	50%	50%	22%	33%	78%	89%	78%	100%
Making a difference	20%	36%	36%	11%	67%	67%	31%	38%	91%	90%	50%	25%	20%	30%	22%	44%	56%	56%	56%	80%
Recognition	0%	57%	36%	33%	11%	22%	15%	12%	55%	40%	8%	19%	10%	20%	22%	56%	44%	22%	33%	60%
Work–life context/balance	10%	14%	18%	56%	56%	56%	23%	13%	100%	80%	17%	25%	50%	30%	0%	11%	44%	56%	44%	60%
Social working environment	40%	21%	18%	22%	11%	33%	46%	25%	100%	100%	17%	0%	10%	30%	33%	11%	22%	22%	67%	30%
Job performance	10%	36%	9%	11%	33%	67%	7%	25%	82%	100%	50%	19%	20%	10%	0%	0%	56%	44%	78%	80%
Self-actualization	30%	29%	27%	11%	11%	44%	15%	13%	91%	90%	42%	19%	20%	20%	22%	11%	44%	33%	44%	80%
Job security	0%	0%	0%	0%	0%	11%	23%	0%	27%	40%	33%	31%	0%	0%	22%	0%	0%	11%	44%	10%
Performing one's role	10%	29%	9%	33%	22%	67%	7%	13%	73%	80%	17%	31%	30%	30%	0%	0%	33%	11%	67%	60%
Material output	20%	29%	9%	44%	0%	0%	7%	0%	100%	100%	33%	38%	0%	0%	11%	33%	67%	56%	78%	30%

Network Contributing to organizational success																			
0%	0%	0%	0%	22%	0%	13%	100%	90%	17%	0%	0%	10%	0%	0%	0%	33%	0%	11%	10%
0%	7%	0%	33%	0%	22%	7%	0%	18%	20%	0%	6%	0%	0%	0%	0%	11%	11%	22%	20%

Notes:
Y = younger age group, O = older age group.
Cells highlighted in gray indicate categories where at least a 20 percent difference between the groups exists.

Table 6.3 Top three most mentioned career success categories across age group and country

Country	Younger age group	Older age group
Austria	Satisfaction, achievement, learning and development, job/task characteristics.	Satisfaction, achievement, learning and development, performing one's role, social working environment.
China	Achievement, job/task characteristics, satisfaction, social working environment.	Achievement, material output, job security, performing one's role.
Israel	Achievement, job/task characteristics, satisfaction, material output, social working environment.	Satisfaction, job/task characteristics, learning and development, self-actualization, social working environment.
Japan	Satisfaction, job/task characteristics, recognition.	Job/task characteristics, satisfaction, achievement.
Malaysia	Achievement, work–life balance, satisfaction, learning and development, making a difference, job security, self-actualization.	Making a difference, learning and development, achievement, satisfaction, material output.
Mexico	Job/task characteristics, achievement, satisfaction, material output.	Achievement, satisfaction, job/task characteristics.
Serbia	Satisfaction, achievement, job/task characteristics, social working environment, network, recognition, work–life balance, making a difference.	Satisfaction, job performance, work–life balance, material output.
South Africa	Achievement, work–life balance, self-actualization.	Making a difference, satisfaction, learning and development, social working environment.
Spain	Satisfaction, job/task characteristics, achievement.	Satisfaction, job/task characteristics, learning and development.
U.S.A.	Achievement, satisfaction, learning and development, making a difference.	Job performance, recognition, job/task characteristics.

Note: Categories listed here were the top three most mentioned for each age group. When more than three are listed, these categories had equal values.

slightly stronger emphasis for the younger generation worldwide. However, it still features strongly for both groups.

These findings would seem to be more in accordance with the maturation or career stage explanations described above, as one might suggest the need for achievement is greater at earlier stages in an individual's career. Indeed, Sturges (1999) found that material achievement becomes less important as people get older. Interestingly, the popular stereotypes of generations suggest that Baby Boomers (aligned with our older age group) have a greater need for achievement than generations X or Y.

Along with achievement, satisfaction is another important aspect of the perceived meaning of career success for both age groups. Table 6.3 shows that satisfaction is almost universal across all groups except in the older Chinese and U.S. interviewees and younger South Africans. Again contextual factors in China may have played a significant role here. A centrally planned economy where individuals lacked freedom to choose their desired career path leaves little room for exploring satisfaction-related career goals. In the U.S.A., the emphasis for the older worker is less on personal satisfaction and more related to finding recognition and success in the work context. In South Africa's case, apartheid-related laws were lifted in the early 1990s, and consequently the younger individuals in the workforce are being exposed to opportunities they previously had little access to. As a result, younger South Africans are moving quickly and believe they can change or have more of an impact on their environment. Does this suggest they are looking for something other than mere satisfaction?

The case for the remaining career success categories is not as clear cut. While job/task characteristics represented another prominent category, there didn't appear to be a pattern in its importance or lack of importance in each group. Interestingly, *none* of the interviewees in South Africa and Malaysia mentioned it as a significant meaning. It appeared to be mainly important for the younger individuals in the other countries, particularly Austria, China and Serbia, where it was not previously a factor for the older workers. In China and Serbia it may be this was a success dimension not considered available in older generations. For Austria this could be due to their particular approaches to work. Across the U.S. sample, it was only mentioned by the older generation, and this may be due to their focus on role and job performance.

Similarly, learning and development did not show a significant pattern amongst the age groups. It was important to both generations in Austria, Malaysia and South Africa. In Israel, Japan, Mexico and Spain only the older individuals placed it high in their preferences. It may be that the younger group in these countries mainly focused upon the job and its basic functions in the early years. In contrast, the U.S.A. is exhibiting this just in the younger generation, as the older generation was more likely to focus upon role and job performance and less on the self or person-centered values. This U.S. picture supports the popular stereotype of the younger generation being more interested in learning and development in order to make themselves more marketable to a range of employers. Conversely, older workers (Baby Boomers) were more focused on a career in a single organization, so are less interested in learning and development. The fact that this picture was not true of other countries demonstrates that generational differences according to the Western model of four generations should not automatically be adopted in other countries. It could also be suggested that the emphasis on learning and development in younger workers is in accordance with the notion of career stages, as younger workers in the exploration stage are said to be more interested in developing their careers and finding their niche.

As Table 6.2 suggests, the remaining categories are mentioned only sparsely by each of the age groups in each country. However, there are a few meanings summarized under the following categories that deserve attention. Performing one's role is important in certain older groups (the U.S.A., Austria, China and Japan) and does not appear at all in the younger generation across the countries. One example from an older blue-collar worker in China describes career success in relation to performing one's role:

> I'm serious about everything I'm doing. Although I may have dissatisfaction and complaint, I've tried to adapt myself to the environment. Therefore I always do a good job. For example, when I was working in the warehouse, with a salary lower than the first-line workers and a workload not necessarily lighter, I always thought that keeping balanced and clear accounts was my role and responsibility. So I tried to perform it well, even though I felt it unfair at the same time.
>
> (Older female Chinese blue-collar worker)

Similarly, an older Japanese individual says:

> I have been challenging my assignments proactively to accomplish continuing and constant job performance.
>
> (Older Japanese businessman)

Related to this, job performance appears important only for the older American and Serbian groups. These categories could be considered more organizationally bound factors which are losing prominence in the new world of work where younger generations are valuing more self-related goals. Recognition from an organizational perspective could also follow this logic; it appeared important only for the older individuals in the U.S.A. and Mexico. This provides evidence suggested by some that the nature of careers has changed from those that occur within a single organization in which job performance and organizational recognition are emphasized to those that are more boundaryless and self-directed.

Interestingly, the younger Japanese in this sample placed importance on recognition to a greater extent than their older counterparts. These ideas will be explored further in the following sections.

Finally, material output is another category that demonstrated differences between the age groups within our sample. Material output was a specific category created to describe career success being equated with certain material career "outputs" such as basic survival and affording material goods. One blue-collar individual from South Africa states that career success is:

> looking after my family, having an income to feed them, and nothing else.

Another goes on to say:

> If you can't work you can't eat. And if you can't eat you're going to go hungry.

Material output seems to appear most prominently in the older groups for China, Malaysia and Serbia and in the younger groups for Serbia, Mexico and Israel. This could reflect the economic uncertainty of these countries and the emphasis placed by these individuals on basic material survival. Interestingly, material output is not mentioned by any of the age groups in Japan, Spain or Austria, which highlights how context plays an important role in careers across the globe. This contextual influence will be discussed in more detail in the following sections.

In sum there are *few* "universals" when it comes to how older and younger individuals perceive career success worldwide, and it is difficult to make generalizations. In most countries and for both age groups, people relate career success in some way to satisfaction, achievement and job/task characteristics. Being "satisfied" in your job appears to be important for everyone, and achievement appears to be relatively universal across the younger individuals. In many cases a country's economic and political context plays an important role, together with career stage and the career competencies characteristic of that time or era. These interweave to shape the differences and similarities we observed.

In Focus: Country Specifics

In our view there is a story to be told about generations and careers, but, as these are not consistent across countries, it is more interesting and useful to examine generational differences on a country-by-country basis.

The following sections will describe some of the more unique country differences observed between the older and younger individuals and their perceptions of career success. We also include more detailed stories that provide a snapshot into the lives of these individuals worldwide.

Table 6.3 outlined the top three career success categories mentioned by each age group according to country. Particularly interesting amongst this are the results seen for China and the U.S.A. In both these countries, what appears important for one age group does not necessarily mirror that of the other group. We first focus on the U.S.A.

Self- Versus Organizational Definitions of Career Success in the U.S.A.

Table 6.4 suggests that each group places a slightly different emphasis on its perception of career success. While both groups share meanings such as satisfaction and making a difference (see Table 6.2), others are more pronounced for each age group. In this case, the key difference is evident in the greater degree to which the older workers give deference to the job itself as well as the employing organization. The following stories from our U.S. sample provide more evidence of this.

Table 6.4 Most mentioned career success categories for younger and older groups in the U.S.A.

	Younger group	Older group
U.S.A.	Achievement, satisfaction, learning and development, making a difference.	Job performance, recognition, job/task characteristics.

(Contributed by Jon P. Briscoe)

John is an older blue-collar worker who has worked in many jobs as a toolmaker in his career. He prided himself on his work and being recognized as being good at what he did. He moved frequently for work and geographic variety, and in terms of organizational mobility would have been labeled "boundaryless" (Arthur & Rousseau, 1996), using contemporary career language. But his definition of career success was quite traditional. He spoke primarily in terms of performance and recognition:

> Well, I made a lot of money. I had people probably that looked at me as a pretty good toolmaker and that's important in your life that you—

people might not like you but they at least acknowledge that you're good at what you do. I made a lot of money when I was working and that's a whole lot of, that's a whole lot of being happy with your job, 'cause I was doing a good job.

Other late career interviewees also spoke about recognition and performance, although they defined it in more affective terms that also reflected their desire to help others. Consider the statement of this nurse:

working in a job where you think you are appreciated and where you are able to mentor and be preceptor and help other young nurses to come up to your standard and share your experience.

Younger workers interviewed in the U.S.A. were less likely to offer definitions of career success reflecting recognition and validation by others or by an organization. They did share with older career actors a desire for achievement, but they were more likely to want to obtain success via their own path defined by learning and/or self-actualization. A good example of this is observable in the following quote from Jan, a young nurse describing her version of career success:

Well, I suppose it's a job or a position where it allows you to grow as a whole person. You can develop very practical skills that hopefully you can apply to other things, but not necessarily. It allows you to grow in your personal skills—working with other people. So it's not just you as a wonderful person, but there's the team synergy that you're growing, and they're improving as well. But it also allows you to have person time outside as well. Then those skills then can carry over to other things, whether it's with your family or with friends. In a way, when you're with other people outside of the work environment you gather energy to go back into the work environment. And the other way, if you spend all your time with your friends—that would be exhausting. So you need a balance between the two. So it would be a job or a career that would allow that . . . something that will allow you to fulfill all aspects of your personality.

While it does not apply to everyone, there seems to be an observable trend for many of the U.S. sample in which older workers focused upon performance through organizational contexts, whereas younger workers displayed elements of contemporary career theory and being more "protean" (Hall, 2002) in defining career success according to more idiosyncratic terms. In our view, both groups strive for achievement, but as in research outlined by Bennis and Thomas (2002) the older interviewees relied more upon the defined status quo, whereas organizations are not seen as essential for self-defined success with the younger generation. This also supports generational research in that older generations appear more focused on intra-organizational loyalty and achievement, while younger individuals are more likely to see their careers as occurring across organizational boundaries.

While this theme is clearly seen in the U.S.A., it is not as prominent in other countries. As we noted earlier, older workers emphasized job performance and performing one's role in Austria, China, Japan and Serbia, while these categories were not as apparent for the younger groups across the other countries. What do these results suggest? Is the younger age group in the U.S. sample exhibiting a profile of career success values indicative of today's working environment? Where does this leave the older workers and the values they associate with?

These results need to be taken with some degree of caution owing to the cross-sectional nature of our study; however, we can make some tentative conclusions. The results seen for the U.S. sample provide support for current Western career theory and the common generational stereotypes seen in the literature. Alongside this, our results also suggest generational diversity across countries and reinforce the need for more research outside of the Western model. Factors such as national context play an important role, and we will focus on this in the following section.

The Effect of National Context

Together with the U.S.A., China also has a relatively different picture of what was perceived as important career success factors in both age groups.

As shown in Table 6.5, the older group places more emphasis on achievement, job security and material output, thus focusing more on survival and making enough money to live. Conversely, the younger

Table 6.5 Most mentioned career success categories for younger and older groups in China

	Younger group	*Older group*
China	Achievement, job/task characteristics, satisfaction, social working environment.	Achievement, material output, job security, performing one's role.

interviewees had a broader sense of career success, which included factors such as satisfaction and social working environment. This may reflect the changes seen in China's political and economic history over the past 30 years (see below). Interestingly, none of the older age group mentioned work–life balance, and satisfaction was only mentioned by 13 percent of the older sample. The following story from a Chinese father and his daughter help explain this dramatic effect of culture in more detail.

Jun and his daughter Ling

(Contributed by Yan Shen)

The following two stories provide some insights into how older and younger generations in China perceive their career success differently. By the time of the interviews, Jun was in his mid-50s, and Ling was in her mid-20s. The key differences between Jun and Ling's careers are the flexibility and freedom the latter enjoys in her career development, as well as the associated career and life satisfaction. As Jun mentioned in his interview, he considered his 50-plus years of life, including his 30 years of career, a waste of time. By contrast, Ling had a clear career goal and actively managed her career transitions towards this goal. Their career stories reflect the significant social and institutional changes China has undergone in the past three decades.

Jun graduated from junior high school and was assigned to work in a state-owned company at the age of 18. In the early 1970s, a new plant was established in a city in inland China owing to the government economic development focus in poverty-ridden regions. Consequently, he was relocated to and worked for the new plant until the late 1990s, when he met the age requirement of early retirement because of the government layoff policy. When he retired and returned to his hometown, he got a net monthly pension of just over RMB 400, which was comparable to the average income level at that time. But later his company was acquired by another company and his salary was lowered almost by half. He was forced to find a temporary job, with the help of a former classmate, with a monthly salary of over RMB 1,000. He is unsatisfied with such a result after so many years of hard work, and he considers his life a failure. To him, career success means high income and a good position with opportunities for further promotion and advancement.

Ling, daughter of Jun, holds a master's degree from a national key university in China. During her four-year undergraduate study, she took many part-time jobs, from customer service and marketing to training and consulting. After she got her master's degree, she worked for a consulting company for about half a year. She quit this job because of lack of learning opportunities, bad relations with her boss, and person–organization misfit. She then actively engaged in job-hunting and received several interview offers till she joined her current private company in which she is assistant to the company president. She likes challenges and a new environment. Her short-term career goal is to become a senior consultant by the age of 35. Therefore she is now trying to accumulate practical knowledge in the real world and to understand an industry well. To her, career success is more than a decent income and hierarchical advancement, though they are necessary. She desires a job that embodies challenges, learning opportunities and a good work–life balance. More importantly, it should be something that she would like to do and has a strong interest in.

As Jun's story shows, his career path was shaped by the evolution of government policies at various periods, from the government-assigned relocation to a remote place to forced early retirement. He had little control over the type of work he wanted to do. Therefore he did not concern himself too much about individual learning and development, the task scope and variety, and work–life balance. A major pattern across the older interviewees in China is that most of them defined career success primarily from an objective, material-focused perspective and paid a lot of attention to job security and stability. They considered their work and life experiences as "fate" and beyond their control.

Ling's story presents a very different picture from her father's. With the rapid change of the economic and social landscape in China, she is much freer to design her own career path out of various alternatives, including working for different types of companies in different industries. Her definition of career success is much more diversified and incorporates both objective (e.g. financial achievement and career advancement) and subjective (e.g. job/career satisfaction, individual learning and development, and working environment) dimensions. Generally speaking, the younger interviewees in China are more innovative, flexible, confident, ambitious and individual-oriented. They attribute their career success more to individual and work context-related factors than to macro-institutional contexts.

Apart from China and the U.S.A., other countries exhibiting relatively big differences or shifts in conceptions of career success between age groups are South Africa, Malaysia and Serbia (see Table 6.3). South Africa has had significant change over the past 30 years, with the apartheid laws being lifted in the early 1990s and "previously disadvantaged individuals" now having equal access to education and job opportunities. Our interviews were able to capture the perspectives of both the older workers, who were very much part of the apartheid era, and the younger individuals, who are now experiencing equal opportunities and significant changes. Our results found that the younger group had broadened or changed their career success focus, with achievement, work–life balance and self-actualization becoming more prominent. One younger individual describes his concept of work–life balance as an important feature of his career success:

> I think if you're successful you have a balance. Being good at your job, being brilliant at your job, but you just have work, you are so buried, you have to have other parts of your life. I mean for me a good healthy balance between the two is what I think. So, yeah, to me that would be successful, so, yeah, having a good human relation with a good balance between work and life. But not when work becomes the "be all," you know.
>
> (Younger South African businessman)

Similarly, another young woman talks about how possessing goals and what could also be described as a self-actualizing approach is important to her career success:

> Since a young age, I lived my life possessing goals as high as possible. And I feel a lot of people live the same way. But a lot of people are not aware of the fact that you are responsible for reaching this goal. I think of lot of people are too passive in their lives. And I think if you're gonna reach any kind of success in anything you need to take responsibilities for the great moment and the failures.
>
> (Younger South African businesswoman)

Apart from South Africa, the younger individuals in Serbia are also experiencing significant change owing to their national context (see below). In this case the younger individuals have retained many of the career success values important to the older generation; however, they also emphasize other important aspects in their careers. Achievement, job/task characteristics, making a difference, social working environment, networks and recognition are all important in their definitions of career success. The following story of an older individual in Serbia describes in more detail how she perceives her career success and how the country's turbulent history has played a role in shaping this.

(Contributed by Biljana Bogićević Milikić and Jelena Zikic)

Slavica is a nurse in her mid-50s. She lives in Belgrade, the capital of Serbia. She graduated from the secondary medical school and started her career in a day nursery, working with babies up to three years old. She is awaiting her retirement, which is due in the next few years, when she fulfills the legally required retirement criteria.

As a nurse, Slavica earns a rather small salary, much like her husband, who is employed in the Serbian Ministry of Defense as a military officer. They live together with their two daughters, who are in their late 20s. Both of their daughters finished secondary school (high school) and found employment immediately after their graduation in order to contribute to the family budget.

Slavica's family is a good example of a typical Serbian family in the 2000s. It is commonly the case in Serbia that the older generation still have a very close relationship with their children, despite the latter often being married, employed and with their own families. Older age groups would often still provide financially for their adult children, as in the economy in transition, while younger people may often lack enough financial security to maintain themselves.

With political changes happening in the country in the late 2000s, Serbia has again started the process of transition toward a market economy through much faster privatization, restructuring of enterprises, downsizing of public enterprises, macroeconomic stabilization and liberalization. All this has led to a very high unemployment rate (above 30 percent during the 2000s), a significant role for the informal sector (hidden economy), high corruption generally, high political involvement in the economic sector and a very low standard of living (around 15 percent of the population are considered to be poor). As a consequence, many young people cannot find adequate employment. They often do not have the financial means to continue with their education or commonly, given these bleak career prospects, they simply lack the motivation for further study. Therefore many young people live together with their parents and are trying to postpone the moment of separation and starting their own families.

Slavica is generally satisfied with her career, since she does the type of work she loves, and she was also able to stay on the same career path and within a single organization for most of her career.

She loves her autonomy on the job and the opportunity to apply her own life experience in her everyday working environment. However, Slavica believes that the main indicator of career success is material security. For her:

> You are successful if you succeed in being financially secure, to satisfy your basic needs, to live a normal live and to support your children in their lives.

Slavica believes that the macroeconomic situation in Serbia nowadays is so poor that you have to struggle every day in order to survive. She says:

> If you do not have good personal network connections, you cannot find a job, while living costs are permanently rising. Young people are leaving the country in order to find better opportunities in other countries. I cannot see any prospects for young people here.

Looking after basic survival needs is often expected in a society faced with deep economic crisis and transitional changes leading to privatization, restructuring, downsizing and layoffs. Much of the middle class in Serbia has almost disappeared, while the majority of the society perceive themselves as being very "poor," and less than 1 percent of the population is considered to be wealthy (according to Western standards). However, their wealth is often perceived to be earned in illegal ways.

These examples suggest that context plays an important role in shaping the differences we saw in our two age groups. As is the case with China, these results could be explained by the increased opportunities seen for younger individuals as apartheid, civil war and religious segregation have eased. Accordingly, the younger individuals are being exposed to similar opportunities to other countries globally, and their career success priorities include a broader array of elements. It will be interesting to see how these profiles or career success priorities continue to change over time and with new context effects. For example, will job security be a more prominent feature of the younger generation in light of today's less than certain economic climate in certain countries like the U.S.A.?

Conclusions

Returning to our discussion at the beginning of the chapter regarding the impact of age on careers and more specifically how career stage, maturation effects and generational differences influence careers, what light does our research shed on this issue? In many cases we have provided more evidence for generational theory than for career or life stage models.

In a number of cases the differences we observed between the older and younger groups were influenced by the national context. In particular, those countries experiencing significant economic and social change had bigger differences between the two age groups, as each had different life experiences during the normative years (Mannheim, 1952). If we assume to some extent that the results we found are due to generational effects, then our research demonstrates an important finding. Generations and the attitudes and characteristics associated with them are not universal across countries. Indeed, for individuals to share a "social location" they must share both a geographical proximity and a temporal proximity in their year of birth (Mannheim, 1952). Accordingly, we also have limited evidence of Edmunds and Turner's (2005) suggestion that the increase in "global events" has led to the development of global generations that share similar attitudes and values.

It should be noted however that, while the differences we observed between the age groups were genuine, we need to be cautious about these conclusions owing to our research design. In order to establish whether the differences we observed are enduring over time and therefore to disentangle generational rather than age or career stage effects, we must conduct longitudinal research (Parry & Urwin, forthcoming; Twenge, 2009). We have also based our results on a relatively small sample size, and therefore it is difficult to generalize our findings.

Further research of a quantitative nature is needed to validate whether the differences we observed apply to other individuals within the countries identified. A question that remains is whether, and in what situations, national context or culture is a more salient influence upon career experience than age, career stage or generations. Do these two factors interact, or is one decidedly more important than the other? Or can career stage and generations meaningfully be regarded outside of country context? We are doubtful that they can be. Our research would suggest it is a complex interplay between all factors, with turbulent economic and social changes in countries playing a moderating role.

Despite the issues raised above, this research has allowed us to make intriguing observations about the impact of age on career experiences and also the effect of culture or national context. The trends we saw in our research also leave us with some interesting questions and areas for future research. Our results showed some evidence of younger individuals taking a more self-directed orientation in their definitions of career success and more interest in managing their careers. To what extent, then, are younger individuals taking more responsibility for managing their careers than older workers? Is this profile of career success values indicative of surviving in the new world of work? Following on from this, countries experiencing significant change have seen a clear shift in career success priorities among the newer or younger individuals in the workforce. What model are these new workers aspiring towards, and what career success values are we losing from the older generation? What other cycles or shifts could we predict in how people define career success in the coming decades as a result of the current context?

Practical Implications

Taking the results we described above into consideration, what can we now say about managing younger and older individuals in the workforce? The data we have provided on conceptions of career success provide a number of suggestions for where the emphasis in rewards systems, leadership and working conditions could be placed when considering these individuals. For instance, achievement-related goals amongst the younger generation appear to be a relatively good source of career motivation. Career paths and reward systems that provide opportunities for promotion, advancement and financial reward will bode well for this group.

Career success was not only about achievement, however, particularly for the older age group. Satisfaction is also important for both groups of workers, and tapping into what these individuals find satisfying will provide better results. The development of appropriate learning and development opportunities should also be investigated in order to attract and retain younger workers. In addition, there is evidence that younger workers want to make a difference through their work. Therefore employers need to consider the content of individual roles and whether these are worthwhile and allow people to have an impact on the organization or wider community.

Our results also suggest that a younger employee is going to be motivated by achievement, satisfaction and job characteristic-related goals to a *greater* extent than more traditional factors such as job performance, performing one's role and material output. Organizations are therefore going to have to be more creative with these groups to promote productivity and incentivize their younger employees. It is also important, however, especially in light of the aging workforce, to retain more traditional financial and other recognition systems in order to motivate older employees.

Overall, our research has suggested there are some differences in the factors that are likely to motivate older and younger individuals to progress in their careers. In addition, national context or culture has an important effect. This would seem to suggest that a one-size-fits-all approach to career management and rewards will not be sufficient in order to motivate and retain workers of all ages and cultures. While it is not possible or practical to tailor benefits or career management packages to each individual (there are bound to be differences by gender as well), it is important for employers to recognize that not everyone is the same. The use of practices such as cafeteria benefits packages where people can choose their benefits within a predefined financial limit may help to address this issue.

It should also be noted that this research was conducted before the recent economic downturn. It would be interesting to repeat this research now, after the global economic crisis, and see if this has affected the views of the younger age group in particular. For instance, could the lack of a focus on material output and job security be reversed after recent layoffs and increases in unemployment?

Case Study

Yoshihiko was excited to have his big opportunity. He had requested an expatriate transfer years ago, because he knew it was required if he were ever to have the future opportunities he was hoping for in TechCo Manufacturing Group. He had experienced great success in Japan, while making improvements to the company's leading product line, with greater quality margins and profits as team leader of the Innovation 2050 team. He knew it was time for an overseas move and accepted the position at the U.S. branch gratefully.

Yoshihiko was transferred to a plant in Cincinnati, Ohio, and he already had some difficult decisions to make only one month into the job. After the quality manager left for a job at a competitor, standards and productivity were slipping. Yoshihiko knew he would be judged harshly if he could not improve results quickly.

He knew from the outgoing manager that motivation had been a problem with his current staff, who were of varying ages and cultures owing to the specialized skills required for their positions. The older workers seemed content to continue working at their regular pace and appeared to spend a lot of time conversing with their colleagues. Younger workers were more assertive but seemed to want a reward for everything. Also, like the quality manager, they left for more money or talked about better opportunities with other companies and better wages.

Yoshihiko was discouraged, because in Japan people rarely left such jobs owing to stability and the chance to progress in a single company. He felt he needed to find a way to keep people motivated and performing well without constant bonuses.

After reading this chapter, what does Yoshihiko need to consider for incentivizing his staff to perform better? How can Yoshihiko create a motivating environment for his staff from various contexts? What kind of career development plan could he implement for older and younger employees? What cultural influences does Yoshihiko bring as a younger Japanese individual that may influence his decisions?

References

Arthur, M. B. & Rousseau, D. M. (Eds.). 1996. *The Boundaryless Career: A New Employment Principle for a New Organizational Era.* New York: Oxford University Press.

Baruch, Y. 2006. Career development in organizations and beyond: Balancing traditional and contemporary viewpoints. *Human Resource Management Review,* 16(2): 125–138.

Bennis, W. G. & Thomas, J. R. 2002. *Geeks and Geezers: How Era, Values and Defining Moments Shape Leaders.* Boston, MA: Harvard Business School Press.

Edmunds, J. & Turner, B. 2005. Global generations: Social change in the twentieth century. *British Journal of Sociology of Education,* 56(4): 559–577.

Egri, C. & Ralston, D. 2004. Generation cohorts and personal values: A comparison of China and the United States. *Organization Science,* 15(2): 210–220.

Filipczak, B. 1994. It's just a job: Generation X at work. *Training and Development Journal,* 31: 21–27.

Hall, D. T. 2002. *Careers In and Out of Organizations.* Thousand Oaks, CA: Sage.

Hall, D. T. & Mirvis, P. 1996. The new protean career: Psychological success and the path with a heart. In D. T. Hall (Ed.), *The Career Is Dead—Long Live the Career.* San Francisco, CA: Jossey-Bass.

Hui-Chun, Y. & Miller, P. 2003. The generation gap and cultural influence: A Taiwan empirical investigation. *Cross-Cultural Management,* 10(3): 23–41.

Kupperschmidt, B. 2000. Multigenerational employees: Strategies for effective management. *Health Care Manager,* 19(1): 65–76.

Levinson, D. J. 1978. *The Seasons of a Man's Life* (17th ed.). New York: Ballantine Books.

Loretto, W., Vickerstaff, S. & White, P. 2005. *Older Workers and the Options for Flexible Work.* Working Paper No. 31. Manchester: Equal Opportunities Commission.

Mannheim, K. 1952. The problem of generations. In *Essays on the Sociology of Knowledge.* London: Routledge & Kegan Paul.

Ornstein, S., Cron, W. L. & Slocum, J. W., Jr. 1989. Life stage versus career stage: A comparative test of the theories of Levinson and Super. *Journal of Organizational Behavior,* 10(2): 117.

Parry, E. & Urwin, P. forthcoming. Generational differences in work values: A review of theory and evidence.

Ralston, D. A., Egri, C. P., Stewart, S., Terpstra, R. H. & Kaicheng, Y. 1999. Doing business in the 21st century with the new generation of Chinese managers: A study of generational shifts in work values in China. *Journal of International Business Studies*, 30(2): 415–427.

Rhodes, S. 1983. Age-related differences in work-attitudes and behaviour: A review and conceptual analysis. *Psychological Bulletin*, 93(2): 328–367.

Schein, E. H. 1978. *Career Dynamics: Matching Individual and Organizational Needs*. Reading, MA: Addison-Wesley.

Sterns, H. L. & Miklos, S. M. 1995. The aging worker in a changing environment: Organizational and individual issues. *Journal of Vocational Behavior*, 47(2): 248–268.

Strauss, W. & Howe, N. 1991. *Generations: The History of America's Future, 1584–2069*. New York: William Morrow.

Sturges, J. 1999. What it means to succeed: Personal conceptions of career success held by male and female managers at different ages. *British Journal of Management*, 10(3): 239–252.

Super, D. E. 1957. *The Psychology of Careers*. New York: Harper & Row.

Twenge, J. M. 2009. Change over time in obedience: The jury's still out, but it might be decreasing. *American Psychologist*, 64(1): 28–31.

Twenge, J. M. 2010. A review of the empirical evidence on generational differences in work attitudes. *Journal of Business and Psychology*, 25(2): 201–210.

Whiteoak, J. W., Crawford, N. G. & Mapstone, R. H. 2006. Impact of gender and generational differences in work values and attitudes in an Arab culture. *Thunderbird International Business Review*, 48(1): 77–91.

Part III

Analysis

7

Culture and Context: Understanding Their Influence Upon Careers

Katharina Chudzikowski, Enrique Ogliastri,
Jon P. Briscoe, Afam Ituma, Astrid Reichel,
Wolfgang Mayrhofer and Svetlana N. Khapova

The findings revealed in previous chapters show that individuals across countries share common understandings of career dimensions as well as differences. These different concepts across countries can be interpreted and explained from different angles that are not necessarily exclusive. Cultural dimensions including socialization in different contexts shape perceptions of careers. Additionally, formal and informal education and occupational settings shape perceptions and career opportunities that are linked to socio-economic or political status and culture. Besides those factors, age as it pertains to life stage or era plays an important role. This is based on the assumption that careers are socially embedded. Consequently, analyzing careers requires a consideration of context (Mayrhofer, Meyer & Steyrer, 2007). Beyond individual influences such as dispositional differences, various layers of external factors influence the course of careers. These include the context of origin, the context of work, the context of society and culture and the global context.

In comparative careers research across countries the cultural perspective is most often used to explain differences across countries (see also Chapter 2) (Arnold & Cohen, 2008; Inkson, Khapova & Parker, 2007; Tams & Arthur, 2007). Second, besides taking a cultural perspective, there are also authors who look at influences on careers from an institutional angle (e.g. Ituma & Simpson, 2009). The results of the previous chapters establish that differences across countries can be explained by concepts that also focus on institutional context. Therefore this chapter addresses the issues both of cultural values and of institutional context influencing careers.

When reflecting on our empirical results on career success, aspects of generations and career transition across countries, we proceed as follows. First, we summarize the results of the comparative analysis across countries (see also Chapters 4, 5 and 6). Second, we take the cultural perspective (as outlined in Chapter 2) to discuss our results. Third, we introduce the institutional perspective in greater detail and use it to discuss our empirical results.

Empirical Insights

In this section, we summarize the empirical results for career success, career transitions and generational aspects.

Career Success

In deciphering the commonalities of career success, four themes emerge: achievement, certain job/task characteristics, satisfaction, and learning and development are crucial career success dimensions in most countries. Basic experiences such as achievement and satisfaction are critical elements in the definition of success. The role of financial achievement as a common theme and career objective needs to be contextualized. On one hand, reference groups are important for defining achievement on the individual level, depending on industry, profession, gender or age group. On the other hand, opportunity structure links to levels of achievements within specific contexts. Thus the economic and social environment influences how individuals conceptualize their need for mastery and capabilities. Our findings reflect this influence, especially in those countries that go through turbulent economic and social change (e.g. China and Serbia). In those countries, achievement is more frequently related to meeting basic human needs, such as having a place to live or being able to feed one's family.

While job and task aspects of career success—responsibilities and challenges—cover both objective and subjective aspects of careers, satisfaction expresses the subjective side of individual values. It is less linked to the specific work context. Satisfaction is not directly related to what others grant the person for doing the job, but instead comes from doing the job itself, irrespective of the actual outcomes or rewards.

The most frequent theme when discussing factors of career success across countries is the context of work, with particular emphasis on the company, superiors, peers and work networks, which are external to a person and refer to the opportunity structure within organizations or professions. All other themes that are identified are specific to the person. They include personal history (educational history, job history and family background), traits (e.g. persistence and diligence, positive attitude and work ethic) and motives (e.g. goal-related drivers such as efforts and emotional drivers such as enthusiasm).

Looking at age groups, the younger age group agrees more homogeneously on the importance of achievement as a major element of career success. However, there are countries that do not rank achievement as the most dominant theme, for example Japan, Israel and Spain. Satisfaction is emphasized in countries belonging to the following clusters of Schwartz's (2006) concept: the Western (Spain and Austria) and the Eastern (represented by Serbia) European clusters, and Japan representing the Confucian cluster. Furthermore, Mexico of the Latin American cluster stresses the characteristics of job and task as meaningful to career success. In general, the older age group generates a more heterogeneous ranking of themes (see also Chapter 6).

The data show differences between older and younger age groups (broadly), but also depend on the respective national contexts. Some countries show greater differences between the two age groups when there are strong contextual forces. An example is China, which has gone through major economic transitions.

Career Transitions

Dominant themes relating to recent "career-related change(s)" include respondents' subjective feelings, their interpretation of influencing factors and their report of outcomes. Over half of our interviewees had gone through at least one job transition. Looking at commonalities, the most mentioned driver for recent career-related changes is specific to the person and summarized as taking one's own initiative. A closer look reveals that the main reasons for transitions varied from seeking development, to seeking balance, to looking for higher pay. This is also an indicator for a perceived individualization of careers and internal control, which mirrors the respective context and labor market conditions within each country, profession and industry, as well as cultural patterns. Differences can also be observed across countries when looking at how individuals perceive career transitions. Persons from highly individualized countries like the U.S.A. attribute more individual and less macro control (e.g. markets, politics, etc.). Conversely, countries in transitions like China, Serbia and South Africa see changes in career opportunities driven by educational opportunities and governmental policies. In particular, there are differences across generations; older workers are more externally driven, younger workers more internally.

Looking at influencing factors, network connections—work, personal or professional—play an important role for transitions. Relationships are an important source for support and for managing transitions across the country samples. On an individual level, planning/goal setting and formal education strategies in managing career transitions are prevalent in countries categorized by high mastery such as the U.S.A., China, Japan and Israel.

Looking at drivers of career transitions for both age groups, younger workers mostly identify the theme of taking their own initiative, and emphasize internal sources for transitions (e.g. desire for a new job or seeking further development). Moreover, graduation is an important driver for younger workers, as they are referring to their experience of school-to-work transitions in the early career stages. In contrast, older workers tend to describe their transitions as self-initiated, but also state that they are mostly stimulated externally, by superiors or peers. Furthermore, themes of drivers initiated by organizations, like restructuring arrangements or changes in leadership, are more emphasized by older workers. The exceptions are China and Japan, where both age groups highlight organizations as the most frequent driver. Thus, in general, members of the older generation emphasize external sources for career transition, whereas the younger generation resemble the patterns of countries mentioning internal drivers.

Cultural and Institutional Perspectives on Careers

Over the past few years, there has been a proliferation of country-specific and cross-national career studies. This is partly due to the increasing recognition that careers are embedded within a wider cultural, economic and political arrangement (Mayrhofer et al., 2007; Tams & Arthur, 2007; Thomas & Inkson, 2007). The multi-faceted literature in this area has provided valuable insight into how contextual factors inform career development. Theories that help to explain cultural differences in work contexts were described in Chapter 2. This chapter will add another concept, drawing from different sources of literature, after we discuss our data though the lens of cultural concepts.

Applying the Cultural Perspective

This section discusses our results from the cultural angle. We will reflect first on career success and generational aspects and second on career transitions by using the cultural concepts discussed in Chapter 2.

Cultural Context

This section analyzes the influence of cultural values on careers as reported in the previous empirical chapters. Career success meanings and drivers for career transitions are studied using Schwartz's (2008) three polar values of embeddedness/autonomy, hierarchy/egalitarianism and mastery/harmony.

Career Success and Cultural Values

A summary of results about career success meanings and culture according to Schwartz's (2008) variables is presented in Table 7.1. To provide the clearest contrast, four countries included in the 5C study were left out of Table 7.1 for having "middle" or average values in the dimensions, thus being inconclusive. There is a general support for the influence of cultural values on career success.

Embeddedness in Schwartz's (2008) study means the values highly emphasizing social order, obedience and respect for tradition; the opposite values are autonomy, made up of two dimensions, intellectual and affective autonomy. This variable is related to collectivism/individualism in other culture studies (i.e. Hofstede, 1980; and GLOBE: see Chhokar, Brodbeck & House, 2007) and to "traditional authority" cultures in the World Value Survey (WVS) (Inglehart & Carballo, 1997). It is a paradox that all the countries with a culture of embeddedness (China, Japan and South Africa) value highly objective achievements as indicators of career success, while two of the four countries with autonomy values (Austria

Table 7.1 Career success meanings

Career success by cultural variables	Embeddedness	Hierarchy	Mastery
Objective career success (i.e. achievements)	**China** **Malaysia** **South Africa**	Japan **China** **South Africa**	**U.S.A.** Japan **China** Israel
Subjective career success (i.e. satisfaction)	U.S.A. **Austria** **Spain** Israel	**Spain** **Austria** **Costa Rica** Israel	**Costa Rica** **Spain** **Austria**
	Autonomy	*Egalitarianism*	*Harmony*

Notes:
Countries in bold letters show consistency between cultural variables and type of career success meanings.
Four countries with "middle" or average cultural values are not part of the table.

and Spain, but not the U.S.A. and Israel) value subjective success (i.e. personal satisfaction).

One line of explanation is that it is more remarkable to be successful for reasons other than the "normal" in the culture. Another possible explanation for the results is in the trend towards post-materialist values of the world, found by the World Value Survey (Inglehart & Carballo, 1997). The trend from "traditional" (work important) to "survival" values (hard work, money) and to "well-being" values was noticeable among the northern countries of Europe and America as well as Catholic Europe (Austria and Spain). "Satisfaction" may be part of this trend towards life satisfaction and post-materialist concerns, and those more economically and socially advanced countries value personal satisfaction over achievements.

Regarding the hierarchy/egalitarian cultural values, we found a good fit between culture and career success meanings in the countries studied. Hierarchy is related to the power distance concept (Chhokar et al., 2007; Hofstede, 1980) and to the traditional authority values of the WVS. For Schwartz these values are centered on authority and humility on one side, and social justice and equality on the other extreme.

In two-thirds of those countries having a value system of authority and hierarchy we found individuals valuing objective achievements (China and South Africa) over personal satisfaction as a significant meaning of career success. Japan is the exception, probably because (along with Confucian values of respect for elders) it has been a society of high achievement motivation values (McClelland, 1961). Schwartz comments on the "striking exception" of an "unusual combination of cultural elements" in Japan: "a culture in tension and transition" (Schwartz, 2008, footnote 4). Regarding perceived meanings of career success, Japan is also the exception. According to the GLOBE study, South Africa and China are also among the high performance orientation cultures (Chhokar et al., 2007), and it may explain these results valuing objective achievements. Conversely, three of the four countries having egalitarian cultures rank personal satisfaction highest in terms of meanings of career success. Israel is the exception, and the reason may be that it is a high achievement motivation culture as well.

One explanation for the main results is that China and South Africa are striving to achieve economic development and modernization, while Austria, Costa Rica and Spain are part of the post-materialist values trend which places emphasis on life satisfaction and well-being (Inglehart, 1997).

The last continuum variable of our study is mastery/harmony. Schwartz focuses the mastery pole with ambition and daring values, while the pole for harmony values unity with nature, and world at peace (Austria, Costa Rica and Spain are the countries in such a pole). We found a good fit between cultural values and the objective/subjective meaning of career success (the exceptions are again Israel and Japan).

In all those countries where the culture is for harmony with nature and peace, we found a subjective satisfaction meaning of career success. It is probably due to the fact that these countries (Austria, Spain and Costa Rica) are in the post-materialist value set, where according to the WVS ecology and tolerance values are part of the cluster with life satisfaction and well-being. The emphasis is not "on *having* work, for the sake of survival; in economically more developed societies, people place much greater emphasis on work as a source of personal *satisfaction*" (Inglehart & Carballo, 1997: 38, italics in the original).

Cultural Values and Career Success for Generations

We have seen in earlier chapters how, across countries, generations and career success are manifest in one another on a global scale. We now explore whether broad cultural dimensions can be used to illuminate these relationships as well.

We looked at the three major meanings of career success that countries had in common—achievement, satisfaction and job/task characteristics

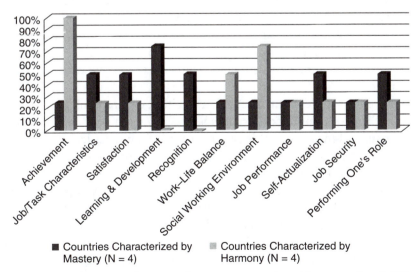

Figure 7.1 Percentage of mastery/harmony countries with generational differences (of at least 20 percent) for given success meanings

according to each of Schwartz's (2008) polarities (autonomy/embeddedness, hierarchy/egalitarianism and mastery/harmony)—and found that type of cultural dimension had very little variability in terms of impact upon these top career success meanings (when considering country samples as a whole). However, when looking across generations and cultural dimensions, more differences became apparent.

Figure 7.1 displays the percentage of countries that were relatively high in mastery or harmony (average countries were left out to illustrate contrasts) and for which they had at least a 20 percent difference between how generations expressed a particular meaning of career success.

What is immediately striking is that each country characterized by harmony (Austria, Mexico, Spain and South Africa) had at least a 20 percent difference between older and younger generations in achievement. This indicates more tension, or at least differences in thinking. Countries higher in harmony were also more likely to have generational differences in work–life balance and social working environment. In most cases the younger generations in these countries are interested in dimensions of career success that their older counterparts are not.

On the other hand, countries higher in mastery (China, Israel, Japan and the U.S.A.) show more generational differences in job/task characteristics, satisfaction, learning and development, recognition, self-actualization and performing one's role. In some of these countries (such as the U.S.A.) older generations retain more organizational views of career success (i.e. with more emphasis upon the work role, recognition, etc.), while younger ones seek more "expressive" and individualized career success manifestations. However, this is not uniform. Other countries such as China show more of the same "organizational" views of career success in the younger generation. These mastery countries are more likely to differ between generations on the above career success meanings.

Figure 7.2 profiles countries higher in either egalitarianism or hierarchy, with corresponding differences between generational ascriptions of career success meanings (at least 20 percent). Countries leaning toward hierarchy (China, Israel, Japan, Malaysia, South Africa and the U.S.A.) showed a greater propensity to report differences in career success meanings of job/task characteristics, learning and development, and recognition. There was not a clear pattern (beyond showing differences) in terms of whether the younger or older generation was higher. Job/task characteristics and recognition reflect a culture of hierarchy. Job/task characteristics and learning and development speak less to hierarchy and more to individuals' own needs in spite of hierarchical realities.

Countries more associated with egalitarianism values (Austria and

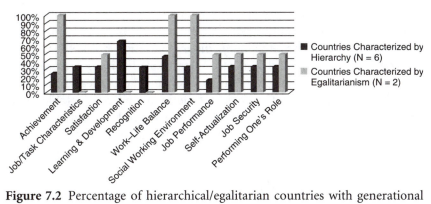

Figure 7.2 Percentage of hierarchical/egalitarian countries with generational differences (of at least 20 percent) for given success meanings

Spain) were much more likely to show generational differences for work–life context/balance, achievement and social working environment. However, the direction was flipped, with older workers in Austria preferring these career success meanings, while younger workers in Spain sought the same. It is interesting to us that each of these career success meanings appears compatible with egalitarianism (with the possible exception of achievement) and yet the generations seemingly differ greatly over its value. It may suggest cultures in transition.

In Figure 7.3 countries characterized by autonomy (Austria, Israel, Japan, Mexico, Spain and the U.S.A.) were more likely to demonstrate generational differences only in the area of work–life context/balance. However, those countries associated with the value of embeddedness (China, Malaysia and South Africa) were more likely than their counterparts emphasizing autonomy to have generational differences with the

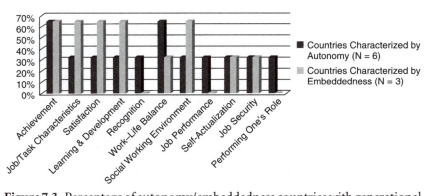

Figure 7.3 Percentage of autonomy/embeddedness countries with generational differences (of at least 20 percent) for given success meanings

career success meanings of job/task characteristics, satisfaction, learning and development, and social working environment. In South Africa these values were more cited by the older generation, while the younger generations in China and Malaysia were more likely to seek them. It strikes us that this last set of highlighted career success meanings are in a way "luxuries" common to a socially functional and comfortable workplace. Are these "perks" that are usually considered unneeded or taken for granted in either embedded or autonomy-driven cultures?

Career Transitions and Cultural Values

A second set of results relating cultural values of the Schwartz framework to our results in this careers study focuses on career transitions, as shown in Table 7.2. We are using the seven country cultures in each polar variable for which we have a classification in one pole (leaving out those in the average or middle point). We have embeddedness in China, Malaysia and South Africa, while autonomy values are predominant in Austria, Israel, Spain and the U.S.A. Hierarchy is high in Japan, China and South Africa, while the opposite pole of egalitarianism is the predominant value in Austria, Costa Rica, Israel and Spain. Dominant values of mastery are prevalent in China, Israel, Japan and the U.S.A.; the opposite, harmony, values are dominant in Austria, Costa Rica and Spain.

Our results show two basic drivers for career transitions. One is focused on internal drivers, such as workers' own initiative for the career

Table 7.2 Career transitions—main drivers of transitions in each country

Career transitions by cultural variables	Embeddedness	Hierarchy	Mastery
External driver (organization, macro, family-influenced)	**China** Malaysia South Africa	**China** **Japan** South Africa	**China** Israel **Japan** U.S.A.
Internal driver (own initiative)	**Austria** **Israel** **Spain** **U.S.A.**	**Austria** **Costa Rica** **Israel** **Spain**	**Austria** **Costa Rica** **Spain**
	Autonomy	Egalitarianism	Harmony

Notes:
Countries in bold letters show consistency between cultural variables and type of driver for career transitions.
Four countries with middle or average cultural values in each dimension are not part of the table.

change. The second driver is external, a transition originating in organizational, macro and family-influenced factors.

As predicted, the values of autonomy are clearly associated with workers' own initiative and other internal drivers for career success, as demonstrated by Austria, Israel, Spain and the U.S.A. The opposite value (embeddedness) was not found to be associated with external drivers for career transitions such as organizational influences, macro factors and family-influenced career changes. The conclusion is that values for social order, obedience and respect for tradition are in a different sphere or dimension, unrelated to personal decisions and reasons for career changes.

The values of egalitarianism were clearly associated with internal drivers such as workers' own initiative for career changes, as is prevalent in Austria, Israel, Spain and the U.S.A. The values of social justice and equality are probably linked to democratic systems (economic, political and social dimensions of "democracy" included), where tolerance for individual decisions and freedom of choice are prevalent in the career patterns of societies.

On the other side, the hierarchy polar values are more associated with external drivers for career transitions in two-thirds of the countries, China and Japan but not South Africa being in this corner. It is not surprising that in hierarchical societies people depend more on external sources of career changes, since probably there would be more attitudes of dependency.

The values of harmony with nature and peace are prevalent in Austria, Costa Rica and Spain. Here the sources for career changes are internal, such as workers' own initiative. Probably this is due to postmodernization values related to well-being and the belief in individual responsibility for one's own life (Inglehart, 1997). Such a movement of social values from modernization to postmodernization is true as well of the U.S.A., an exception to the other polar set of values (mastery).

The mastery set of values (ambition and daring) is prevalent in China, Israel, Japan and the U.S.A. In the two Confucian cultures we found external sources for career transitions, while in Israel and the U.S.A. there is not such a conclusive result. The reason for the difference might be that the cultures of China and Japan are still in the "survival" set of values more closely related to modernization (Inglehart & Carballo, 1997), while Israel and the U.S.A. are in the postmodernization values set. As mentioned previously, the shift in economically advanced countries from reliance on the state and the preference for state/employee management to a preference for leisure and well-being (postmodernist values) has been found to be the case in the U.S.A., but the Confucian cluster has been closer to being anchored in the survival pole of values (Inglehart, 1997).

The Institutionalist Approach

The institutionalist approach is increasingly gaining attention in international management literature. Scott (2004: 2) points out that institutional theory "considers the processes by which structures, including schemas, rules, norms and routines, become established as authoritative guidelines for social behavior." Institutional theory is dominated by two main research traditions, which are premised on different analytical foci and predilection. The first tradition, which is grounded in the work of early institutionalists, focuses on "institutional effect" and institutional isomorphism (Scott, 2004) in the sense that "cognition was thought to be channeled by values, norms and attitudes, and the individual was considered deeply socialized and committed in every action" (Grendstad & Selle, 1995: 8). The second tradition, which is commonly referred to as neo-institutionalism, focuses on the process of institutionalism and pays attention to "institutional change" in terms of accounting for the role of agency and structure in shaping organizational fields (Scott, 2008).

Inherent to the work of all institutionalists, although to a varying degree, is a claim that organizations operating in a similar environment are likely to seek legitimacy and recognition by adopting practices, processes and structures prevalent in their environment (Fogarty, 1996). This general proposition has been the foundation on which a number of institutional mechanisms have been conceptualized. DiMaggio and Powell (1983), for instance, argue that the tendency of organizations to seek homogeneity is influenced by three key mechanisms: coercive (laws and regulations used for control), mimetic (adoption of a success formula) and normative (professional norms and standards) isomorphism.

Pillars of Institutions

Building on this foundational work of institutionalists, more recently Scott (1995) proposed a very broad framework integrating perspectives from the whole field of institutionalism. The framework is based on a broad definition of institutions that takes into account the close relationship between the entity and the process view on institutions: "[i]nstitutions consist of cognitive, normative, and regulative structures and activities that provide stability and meaning to social behavior. Institutions are transported by various carriers—cultures, structures, and routines—and they operate at multiple levels of jurisdiction" (Scott, 1995: 33). Scott (1995) argues that individuals and organizations are likely to adapt and copy "what is obtainable" in a given institutional context in order to achieve legitimacy. This perspective does not view culture and institution as irreconcilable; rather, culture is viewed as a subset of institutional analysis and is fused with other institutional factors to provide for a dialectical relationship. Along similar lines, Sorge (2005: 39) argues that "cultural orientations, such as fundamental values, and institutions are really two sides of the same theoretical coin." In essence, culture and institutional perspectives are viewed as complementary. Thus the actions of individuals and organizational policies and practices are viewed as being contingent on particular national institutional arrangements, which include cultural, economic, political and historical contexts.

The framework suggests that institutions consist of three key pillars—cognitive (shared perceptions), normative (norms and value systems) and regulative (rules and regulations). These pillars shape and circumscribe individuals' and organizations' action within a given institutional environment and are described as followed:

- The regulative pillar stresses that institutions constrain and regularize behavior. Regulative processes involve the capacity to establish rules, inspect others' conformity with them and sanction behavior not compliant with the rules in an attempt to influence future behavior. These processes can operate through informal or highly formalized mechanisms.
- The normative pillar emphasizes normative rules that introduce a prescriptive, evaluative and obligatory dimension into social life. Normative systems include values and norms. Values are defined as "conceptions of the preferred or the desired together with the construction of standards to which existing structures or behavior can be compared and assessed. Norms specify how things should be done" (Scott, 1995: 37). Normative systems define goals and appropriate ways to pursue them. If values and norms apply only to selected types of actors or positions they are called roles.
- The cognitive pillar of institutions is concerned with "the rules that constitute the nature of reality and the frames through which meaning is made" (Scott, 1995: 40). The cognitive dimension points out that a collection of internalized symbolic representations of the world is mediating between the external world of

stimuli and the responses of individuals. Symbols shape the meanings individuals attribute to objects and activities. Meanings arise in interaction and are preserved and modified as they are employed to make sense of what is happening. Neo-institutional sociology (e.g. Berger & Luckmann, 1967) treats symbolic systems and cultural rules as objective and external to individual actors.

Institutions are embedded in various types of repositories or "carriers" (Jepperson, 1991: 150). Scott (1995) distinguishes three carriers: cultures, social structures, and routines. The carriers are orthogonal to the pillars and can be viewed as associated with, and affected by, the regulative, the normative and the cognitive pillars. Each of the carriers involves structure and action.

Cultures are carriers that primarily rely on interpretative structures. Interpretative schemes are codified patterns of meaning and rule systems that constrain and reinforce behavior, but can also be changed by behavior. Cultural beliefs can be widespread, for example across a country or specific organization. Cultural beliefs are ideas and values in the heads of organizational actors but also exist in the environment as widely held beliefs (Scott, 1995).

Social structures also carry institutions. This carrier relies on role systems, i.e. patterned expectations connected to networks of social positions. Rules and belief systems are coded into structural distinctions and roles (Scott, 1995: 54). Like cultures, social structures constrain and empower actors' behavior and can be transformed by behavior. They can be widely shared across organizations, creating isomorphism, or be distinctive.

Routines can also act as carriers of institutions. Structured activities in the form of habituated behavior and routines rely on patterned actions that reflect deeply ingrained habits and procedures based on the unarticulated knowledge and beliefs of actors. Routines form the basis for the stability of (organizational) behavior but also account for its rigidity.

Applying the Institutional Perspective

The following section analyzes the influence of institutional contexts. It refers to Scott's (1995) framework of the three pillars (regulative, normative and cognitive) and three carriers that are orthogonal to the pillars (cultures, social structures and routines). As our analysis has also allowed us to compare findings in different national contexts, we can hypothesize on possible explanations for the differences in career con-ceptualizations by using Scott's framework in addition to the presented cultural frameworks.

Career Success and Institutional Context

The universal themes of career success reflect cultural values and contex-tual factors and also influence the preferences for outcomes and goals. As mentioned above there are some universal elements of career success across countries: achievement, satisfaction and job/task characteristics. The first two themes according to Scott's framework show the signifi-cance of normative (e.g. underlying values and expectations) as well as cognitive pillars (e.g. scripts and perception of professional role) which shape primary meanings of career success, achievement and satisfaction, on the level of culture and social structures. Responsibilities and chal-lenges of job and task characteristics can be described by all three pillars. While the themes play a role for most countries, the way these themes are expressed in each context can be diverse. They reflect specific values, typifications, regimes and authority systems as well as the construction of identities.

Furthermore, the institutionalist framework points towards the potential importance of various types of boundaries and segmentations. They include boundaries constituted not only by countries and cultures, but also by occupation and age.

First, the source of routines across three pillars shows that the impor-tance of boundaries is clearly demonstrated between occupational groups within each country. Particularly, routines for work differ between occu-pational groups and how career success is shaped within each country. Likewise, countries differ in terms of how they organize occupations. Routines are also linked to the historical development of occupations that develop over time (Scott, 1995).

Along these lines, within each country nurses seem to be distinct from both other occupational groups. They represent different values under-lying their daily working routines. In most countries, nurses are the only professional group that expresses specific meanings not shared by the other professional groups, for example helping others and making a dif-ference. Likewise, they tend to mention calling, serving others or being passionate about your job as indicators for career success. Unlike blue-collar workers and business school graduates, nurses most often work in organizations and a sector that partly or fully differ from traditional for-profit organizations where market logics are dominant.

Second, age groups play a role when looking at differences within countries. Some countries show differences across age groups to the extent that the younger age group agrees more homogeneously on achievement than the older one. This can be explained by career stage theory and maturation effects, as accumulated career experience leads to more diverse perception of careers in older age. Additionally, age groups show a different perception in countries that go through political and economic changes like China. Here, only younger people bring up themes like satisfaction, and show more self-related orientation in their definitions of career success and also more interest in managing their careers. In this case the regulative context has changed, as well as the normative resources of culture, social structure, and routines. In addition, this has an impact on the cognitive dimension, especially for categorizations, creating identities, scripts and so on. Moreover, meanings of career success shared among the younger age group are a reflection of the—arguably increasing—dynamic and turbulence in the career-relevant environment of individuals. It includes developments in the private sphere such as new forms of partnerships, lifestyles and life concepts as well as changes in the career landscape such as new forms of careers, less predictability and greater career complexity.

Looking at influencing factors, it seems that across the globe both the context of work (embracing good relationships with superiors and peers and from the organization) and individual factors (experiences, traits and motives) are vital for individuals' career success. Therefore regulative, normative and cognitive pillars are significant for these results, as well as their carriers within institutions: culture, social structures, and routines. Moreover, this suggests that the emphasis lies in the necessity to take a relational perspective when examining individuals' career success. This is in line with King, Burke and Pemberton (2005: 281), who argue that work context is important because "careers are bounded not only to prior career history, occupational identity, but also to institutional constraints imposed by 'gatekeepers' to job opportunities."

Career Transitions and Context

In terms of career transitions, there are factors beyond culture that have an impact on the course of careers and transition phases. They contain factors such as the impact of the regulative pillar, including economic dynamics or boundaries surrounding immigration. Thus they reflect not only cultural values, but also the institutional context of each country.

Therefore the pace of change seems relevant (Elder, 2003). Respondents from economies with less dynamic change emphasize causes of career transitions that are closer to the person. This is the case especially in the U.S.A., where individuals perceive the dynamic of change as imminent. Countries with more dynamic economic change show a stronger emphasis on organizational and macro factors. In general, the person and the work context strongly influence the perceptions of causes. Thus societal issues are important for career transitions, and individual factors reflect the financial and economic situation of the country.

In China, a country undergoing major transitions, the organizational context and macro factors (e.g. governmental policies) are more emphasized than personal factors. However, in countries with relatively stable economic and societal conditions, macro factors are mentioned less across all occupational groups than in countries going through economic transitions. Serbia and China—both countries in transition—show similar results regarding their perceived causes of career transitions. While Serbian interviewees still mention internal sources, although focusing on organizational and macro factors, people from China exclusively highlight the latter ones. Individuals in China describe "organizationally driven factors" as being more important than personal, internal ones. Particularly in China and Serbia, there are different working conditions for both generations reflected in our interviews.

Similarly to career success conceptualizations in China, for most interviewees who belong to the older generation, career paths are shaped by the emergence of government policies representing the regulative functions of social structures. On the contrary, the younger generation highlight internal sources for change, indicating that they take responsibility for their own career transitions. A similar picture is shown in Serbia, where causes of career transitions of younger interviewees are expressed by emphasizing internal sources.

Closely linked to the above, the developmental status of economies and the historical background within which careers are embedded seem to influence the perceptions of professional identities represented by the cognitive pillar of Scott's framework (1995). In the results of the perceived causes of career transitions common to all occupational groups, data show that in some countries occupational groups have very few factors in common, for example in the U.S.A., Spain and Austria. A greater variety of themes common to all occupational groups is mentioned in countries that are going through transitions. Thus Serbia and China show a more consistent pattern across all occupational groups. Another factor that seems important when considering occupational boundaries is that in most countries different occupational groups have a different work history and educational background. Presumably, this also leads to different perceptions of causes of career transitions.

Conclusion and Outlook

Our findings show a potential avenue for future theoretical development. While culture already has some significance in careers research, the discussion about different elements of the institutional context is still in its infancy.

Besides our discussion on cultural dimensions, we were drawing on Scott's (1995) three institutional pillars to demonstrate the significance of the regulative pillar (e.g. governmental policy), the normative pillar (e.g. through the role of family obligations) and the cognitive pillar (e.g. perception of different age groups) in describing the careers of individuals across 11 countries. Our analysis has allowed us to compare findings in different national contexts and hypothesize possible explanations for the differences in career conceptualizations by using a framework that highlights institutional context beyond the cultural perspective as an explanatory lens.

Overall, both perspectives applied show interesting insights. Besides insights taking a cultural perspective, implications for institutional theory show that individual perceptions of career success and transitions reflect as well those underlying cultural patterns embedded in the institutional context in which careers emerge. Thus career development is not exclusively driven by individuals, but the wider contextual factors should be taken into consideration that create opportunities but also constraints for individual career development as well as influence the value systems expressed in cultural patterns.

References

Arnold, J. & Cohen, L. 2008. The psychology of careers in industrial and organizational settings: A critical but appreciative analysis. In G. P. Hodgkinson & J. K. Ford (Eds.), *International Review of Industrial and Organizational Psychology*. London: Wiley.

Berger, P. L. & Luckmann, T. 1967. *The Social Construction of Reality*. New York: Doubleday Anchor.

Chhokar, J. S., Brodbeck, F. C. & House, R. J. E. (Eds.). 2007. *Culture and Leadership Across the World: The GLOBE Book of In-Depth Studies of 25 Societies*. Mahwah, NJ: Lawrence Erlbaum Associates.

DiMaggio, P. J. & Powell, W. W. 1983. The iron cage revisited: Institutional isomorphism and collective rationality in organizational fields. *American Sociological Review*, 48(2): 147–160.

Elder, G. H. 2003. The life course in time and place. In W. R. Heinz & V. W. Marshall (Eds.), *Social Dynamics of the Life Course: Transitions, Institutions, and Interrelations*. New York: Aldine de Gruyter.

Fogarty, T. J. 1996. The imagery and reality of peer review in the US: Insights from institutional theory. *Accounting, Organizations and Society*, 21: 243–268.

Grendstad, G. & Selle, P. 1995. Cultural theory and the new institutionalism. *Journal of Theoretical Politics*, 7(1): 5–27.

Hofstede, G. 1980. *Culture's Consequences: International Differences in Work-Related Values*. Beverly Hills, CA: Sage.

Inglehart, R. 1997. *Modernization and Postmodernization: Cultural, Economic and Political Change in 43 Societies*. Princeton, NJ: Princeton University Press.

Inglehart, R. & Carballo, M. 1997. Does Latin America exist? (And is there a Confucian culture?): A global analysis of cross-cultural differences. *Political Science and Politics*, 30: 34–47.

Inkson, K., Khapova, S. N. & Parker, P. 2007. Careers in cross-cultural perspective. *Career Development International*, 12(1): 5–8.

Ituma, A. & Simpson, R. 2009. The "boundaryless" career and career boundaries: Applying an institutionalist perspective to ICT workers in the context of Nigeria. *Human Relations*, 62(5): 727–761.

Jepperson, R. L. 1991. Institutions, institutional effects, and institutionalism. In W. W. Powell & P. J. DiMaggio (Eds.), *The New Institutionalism in Organizational Analysis*. Chicago, IL: Chicago University Press.

King, Z., Burke, S. & Pemberton, J. 2005. The "bounded" career: An empirical study of human capital, career mobility and employment outcomes in a mediated labour market. *Human Relations*, 58(8): 981–1007.

Mayrhofer, W., Meyer, M. & Steyrer, J. 2007. Contextual issues in the study of careers. In H. P. Gunz & M. A. Peiperl (Eds.), *Handbook of Career Studies*. Thousand Oaks, CA: Sage.

McClelland, D. 1961. *The Achieving Society*. Princeton, NJ: Van Nostrand.

Schwartz, S. H. 2006. A theory of cultural value orientations: Explication and applications. *Comparative Sociology*, 5(2–3): 136–182.

Schwartz, S. H. 2008. *Cultural Value Orientations: Nature and Implications of National Differences*. Moscow: State University Higher School of Economics Press.

Scott, R. W. 1995. *Institutions and Organizations*. Thousand Oaks, CA: Sage.

Scott, W. R. 2004. *Institutions and Organizations*. Thousand Oaks, CA: Sage.

Scott, W. R. 2008. Lords of the dance: Professionals as institutional agents. *Organization Studies*, 29: 219–238.

Sorge, A. 2005. *The Global and the Local: Understanding the Dialectics of Business Systems*. Oxford, U.K.: Oxford University Press.

Tams, S. & Arthur, M. B. 2007. Studying careers across cultures. *Career Development International*, 12(1): 86–98.

Thomas, D. C. & Inkson, K. 2007. Careers across cultures. In H. P. Gunz & M. A. Peiperl (Eds.), *Handbook of Career Studies*. Los Angeles, CA: Sage.

8

Implications for the Management of People and Organizations

Douglas T. Hall, Jon P. Briscoe,
Michael Dickmann and Wolfgang Mayrhofer

Now that we have seen in great detail what the variations are in career experiences around the world, how can these findings be used to produce practical benefit in contemporary work settings? As we said at the beginning of this research journey, our aim was to see if culture and country made a difference in the ways that career dynamics play out in the global economy. As much of the existing research on careers has been rooted in particular cultures, mainly Western and developed, we saw a strong need for good empirical data to guide future career management practice around the world.

In terms of this initial aim of our research, the short answer is, yes, location and culture and related influences, such as institutional factors, do make a big difference in the ways that people experience their careers. In this chapter we will discuss the practical implications of these country differences. But also we found that there are certain universal or constant features of careers in most of the countries that we studied. Let us start with those.

Universal Qualities of Careers

The main findings indicate that achievement is the most common meaning ascribed to career success across countries. The other two universal sources of the meaning of success are satisfaction and job/task characteristics.

While these may not seem like remarkable categories, as we reflect on their implications, the three together seem to capture three fundamental aspects of human motivation. One way to think about this is to consider the basic question "Why do we work?" First, consider the nature of work. Work is generally defined as a goal-directed activity (Schein, 1979). It is this notion of being focused on a goal that differentiates work from other forms of human activity, such as leisure or play. Thus one reason we work is to *accomplish something*. We express accomplishment in terms of achievement, and when our work results in achievement we feel successful.

Another basic reason for working is that the nature of our work or job, the task activity we perform in our work, is *intrinsically rewarding*. Going back to the job design theory of Hackman and Oldham (1980), we know that jobs can be designed so that mere engagement in the task activities of the job is in and of itself rewarding. Thus another reason for working is to experience the pleasure of work, and when we experience the pleasure of working we can also feel (subjectively) successful.

Thus, when we put these ideas together, we obtain a simple model of the ways that these three universal factors can represent career success, as shown in Figure 8.1. The starting point in all careers is work. This is true by definition, as the career is the sequence of work-related activities over the life span (Arthur, Hall & Lawrence, 1989). Work (i.e. paid employment) is inherent in all careers, and there are at a minimum two outcomes that can result from a person's engaging in work activity, two ways that the person can feel successful. One way is when the person achieves or accomplishes something, so that she has something to show for this work (e.g. monetary rewards and/or advancement). The other way to achieve success, subjective or psychological success, is when the person finds the mere act of doing the work to be satisfying. Thus what we do, how we feel about it and what we accomplish seem to be three of the most basic ingredients in the experience of success in the career.

Figure 8.1 A model of the universal sources of career success

Source: Demel, Yan, Unite, Briscoe, Hall, Mayrhofer, Chudzikowski, Abdul-Ghani, Bogicevic Milikic, Colorado, Zhangfeng, Las Heras, Ogliastri, Pazy, Poon, Shefer, Taniguchi & Zikic (2010).

The practical implications of these simple ideas about the human meaning of work are profound. One is that, whatever kind of work a person is doing, wherever he or she is doing it, these three factors are motivating that individual. Even though other specific rewards might be important in a particular culture, such as family connectedness in Spain, it is also important to workers that they do tasks that provide for a sense of accomplishment, job satisfaction, and intrinsically interesting activities. This means that executives and managers should be attentive to the design of jobs as well as to the rewards, working conditions, benefits and other factors related to the context of the jobs. In short, workers around the world *care* about the meaning of the work that they do, and the leaders of their organizations would be wise to respect that caring.

Universal Factors That Influence Success

In terms of the factors that influence success, again we found three universal factors. The first influencing factor is the context of work. This is elements in the work environment, such as support from the company, superiors and peers. While previous studies have attached significant attention to individual differences as the determining factors of career success (Judge, Higgins, Thoresen & Barrick, 1999), our findings emphasize supportive relationships within the context of work. Across the globe, support from superiors, peers and the organization is vital for career success, thus highlighting the necessity to take a relational perspective when examining individuals' career success (e.g. Hall & Associates, 1996; Kram & Hall, 1996).

Therefore this means that, in all of the countries in our sample, it is important for organizations to work to provide conditions that support the development of their employees. At the organizational level, examples would be programs for self-assessment and career development, in which individuals can increase their self-awareness of their career interests, their career values, their strengths, and their personal definition of what constitutes work–life balance. This would also mean a commitment by the organization to assist employees in finding job assignment opportunities and in designing particular jobs so that each person can create a good person–job fit.

It is important to point out that this does not necessarily mean that the organization should find ways to help people move up the formal hierarchy. Support here means helping people find ways to experience the three types of success that we have just discussed—achievement, satisfaction and positive job/task characteristics. A person does not necessarily need advancement to experience these three sources of success.

The second critical factor influencing success, as we find in our data, is the personal history of the individual (such as educational history and job history). Since we know that one of the best predictors of future behavior is past behavior, it makes sense that future success would be strongly influenced by past success and other socializing and shaping experiences. One important implication of this finding is that early success predicts later success. Thus the "name of the game" becomes: How can the chances for early success be maximized? For organizations and managers, one way to do this is to provide high levels of initial job challenge for new employees, as early challenge leads to early success (Hall, 2002).

Of course, challenge may be in the eye of the beholder. What some employees see as a great stretch experience others may see as unrewarding or lacking in purpose. It would help, then, to provide new employees with rotational development programs, where they are rotated through assignments in different parts of the organization for the first year or two. The goal would be to make this an explicit trial period, which would fit with career stage theory (Super, 1957), after which the person and the organization could decide together what kind of permanent position would constitute the best fit and the most challenge for the person.

Since educational history is also such an important facilitator of success, this implies that organizational assistance with time and money for further education and training is a very sound investment in the firm's human capital. In many parts of the world, however, employers have been cutting back on these education investments owing to the economic crisis. In our opinion, however, there is a paradoxical dynamic at work: those firms that take the counter-cyclical action of increasing their human capital investments during lean economic times will reap a double benefit. Not only will they enhance the capacity of their workforce, but they will also make giant strides in relation to their competitors that are cutting back on these capacity-building investments.

Finally, the third source of influence on success is personal traits, such as persistence and diligence, and positive attitude. (Thus we are not saying that individual differences are not at all important.) These personal traits to a large extent represent a personal belief system, unique to the person. Personal traits and personal history together are similar to what Bourdieu (1977) called the *habitus*, which is the person's phenomenological response to the objective structural context. A clear implication of this finding is that, again, person–role fit is tremendously important. This attests to the importance of industrial-organizational psychology methods in the psychological assessment and placement of human talent. While, in some ways, this may sound like a very old and traditional methodology, the advances in research and measurement technology have led to comparable advances in employers' ability to identify these personal orientations that lead to success. The caveat, however, is that any tools that are used must be validated and also be shown to be fair to all groups of employees.

One Size Does Not Fit All: Occupational Differences Matter

The reader will remember that we wanted to compare the career experiences of people in three kinds of occupation that one would find anywhere in the world: business, nursing and manual labor. We found major differences in the careers of workers in these three fields.

Nurses

As a group the nurses were the most distinctive of the three, and nurses in any one country seem to have more in common with people in the same occupation in other countries than do businesspeople or manual laborers. The intrinsic nature of nurses' work was highly important, and this usually centered on providing the best possible care to their patients. Many nurses seemed to have a sense of calling about their work, that this was their purpose in life, one to which they felt highly committed.

The flip side of this intrinsic orientation is that the nurses were the lowest of the three occupational groups in their concern for material rewards for their work. This should not be taken to mean that money and other material benefits are not important, just that they are not the nurses' primary motivators. (Considering that one of the most important sources of differences in the work experiences of nurses around the world is the available resources of the organizations in which they work, it is perhaps a blessing for their employers that these material rewards are often not of primary importance.)

The implication then is that, because of this need to care for their patients, nurses (and perhaps more generally other types of care providers) need to receive clear feedback that they have indeed provided this care and comfort. This feedback could come from at least three sources: the patient (or the patient's family), the medical staff and the nurse him- or herself. From the patient perhaps the most sincere form of feedback is the spontaneous responses that the nurse's care evokes from the patient.

When the patient's pain subsides in response to the nurse's activities or when the patient sees noticeable improvements in his or her condition, the nurse can also see these changes and, as a result, the nurse experiences great satisfaction.

However, in addition to these natural expressions of patient gratification, it is also possible to collect formal evaluation feedback from the patient, in the form of brief surveys or interviews that can assess the quality of the nurse's care. These quality surveys can also be given to family members and friends who come to visit. With the proliferation of web-based surveys it would be a very simple task to administer short, user-friendly surveys via text messages, email and smart phones.

Similar formal feedback could also be provided by medical staff using the same technology as that used for patients. With so many nurses providing care to a particular patient over the course of the day, it might be more practical to ask the staff to cite nurses for particularly noteworthy incidents of care, when the nurse clearly went out of his or her way to provide some exceptional service. Forms could be posted in convenient locations, such as on a bulletin board or at the nurses' station, and a doctor could just date them and indicate with check marks or in a few words what the specific care activity was that the nurse provided.

Another powerful form of recognition is self-feedback. (Again these ideas might be applied more generally to other types of helping professionals.) This might be accomplished through a process of weekly journaling by nurses. One method might be a daily automatic email to the nurse from the nurse's blog, with one or two diagnostic questions such as "What special care, above and beyond the call of duty, did you provide for a patient today? What specifically did you do? How did the patient respond? What changes in procedures on the floor might increase your ability to provide care like this more often?"

People in Business

For people in business, beyond the three universal success factors, the most important element of success was work–life context balance. To them, this means being able to combine personal and professional objectives, to live well and to have a good life. Part of the reason this factor is more important for businesspeople than it is for nurses and manual laborers may be that it requires a certain level of affluence to give people the "luxury" of worrying about work and family life. But another reason may be that by its nature business activities are largely mental, and this makes it very easy for people to "carry" work and work concerns home with them, whereas the work of manual laborers (e.g. a building) and of nurses (e.g. patients) remains behind when the worker leaves the work site.

One implication of this concern for work–life dynamics for business-people is that it is in the interests of organizations and managers to help people at all levels in business attend to and resolve work–life issues when they arise (Las Heras & Hall, 2007). Many organizations already have wide-ranging work–life initiatives, and there are many effective research centers and institutes, such as the Boston College Center for Work and Family (CWF, http://www.bc.edu/centers/cwf/rt.html) and the International Center for Work and Family (ICWF, at the IESE School of Business in Barcelona, http://www.iese.edu/en/Research/Centersand-Chairs/Centers/ICWF/Home/Home.asp). The Boston College CWF has recently started a global workforce roundtable, which will explore ways that employing organizations might respond to employees' integrating work and life concerns. So the good news in these activities, as well as in the many other institutionalized responses to work–life concerns, is that work is being done to be responsive. However, the less good news is that the problems around work–life integration are fundamental, and real progress is slow. Therefore the implication of our findings about the work–life concerns of people in business is that we need to strengthen our resolve to find new and more powerful ways to help employees manage the relationships between their work lives and their professional lives in business.

Another major career success factor for people in business is making a difference. This includes activities such as helping others, having a positive impact on society and finding meaning in one's work. One implication of this finding is that there is great value in providing businesspeople with self-assessment activities in which they discern for themselves what kind of jobs and assignments would be the most meaningful for them personally. This is a highly individualized discernment process. Helpful elements would include time for personal reflection, measurement tools for self-assessment, and coaching to help the person think through issues of meaning and purpose for him or her personally.

Blue-Collar Workers

For blue-collar workers, the most important aspect of success was the job and more specifically job security, or having a job. Perhaps the most basic problem that work can create for people's personal lives is that, when job insecurity is high, this can create a sense of career failure, and this stress can spill over into the person's family life. The cure here is economic recovery, and different countries are making progress here at different rates. As we have seen in many countries, this economic insecurity can lead to powerful social unrest in a society.

Although we do not have the cure for unemployment, careers researchers do have ideas to contribute on how to help workers develop higher employability. As Fugate, Kinicki and Ashforth (2004) have shown, employability consists of high levels of self-awareness, adaptability, social capital and human capital. Formal programs for career development, with their activities for self-assessment, developing proactivity and learning agility, developing networking skills and creating developmental networks, as well as continuous learning and training, are excellent activities for building employees' employability. Research has shown that unemployed workers in a wide range of jobs who have high levels of employability are faster in finding new employment than are people with lower levels of this capacity (McArdle, Waters, Briscoe & Hall, 2007).

We would also encourage people who manage employees in other occupations to consider these ideas, as well. Practices such as self-reflection, feedback and work–family initiatives have been applied with success in other settings. We would encourage thoughtful managers to examine the motivations and success factors for the groups that they supervise and to consider employing some of these practices for these groups.

Managing the Generations

In general, we found the biggest country differences among the older generation of workers. The younger members of our sample had much more in common around the world than did our older participants. Undoubtedly, technology plays a major role in creating common experiences for younger people, and there is a "universal language" of technology. However, we also found some important differences by country in the generations, and we found limited evidence of a "global generation" among our younger respondents.

One implication of this general finding is that employers can apply more universal methods of career and human resource management to their younger employees than to their older ones. Younger employees are generally more concerned about factors such as achievement, learning and growth, feedback and recognition, and making a difference, and less concerned about performance and security. It is more important to them to have self-expression and autonomy or self-direction in their careers. Thus it appears that discussions about "new careers" may be more valid for the younger generation than for their parents' generation. This means that career and human resource management practices that allow for a more agentic role for the individual employee would be more appropriate and effective for younger employees. We will discuss the meaning of this more agentic approach in the following sections.

It is also important to be mindful of and responsive to the dire social and economic condition of older workers in many countries. This is especially true in rapidly growing economies such as China. Here, the older employees are truly living in a different world from that of their children. The older workers have had the social contract change in a drastic way. They have lived up to their end of the contract and have provided commitment and service during their early and middle working years, but now the expected benefits of income security and health coverage are not being provided, so they have to continue to find paid employment.

This phenomenon of the broken contract is also particularly vivid in countries that have been hit hard by the economic crisis. Although our data in Spain were collected before the crisis, we know from other research and writing that the plight of older workers and retirees in Spain and other distressed economies such as Greece and Ireland is serious. National policies regarding retirement ages, retirement benefits and health care coverages are being revised so that people will be working later in life, and pension and health benefits will be curtailed. All of this means that more support to older employees will be required to strengthen their employability, lifelong learning skills and proactive career coping skills.

There will also be a need for more effective ways to assist older couples in managing work–family issues, as the pressures on the family unit increase, including the needs of their children for help with providing for grandchildren. The demands on family units are growing precisely at a time when the family's resources are declining.

Implications for Human Resource Management (HRM)

Notwithstanding the necessities for HRM to streamline its activities to a certain extent, to focus on groups of employees rather than on individuals and, in particular in MNCs, to rely on a substantial amount of standardization, our results lead to a number of practical implications for a context-sensitive HRM.

First, our results suggest that organizations need to incorporate an agentic element in their HR development processes. The need for this agentic perspective is based on our finding that, in the countries we have sampled, individuals perceive their careers to be strongly governed by their own motivations and actions. Organizations no longer have an "automatic" or determining voice in these decisions. If the organization's interests are the sole determining influence on career moves, this leads to the risk that the link between individual career and organizational performance is neglected. Hence HRM has to make sure that this employee input is part of the decision-making processes.

This makes organizational career planning at the same time more crucial and more difficult. It is more crucial because, unless HRM is able to synchronize the career decisions of its members and link those to organizational goals, overall organizational performance will be reduced, owing to an imbalance of individual and organizational needs. With an agentic input, organizational career planning becomes more difficult because individuals showing marked agentic behavior are not easy to include into a planning system relying on standardization and mid-range predictability.

Most organizations today refrain from highly sophisticated career and succession planning systems which often require a considerable amount of stability and predictability. Nevertheless, career planning is essential for organizations. In conjunction with a more turbulent work context, agentic career actors with highly autonomous decisions make this task more difficult. This increases the need for dialogue between individual employees and the organization, for example by including this topic in yearly service reviews or putting a stronger emphasis on this topic in the ongoing conversations between employees and their supervisors.

Second, individual and organizational career decisions usually have a significant legal and cultural component, for example under what circumstances career changes are legally possible or culturally adequate. Consequently, large multinational corporations, as well as small and medium-sized enterprises with border-crossing activities in a more regional sense, require a great amount of legal and cultural expertise. Again, there is a certain tension between the efforts of organizations in general and MNCs in particular to standardize. Yet local knowledge is crucial for successful action in HRM. This goes beyond the self-evident requirement of being accustomed to the respective legal regulations and the role of institutional players such as trade unions or works councils—difficult enough, as it turns out to be, in particular for U.S. multinationals in certain contexts (Gooderham, Nordhaug & Ringdal, 1998). It also touches on the cultural aspects of how standard operating procedures can be applied in a local context.

There is ample literature showing that there is no such thing as an identical replication or exact transfer of HR policies and practices from headquarters to subsidiaries or between subsidiaries. Rather, there are inevitably modifications that adapt these policies and practices to the local context. Some of these modifications can be small, hardly noticeable and ultimately irrelevant for the "spirit of the rules." An example for this is the adaptation of the number and kind of individuals present during a selection interview to accommodate for legal and/or cultural requirements, for example by including a member of the works council even if this is not required in the country of the headquarters, or to bring in both the future supervisor and a member of the level above if this is culturally adequate. Sometimes these changes can be substantial. For example, hiring and promotion practices based on individual merit can collide with cultural values emphasizing familial ties. This is the case with *vartan bhanji*, a basic framework of social organization, in contemporary Pakistani organizations and their management of human resources (Khilji, 2003).

Third, results from the study underline the importance of social networks at work for career progress. Mentoring and coaching, an important way of supporting individual decisions and linking individuals to relevant social networks, belong to the role set of supervisors when being part of HRM and contributing to individual, HRM and organizational outcomes. In this role, supervisors take a nurturing perspective and focus on the personal development of the individuals they are responsible for. This role becomes crucial both to support individuals in their career decision making and to strengthen organizational performance interests. Yet supervisors often are not very eager to take on this part of their role set. One main reason for this is that they put more emphasis on their technical expertise than on genuine leadership behavior. This is especially true for supervisors at the lower levels of the organizational hierarchy, who are usually still strongly involved in the operative business. They often see time devoted to "soft issues" such as coaching and mentoring as a distraction from their core tasks. In addition, they are sometimes not sufficiently trained in these soft areas.

Clearly, HRM has a role to play in supporting the use of internal social networks. Such networks bring immediate advantages for both the individual and the organization. Technology can be a powerful facilitator here. Examples include job posting boards, providing knowledge about internal job opportunities; the possibility of gaining access to information for one's job beyond the official lines of inquiry, thus better equipping individuals for doing their jobs, which in turn increases the likelihood for a desired job offer or change; the use of internal role models demonstrating the variety of opportunities in the internal labor market; and the positive reward effects that the establishment of social contacts usually have, which in turn strengthens the bond between individuals and the organization.

Fourth, the results point towards the importance of specific types of career capital when dealing with organizational careers. Take the example of achievement, which has turned out to be of overarching importance for members of very different cultural settings. Even in light of the differences about what kind of achievement is addressed, it is obvious that it matters. Linked to this are issues like making a difference, performing one's role in the organization or making a contribution to the organization. All these issues point towards the importance of various career capitals, in particular various competencies of individuals, for example technical expertise, the relationship with the supervisor or making use of social networks.

For HRM more specifically, this underscores the importance of investing in human resources for creating adequate career capital through training and development. As already outlined, HRM is always linked with a certain amount of standardization. Yet, by investing in nonspecific competencies which can be used across a broad range of concrete situations, HRM not only contributes to organizational performance, individual development and the bond between the organization and the individual, but also supports individualization and a tailored application of these competencies. Employees equipped with such competencies know best what it takes to apply them in a concrete setting. Inevitably, they will adapt and modify the use of these competencies in accordance with the respective situation. In this way, investing in training and development contributes both to individual careers and organizational performance and to culture-sensitive organizational action.

Overall, we argue in favor of sustaining both poles of the built-in tension between differentiation and standardization in HRM. Our results show systematic differences in careers of individuals with different cultural, professional and age-related backgrounds, thus strengthening the differentiation pole. Yet standardization is important, too, in order to conduct efficient HRM. As outlined above, this is not necessarily a contradiction, but can, at least to some extent, be done in parallel.

Implications for Leadership and Management

As has been discussed in regard to career development earlier in this chapter and implied throughout the book, the implications for leadership and management are abundant but not of the one-size-fits-all variety. These implications are complicated by the fact that managing and leading go beyond the leader's own career to impact the careers of others as well as the stakeholders of the leader, the followers and the organization.

Consider an actual case in which a local manager is placed on the "fast track" at a U.S. multinational's regional office. At first she is excited and proud to have made the mark and she feels a sense of achievement. However, after many months the mobility required of the new role tears at her concerns for family and the immediacy with which they need her and she them. The glow of achievement is heavily tempered by the subjective shortcomings the new role implies for her family. Similar complications exist in many countries, often stemming from differing generational needs and expectations and other times from the juxtaposing of cultures (national, ethnic and organizational) that are not quite ready for each other.

As with other organizational theory and practice—and even more so—the status quo of global corporate leadership development has a decidedly U.S. or Western feel to it. "Leadership" is largely considered to be achieved by an individual rather than a group of people. Leadership development is often more scientific and atomistic in tone than holistic (Briscoe & Hall, 1999).

The global demand for more leadership talent extends the "leadership mill" mentality even further. People are seen as needed commodities, and competition for them is fierce (Ready, Hill & Conger, 2008; Tarique & Schuler, 2010). In this war for talent both the organization and the potential leader may get caught up in a script that is not as rich or reflective of the home culture as it might be.

Jackson (2009) reflects in particular on the case of non-governmental organizations (NGOs) in Sub-Saharan Africa and the frequent attempt to bring Western ways of doing things to cultures that are not in sync. Jackson points out that, while African cultures can seem hierarchical and arbitrary, they also tend to value people for their own sake and less as a means to an end. Further, while work is not everything to many people's identity in these cultures, they are nonetheless loyal to their organizations. Such subtleties are reflected in our own research experience as well, and corporations would be wise to try to reflect the local culture and, as Jackson suggests, hybridize outsider ways of creating management and leadership skills with insider ways of knowing and doing.

Beyond developing global high potentials, our 5C research probably has as many implications for managing and leading people horizontally and vertically *within* the local culture who will never be global in the same sense as those targeted as global managers. How can a manager be more sensitive and effective with local culture in a way that is reflective of some of our research findings on careers?

Our findings on career success indicate a diversity of meanings in each given culture. Past research on career success which emphasized only the rawest performance measures (pay and promotion) and most simple subjective success (satisfaction) is not adequately informative to guide today's leaders in any culture.

Part of the key in effectively leading diverse followers is to lead "inside out" by giving followers the same courtesy one gives to oneself—not simplifying their values and career aspirations, but discovering them. While the U.S. approach to leadership development is not the only way, some recent research reflects trends which seem to be valuable in all cultures. Especially salient to this conversation is the idea of authenticity in leadership.

Avolio and Gardner (2005) identify authenticity as a key thrust of current leadership research and theory. Authentic leadership involves self-awareness and the ability to be reflective in considering options. This approach to self-leadership seems like good advice to us for leading self and others, as well as in career self-management (Hall & Mao, forthcoming). Especially when in doubt, do not assume a one-dimensional approach will be adequate. Lead in ways that invite others' contributions. In high context cultures, follower participation and input may need to be "invited" in less explicit and more symbolic ways. They may even need to be diagnosed furtively if followers are looking for a more authoritarian style. In lower context and/or autonomy-seeking cultures a more transparent "dance" with followers may be more advisable.

We were struck by how often our research participants saw their career path as subject to their own influence and not overly influenced by their boss (in most cases). This implies that leaders may provide a helping role in many cases as they help the followers discover their own path. One consequence of this is that systems which overly prescribe rewards or competencies may overly constrain followers and not allow the sense of authenticity that will motivate them to better performance (Ryan & Deci, 2000).

Various authors emphasize the importance of the life path and finding meaning in transition as being key to developing leadership identity (Avolio & Hannah, 2008; Boyatzis, 2008; Hall, 2004; Riggio & Reichard, 2008). We would echo this not just for leaders but for everyone. Only a small portion of our interviewees adequately reflected upon their career transitions, and in this sense they did not take full advantage of the lessons their career successes and failures offered (McCall, 1998).

Leaders should be aware of the power of transition, for themselves and for their followers, and recognize times of transition as teachable moments. Action planning and more overt self-development may be appropriate in some cultures and have been shown to be successful in U.S. business schools (Boyatzis, 2008).

The social context is also cited as an area that has been neglected in leadership development (Avolio, Walumbwa & Weber, 2009; Riggio & Reichard, 2008). The context in which one discovers the authentic "path with a heart" (Hall & Mao, forthcoming; Shepard, 1984) will be different in different cultures. In the U.S.A. this is sometimes perceived as a heroic journey that must be traveled alone; in other cultures leaving one's community behind is tantamount to failure. The leader must recognize the needs of followers and try to provide a context that will allow them to reflect in ways that are meaningful to them.

With the above being said, lessons might be gleaned from other cultures that can be applied to one's own. We recall a Malaysian man who attended a U.S.-type career development seminar from a visiting consultant, and he considered his future in a way he had not before (in a positive way). On the other hand, we noticed that some of our U.S. sample interviewees had help along the way in their careers (as everyone does) but had a harder time recognizing this support owing to how they constructed their narrative in individualistic ways. Thus we believe our research has lessons for leaders that imply staying "close to home" yet also invite a learning orientation toward other cultures' advantages.

Implications for International Organizations and Multinational Corporations (MNCs)

While modern career theory and research show that the locus of career agency and mastery has shifted towards the individual (Arthur, Hall & Lawrence, 1989; Baruch, 2004), the role of organizations is still substantial. It goes beyond simply setting the context for careers to unfold to retaining some part in providing career opportunities, career patterns and career support (Dickmann & Doherty, 2010; Kidd, 2007). The role of organizations that operate across borders is, therefore, continuing to be crucial for individual careerists.

It is clear that various forms of organizations—including MNCs, international governmental organizations (IGOs) and international non-governmental organizations (INGOs)—have created career systems and have attempted to manage the careers of their staff (Black, Gregersen, Mendenhall & Stroh, 1999; Dickmann, Parry, Emmens &

Williamson, 2010; Mendenhall & Stahl, 2000; Thomas & Inkson, 2007; Toomey & Brewster, 2008). While writers discussing "best-practice" HRM are prone to suggest internal career patterns and high investment in training and development (Evans, Pucik & Björkman, 2011; Huselid, 1995; Pfeffer, 1998), it is less clear how exactly MNCs should go about developing and implementing their global career approaches.

In order to assess whether organizations want to develop and integrate their career approaches across countries, we need to evaluate a range of levels of decisions. First is the level of organizational strategy and structure, as this will shed some light on how responsive MNCs, IGOs and INGOs are to their domestic context. Second, we need to discuss the level of policies and practices in order to determine what actual career approaches in specific contexts could look like. Third, we will reflect on issues regarding the individualization of career management, the psychological contract and flexibility implications. Especially in the second and third areas we will be able to pull the 5C findings into the discussion.

The discourse in the first area has also often been labeled a discussion of organizational configurations. There has been a long-standing argument that organizations that operate across the world have a range of choices as to what strategies, structures and processes they want to adopt (Bartlett & Ghoshal, 1989; Heenan & Perlmutter, 1979). MNCs can choose to be highly standardized and integrated around the world (e.g. "global" companies such as Microsoft, Coca-Cola or Procter & Gamble), they can elect to be highly responsive to their local environments ("multidomestic" organizations such as Nestlé in human food, some "front office" operations of HSBC, or Siemens in India) and they can attempt to have strong knowledge exchange activities in order to increase the creation and exploitation of innovation ("international" firms such as 3M or Nokia).

The 5C research design is testament to our skepticism with regard to one-best-way, universalistic career approaches. In fact, it is in the country, occupational and age details that some of the strengths of the data presented in earlier chapters lie.

In tune with the literature on modern careers (Gunz & Peiperl, 2007; Hall, 2002), the majority of people in the 5C research regard their career transitions as self-initiated. In a world where many MNCs have argued for more than a decade now that they are engaged in a "war for talent" and where competition through knowledge and innovation is for many organizations crucial, a flexible yet sophisticated career approach will be of paramount importance for many globally operating organizations if they want to construct leading-edge HRM (O'Toole & Lawler, 2006).

What does this mean in the career system reality within MNCs and other internationally operating organizations? It is important to look at the quality of the employer–employee career relationship. While we foresee a large variety of career approaches in diverse organizations, we would like to remind the reader about our belief that individuals are increasingly the key determinants of their careers and that organizations have lost their predominant role of "career masters" (if they ever have been).

HRM and career management are at their core mostly designed for large groups of people to reach their limits when confronted with high degrees of diversity. In the recent past we have experienced that organizations build ever more complicated career systems, which invariably experience the international tensions that we have described above. We would urge MNCs to factor in our and other recent career preference findings. What does this mean in the career system reality within MNCs and other internationally operating organizations? It is important to look at the quality of the employer–employee career relationship. While we foresee a large variety of career approaches in diverse organizations, we would like to remind the reader about our belief that individuals are increasingly the key determinants of their careers and that organizations have lost their predominant role of "career masters" (if they ever have been) (Shen & Hall, 2009).

However, while this is one possible way forward, we would also like to advocate another alternative which we have observed taking root in organizations. In essence, we have seen increasing trends to react to the changing psychological contracts in diverse countries and firms and to the individualization of the employment and career relationship (Conway & Briner, 2005; Dickmann & Baruch, 2011; Karaevli & Hall, 2008; Lips-Wiersma & Hall, 2007). Starting from the premise that individuals are the masters of their careers, the organization's core career approach would be in the development of trust and openness and the identification of career ideas, anchors and dreams of individuals. After individuals have done this self-assessment work and created career plans that would represent a "path with a heart" for them, they and the organization (e.g. line managers and the HR organization) would help to implement their plans.

O'Toole and Lawler (2006) see this kind of individualized process as the best course of action for utilizing talent and building organizational competitiveness:

> In all, the self-directed career model offers the potential for more people to develop satisfying careers than the traditional lifetime-loyalty model did.

> Because the new model allows individuals to define success for themselves and offers them many more career options, there is a far greater chance that the wide range and variety of career interests found in the workforce can be met than under the traditional model.
>
> (O'Toole & Lawler, 2006: 91)

As the authors point out, however, this individualized approach works only if the organizational and social policies are aligned to support this new model. Multinational companies such as IBM, Deloitte Touche, Nestlé, GE and Shell have revised their development practices so that employees can obtain information about job openings and required skills and experience and can self-initiate their applications for promotions and transfers. They do not have to wait for a supervisor or other corporate official to nominate them, and they can thus be much more agentic than employees were able to be in previous generations.

What Global Leaders Should Know

We would argue that organizations in all parts of the world that implement these agentic HR development practices will be the ones that thrive and survive the vicissitudes of future economic cycles. And, for employees, while these activities could start well before individuals join an organization, career coaching (including career peer coaching relationships), counseling, performance appraisals and other similar interventions through experts, direct superiors and colleagues could be utilized more often. A host of HR activities and options—such as job rotations, job enlargement, functional diversity, exchanges between the profit and not-for-profit sectors, expatriation, etc.—could be integrated.

What this calls for is boundary spanning leadership (Ernst & Chrobot-Mason, 2011). It is important for leaders to be able to be clear on cultural and institutional differences and to be able to manage boundaries between their organizations and other entities—the corporate home office in the case of MNCs, host-country organizations, different groups of employees and so on. This requires skills in buffering different groups and facilitating respectful reflection on these differences. This provides psychological safety that enables each entity to feel internally secure and also able to reach out and create common ground across the differences. In the case of an MNC's country organization, this means connecting to other companies in the host country, to groups of international employees, to the corporate headquarters office and so on. This entails skills in mobilizing and connecting, to build trust and develop community, with the result of building common ground. Ultimately the skillful global leader is able to weave together differences in a synergistic way that creates transformation and invention of new possibilities. When this valuing and synthesizing of differences is successful and transformative, Ernst and Chrobot-Mason (2011) call the result the *nexus effect*.

These ideas and our 5C results constitute important starting points on which to base these interventions. Overall, the pragmatism of organizations as well as cost and other pressures might lead to a diverse range of career approaches within each organization targeted at segments of their workforce. Nevertheless, it could be one answer to the global talent challenges of MNCs and would represent a further strategic opportunity for international HRM (Schuler, Jackson & Tarique, 2011).

References

Arthur, M., Hall, D. T. & Lawrence, B. 1989. *Handbook of Career Theory*. Cambridge, U.K.: Cambridge University Press.

Avolio, B. J., & Gardner, W. L. 2005. Authentic leadership development: Getting to the root of positive forms of leadership. *Leadership Quarterly*, 16: 315–338.

Avolio, B. J. & Hannah, S. T. 2008. Developmental readiness: Accelerating leader development. *Consulting Psychology Journal: Practice and Research*, 60(4): 331–347.

Avolio, B. J., Walumbwa, F. O. & Weber, T. J. 2009. Leadership: Current theories, research, and future directions. *Annual Review of Psychology*, 60: 421–449.

Bartlett, C. & Ghoshal, S. 1989. *The Transnational Solution*. Boston, MA: Harvard Business School Press.

Baruch, Y. 2004. *Managing Careers: Theory and Practice*. London: FT Prentice Hall.

Bilimoria, D. & Piderit, S. K. 2007. *Handbook on Women in Business and Management*. New York: Elgar.

Black, J. S., Gregersen, H., Mendenhall, M. E. & Stroh, L. K. 1999. *Globalizing People Through International Assignments*. Reading, MA: Addison-Wesley.

Bourdieu, P. 1977. *Outline of a Theory of Practice*. Cambridge, U.K.: Cambridge University Press.

Boyatzis, R. E. 2008. Leadership development from a complexity perspective. *Consulting Psychology Journal: Practice and Research*, 60(4): 298–313.

Briscoe, J. P. & Hall, D. T. 1999. Grooming and picking leaders using competency frameworks: Do they work? *Organizational Dynamics*, Autumn: 37–52.

Conway, N. & Briner, R. B. 2005. *Understanding Psychological Contracts at Work: A Critical Evaluation of Theory and Research*. Oxford, U.K.: Oxford University Press.

Demel, B., Yan, S., Unite, J., Briscoe, J. P., Hall, D. T., Mayrhofer, M., Chudzikowski, K., Abdul-Ghani, R., Bogicevic Milikic, B., Colorado, O., Zhangfeng, F., Las Heras, M., Ogliastri, E., Pazy, A., Poon, J. M. L., Shefer, D., Taniguchi, M. & Zikic, J. 2010. Defining and influencing career success across cultures: Implications for international business, Unpublished technical report, Vienna University School of Business and Economics.

Dickmann, M. & Baruch, Y. 2011. *Global Careers*. New York: Routledge.

Dickmann, M. & Doherty, N. 2010. Exploring organizational and individual career goals, interactions and outcomes of international assignments. *Thunderbird International Review*, 52(4): 313–324.

Dickmann, M., Parry, E., Emmens, B. & Williamson, C. 2010. *Engaging Tomorrow's Global Humanitarian Leaders Today*, Report for Enhancing Learning and Research for Humanitarian Assistance (ELRHA). London: People in Aid and Cranfield University.

Ernst, C. & Chrobot-Mason, D. 2011. *Boundary Spanning Leadership: Six Practices for Solving Problems, Driving Innovation, and Transforming Organizations*. New York: McGraw-Hill.

Evans, P., Pucik, V. & Björkman, I. 2011. *The Global Challenge* (2nd ed.). New York: McGraw-Hill.

Fugate, M., Kinicki, A. J. & Ashforth, B. E. 2004. Employability: A psycho-social construct, its dimensions, and applications. *Journal of Vocational Behavior*, 65(1): 14–38.

Gooderham, P., Nordhaug, O. & Ringdal, K. 1998. When in Rome, do they do as the Romans? HRM practices of US subsidiaries in Europe. *Management International Review*, 38(2): 47–64.

Gunz, H. & Peiperl, M. 2007. *Handbook of Career Studies*. Thousand Oaks, CA: Sage.

Hackman, J. R. & Oldham, G. R. 1980. *Work Redesign*. Reading, MA: Addison-Wesley.

Hall, D. T. 2002. *Careers In and Out of Organizations*. Thousand Oaks, CA: Sage.

Hall, D. T. 2004. Self-awareness, identity, and leader development. In D. V. Day, S. J. Zaccaro & S. M. Halpin (Eds.), *Leader Development for Transforming Organizations: Growing Leaders for Tomorrow*: 153–170. Mahwah, NJ: Lawrence Erlbaum Associates.

Hall, D. T. & Mao, J. forthcoming. Authenticity and careers.

Hall, D. T. & Associates 1996. *The Career Is Dead—Long Live the Career: A Relational Approach to Careers*. San Francisco, CA: Jossey-Bass.

Heenan, D. & Perlmutter, H. 1979. *Multinational Organization Development*. Reading, MA: Addison-Wesley.

Huselid, M. 1995. The impact of human resource management practices on turnover, productivity, and corporate financial performance. *Academy of Management Journal*, 38(3): 635–672.

Jackson, T. 2009. A critical cross-cultural perspective for developing non-profit international management capacity. *Nonprofit Management and Leadership*, 19(4): 443–466.

Judge, T. A., Higgins, C. A., Thoresen, C. J. & Barrick, M. R. 1999. The big five personality traits, general mental ability, and career success across the life span. *Personnel Psychology*, 52(3): 621–652.

Karaevli, A. & Hall, D. T. 2008. The use of strategic career development in promoting organization effectiveness: A multilevel view. In T. G. Cummings (Ed.), *Handbook of Organization Development*: 367–384. Thousand Oaks, CA: Sage.

Khilji, S. E. 2003. To adapt or not to adapt: Exploring the role of national culture in HRM—a study of Pakistan. *International Journal of Cross Cultural Management*, 3(1): 109–132.

Kidd, J. 2007. Career counseling. In H. Gunz & M. Peiperl (Eds.), *Handbook of Career Studies*: 97–113. Thousand Oaks, CA: Sage.

Kram, K. E. & Hall, D. T. 1996. Mentoring in a context of diversity and turbulence. In E. E. Kossek & S. A. Lobel (Eds.), *Managing Diversity: Human Resource Strategies for Transforming the Workplace*: 108–136. Cambridge, MA: Blackwell.

Las Heras, M. & Hall, D. T. 2007. Integration of career and life. In Diana Bilimoria & Sandy Kristin Piderit (Eds.), *Handbook of Women in Business and Management*: 178–205. Cheltenham, U.K.: Edward Elgar Publishing.

Lips-Wiersma, M. & Hall, D. T. 2007. Organizational career development is *not* dead: A case study on managing the new career during organizational change. *Journal of Organizational Behavior*, 28: 771–792.

McArdle, S., Waters, L., Briscoe, J. P. & Hall, D. T. 2007. Employability during unemployment: Adaptability, career identity and human and social capital. *Journal of Vocational Behavior*, 71(2): 247–264.

McCall, M. W. 1998. *High Flyers: Generating the Next Generation of Leaders*. Boston, MA: Harvard Business School Press.

Mendenhall, M. E. & Stahl, G. K. 2000. Expatriate training and development: Where do we go from here? *Human Resource Management*, 39: 251–265.

O'Toole J. & Lawler, E. E., III. 2006. *The New American Workplace*. New York: Palgrave Macmillan.

Pfeffer, J. 1998. *The Human Equation: Building Profits by Putting People First*. Boston, MA: Harvard Business School Press.

Ready, D. A., Hill, L. A. & Conger, J. A. 2008. Winning the race for talent in emerging markets. *Harvard Business Review*, Nov.: 63–70.

Riggio, R. E. & Reichard, R. J. 2008. The emotional and social intelligences of effective leadership: An emotional and social skill approach. *Journal of Managerial Psychology*, 23(2): 169–185.

Ryan, R. M. & Deci, E. L. 2000. Self-determination theory and the facilitation of intrinsic motivation, social development, and well-being. *American Psychologist*, 55: 68–78.

Schein, E. H. 1979. *Organizational Psychology* (3rd ed.). Englewood Cliffs, NJ: Prentice-Hall.

Schuler, R., Jackson, S. & Tarique, I. 2011. Framework for global talent management: HR actions for dealing with global challenges. In H. Scullion & D. G. Collings (Eds.), *Global Talent Management*: 17–36. New York: Routledge.

Shen, Y. & Hall, D. T. 2009. When expatriates explore other options: Retaining talent through greater job embeddedness and repatriation adjustment. *Human Resource Management*, 48(5): 793–816.

Shepard, H. A. 1984. On the realization of human potential: A path with a heart. In M. B. Arthur, L. Bailyn, D. J. Levinson & H. A. Shepard (Eds.), *Working With Careers*: 25–46. New York: Center for Research on Careers, Graduate School of Business, Columbia University.

Super, D. 1957. *The Psychology of Careers*. New York: Harper & Row.

Tarique, I. & Schuler, R. S. 2010. Global talent management: Literature review, integrative framework, and suggestions for further research. *Journal of World Business*, 45: 122–133.

Thomas, D. & Inkson, K. 2007. Careers across cultures. In H. Gunz & M. Peiperl (Eds.), *Handbook of Career Studies*: 451–470. Thousand Oaks, CA: Sage.

Toomey, E. & Brewster, C. 2008. HRM and international organizations. In M. Dickmann, C. Brewster & P. Sparrow (Eds.), *International Human Resource Management: A European Perspective*: 298–306. London: Routledge.

9

The 5C Project: Harvesting Lessons for Future Career Research

Wolfgang Mayrhofer, Jon P. Briscoe and Douglas T. Hall

The results presented in the chapters above have considerable implications not only for career actors (i.e. individuals interested in their own careers) but also for those career practitioners managing and consulting to people and organizations (see the previous chapter). They also provide some lessons for career researchers. In essence, the work of 5C as research collaboration has generated insight in three areas. First, we have looked at various facets of career success and career transitions and what individuals from different countries and cultures, occupations and age groups regard as important in this respect. This has consequences for career theory in terms of future research themes and the available theoretical concepts. Second, we have experienced the potential, but also the limits, of applying a specific combination of qualitative methods in a culturally and language-wise mixed setting, in terms of the respondents we asked, their context and the research team. This contains some lessons concerning methods and methodology. Third, we gained experience about managing a research network spread out over all the major culture clusters of the world and over an extended period of time. This offers some insight for similar endeavors. In the remainder of this chapter we will address these issues in turn.

Career Theory

After highlighting emerging future research themes with regard to career success, career transitions and age groups, we discuss in this section the consequences for further developing career theories.

Research Themes

Results from our work led to various suggestions for themes in future career research.

Career Success

Looking at the highly differentiated views of our respondents regarding career success shows that there are myriad definitions of career success. Yet some major themes emerge (see Chapter 4 on career success and Figure 9.1).

Individuals around the globe implicitly or explicitly concentrate on four major dimensions when talking about career success. First, they address issues directly related to them as persons. Examples include achievement, satisfaction, learning and development or self-actualization. Second, career success is linked to material output. Depending in particular on the economic situation of the country as a whole and/or the situation of the individual within society, this ranges from purely securing basic survival to the more general ability to afford desired material goods. Third, the job and its embeddedness in the organization come into sight. Issues touched range from job security and job/task characteristics to one's performance or contribution to organizational success. Fourth, the interaction with the broader environment constitutes an issue. Here it is the social working environment within one's sphere of working, as well as the work–non-work interface and the urge to make a difference in society as a whole, which emerges. Against this backdrop, three issues deserve special attention when analyzing potential consequences for future career research in terms of themes addressed: the multi-faceted nature of perceptions of

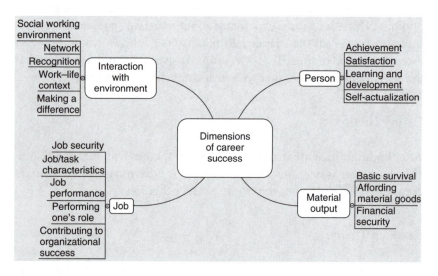

Figure 9.1 Major dimensions of career success and examples

career success; the prominence of individual achievement in conceptualizations of career success across the globe; and the importance of organizations as a primary context for careers.

Much of career success research applies a basic distinction between objective and subjective career success. Our data reflect this. More importantly, the data also suggest going beyond the simple bipolar objective–subjective divide (which at closer range becomes increasingly fuzzy anyway) towards a more multi-faceted approach when analyzing career success. The richness of themes emerging when asking respondents for their views on career success seems to indicate that future research has to take into account this multi-dimensional nature of career success. Instead of primarily or exclusively taking a top-down approach, focusing on meanings of career success determined beforehand, a more self-directed approach seems adequate, at least as a supplement. In this way, individuals can express dimensions that are important for them and not only for the researchers. In qualitative studies, this is usually the case. We suggest such a course of action for a more survey-type quantitative approach too, for example by including open-ended questions or letting individuals decide about the relative importance of various elements of career success as expressed in survey questions.

Within the multi-faceted nature of career success, achievement is of overwhelming importance, as represented by the proportion of responses reflecting it. It regularly appears when talking to a Chinese nurse, a South African blue-collar worker or a U.S. business school graduate, to mention a few examples. In a way, this is highly surprising. Remember that our research did not direct respondents to certain dimensions or themes. Still, achievement emerges as a dominant theme in the narrations of our respondents. Two major issues for future research are the meaning of achievement and the reasons for its prevalence. Regarding the former, potential research questions include, for example, what achievement exactly means for different groups of individuals, which factors influence their respective understanding, how different interpretations of achievement influence the course of careers, personal satisfaction, and the choice of labor arrangements, e.g. working for certain types of organizations or freelancing.

Regarding possible reasons for the prevalence of achievement, one line of reasoning comes from institutionalist thinking, for example the world polity approach (Meyer, Boli, Thomas & Ramirez, 1997). Its argument goes roughly as follows. By and large, we can observe a worldwide replacement of traditional particularistic schemes through universal standards associated with modernity. Global myths such as rationality or equality exist that exert considerable influence on all kinds of actors, individual or collective, economic or political. To be sure, such global myths do not lead to uniformity. On the contrary, owing to specific local conditions, there is a great variety of differences in how these global myths are actually realized and lived out. Consequently, for career research this could lead to studies about: how such global myths influence the perception of career success in different regions of the world; how the perception of these myths and their role for career success differ according to age, occupation or gender; how individuals and organizations modify the career-success-relevant parts of such global myths in line with their cultural beliefs and assumptions; or which kind of global myths do play a role when individuals conceptualize career success.

Another line of inquiry when explaining the prevalence of achievement is the increasing dominance of economic logic over various spheres of life. Some voices claim that we are witnessing a fundamental change in the role of the economic system in society: "The economy no longer is embedded into social relationships, but social relationships are embedded into the economic system" (Polanyi, 1978: 88f.). For example, a qualitative study found that Austrian managers describe and analyze their family life in economic terms and with an economic framework, heavily using concepts like efficiency and effectiveness. Vice versa, they describe their work life in terms hitherto reserved for the private sphere, such as erotic or emotionally fulfilling (Kasper, Scheer & Schmidt, 2002; see also Hochschild, 1997). This illustrates the increasing hegemony of the economic logic. In turn, this questions the established relationship between individual life spheres and the division between "life" and "work." For example, can one still speak of spill-over effects between various spheres of life if these spheres follow a joint logic? What are the consequences of a "holistic" lifestyle with few, if any, boundaries between work and private life (see Fleming & Spicer, 2004, for an example in high commitment organizations)? It also reframes the characteristics of highly personal activities, for example participating in a language course. Suddenly, this is no longer just merely a personal development activity. Under an economic logic, this is also an investment in one's cultural capital and competencies, with potential effects on one's employability.

Explanations of the importance of achievement in conceptualizations of career success across the globe provide career research with some fascinating lines of inquiry. These include, for example, an analysis of: the boundaries between career and life success; the role that achievement plays in both spheres of life; and the extent to which individuals from different regions of the world, of different occupation and age, are influenced by this. In addition, this can lead to an analysis of the role of cultural and religious convictions about individual performance and achievement for definitions of career success, a line of inquiry with considerable tradition (see Weber's [1905] 2002 arguments about the role of religion for the development of capitalism). Finally, the results also raise the question of how individuals interpret the role of achievement in their view of career success depending upon their personality characteristics, age, occupation and cultural heritage.

The context of work as an important influence upon career success is a third major theme. Organizations have been a traditional theme throughout much of the history of career research (see, for example, seminal works such as Dyer, 1976; Glaser, 1968; Hall, 1976; Schein, 1978; Van Maanen, 1977). Yet, for the past decade or so, there has been some neglect here. The useful, nevertheless partly one-sided, reception of the boundaryless career concept (Arthur & Rousseau, 1996) has partially discouraged analyses of organizational careers.

Our results support a renewed focus on the organization and its role for careers in general and career success and career transitions in particular. For example, we know relatively little about how recent organizational concepts with labels such as "cellular" (Miles, Snow, Mathews & Coleman, 1997), "empowering" (Chakravarthy & Gargiulo, 1998), "fractal" (Warnecke, 1993), "heterarchical" (Hedlund, 1986), "learning" (Cohen & Sproull, 1996) or "differentiated network" (Nohria & Ghoshal, 1997) influence their employees' views on careers. The same is true for virtualization, i.e. the decoupling of processes or actions and the underlying material basis, especially through the means of information technology. Virtualization is visible in many aspects of the organization and organizing, yet we have little evidence how it influences conceptualizations of career success, for example in terms of the importance of material aspects of career outcomes or its link to "ranks and titles," which is often hard(er) to detect in such types of organizations.

Career Transitions

Looking at the results presented in Chapter 5, two major aspects regarding career transitions stand out: the intricate interplay between individuals' own initiative and the immediate context; and the role of national culture in individuals' perceptions about key elements of career transitions. We will deal with the relevance of these aspects for future career research in turn.

Looking at career transitions inevitably also means looking at who or what drives them—in particular what causes and triggers career transitions and guides their overall progression. Our respondents' views fit neither the (slightly oversimplified) notions of free, self-determined career agents deciding independently of their respective contexts nor those of external forces such as organizational structures or chance coercing individuals into action. Rather, they take a balanced view and acknowledge the importance of both individual and contextual factors. The majority of individuals see their transitions as self-initiated, indicating the importance of self-directed career behavior across cultures. At the same time, they also recognize the importance of contextual factors in the organizational environment such as the boss or organizational and relational dimensions. While the relative emphasis on individual and contextual factors varies according to the cultural background (see below), the importance of the interplay between these two elements stays constant across the cultures researched in this study.

For future career research, this contains several lessons. While conceptualizations of career transitions usually include both individual and contextual, in particular organizational, factors, the interplay between them often remains somewhat unclear. Research questions that deserve further attention include in particular: Do they exist side by side without any interaction and "somehow" are integrated within the individual in a kind of black box? Using the differentiation between predictor and moderator variables, what kind of relationship do these factors and the underlying variables have: are there specific configurations of personality and/or cultural context where individual agency takes precedence over contextual factors, i.e. is a predictor moderated by context or vice versa? Is the relationship merely a matter of well-known attributional tendencies where individuals in hindsight frame career transitions that went well as "driven by me," whereas they regard difficult or failed ones as triggered and guided by external forces? Assuming that "the boss" and other factors in the organizational environment do play an important role, further questions arise: What exactly are the variables within this broad category which are relevant for career transitions? Do they vary systematically with the cultural background of the organization and its employees, or the age or the occupation of the individuals, for example the older, the more self-reliant or the better the formal education and the higher its regard in society, the more emphasis on autonomy? To what degree does it play a role that individuals possibly mention less or even completely blank out factors that they take for granted, for example networks in the U.S.A. or family in Spain, Mexico, Japan and Malaysia?

Besides the interplay between individual agency and contextual influence, the role of national culture in career transitions is a second major topic in our results that has relevance for future career research. Our empirical evidence indicates that national culture influences the perception of career transitions. For example (for more details see Chapter 5), in countries characterized by low uncertainty avoidance, autonomy, egalitarianism and harmony, a greater proportion of research participants see their career transitions as internally driven. To the contrary, participants from mastery-driven countries are more likely to report organizationally driven career transitions. Furthermore, on an individual level, mastery country interviewees were more likely to report both planning/goal setting and formal education strategies in managing their career transitions.

Again, while these results are in line with the culture-theoretical background, they also trigger further research. For example, do cultural differences lead to different perceptions of career transitions or also to differences in "hard evidence"? It is one thing for individuals to report an important role of the boss and organizational circumstances in triggering career transitions. It is another thing to produce some corroborating "hard evidence." Examples for such a kind of evidence include showing: that supervisors in mastery-driven countries have more face-to-face contact with their subordinates; that future career development is more often a topic in their conversations; and that supervisors' role in organizational decision making about employees' careers differs systematically between cultures along the degree of mastery. Another example for the role of culture relates to the interplay between cultural and institutional dimensions. Are the cultural dimensions relevant for different views on career transitions or do institutional factors such as the ease of job moves, governed by labor law, collective agreements and firm-level regulations, play a role? What is the influence of the labor market situation on such considerations, for example do we see a systematic change in the descriptions within and between cultures in times of a labor shortage or a surplus?

Generations

Our analyses show that the views of younger and older members in our sample regarding various career-related issues differ substantially. For example, members of the younger generations across the world seem to be taking more control of their careers. This is most likely due to external conditions in career systems, such as the reluctance of many organizations to offer long-term perspectives, rather than some unconnected change at the level of individuals. Likewise, a major and somewhat overlooked related issue is that the older generations in many cultures see themselves as left behind. Potentially, this has serious repercussions. Examples at the individual level include a lack of self-esteem or a difficult economic situation. At the societal level, one can mention negative effects on the available knowledge and competency base of an economy or the social fabric owing to tensions between different age groups.

For future career research, these results contain a number of starting points. One issue is the theoretical framing of these findings. We are confident about the existence of age-related differences in a great number of career-related issues in various cultures around the globe, yet the source of those differences and their theoretical significance are by no means clear. Owing to the design of our study, we are not able to differentiate between age, cohort and period effects. Our data do not allow us to set apart changes attributed to individual developments over time (age), to specific circumstances of one cohort only, for example belonging to the Baby Boom generation (cohort), or to specific circumstances affecting all cohorts, such as increasing internationalization of businesses or the prevalence of the internet and its growing significance for all parts of life (period). Furthermore there are career stage theories (e.g. Super, Crites, Hummel, Mose, Overstreet & Warnath, 1957) which may explain some of our generational data but will certainly vary by culture. Yet a comprehensive understanding of career-related differences between young and old requires a more thorough understanding of the relative contributions of these effects. Hence studies that at least partially take into account these effects, for example by exploiting existing longitudinal large-scale data sets such as the German Socio-Economic Panel (SOEP, see www.diw.de/en/soep), the Wisconsin Longitudinal Study (see www. ssc.wisc.edu/wlsresearch/) or three-cohort designs such as the Vienna Career Panel Project (ViCaPP, see www.wu.ac.at/project/vicapp/), can shed more light on this. It will be relatively difficult to establish such studies in a similar way across a great number of countries (although efforts such as the World Values Survey, see www.worldvaluessurvey. org, at least have several waves of cross-sectional investigations). Nevertheless, steps in that direction would offer partial progress.

In addition, we suggest that future career research takes a more indepth look at the actual significance of age-related differences. Per se, age is meaningless unless it is contextualized. If so, it usually becomes shorthand for a variety of things, for example degree of experience, social status, biological state, career stage, time to retirement and so on. Since our findings indicate that age makes a difference, some follow-up questions arise. For example, related to the finding that members of the younger generation usually emphasize more the issue of achievement in their career and take a more active stance in shaping their career: Is this an age, cohort or period effect? Does past experience have an effect, for example do individuals with many years of experience realize that a lot of things happen irrespective of one's own efforts, and are individuals with little work experience convinced about the effects of their individual efforts? Do different time horizons play a role, for example do feelings of being in charge wane when seeing a comparatively short time span in one's work career left, whereas having decades ahead leads to feelings of agency? Is the importance of age the same in all cultures or can one detect specific differences, for example in line with the social status that is ascribed to individuals at a certain age in their respective cultures, such as older people being wise or being out of date? How can our understanding of generational differences be better illuminated in light of the interaction between cultural variables and institutional variables or macro-level phenomena such as technology shifts and so on?

Career Theories

The 5C results not only inspire future research themes, but also raise the question of whether adequate theoretical concepts are available to address these themes. The theoretical landscape in career research is rich but, owing to the great array of contributing disciplines, also highly diverse and even fragmented. Hence it is futile to go through a detailed list of theories or conceptual frameworks (and analyze their suitability for single research themes for the debate on what constitutes a theory; see, for example, Bacharach, 1989; Poole & Van de Ven, 1989; Weick, 1995; in the following we will use the term "theory" and employ it in a broad sense). Yet, on a more general level, we can formulate general requirements for career theories which support the suggested future agenda. In this respect, theories are especially helpful which:

- avoid one-sidedness in terms of "structure or agency" and acknowledge that actual individual career behavior is the result of an intricate interplay between agentic behavior and contextual forces;
- emphasize the role of the organizational as well as the broader cultural and institutional context;
- allow multi-level analyses, including all levels ranging from individual characteristics to cultural and institutional factors;
- go beyond simplistic mono-causal explanations and have potential for analyzing the interplay between the various factors and levels;

- cut across different contexts;
- explicitly include the time dimension, especially in terms of the ages of individuals; and
- support a country- and culture-comparative angle.

It is safe to say that no one theory fulfills all these requirements. Even so, we would like to point towards four groups of theories that seem especially suitable for the outlined research agenda.

One group of potentially promising theories is concepts that go beyond the traditional boundaries of organizations and occupations, and even beyond the boundaries of developmental networks—in particular the idea of communities of practice (see, for example, Brown & Duguid, 1991; Lave & Wenger, 1991; Mutch, 2003; Wenger, 1999). This social constructivist theory of learning emphasizes that much of relevant learning happens outside formal organizational or educational structures in highly autonomous, self-directed and self-organizing systems. Learning is not an individualized effort guided by some formal structures such as company training or educational courses. Rather, it is a social practice, usually between established and more recent members of such a community, that is never fully integrated in the formal structures. This theory provides a theoretical basis to better understand how individuals learn in the course of their careers beyond official and traditional learning opportunities. In addition, it offers a starting point to explain commonalities in the understanding of career, career success and career transitions across cultural, geographical, age-related and occupational boundaries. Take, for example, the case of business school graduates. It is debatable whether they form a conscious community of practice. Still, this theoretical angle can provide insight into the partly homogeneous world- and career views of this group.

A second group of theories takes a broad view of social action and serves as a meta-framework for more fine-grained, directly career-related theories and concepts. Sometimes called grand social theories, they explain the overall functioning and dynamics of a given social order instead of analyzing more restricted parts of the picture only. One example is Bourdieu's theory of practice (Bourdieu, 1977), which has received attention both in organizational research (e.g. De Clercq & Voronov, 2009; Golsorkhi, Leca, Lounsbury & Ramirez, 2009; Kerr & Robinson, 2009; Özbilgin & Tatli, 2005) and in career research (e.g. Chudzikowski & Mayrhofer, 2011; Iellatchitch, Mayrhofer & Meyer, 2003). In a similar way, new structuralism emerging in organizational theory over the past decade (e.g. Jones, 2001) holds some promise for career research too. As Lounsbury and Ventresca (2003: 459) point out, "the time is ripe for organizational theorists to renew their attention to broader social structures and to bring 'society' back to center stage." Theories within this group place heavy emphasis on various layers of context for explaining individual and collective action and cut across several levels of analysis.

A third group of theories puts time at the center of its considerations. Two career families are especially prominent. Life and career stage theory (e.g. Graves, Dalton & Thompson, 1980; Levinson, Darrow, Klein, Levinson & McKee, 1978; Super et al., 1957) holds some promise if adapted to allow for shorter and more frequent cycles, as well as irregular schedules in working lives. Its focus on the developmental aspect and the overall life span constitutes a good starting point for the differences between members of the young and the old generations about core career aspects. Alternatively, generational theories explain differences between young and old by looking at the conditions under which the members of a specific cohort were born, raised and continue to live. Examples are concepts looking at Baby Boomers, Generation X (e.g. Ulrich & Harris, 2003), Generation Y (e.g. Martin & Tulgan, 2001), Millennials (e.g. Howe & Strauss, 2000) and Generation Me (e.g. Twenge, 2006), to name a few.

A fourth group of theories focuses on the cultural and institutional context. Unlike grand social theories cutting across different levels of social complexity, they stay on the macro-level. On the one hand, this group contains culture concepts such as the ones the 5C group related to, in particular the concepts of Schwartz (1999), Hofstede (1980) or the culture-related work emerging from the GLOBE study (Chhokar, Brodbeck & House, 2007). On the other hand, this points towards institutional theory (e.g. Djelic & Quack, 2003; Meyer & Rowan, 1977; Scott, 2001), which argues that organizations are socially embedded in their external environment and affected by respective forces that require them to adapt their structures and behavior: "A firm's action is seen not as a choice among an unlimited array of possibilities determined by purely internal arrangements, but rather as a choice among a narrowly defined set of legitimate options" (Hoffmann, 1999: 351). By and large, within HRM two positions have emerged in the discussion about the significance of the context. The universalist angle assumes a basic similarity of successful organizational structures, processes and organizational cultures across the globe and favors a best-practice approach. Conversely, the contextual position focuses on understanding what is distinctive between and within various contexts, and what the antecedents of those differences are, and leans towards best fit rather than best practice (Brewster & Mayrhofer, 2009). This can guide career research in particular when looking at organizational career management.

Contributing to such a contextualist view, a growing body of theoretical literature is exemplified in the work of the so-called varieties of capitalism theorists (e.g. Amable, 2003; Hall & Soskice, 2001; Whitley, 1999). They explore the differences between various forms of capitalism, in particular looking at the way in which societies conceive of and manage the relationship between employers and their employees. In line with our results, which reject a one-size-fits-all perspective for career transitions and career success, these theories allow a more differentiated view of what careers are, depending on various cultural and institutional contexts. In turn, this can help career research, which has no coherent and convincing theoretical explanations for the antecedents of those differences and for the interplay between cultural and institutional forces relevant for career behavior.

Methods and Methodology

Pursuing research in 11 countries through conducting and analyzing interviews in the local language(s) raises not only theoretical issues, but also questions regarding methods once you have made your basic methodological choices. The problems related to data gathering and interpretation in a cross-cultural setting are well documented (e.g. Leung, 2008; Marschan-Piekkari & Welch, 2005; Matsumoto & van de Vijver, 2011). Against the backdrop of our experience in this area, we would like to selectively address a few issues which turned out to be especially crucial and are most likely to be important in similar activities in the future.

Local Expertise

In comparative research, the problem of making sense of the local environment regularly occurs when designing studies and interpreting results. There has been considerable criticism of a "safari research" (Peterson, 2001) type of approach. Here researchers with very limited, if any, contact with local experts analyze countries or cultures about which they have little first-hand knowledge. We strongly subscribe to the dictum of avoiding ethnocentric biases by forming a research group including the respective local experts. Without them it would have been much more difficult to get access to the target population, in particular groups that tend not to be too visible on an international scale, in our case blue-collar workers and nurses. Even more important was the access to local knowledge during data interpretation. For example, when discussing whether the results of the analysis were "typical," what they actually meant and how they fit into the overall career landscape of a specific country, it would have been close to impossible to do this without local experts.

Local Language(s) for the Interviews

Linked to the issue raised above, the 5C group decided to conduct all interviews in the local language(s) most familiar to the respondents. For some groups in some countries, there was no alternative to this, since their command of English was, at best, marginal. For other groups, in particular the business school graduates, English most often would have been an option. Nevertheless, we decided to go for the local language option, in particular because of the better ability to express oneself in one's native language, the resulting richer nuances in the resulting text corpus once the interviews are transcribed, and the avoidance of one element of awkwardness in the interview situation. Inevitably, there is a certain trade-off involved. In some cases, choosing the local language closes the rest of the research team off from the original texts, for example if only the local experts speak the language, as was the case in many 5C countries. Consequently, this excludes data interpretation with methods requiring access to the original text. Yet overall we feel that the advantages clearly outweigh the drawbacks.

English as Lingua Franca During Data Analysis

English was not only the language allowing the research team to communicate with each other (see also the next section), but also the lingua franca for later stages of data analysis. The chosen variant of content analysis (see Mayring, 2007) requires, roughly speaking, a stepwise condensation of the text. It starts with coding the basic units of analysis and then, via paraphrasing, generalized paraphrases and reduction, formulates categories as the endpoint of analytical material reduction. The original text, transcribed in full from the interviews, was in the respective local language(s). The 5C group decided that in a first round all the analytic steps should be conducted by the local researchers in their local language(s). In this way we would ensure that the analytical process would permit as much justice to the interview material as possible. In a next step, the labels for the categories and their descriptions were translated into English, as were some verbatim quotes typical for the categories. In this way, the essence of the content analysis became available to the whole research team. As a side effect, the robustness of the results increased, because the team concentrated on main issues that "survived" the translation. We are still convinced that such a procedure represents the best of both worlds. It combines necessary elements of culturally sensitive data collection and analyses with transparency and accessibility for the whole research team.

Again, however, there is a certain amount of trade-off involved. First, "classical" translation problems emerge. Some concepts with a specific meaning in one culture are difficult to translate without losing a lot of connotations. For example, a number of translations for *Wirtschaft*—often mentioned as a major influencing factor for careers—exist, such as economy, industry, commerce or business world, yet some aspects in its German use, such as mythical-religious undertones (*Wirtschaftswunder*), are hard to get across the language barrier. Second, translating original interview passages for verbatim citations into English often reduces or even nearly erases the specific flavor of the quotation. Third, the switch from the local language(s) to English resulted in a varying number of barriers for members of the research team. For example, there can be no change from the original language when U.S. members of the team look at South African core categories; one language change in the case of Austrian researchers looking at U.S. interviews; or two language changes when Malaysian members look at Spanish core categories formulated in English. This leads to an uneven information base, a loss of nuances, difficulties in consulting the original interview texts which sometimes is practically impossible to access for non-native speakers, or a lack of density when analyzing texts in culturally mixed interpretation groups. Overall, however, we still see this as a reasonable way of dealing with the inevitable variety in culture-comparative qualitative research.

Conducting Comparative Career Research in Culturally Mixed Teams

Working in a culturally mixed research team is a *conditio sine qua non* in comparative research, not the least for reasons outlined in the previous section. Again, we do not repeat all that is easily accessible through literature on the management of international research collaborations (e.g. Mayrhofer, 2000). Instead, we emphasize three issues that in our experience have been crucial success factors for the completion of this project: the bottom-up formation of the research team, synchronization of team members on a number of dimensions, and handling the dynamics of team development.

Bottom-Up Formation

In order to develop international cooperation in research, policy makers and grant agencies in many countries offer support for cross-border research activities. The criteria of some funds have the effect that research consortia are sometimes partly formed around criteria beyond technical knowledge and established personal relationships, for example with an emphasis on geographical location of the respective partners owing to explicit or assumed criteria of grant agencies about geographical spread of the consortium. As a result, there is sometimes very little, if any, knowledge of the prospective team members in advance. This leads to a number of potential pitfalls. Examples include different explicit or implicit interest and agendas of consortium partners, for example in terms of the degree of scientific interest, interest in building networks or learning from others without being able and/or willing to adequately give in return. Beyond the immediate effects on the research team itself, this also leads to an increasing commercialization of research. When grant money becomes the major or sole driver for establishing an international research team, it is more than likely that "research mercenaries/ funding vultures" will appear whose interest and capacity for comparative work will fade once the money is gone.

We chose a different approach when forming 5C and started with a small core group. Its members had expertise and enthusiasm with regard to the research issues and fit into the culture clusters according to the theoretical framework by Schwartz (1999). In addition, they possessed a learning rather than performance orientation toward the research (Button, Mathieu & Zajac, 1996), i.e. they were not overly committed to one particular theoretical position, but open-minded and with a strong curiosity and willingness to explore and learn. This core group was enlarged stepwise with additional collaborators.

In all instances, personal chemistry and the right mix of technical competencies, motivation and seniority were of equal, if not greater, importance. To us, the latter seems to be an extremely crucial success factor. Any comparative project of a certain size will need a mix of technical competencies, motivation and seniority to handle unforeseen contingencies. Examples include: language capabilities to form bridges between members less fluent in the lingua franca; access to resources for organizing global conference calls; the willingness and financial resources of some members to invest in extensive traveling in order to facilitate coordination and control within the collaboration; a long-term perspective for at least some of the members in order to sustain a helicopter-view in times of crises or ground-work overload; junior members willing and able to put a lot of effort into often less visible, but indispensable, operative work, showing a lot of motivation and eagerness to make a name for themselves through the project; senior members bringing in their expertise in terms of overview of the field, reputational capital in terms of opening doors to conferences and invitation-only publications such as edited volumes, and giving credibility to the project; and a balance between individuals focusing on output and on group processes which takes into account two classical dimensions in group research, locomotion and cohesion.

We are well aware of successful collaborations with a very different set-up, and there is no one best way to ensure success of culturally mixed research teams in comparative (career) research. Still, we would argue in favor of a bottom-up approach along the lines highlighted above. From a holistic perspective we are convinced that such an approach increases the technical output in terms of completion of the project, publications and conference presentations, as well as the influencing of the field, the professional and personal development of the members of the collaboration and, last but not least, the enjoyment of one's joint work.

Synchronizing Team Members

Not only the formation but also the continuous management of long-standing research teams across national and cultural boundaries faces a number of problems. Examples include: the high degree of diversity in terms of time spent in the academic system and preferences for scientific work; vastly differing resources leading to varying contributions and to questions of relative fairness and sharing of the workload; and different objectives for members' academic work, for example heavily practitioner versus clearly science oriented. All of this regularly leads to sometimes fruitful, sometimes dysfunctional tensions within the research team.

One especially crucial aspect in our case was the great diversity in terms of schedules and priorities, which are in constant flux and change over time. For example, highly varying degrees of priority lead to tensions because of different attitudes towards the project, a varying readiness to devote time and energy, a differing degree of keeping deadlines and the like. This is especially true when the collaboration's activities face certain deadlines such as submitting conference papers or contributions to special issues.

Of course, there is no general recipe for dealing with these problems. In the end, they are not so different from leadership problems faced by any group. What helped greatly in the case of 5C was the personal bonds that emerged over the course of the project, establishing a relational rather than a transactional psychological contract (Rousseau, 1995; Rousseau & Schalk, 2000). Owing to a commitment to the project by many members which went beyond polite professional interests, it was always possible to overcome the inevitable conflicts arising without too many transaction costs, too much time delay and formal dispute resolution. From our perspective, three things were crucial for this. First, the bottom-up process of team formation paid some dividends. It increased the likelihood of good personal relationships. Second, meeting twice a year in person for about two days was crucial. It allowed intensive work, but also time for joint leisure activities (and was usually linked to some large conference which many members attended anyway). These meetings made it easier to form and strengthen personal bonds and deepen our understanding of what we were doing in terms of research. It also allowed the 5C group to address difficult issues comparatively early on and look for joint solutions. Third, a lack of central funding had its advantages. While it complicated joint meetings or conducting the practical research, it had a number of positive effects too. The lack of funding constituted a barrier against "research mercenaries/funding vultures," i.e. people who are primarily interested in the research because of monetary reasons, and favored individuals with a primary interest in the topic and the team. At the same time, the lack of funding also underscored the egalitarian and network-based characteristic of the collaboration. Central money usually involves some kind of formal hierarchy owing to the requirements of the funding source. If the latter is absent, the partners with their local ways of running their national activities are more of a loosely coupled network of egalitarian entrepreneurs. In addition, a lack of central funding keeps members of the collaboration alert and constantly questioning the basic motivation ("Is it still worth it?"). A positive answer boosts intrinsic motivation, which in turn helps in keeping the collaboration.

Handling Team Dynamics

As might be expected, the history of a research collaboration such as 5C is no linear process. On the contrary, turning points and a variety of dynamics characterize the joint work. Dealing with this in great detail goes beyond the scope of this chapter, yet we would like to address a few issues which we regard as crucial for the management of such research collaborations.

During the start-up phase, a core issue is to integrate new members in terms of content as well as socially. Regarding the former, this leads to some kind of repetitious element, in particular in joint meetings. Old-timers see valuable time wasted when newcomers are brought up to date and, conversely, new members easily lose track and cannot fully contribute if there is no deliberate effort to include them. A revolving and phased approach turned out to be useful here. During the early stages, with a greater number of new members, deliberate efforts to bring everybody up to the same standards dominated. In the later stages, this was less the case during joint meetings or in plenary time, but was done "by the side" in personal conversations prior to meetings or outside the official agenda.

Another, more difficult issue relates to the dynamics relating to changes in membership and status/role changes of members during the course of the collaboration. Inevitably, there is a certain amount of fluctuation, with some individuals dropping out while others are joining the team. In addition, role changes for continuing team members occur owing to factors such as seniority, priorities, personal life circumstances or acceptance within the team. For example, when doctoral students form part of the team and reach the end of their dissertation, they are at a personal cross-road in their life. If they decide to continue in the project, in line with a changed formal status and their increasing experience, they grow into different roles. This changes the whole system of mutual understanding at a technical level, i.e. who does what under which supervision. The same is true at the level of the social fabric, for example who relates to whom in what way, who is seen in which role and so on. Sometimes geographical moves of members influence the practical aspects of communication or question the basic design of the study, for example if a member moves from a country which was part of the study design, and for which he or she was an expert, to a country which was not part of the original plan.

Especially in academia with its notions of equality and skepticism towards formal relations, handling the dynamics in a long-standing research team across national and cultural borders is not easy. The intensity of qualitative versus quantitative research makes this even more complex, but because so much "face time" is necessary it also makes it easier in some ways. Still, there is no easy solution we can offer. Besides being aware that these problems will arise and consciously monitoring group processes and individual developments along these lines, the following things helped 5C to deal with these issues: the great interest of participating members, paired with considerable intrinsic motivation; at least for some of the members good personal relationships which helped us see beyond the professional self and detect the "human being" in other members; and a readiness to find creative and non-traditional solutions for some of the problems that arose. For example, we were often mutually making up uneven inputs owing to understandable reasons, such as high pressure because of private circumstances, or developing a specific "Skype culture" across different time zones in order to counter-balance the lack of personal meetings. This increased the willingness to bear some kind of temporal inequity because of a basic trust that "in the long run" things would even out, which helped in coping with the dynamics of the group development.

Conclusion

Our purpose with the 5C project and this book has been to better represent and understand careers on both local and global scales. It should be stated that, while we did not wish to engineer findings, we did hope to use those findings for the betterment of individuals, management, organizations and societies. Our motivations in that sense were not "neutral." We believe we have succeeded in at least bringing to light some careers perspectives that have been unseen or at any rate underappreciated, and our ongoing goal is to add value to working lives and careers with this research.

We have used data from over 200 people around the world to generate a framework for defining career success meanings that can truly be said to be global. This helps in understanding career success better as a topic, and allows for hypothesis testing and much more detailed query on a worldwide scale. We have shown that the new career really is becoming global, but the old career has not gone away. In viewing transitions, it is clear that many feel they control their careers, but they also recognize that their organizational and other contexts anchor and moderate their actions. So, the more things change, the more they stay the same.

We would strongly urge readers not to be tempted into drawing global conclusions and generalizations where they are not merited. While some findings, such as the universality of achievement as a career success meaning, are not a reach, other conclusions about careers vary on a country-by-country basis. Perhaps most striking is the realization that generations are largely a nationally contained phenomenon. True, there are some broad commonalties amongst older and younger career cohorts, respectively, but more detail and insight are gleaned when seeing each country in isolation as an N of 1.

While our research points the way toward new career theory and research in career success, career transitions and comparative research in these and other areas, practical research questions also beckon. How can our findings and findings yet undiscovered be used to stimulate better career practice around the world—for individual career actors and those managers, organizations and career practitioners that would help them? When can a Western approach add value in South Africa, and when might a South African maxim add value elsewhere? This is a realm of research largely untapped but hopefully primed by our research.

In spite of its limitations, we are pleased to make a unique offering in the field of career research that has attempted to go beyond the West and beyond isolated corners of the world. We hope that it will inspire similar efforts amongst our colleagues studying careers and that they will improve upon our study and further drive career studies toward a truly global field.

References

Amable, B. 2003. *The Diversity of Modern Capitalism*. Oxford, U.K.: Oxford University Press.

Arthur, M. B. & Rousseau, D. B. (Eds.). 1996. *The Boundaryless Career: A New Employment Principle for a New Organizational Era*. New York: Oxford University Press.

Bacharach, S. B. 1989. Organizational theories: Some criteria for evaluation. *Academy of Management Review*, 14(4): 496–515.

Bourdieu, P. 1977. *Outline of a Theory of Practice*. Cambridge, U.K.: Cambridge University Press.

Brewster, C. & Mayrhofer, W. 2009. Comparative human resource management policies and practices. In D. G. Collings & G. Wood (Eds.), *Human Resource Management: A Critical Approach*: 353–366. London: Routledge.

Brown, J. S. & Duguid, P. 1991. Organizational learning and communities of practice: Toward a unified view of working, learning, and innovation. *Organization Science*, 2(1): 40–57.

Button, S. B., Mathieu, J. E. & Zajac, D. M. 1996. Goal orientation in organizational research: A conceptual and empirical foundation. *Organizational Behavior and Human Decision Processes*, 67: 26–48.

Chakravarthy, B. & Gargiulo, M. 1998. Maintaining leadership legitimacy in the transition to new organizational forms. *Journal of Management Studies*, 35(4): 437–456.

Chhokar, J. S., Brodbeck, F. C. & House, R. J. 2007. *Culture and Leadership Across the World: The GLOBE Book of In-Depth Studies of 25 Societies*. London: Routledge.

Chudzikowski, K. & Mayrhofer, W. 2011. In search of the blue flower? Grand social theories and career research: The case of Bourdieu's theory of practice. *Human Relations*, 64(1): 14–32.

Cohen, M. D. & Sproull, L. S. (Eds.). 1996. *Organizational Learning*. Thousand Oaks, CA: Sage.

De Clercq, D. & Voronov, M. 2009. The role of domination in newcomers' legitimation as entrepreneurs. *Organization*, 16(6): 799–827.

Djelic, M.-L. & Quack, S. (Eds.). 2003. *Globalization and Institutions: Redefining the Rules of the Economic Game*. Cheltenham, U.K.: Edward Elgar.

Dyer, L. (Ed.). 1976. *Careers in Organizations*. Ithaca, NY: Cornell University Press.

Fleming, P. & Spicer, A. 2004. "You can checkout anytime, but you can never leave": Spatial boundaries in a high commitment organization. *Human Relations*, 57(1): 75–94.

Glaser, B. (Ed.). 1968. *Organizational Careers: A Sourcebook for Theory*. Chicago, IL: Aldine.

Golsorkhi, D., Leca, B., Lounsbury, M. & Ramirez, C. 2009. Analysing, accounting for and unmasking domination: On our role as scholars of practice, practitioners of social science and public intellectuals. *Organization*, 16(6): 779–797.

Graves, J. P., Dalton, G. W. & Thompson, P. H. 1980. Career stages in organizations. In C. B. Derr (Ed.), *Work, Family, and the Career*: 18–37. New York: Praeger.

Hall, D. T. 1976. *Careers in Organizations*. Santa Monica, CA: Goodyear.

Hall, P. A. & Soskice, D. (Eds.). 2001. *Varieties of Capitalism: The Institutional Foundations of Comparative Advantage*. Oxford, U.K.: Oxford University Press.

Hedlund, G. 1986. The hypermodern MNC: A heterarchy? *Human Resource Management*, 25(1): 9–35.

Hochschild, A. R. 1997. *The Time Bind: When Work Becomes Home and Home Becomes Work*. New York: Metropolitan.

Hoffmann, A. 1999. Institutional evolution and change: Environmentalism and the U.S. chemical industry. *Academy of Management Journal*, 42(4): 351–371.

Hofstede, G. 1980. *Culture's Consequences: International Differences in Work-Related Values*. Newbury Park, CA: Sage.

Howe, N. & Strauss, W. 2000. *Millennials Rising: The Next Great Generation*. New York: Vintage Books.

Iellatchitch, A., Mayrhofer, W. & Meyer, M. 2003. Career fields: A small step towards a grand career theory? *International Journal of Human Resource Management*, 14(5): 728–750.

Jones, C. 2001. Co-evolution and entrepreneurial careers, institutional rules and competitive dynamics in American film, 1895–1920. *Organization Studies*, 22(5): 911–944.

Kasper, H., Scheer, P. J. & Schmidt, A. 2002. *Managen und Lieben: Führungskräfte im Spannungsfeld von Familie und Beruf*. Wien: Ueberreuter.

Kerr, R. & Robinson, S. 2009. The hysteresis effect as creative adaptation of the habitus: Dissent and transition to the "corporate" in post-Soviet Ukraine. *Organization*, 16(6): 829–853.

Lave, J. & Wenger, E. 1991. *Situated Learning: Legitimate Peripheral Participation*. Cambridge, U.K.: Cambridge University Press.

Leung, K. 2008. Methods and measurement in cross-cultural management. In P. B. Smith, M. F. Peterson & D. C. Thomas (Eds.), *The Handbook of Cross-Cultural Management Research*: 59–76. Los Angeles, CA: Sage.

Levinson, D. J., Darrow, C. N., Klein, E. B., Levinson, M. H. & McKee, B. 1978. *The Seasons of a Man's Life*. New York: Ballantine Books.

Lounsbury, M. & Ventresca, M. 2003. The new structuralism in organizational theory. *Organization*, 10(3): 457–480.

Marschan-Piekkari, R. & Welch, C. (Eds.). 2005. *Handbook of Qualitative Research Methods for International Business* (5th ed.). Cheltenham, U.K.: Edward Elgar.

Martin, C. A. & Tulgan, B. 2001. *Managing Generation Y: Global Citizens Born in the Late Seventies and Early Eighties*. Amherst, MA: HRD Press.

Matsumoto, D. & van de Vijver, F. J. R. (Eds.). 2011. *Cross-Cultural Research Methods in Psychology*. Cambridge, U.K.: Cambridge University Press.

Mayrhofer, W. 2000. Coordination of research networks: Market, bureaucracy, and clan in the Cranfield Network on European Human Resource Management (Cranet-E). In C. Brewster, W. Mayrhofer & M. Morley (Eds.), *New Challenges for European Human Resource Management*: 290–312. London: Macmillan.

Mayring, P. 2007. *Qualitative Inhaltsanalyse: Grundlagen und Techniken* (9th ed.). Weinheim: Beltz.

Meyer, J. W. & Rowan, B. 1977. Institutionalized organizations: Formal structure as myth and ceremony. *American Journal of Sociology*, 83(2): 340–363.

Meyer, J. W., Boli, J., Thomas, G. M. & Ramirez, F. O. 1997. World society and the nation-state. *American Journal of Sociology*, 103(1): 144–181.

Miles, R. E., Snow, C. C., Mathews, J. A. & Coleman, H. J. 1997. Organizing in the knowledge age: Anticipating the cellular form. *Academy of Management Executive*, 11(4): 7–20.

Mutch, A. 2003. Communities of practice and habitus: A critique. *Organization Studies*, 24(3): 383–401.

Nohria, N. & Ghoshal, S. 1997. *The Differentiated Network*. San Francisco, CA: Jossey-Bass.

Özbilgin, M. & Tatli, A. 2005. Book review essay: Understanding Bourdieu's contribution to organization and management studies. *Academy of Management Review*, 30(4): 855–869.

Peterson, M. F. 2001. International collaboration in organizational behavior research. *Journal of Organizational Behavior*, 22(1): 59–81.

Polanyi, K. 1978. *The Great Transformation: Politische und ökonomische Ursprünge von Gesellschaften und Wirtschaftssystemen*. Frankfurt am Main: Suhrkamp.

Poole, M. S. & Van de Ven, A. H. 1989. Using paradox to build management and organization theories. *Academy of Management Review*, 14(4): 562–578.

Rousseau, D. M. 1995. *Psychological Contracts in Organizations: Understanding Written and Unwritten Agreements*. Thousand Oaks, CA: Sage.

Rousseau, D. M. & Schalk, R. 2000. *Psychological Contracts in Employment: Cross-National Perspectives*. Thousand Oaks, CA: Sage.

Schein, E. H. 1978. *Career Dynamics: Matching Individual and Organizational Needs*. Reading, MA: Addison-Wesley.

Schwartz, S. H. 1999. A theory of cultural values and some implications for work. *Applied Psychology: An International Review*, 48(1): 23–47.

Scott, W. R. 2001. *Institutions and Organizations* (2nd ed.). Thousand Oaks, CA: Sage.

Super, D. E., Crites, J. O., Hummel, R. C., Mose, H. P., Overstreet, P. & Warnath, C. F. 1957. *Vocational Development: A Framework for Research*. New York: American Book–Stratford Press.

Twenge, J. M. 2006. *Generation Me: Why Today's Young Americans Are More Confident, Assertive, Entitled—and More Miserable Than Ever Before*. New York: Free Press.

Ulrich, J. M. & Harris, A. L. (Eds.). 2003. *GenXegesis: Essays on Alternative Youth (Sub)Culture*. Madison: University of Wisconsin Press.

Van Maanen, J. (Ed.). 1977. *Organizational Careers: Some New Perspectives*. London: Wiley.

Warnecke, H.-J. 1993. *Revolution der Unternehmenskultur: Das Fraktale Unternehmen*. Berlin: Springer.

Weber, M. [1905] 2002. *The Protestant Ethic and the Spirit of Capitalism*. New York: Penguin Books.

Weick, K. E. 1995. What theory is not, theorizing is. *Administrative Science Quarterly*, 40(3): 385–390.

Wenger, E. 1999. *Communities of Practice: Learning, Meaning and Identity*. Cambridge, U.K.: Cambridge University Press.

Whitley, R. 1999. *Divergent Capitalisms: The Social Structuring and Change of Business Systems*. Oxford, U.K.: Oxford University Press.

Part IV

Country Chapters

Introduction to the Country Chapters

The following 11 chapters allow the reader to get a closer understanding of each of the countries involved in the 5C project (with the exception of Malaysia). As noted in Chapter 1, while the United Kingdom findings were not part of the original data used to generate our collective findings and conceptual frameworks, the country team there used the same methods as the rest of 5C and thus the results can be effectively compared with other country chapters.

Each of the following country chapters provides some historical background and information on the career environment in the respective country context. The chapters cover very similar categories of results, reflecting the primary themes of career success and career transitions found in the earlier chapters. These chapters emerge from a similar methodological process, but vary slightly from one another in reflection of how the respective authors chose to report and display their results.

The country chapters are intended for researchers, educators, students, managers and others—essentially anyone who is interested in how careers play out in the provided country contexts and beyond. As with cross-cultural interactions in real life, the reader should use information from within and across countries to build and extend intercultural competence in other countries. In other words, effective cross-cultural competence allows one to learn how to learn.

We urge the practical audience reading this book—managers, expatriates, career practitioners and employees of all types—to extrapolate the country chapter findings beyond careers to other practical implications. The way that one defines and makes meaning of career success has direct as well as implied lessons for motivation. Career transitions and the paths people take to achieve them have implications for personal, social and organizational change. These are just starting points, of course. The active and insightful reader will extrapolate many more.

10

Careers in Austria

Katharina Chudzikowski, Barbara Demel,
Wolfgang Mayrhofer and Astrid Reichel

Country Background

Culture

Austria is part of the Western European culture cluster, which emphasizes intellectual autonomy, egalitarianism and harmony more than any
other world region. In addition, it is the lowest region on hierarchy and
embeddedness (Schwartz, 2006; for more on this concept see Chapter
2). Austria itself is low on embeddedness, hierarchy and mastery, and is
an autonomy culture. People are viewed as autonomous, bounded entities. They cultivate and express their own preferences and find meaning
in their own uniqueness. Intellectual autonomy, the independent pursuit of one's own ideas and intellectual directions, is especially encouraged in Austria. Such values provide challenges for the social fabric and
are counter-balanced by egalitarianism. Generally, Austrians commit to
cooperate and to pay attention to other people's welfare. Compromise is
important in political decision making. This is especially true for negotiations between actors representing opposite interests, for example trade
unions and employers' associations, and is expressed in social partner-
ship governing labor relations. Harmony governs relations to the natural and social world. This leads to a tendency to appreciate the social
and natural world and fit into it as it is rather than direct or exploit it
(Schwartz, 1999, 2006).

Economic and Demographic Trends

Economically, Austria is well developed and enjoys a high standard of
living. In 2008 it had a GDP per capita (purchasing power parity) of
about $40,400, ranking 21st in the world and fourth in the European

Union. Its economy consists of a large service sector (67.4 percent of GDP), a sound industrial sector (30.7 percent of GDP) and a small (1.9 percent of GDP) but highly developed agricultural sector. Following several years of economic growth, the global downturn in 2008 led to a recession that has only recently stopped. Since the fall of the Iron Curtain around 1989/90, the Austrian economy has greatly benefited from strong commercial relations with Central, Eastern and Southeastern Europe, especially in the banking and insurance sectors. Because these sectors have been very vulnerable to recent international financial instabilities, some of Austria's largest banks have required government support (CIA Factbook, 2009).

At the last official census in 2001, Austria's population was 8,032,926 (Statistik Austria, 2009). In 2007 more than 1.6 million lived in Vienna, Austria's capital. About 15 percent of the population are under 15 years old; 18 percent are 65 years or older. Life expectancy for women is 82.6 years and for men 76.6. The average number of children per woman is 1.39, clearly below the "replacement level" of about 2 and well below the post-war maximum of 2.82. Although the death rate exceeds the birth rate, Austria has a small positive population growth rate of 0.052 percent because of migration (CIA Factbook, 2009). Almost 13 percent of people living in Austria were born abroad, which is beyond the comparable figure for classical immigration countries such as the U.S.A. (11 percent; see Statistik Austria, 2009). The estimation of net migration in 2009 reached +1.85 migrants/1,000 inhabitants (CIA Factbook, 2009). Immigration is dominated by individuals from the former Yugoslavian states, Germans, Turks and Czechs. Austria has a tradition of sheltering refugees from nearby countries, for example the Sudeten Germans fleeing from Czechoslovakia, emigrants leaving their countries after the Hungarian uprising in 1956 and the Prague Spring in 1968, and especially refugees from the civil war in the former Yugoslavia in the 1990s (Statistik Austria, 2009; Szabo & Reber, 2007).

Despite the positive population growth rate, Austria will face severe demographic challenges in the future: 2050 prognoses estimate a population of 9.5 million people, who on average will be six years older than in 2007, with the percentage of inhabitants over 60 years reaching about 34 percent (Statistik Austria, 2008). The aging society is especially challenging because Austria is a welfare state with high expenditures on social welfare (€9,123 per inhabitant per year compared to the EU average of €6,521; see Eurostat, 2009). Owing to generous early retirement arrangements, the actual retirement age is well below the official age of 65 years for men and 60 years for women. For example, Austrian men on average retire more than six years before the official retirement age

(ORF, 2009). Accordingly, Austria has the third highest expenditures for pensions in the European Union (€ 3,949 per inhabitant per year against the EU average of €2,571; see Eurostat, 2009).

Educational System

Education in Austria is compulsory for children between the ages of 6 and 15 years. They spend their first four years in primary education. Secondary education is divided into three streams leading to a comprehensive and demanding final examination called *Matura*: academic secondary schools (eight years); lower secondary school (four years) plus upper secondary school (four years); or lower secondary school plus vocational secondary education (five years). The school system is governed by nationwide uniform regulations. No fees are charged for attendance at state-run schools. About 10 percent of primary and secondary schools are private.

Successfully completing secondary education is necessary for studying at a national university. Austria has 22 public universities. The state almost holds a monopoly for higher education, which is publicly funded and free of charge for students. Private universities have admitted students only since 2001. Most of the 12 accredited private universities have a single focus, often business, psychology or medicine, and have less than 1,000 students (Szabo & Reber, 2007; University of Vienna, 2008). Higher education also includes almost 300 degree programs in about 20 public universities of applied science, a specific type of higher education institution (Fachhochschulen, 2008).

Currently the Austrian system of higher education is completing the so-called Bologna process initiated by 29 European countries (Austria being one of them) in 1999. This process aims at a "European higher education area" in which students and graduates can move freely between countries, using prior qualifications in one country as acceptable entry requirements for further study in another. In line with the Bologna declaration, Austria introduced a three-cycle system: the bachelor's for a first degree of university education of three years ("first cycle"); the master's for subsequent study ("second cycle," most often two years); and Ph.D. studies ("third cycle," most often three years). In addition, the European Credit Transfer System (ECTS) for measuring workload and making it comparable across Europe was established (Austrian Federal Ministry of Science and Research, 2009).

When aiming for a vocational career, young people usually complete lower secondary school and one year of prevocational school. In most cases, formalized apprenticeship training lasts three years and takes places at two different, company-based training and compulsory attendance of a part-time vocational school. This training is only possible in legally recognized apprenticeship trades and is completed with a final exam (*Gesellenprüfung*). Once licensed, journeymen/-women work in their profession or opt for further education towards a master craftsman exam. Currently about 40 percent of all Austrian teenagers enter apprenticeship training upon completion of compulsory education, a number which has been declining since 1981 (Austrian Federal Ministry for Education, Arts and Culture, 2009). The importance of formalized vocational training has had its roots in the traditional, highly regulated system of guilds since medieval times, the quite highly regulated labor market and the amount of regulations that companies face when offering products and services.

Career-Related Trends and Patterns

Over the past two decades, two major trends have had a strong influence on emerging career patterns in Austria. First, there has been an increase in the labor force participation of Austrian women, in particular a trend towards a continuous career with only a relatively short interruption of work due to motherhood. The 2009 level of female participation in the labor force amounted to 54.8 percent. This constituted a strong increase compared to a 48.8 percent rate in the mid-1990s (male 2009 68.2 percent, 1995 70.8 percent; see Statistik Austria, 2010b). Combined with the low total fertility rate this has led to different career patterns for women (Statistik Austria, 2010a).

Second, the fall of the Iron Curtain in the early 1990s led to a strong influx of migrant workers and immigrants, in particular from Central and Eastern Europe, and an increasing internationalization of the workforce. This widened the horizons of both employers and employees for careers beyond national borders. Especially in the regions bordering neighboring states, there is a remarkable exchange of members of the workforce, leading to new forms of international "day travelling."

Sample

We chose our sample—18 individuals (10 males, 8 females)—in line with the idea of dimensional sampling (Glaser & Strauss, 1967: 69)

Table 10.1 Austria sample profile

Occupation	Business graduates		Nurses		Blue-collar workers	
Generation	Older	Younger	Older	Younger	Older	Younger
Gender	1 female, 2 male	1 female, 2 male	3 female	3 female	3 male	3 male
Educational background	University	University	Nursing schools	Nursing schools	Master craftsman's certificate; apprenticeship certificate	Master craftsman's certificate; apprenticeship certificate

Total N = 18 (8 females and 10 males), with 6 business graduates, 6 nurses and 6 blue-collars. The average age is 28.9 for the younger generation and 57.6 for the older generation.

and used: age and career phase, i.e. early (having worked for about two years) versus late career stages (shortly before or after retirement); profession, i.e. blue-collar worker, businesspeople and nurses; and gender, i.e. female versus male.

We approached the members of our sample through institutions and associations, as well as companies representative of specific industries. The younger business graduates all come from the largest business school in Vienna. Nurses were approached through clinical health centers and social services associations. Blue-collar workers were contacted through professional associations or companies. The remaining interviewees were contacted via personal networks. There was an attempt to spread the sample across geographical sub-regions. Almost half of the interviewees work in the countryside (Tyrol and Lower Austria). The remaining half are based in Vienna. Table 10.1 shows the profile of the sample involved in the interviews.

Note that the nurse sample is dominated by females and the blue-collar sample by males. This is more or less representative of the respective gender ratio.

Findings

In this section, we first examine the main themes of career success meanings. This includes a brief discussion of occupational and generational specifics. Second, the main themes of career transitions are summarized, including causes, influencing factors as well as desired and actual outcomes of career transitions. For both issues, we proceed as follows: after summarizing the main themes, we illustrate them by quotes taken from the original interviews and translated into English.

Meanings of Career Success

Across Groups

Most of the perceived meanings of career success are—in order of importance—linked to the person, the job and interaction with the environment. Across occupations, the five most important meanings of career success include satisfaction (mentioned by 16 interviewees), with an emphasis on satisfaction with one's career and enjoyment and fun.

> Career for me is satisfaction with the job, satisfaction with the tasks . . . and ongoing development, getting to know new fields. That is actually career as well as career success for me.
>
> (Younger businesswoman)

Similarly, achievement is mentioned by 16 interviewees, with a focus on promotion or hierarchical advancement and financial achievement.

> To me success means organizing something; meanwhile it has also become my task to lead other people, a team. I am superior in a hierarchical sense; and that means success to me.
>
> (Younger female nurse)

Another central category is learning and development (mentioned by 12 interviewees). Importance is put on formal learning, for example certificates.

> Well, I would say that if I had a master craftsman's certificate then I would consider myself as being successful.
>
> (Younger male blue-collar worker)

Furthermore, certain job/task characteristics are perceived as important success factors. In particular, 11 interviewees regard having autonomy and responsibility in their job as career success.

> It is interesting once you are able to manage or control things and to lead something by yourself; actually reaching that has to be a goal in life, you cannot always be the "slave in a rowing boat."
>
> (Younger businessman)

In addition, recognition is important to ten interviewees; above all it is about receiving positive feedback.

> For me, career success is when one of my patients tells me, "Alexandra, great that you are here today. I have been missing you!" . . . Yes, that means career

success for me, because then I know why I work every day for 12 hours. Yes, indeed that means career success for me.

(Younger female nurse)

Another central category among the most important meanings of career success is one's social working environment (mentioned by nine interviewees), with an emphasis on relationships with peers, superiors and customers.

Well, critical factors for success are interest in your job, technical know-how training . . . good working atmosphere, good relationship to your colleagues, and to have superiors supporting you.

(Younger male blue-collar worker)

Occupational Specifics

Our results show some occupational specifics, in particular for nurses. While satisfaction and achievement are important to all three occupational groups, they are least mentioned by nurses. Further differences relate to sublevel categories. While blue-collars and business school graduates strongly emphasize being satisfied with their career (blue-collars) and their work or job (business), nurses do not show a specific focus. Concerning achievement, both promotion and advancement are most important to all three occupational groups. Additionally, blue-collar workers and business school graduates, but not nurses, emphasize financial achievement. In turn, nurses underline the importance of gaining or extending one's influence.

All three groups show the same pattern for learning and development by particularly emphasizing formal learning. For job/task characteristics, it is again the group of nurses who show a distinct pattern by putting less weight on job/task characteristics. The only job/task characteristic that is mentioned by more than one nurse is challenge. For blue-collar workers, having autonomy, responsibility and challenges at work is most important. Business school graduates see having scope and variety of tasks, autonomy and responsibility as crucial success factors. One meaning of career success that is again more emphasized by nurses is performing one's role.

Generational Specifics

The two most important meanings of career success, satisfaction and achievement, are mentioned a bit more by the older generation. Most

differences can be observed on sublevel categories: The younger generation put slightly more emphasis on satisfaction with one's career as well
as enjoyment and fun. The older generation prefer life quality.

> I think that people of the older generation are actually pretty satisfied with
> what they have achieved, and I believe that younger people are striving for a
> little bit more.
>
> (Younger male blue-collar worker)

Concerning achievement, both generations focus on promotion or
hierarchical advancement. In addition, the older generation mentions
financial achievement as well as gaining or extending influence a lot
more. Another category more central to the older generation is self-
actualization, with a focus on goal fulfillment.

> Yes, I would say being in the leading position within my ward, I would value
> that as being successful in my field.
>
> (Older female nurse)

A further category more central to the older generation is performing
one's role. The same is true for the social working environment, with a
focus on a positive relationship to superiors. The latter is not mentioned
at all by the younger generation.

> When I come home and I can tell myself "Yes, I have done a really good job
> today." I have always been a role model to younger colleagues. They admire
> that I manage to fulfill my duties and at the same time be in a good mood.
>
> (Older female nurse)

Job/task characteristics are important to both generations. On the sub-
level categories, most important to the younger generation is having
responsibility in their job, a category that is hardly mentioned by the
older generation.

> Career success to me is when you are asked to take on more responsibility, and
> when you face new challenges and fulfill expectations then you get ahead.
>
> (Younger male blue-collar worker)

Scope and variety of tasks are also emphasized a lot more by the younger
generation. Autonomy and challenge are quite important to both
generations.

   Clearly, for both generations the kind of work is important, yet differences occur. Satisfaction, fun, having responsibility, and scope and
variety of tasks are more important for the young generation, while

self-actualization and performing one's role are more important for the older generation. Arguably, this is the result of a combined developmental (career stage) and cohort effect. In the early stages of a career, many people are uncertain about what their work will look like and how they will enjoy it. In the later phases of life, it becomes more important to contribute to one's own development and that of the institutions one is part of. In terms of generations, there is some evidence that members of more recent generations put a stronger emphasis on fun and joy in the world of work (see the literature on Gen Y, e.g. Martin & Tulgan, 2001).

Causes of Career Transitions

The three most frequently mentioned causes for career transitions across all occupations are (in their order of frequency): own initiative, both internally and externally attributed; counsel and encouragement by others; and macro factors. In general, intrinsic motives and support from the social working environment trump factors like governmental policies, economic influences and the labor market when looking at triggers for career transition.

> I didn't want to be dependent on others anymore. You are always dependent in any way but I just wanted to try to act independently.
>
> (Older businessman)

Across occupations, family role, especially motherhood obligations, and organization-related causes, for example promotions, redevelopment, organizational restructuring (nurses) or change in organizational leadership (business graduates), are most often mentioned by nurses, followed by business graduates. Moreover, internally attributed motives are influenced by task specifics which are only influential for nurses and business graduates about to change job.

> Well, I never wanted to be a software engineer. I got ahead. Within four days I was system assistant. A system assistant was somebody who was sorting punch cards. . . . I told them I don't want that.
>
> (Older businessman)

For internal motives beyond task-related characteristics, there are some occupational specifics too: business graduates aspire to further development and more work–life balance; nurses share the desire for something new with business graduates; blue-collar workers seek new opportunities.

I had the opportunity to work again as an electrician, but then I thought, "All right, though I will earn a bit less I will do something totally new now [as a snowboard instructor]." I will have a lot of time for reflecting and will experience something completely different, and that is important to me.

(Older male blue-collar worker)

Furthermore, looking at relational influences, the boss seems to be an important key person and influential for changing job, mostly for blue-collar workers and business graduates. Some causes of career transitions can be summarized as driven by certified graduation for nurses and business graduates, and by completing obligations for business graduates. Noticeably, there are particularities in terms of age groups. Internal motives are mentioned twice as much by younger workers, while older workers point to external factors on the organizational and economic levels. Family as well as health issues are only mentioned by older workers.

Well, the transition from the hospital to mobile nursing led to less stress and more time for the family.

(Older female nurse)

Influencing Factors of Career Transitions

Looking at influencing factors of career transitions, relationships play a major role across occupations. Support is a key theme related to superiors and family. The following quote shows an example of lack of support in the work context.

It was also because of my boss. The situation was just not right, a few promises were not kept and you always had to keep track of it yourself so that you at least got something out of it.

(Younger businessman)

Furthermore, professional networks and organizations are influential for career transitions across all occupations. There are also some occupational specifics. Half of the interviewees working as nurses stressed organizational support. Supportive peers are only mentioned by nurses and blue-collar workers. Interestingly, missing support from family was most mentioned by younger female nurses. Support by friends is most mentioned by nurses and to a lesser extent by business graduates. Influencing factors corresponding to the social working environment are an issue for both age groups, although younger workers mention peers more while older workers highlight superiors as the reference group.

Structural factors such as education and training are most highlighted by nurses and business graduates as influential for career transitions. In contrast, blue-collar workers emphasize the role of luck and contingencies for career changes.

> To achieve something at work you definitely need diligence and persistence, and luck too. Yes, I really have to say, luck is always a factor.
>
> (Older male blue-collar worker)

Desired and Actual Outcomes of Career Transitions

Individuals differ considerably in terms of desired outcomes, since there exists no single outcome desired by all professional groups. Two not mutually exclusive explanations emerge. First, because of person-related factors, individuals differ in their expectations regarding career transitions and their ability to express these expectations. Second, career transitions themselves are located on a continuum with two extremes. On the one end there are career transitions that are vague, linked with many hopes and fears, and loaded with a great number of expectations. On the other end of the continuum, career transitions exist linked with a clear major theme and clearly focused outcomes.

Looking at actual as opposed to desired outcomes of transitions, the following themes across all professions emerge: work–life context, stressing time for family and friends; task-related changes emphasizing responsibility; recognition; satisfaction with the job; personal knowledge; and learning. Reflecting these themes in more detail, it is worth noting that mainly female nurses and business graduates mention work–life context, especially work–life balance, and change in lifestyle issues.

As regards task-related issues as actual outcomes, blue-collar workers especially mention a lot of themes besides responsibility: internally, flexibility and freedom and the work becoming more interesting; externally, they perceive a change in workload intensity and working hours.

There also seems to be an occupation-related boundary between occupations concerning recognition as a desired outcome. Business graduates point to recognition in general terms, while nurses and blue-collar workers emphasize positive feedback and appreciation in greater detail. In contrast, salary and the financial situation are a theme for mainly blue-collars and business graduates.

> I got quite a few job offers actually . . . and I turned them down for different reasons. Some didn't pay enough.
>
> (Younger businessman)

Implications

Our analyses lead to a number of implications for dealing with careers in Austria:

- Austria has a lot of legal regulations governing work. Disregarding them leads, at best, to less effective organizational career decisions or, at worst, to costly and tedious legal disputes and estrangement between organizations and their employees.
- Institutional actors play an important role in careers. In particular, trade unions, works councils and employers' associations have a voice in hiring, promotion and dismissal decisions. Examples include their role in the legislative process and in collective agreements which govern employment; and works councils' role in the dismissal process, which is legally guaranteed.
- A legally binding list of descriptions of specific occupations (*Ausbildungsberufe* or *Lehrberufe*) constitutes and governs much of the career space for skilled work. Occupations on this list range from popular choices such as hairdresser or car mechanic to less frequently chosen occupations, for example watchmaker or bookbinder.
- Occupations are an essential element of identity construction and important for individual career decisions. This ranges back to the medieval system of guilds regulating, among others, the access to the craft and the number of craftsmen. For example, many adolescents frequently face the question: "Which occupation will you take in the future?" Less often they hear formulations such as "How will you earn your money?" It also means that flexible concepts of work that do not clearly indicate what job an individual does (as a shorthand for which occupation she or he is in) do meet some resistance.

References

Austrian Federal Ministry for Education, Arts and Culture. 2009. *Medium-Level Secondary Technical and Vocational Colleges.* Available at: http://www.bmukk.gv.at/enfr/school/bw_en/bw_en_bms.xml (accessed Dec. 22, 2009).

Austrian Federal Ministry of Science and Research. 2009. *Bericht über den Stand der Umsetzung der Bologna-Ziele in Österreich 2009.* Available at: http://www.bmwf.gv.at/fileadmin/user_upload/europa/bologna/bologna-bericht_2009.pdf (accessed Dec. 22, 2009).

CIA Factbook. 2009. *Austria.* Available at: https://www.cia.gov/library/publications/the-world-factbook/geos/au.html (accessed Dec. 20, 2009).

Eurostat. 2009. *Volkswirtschaftliche Gesamtrechnung.* Available at: http://epp.eurostat.ec.europa. eu/portal/page/portal/national_accounts/data/main_tables (accessed Dec. 22, 2009).

Fachhochschulen. 2008. *Fachhochschulstudiengänge in Österreich.* Available at: http://www.fach-hochschulen.at/ (accessed May 3, 2008).

Glaser, B. & Strauss, A. L. 1967. *The Discovery of Grounded Theory: Strategies for Qualitative Research.* Chicago, IL: Aldine.

Martin, C. A. & Tulgan, B. 2001. *Managing Generation Y: Global Citizens Born in the Late Seventies and Early Eighties.* Amherst, MA: HRD Press.

ORF. 2009. *Gesetzliches Pensionsalter als Illusion.* Available at: http://orf.at/091015-43681/?href=htt p%3A%2F%2Forf.at%2F091015-43681%2F43682txt_story.html (accessed Dec. 22, 2009).

Schwartz, S. H. 1999. A theory of cultural values and some implications for work. *Applied Psychology: An International Review,* 48(1): 23–47.

Schwartz, S. H. 2006. A theory of cultural value orientations: Explication and applications. *Comparative Sociology,* 5: 136–182.

Statistik Austria. 2008. *Oesterreichs Bevoelkerung waecht und altert, Prognose 2050: 9,5 Mio. Einwohner.* Available at: http://www.statistik.at/web_de/presse/033887 (accessed Dec. 20, 2009).

Statistik Austria. 2009. *Bevoelkerungsstand.* Available at: http://www.statistik.at/web_de/statistiken/ bevoelkerung/volkszaehlungen_registerzaehlungen/index.html (accessed Dec. 20, 2009).

Statistik Austria. 2010a. *Demographic Indicators.* Available at: http://www.statistik.at/web_en/sta-tistics/population/demographic_indices/demographic_indicators/index.html (accessed Dec. 20, 2010).

Statistik Austria. 2010b. *Ergebnisse Mikrozensus-Arbeitskräfteerhebung.* Available at: http:// www.statistik.at/web_de/statistiken/arbeitsmarkt/erwerbsstatus/erwerbspersonen/index. html?ssSourceSiteId=null (accessed Dec. 20, 2010).

Szabo, E. & Reber, G. 2007. Culture and leadership in Austria. In J. S. Chhokar, F. C. Brodbeck & R. J. House (Eds.), *Culture and Leadership Across the World:* 109–146. Mahwah, NJ: Lawrence Erlbaum.

University of Vienna. 2008. *Public and Private Universities.* Available at: http://www.univie.ac.at/ links/uni_uniinoe.html (accessed May 3, 2008).

11

Careers in China

Yan Shen

The Cultural Context

China has long been influenced by traditional Confucian values (Pun, Chin & Lau, 2000), emphasizing hierarchy, discipline, reciprocity, face (i.e. the respectability and/or deference which people can claim for themselves from others) (Ho, 1976: 883) and group orientation (Lockett, 1988) stressing in-group harmony and well-being (Leung & Kwong, 2003). These characteristics echo Schwartz's (2006) framework in which China is categorized as high in embeddedness (interdependence and shared collectivism), hierarchy (ascribed roles and obligations) and mastery (assertive actions to change the world), as well as Hofstede's (2001) cultural dimensions, with China high in power distance and collectivism.

In China, there is a strong cultural preference for continuing, stable, harmonious relations within hierarchical organizations (Ross, 1999: 17). A very salient feature of Chinese culture is its emphasis upon the interpersonal relationship, or *guanxi*, especially with people of higher social status, authority or prestige. Generally speaking, China is a personal relationship-based society (Hui, Lee & Rousseau, 2004: 233). *Guanxi* is defined as the direct or indirect interpersonal relationship to solicit favor (Leung, 2000; Verburg, Drenth, Koopman, van Muijen & Wang, 1999). The importance of *guanxi* in individuals' career development in China is stressed by many researchers (e.g. Bian, 2002; Li & Wright, 2000; Wong & Slater, 2002).

Chow, Deng and Ho (2000: 69) point out that individualism versus collectivism "has been identified as being particularly different between Anglo-American and Chinese-based cultures." However, during the transitional process from a closed, central planning system to an open, market-oriented system, Wong and Slater (2002) argue that the Chinese have become more individualistic, with neo-Confucian social values featuring the coexistence of individualism and collectivism and competing for better career opportunities, higher pay and individual satisfaction.

In China, mastery is represented by individuals' great efforts and desire for personal success and materialistic achievement, and the society values diligence and hard work (Leung, 2008). Learning (e.g. formal education) becomes the means rather than the end for high achievement (Ng, 2003). Consequently, Chinese parents have very high expectations for their children's academic performance in school and are willing to invest a lot of time and money in formal and informal education and training to enhance their children's competitiveness in their future careers.

Economic and Demographic Trends

China had a very limited global economic presence before the 1980s. However, it has progressively become a very important global player since its open-door reform in 1978. According to the National Bureau of Statistics, the average annual growth rate of GDP in China was 10.5 percent between 2003 and 2009. China was the third largest economy in terms of GDP in 2008 (World Bank, 2009), and one of the most attractive foreign direct investment destinations (UNCTAD, 2009).

With the massive layoffs across the state sector owing to the industrial restructuring process and the poor performance of many state-owned enterprises in the 1990s, there has been rapid development in the service industry and in the non-state sectors (such as the prosperity of various forms of foreign-invested enterprises and private companies).

The fast-changing economic and social landscape in China triggered significant shifts in intergenerational values orientation among different generation cohorts, i.e. consolidation (1950–65), cultural revolution (1966–76) and social reform (1977 to the present) (Egri & Ralston, 2004). Egri and Ralston (2004) found that the "social reform generation" attributes significantly higher importance to openness to change than the other generation cohorts, whereas the cultural revolution generation scored the highest in terms of self-enhancement featuring achievement, hedonism and power.

The "after-80 generation" is a more straightforward term used to refer to those who were born between 1980 and 1989 in urban areas of Mainland China when the one-child policy was implemented.[1] Stanat (2005) uses another term, China's Generation Y, to describe those who were born between 1981 and 1995. Compared with their parents, who had experienced the cultural revolution during which economic development was stagnant and education was greatly discredited, the after-80 generation (or Generation Y) is exposed to fast economic growth and intensified globalization, significant social change and a great focus upon university education. Their more entrepreneurial and individualistic values orientations indicate the dramatic organizational changes in a competitive market-based economy in China (Egri & Ralston, 2004; Ralston, Egri, Stewart, Terpstra & Yu, 1999; Stanat, 2005).

Educational System/Occupational Background

The ten-year cultural revolution seriously disrupted China's development in many aspects, including the education sector. Student enrollment in institutions of higher education hit the bottom in 1970, and it was not until 1978 that the number of enrollments in universities went back to the level of 1962 (China Statistics Bureau, 1996). In addition, business and management education was almost non-existent before the mid-1980s.

The past two decades have witnessed fast growth in the enrollment of undergraduate and graduate students across Chinese higher education institutions, particularly in business and management-related disciplines. Today, a bachelor's degree (i.e. four-year university education) is a must for many professional jobs. Nursing education has undergone big changes as well, with increasing requirements for continuing education for associate or bachelor's degrees to boost nursing quality.

Compared with businesspeople, blue-collars and nurses are not seen as high-status occupations. In a study of occupational prestige ratings and job preferences in China (Xu, 2000), blue-collar jobs (e.g. workers in state-owned enterprises, restaurant waiters, bus drivers and shop assistants) are among the lowest occupational prestige categories, whereas those featuring high political power (e.g. government officials), income (e.g. company directors or managers) and professional/technical skills (e.g. university professors, lawyers and computer engineers) are socially admired and preferred.

Career Trends and Patterns

The Chinese employment system was once characterized by lifetime employment, an egalitarian wage structure, state-controlled job allocation, and a rigid rural–urban and worker–cadre dichotomy before the 1990s (e.g. Bian, 2002; Chen, Wakabayashi & Takeuchi, 2004; Ding & Warner, 2001; Lin & Bian, 1991; Warner, 2004; Wong & Slater, 2002; Zhang, Hu & Pope, 2002; Zhu & Dowling, 2002). In terms of work careers, this left individuals with little freedom, leading to low career and occupational mobility. In the 1950s through 1980s people simply performed the job assigned by the government, regardless of their personal interests, abilities and future development plans.

With the transition from workplace-based welfare to a social welfare system (Cooke, 2005), the relaxation of household registration regulation and a free though immature contract-based labor market (Zhu & Dowling, 2002; Zhu & Warner, 2004), individuals now have much more freedom in designing their own future and have had more career opportunities in recent years. A variety of career guidance and counseling services is offered (Zhang et al., 2002) at many organizations, including career centers in most universities.

State-owned enterprises (SOEs) were the "golden bowl" before the 1990s because of their dominant position in the economy. People were proud of themselves if they could get the chance to work in an SOE. There was no strategic human resource planning. The HRM practices tended to focus on control and regulation rather than human resource planning or employee development (Leung & Kwong, 2003). Individuals exchanged job security and other free welfare with their loyalty and commitment to their companies.

The boom of private and foreign-invested enterprises as well as the poor performance of many SOEs has made working in the state sector no longer socially desirable. Human resource management in China has been undergoing a transformation from very traditional personnel management to more complicated strategic human resource management (Wei & Lau, 2005). Personal competencies and skills have become important factors in seeking employment (Ding & Warner, 2001; Zhu & Dowling, 2002) and promotion in the past decade, with much more emphasis on one's educational background (Bjorkman & Lu, 1999).

Walder, Li and Treiman (2000) developed a distinctive dual-path model—professional versus administrative career path in China. Findings from a study of a stratified sample of urban residents drawn from 14 cities in six provinces (Zhao & Zhou, 2004) support this model, indicating that both party membership and college education are important for promotion along the administrative line in the reform era, while education is much more critical for promotion along the professional line.

Findings From the Study

Sample

There were 28 interviewees gathered primarily through convenience sampling in Shanghai, one of the most developed cities in China. There were 12 parent–child pairs (i.e. the younger interviewees and their parents) in the sample. Table 11.1 shows the sample profile involved in the interviews. The reader will note that all the nurse interviewees are females. This is the general pattern in this specific industry.

Meanings of Career Success

Looking across the sample as a whole the following meanings of career success were coded by the research team for seven or more of the 28 research participants:

Achievement	(24 people)
Learning and development	(10 people)
Job/task characteristics	(10 people)
Social working environment	(9 people)
Job security	(9 people)
Self-actualization	(8 people)
Satisfaction	(8 people)
Performing one's role	(7 people)

What Can Be Learned From This?

A common pattern across the two generations and three occupations in China is that most interviewees focused predominantly upon

Table 11.1 China sample profile

Occupation	Businesspeople		Nurses		Blue-collar	
Generation	Older	Younger	Older	Younger	Older	Younger
N =	2	4	2	4	12	4
Gender	2 males	2 females, 2 males	2 females	4 females	5 females, 7 males	2 females, 2 males
N =	N = 6		N = 6		N = 16	

Total N = 28 (13 males and 15 females). The average age is 25.6 for the younger generation and 55.7 for the older generation.

achievement, such as financial achievement and advancement up the company ladder (see the two quotes below). Learning and development, particularly the opportunity for formal education and training, and job/task characteristics (e.g. the scope and variety of tasks) were another two important career success dimensions. The former one was salient for nurses (five out of six interviewees mentioned this), whereas the latter one was important for nurses and businesspeople (half of the interviewees mentioned this).

> An ideal career means progressive mobility, step by step, from basic business operations to real practices.
>
> (Younger businessman)

> From nurse, to head nurse, to the director of the whole nursing department, which is the highest position to me, I think it is a successful career.
>
> (Younger female nurse)

The subjective meanings of career success centered on dimensions related to the social working environment (including having a positive work environment and/or positive relationships with peers and colleagues), satisfaction and self-actualization.

> First, one must be happy and enjoy what he or she is doing. Unhappiness and non-interest do no good [in one's career].
>
> (Older businessman)

> Success means seeing my patients leaving the hospital with a healthy body— this gives me a sense of fulfillment.
>
> (Younger female nurse)

Except for the common drive for achievement, the younger and older groups conceptualized their meanings of career success quite differently. Most interviewees in the older group defined career success from an objective perspective. They were not concerned with satisfaction, social working environment and job-related characteristics. They also had lower expectations for learning and development, as well as self-actualization. Some interviewees regarded their lives and careers as "fate" or "a complete failure."

Traditional attitudes and behaviors such as stability, security and hard work were very evident in the older group. A typical statement was "No matter what you do, you should love it and try your best to perform it well." The older interviewees did not have the freedom to choose their own career paths when they were young; however, they valued loyalty and tried their best to perform their jobs well. Some interviewees believed that these qualities were missing in the younger generation, whom they regarded as overly oriented toward money and short-term gains:

> At that time, we were rewarded with a certificate rather than money. However, we still worked very hard because what we valued was not money, but things at the spiritual level. However, in today's market economy, money is over-stressed. . . . The younger generation considers money as the symbol of success and cares too much about money.
>
> (Older female blue-collar worker)

For the younger group, the definitions of career success were more diversified, although objective career success (such as achievement) was still emphasized by many younger interviewees. The younger group pursue change and challenge, value personal growth and opportunities to learn, and are not afraid of uncertainties. Some younger interviewees viewed their elderly colleagues as more family-oriented and less ambitious, and easily content with the status quo. As one younger interviewee mentioned, "The senior people work for the present and for their family; I'm working for my future." One interviewee explicitly differentiated her senior colleagues from herself:

> The senior colleagues are more principled and conservative. Their basic attitude towards work is doing their job well without committing any errors. To them, a successful career means staying with the same employer and securing a good pension after retirement. Because of their age, they are less competitive in society. They have closely linked their fate with that of the company. . . . I am more flexible and ambitious. . . . I like challenges and new environments. I prefer to work in a fast-growing company or industry, with an acceptable salary and task variety.
>
> (Younger businesswoman)

Career Success Themes in China

Tu, Forret and Sullivan (2006) suggest that people in transitional or less affluent economies tend to focus more on extrinsic rewards and job perks. Our findings provide some support for their arguments, in that "career success" in China seems to be largely defined by achievement and other external rewards. In addition, the findings are consistent with Schwartz's (2006) framework regarding the embeddedness and mastery cultural dimensions.

For the older group, since they had little control over the type of work they wanted to do, they simply forced themselves to like their jobs and worked hard to fulfill their assigned responsibility. Their traditional cultural values of being non-confrontational, tolerant and accommodating influence how they perceive their work experience. By contrast, the younger interviewees, particularly the younger businesspeople, are more protean-oriented. They want to achieve many things in their careers.

Generally speaking, the more autonomy and freedom individuals enjoy in their career development, the more diversified are career success definitions. This is a pattern clearly demonstrated by the businesspeople, who have a stronger educational background, more job alternatives and clearer career developmental goals.

It should be noted that, though "helping others" and "making a positive impact upon society" are doctrines always emphasized throughout the different levels of education in China, they were rarely mentioned as career success dimensions. There are three possible reasons for that. First, in a fast-changing transitional society, success is largely judged by material fortunes, and quick returns are desired and encouraged. That's why some older interviewees were proud of past "personal sacrifice" in their work life and criticized the shortsighted money-oriented behavior of the younger generation. Second, the younger individuals are seeking different types of expression in terms of career success and becoming more individualistic when their careers are much less determined by external institutional factors and they have the opportunity to manage and direct their own careers. They have learned that individual success is attainable if they work hard for it. Their values and beliefs have already shifted away from the traditional ones to some extent, particularly for those in Shanghai, where local economic development has already been highly integrated with the outside world. Third, it might be seen as superfluous to emphasize the above two categories, i.e. what is taken for granted.

"Job security" is much more valued in China than the other countries in our study. It is possibly due to fast economic development, with job insecurity as the norm rather than the exception. It is especially important for blue-collars because of their relatively weak competitiveness in the job market and the difficulty in landing other jobs if they lose their current ones.

Career Transitions

Career Transition Frequency

Many older interviewees remained at the same company or companies under the same administrative authority[2] for many years until their (forced) retirement or layoff. By contrast, the career lives for the younger group were much more diversified, particularly for the younger businesspeople, who had already worked for at least two companies on average in their 20s. Most nurses have remained at the same hospital since their graduation from nursing school or university, though they have rotated among different wards.

Internal/External Causes/Triggers

Career transitions can be the result of individuals' own initiatives and/or external factors. Among the various reasons, "organizationally driven factors," "macro factors" (e.g. government policies) and "individuals' own initiative" rank as the top three reasons that were frequently mentioned by interviewees.

The role of the external environment was so salient in the older interviewees' lives and work that their career paths were actually shaped by a series of external forces, such as assigned job relocation to less developed regions because of government calls to facilitate the economic development of the inland area, and layoff or forced early retirement because of national industrial restructuring.

> There are a lot of layoffs. Social reform requires the absorption of new blood and drainage of the old. I am old, and should follow the company's policy without objections and extra requirements. . . . I think life has its own course. Many things do not change with one's own will. Sometimes, even you work very hard, you may fail to realize what you want. . . . I believe in fate. Our life is already arranged by our destiny, though sometimes opportunity is also important.
>
> (Older female blue-collar)

For the older interviewees who either voluntarily or involuntarily accepted layoff or an early retirement package, many of them are now still working as temporary workers. In this sense, their career lives can be viewed from two different perspectives: before their (early) retirement, their careers were controlled by the government or organization, whereas their career transitions after retirement were mainly the result of their own initiative, such as the desire to get more money or overcome survival pressure.

The effects of the macro environment upon the younger interviewees' career paths were very limited (only one of the 12 younger interviewees mentioned the role of macro factors in his career development). On the contrary, individual initiatives play a much more significant role in the younger group, such as their desire for something new or more challenging tasks, bad relations with the boss and/or lack of learning opportunities. In addition, organization-related factors (e.g. company bankruptcy or downsizing, internal transfer, or merger and acquisition), graduation, counseling and encouragement from other people are important externally driven causes or triggers of individuals' career transitions.

> People like us have the lowest salary, while at the same time we have to consider so many things. . . . I hope I can earn more money and learn more skills. . . . Having stayed in a company for a long time and learned everything, I would like to jump to another company so that I can learn more and meet more people in a new environment.
> (Younger female blue-collar worker)

Within the younger group, there are clear differences as well. Businesspeople with a higher educational background and expertise usually have stronger self-confidence and are more willing to challenge themselves. They have a clearer career goal and more career opportunities. As regards the blue-collar workers and the nurses, their educational background limits their career mobility to some extent. They are relatively passive in their career changes. Most nurses (five out of six) and blue-collars (13 out of 14) had experienced career changes owing to merger and acquisition, internal transfer and job rotation.

Individuals' Career Management

Career management in China has experienced tremendous change over the past two decades. There are very salient generational differences. The younger interviewees used multiple approaches to manage their career transitions, such as active job search, and formal education and training. The younger business school graduates were the most active in managing and designing their career paths. Most of their career moves were individually and purposefully initiated, aiming towards their ultimate career goals.

External Influencing Factors of Career Transitions

The main influencing factors of career transitions include support from organizations, boss and superior, family and friends, as well as education and training, mentioned by at least 12 out of the 28 interviewees.

Guanxi not only plays a role in one's job-seeking process (e.g. ten interviewees found their current jobs through relationships with friends, former colleagues or some high-ranking people in the companies) but also partly determines one's promotion opportunities, particularly in state-owned enterprises.

> Promotion is dependent upon "relationship" rather than educational background. If I am the plant director and think that your overall moral quality and individual ability are OK, I will develop you, sometimes even regardless of your individual competence, because it can be enhanced in future work. Then your fate is linked with mine—you are promoted or demoted together with me.
>
> (Older male blue-collar worker)

> My educational background enables me to secure this job . . . the key is that you have learned relevant knowledge and undergone the university training process . . . you have learned how to study.
>
> (Younger businessman)

Family influence cannot be ignored, particularly in the nurse group. For example, some nurses mentioned that they chose this occupation because their parents thought it was quite stable. Considering that the older generation in China usually values job stability and nursing is often regarded as "a female job," it is not surprising to see the strong family influence upon these interviewees' career lives.

One clear difference among the three occupations is that the blue-collar group more frequently referred to "support from family and friends," "network" and "job search assistance" as the important influencing factors in their career transitions. Compared with the other two groups, most of the blue-collars lacked competitiveness in the labor market, particularly the older ones in terms of their educational background, financial situation and individual competences. Therefore they might have to rely more on external help in their career transitions.

Themes and Implications

Several themes emerge from the findings that are important for practitioners, particularly for global companies.

The Strong Need for Achievement

- Achievement is the single dominant career success dimension in China.

- A well-designed career development plan based on effective performance assessment and motivation is critical.
- The management needs to understand the various achievement-related needs of the younger generation, such as financial achievement, career/job mobility, and employability.

The Importance of Education and Training

- Education and training are very important in today's job-hunting and career-building process. The younger generation are much more proactive in managing their career development, trying hard to strengthen their personal abilities through various kinds of formal and informal educational programs.
- Companies need to offer effective training programs, since learning and development are among the key career success dimensions for the younger generation.

The Psychological Contract Has Changed

- Individuals have reconstructed their psychological contract with their employers, replacing organizational commitment with the desire for individual growth and success.
- Person–job and person–organization fit, which were seldom considered by the older generation, are now important in individuals' career-related decisions.
- The younger generation are more demanding as regards what kind of leadership they want to follow in terms of role model ability and leadership competencies. "Conflict with boss and superiors" has become one of the reasons for their career changes.
- It is important to consider the more diversified needs of younger employees in addition to financial achievement.

Notes

1 http://en.wikipedia.org/wiki/After-eighty_generation.
2 Under the central planning system, even though people might have worked in different companies, these companies were subordinate to one administrative bureau that controlled personnel relocation across the different companies.

References

Bian, Y. 2002. Chinese social stratification and social mobility. *Annual Review of Sociology*, 28: 91–116.

Bjorkman, I. & Lu, Y. 1999. The management of human resources in Chinese–Western joint ventures. *Journal of World Business*, 34(3): 306–324.

Chen, Z., Wakabayashi, M. & Takeuchi, N. 2004. A comparative study of organizational context factors for managerial career progress: Focusing on Chinese state-owned, Sino-foreign joint venture and Japanese corporations. *International Journal of Human Resource Management*, 15(4/5): 750–774.

China Statistics Bureau. 1996. *Student Enrollment by Level and Type of School*. Available at: http://www.stats.gov.cn/ndsj/information/zh1/r051a (accessed July 10, 2007).

Chow, C. W., Deng, F. J. & Ho, J. L. 2000. The openness of knowledge sharing within organizations: A comparative study of the United States and the People's Republic of China. *Journal of Management Accounting Research*, 12: 65–95.

Cooke, F. L. 2005. Women's managerial careers in China in a period of reform. *Asia Pacific Business Review*, 11(2): 149–162.

Ding, D. Z. & Warner, M. 2001. China's labor-management system reforms: Breaking the "three old irons." *Asia Pacific Journal of Management*, 18(3): 315–334.

Egri, C. P. & Ralston, D. A. 2004. Generation cohorts and personal values: A comparison of China and the U.S. *Organization Science*, 15(2): 210–220.

Ho, D. Y. 1976. On the concept of face. *American Journal of Sociology*, 81(4): 867–884.

Hofstede, G. 2001. *Culture's Consequences* (2nd ed.). Thousand Oaks, CA: Sage.

Hui, C., Lee, C. & Rousseau, D. M. 2004. Employment relationships in China: Do workers relate to the organization or to people? *Organization Science*, 15(2): 232–240.

Leung, A. S. M. 2000. Gender differences in guanxi-behaviors: An examination of PRC state-owned enterprises. *International Review of Women and Leadership*, 6(10): 48–59.

Leung, K. 2008. Chinese culture, modernization, and international business. *International Business Review*, 17(2): 184–187.

Leung, K. & Kwong, J. Y. Y. 2003. Human resource management practices in international joint ventures in Mainland China: A justice analysis. *Human Resource Management Review*, 13(1): 85–105.

Li, J. & Wright, P. C. 2000. Guanxi and the realities of career development: A Chinese perspective. *Career Development International*, 5(7): 369–378.

Lin, N. & Bian, Y. 1991. Getting ahead in urban China. *American Sociological Review*, 97(3): 657–688.

Lockett, M. 1988. Culture and the problems of Chinese management. *Organization Studies*, 9(4): 475–496.

Ng, C. 2003. Re-conceptualizing achievement goals from a cultural perspective. Paper presented at the Joint Conference of NZARE and AARE, Auckland, New Zealand.

Pun, K. F., Chin, K. S. & Lau, H. 2000. A review of the Chinese cultural influences on Chinese enterprise management. *International Journal of Management Reviews*, 2(4): 325–338.

Ralston, D. A., Egri, C. P., Stewart, S., Terpstra, R. H. & Yu, K. C. 1999. Doing business in the 21st century with the new generation of Chinese managers: A study of generational shifts in work values in China. *Journal of International Business Studies*, 30(2): 415–427.

Ross, D. N. 1999. Culture as a context for multinational business: A framework for assessing the strategy–culture "fit." *Multinational Business Review*, 7(1): 13–19.

Schwartz, S. H. 2006. A theory of cultural value orientations: Explication and applications. *Comparative Sociology*, 5(2–3): 136–182.

Stanat, M. 2005. *China's Generation Y: Understanding the Future Leaders of the World's Next Superpower*. Paramus, NJ: Homa & Sekey.

Tu, H. S., Forret, M. L. & Sullivan, S. E. 2006. Careers in a non-Western context: An exploratory empirical investigation of factors related to the career success of Chinese managers. *Career Development International*, 11(7): 580–593.

UNCTAD. 2009. *Expansion of FDI Flows Through 2009 Anticipated by Transnational Corporations.* Available at: http://www.unctad.org/TEMPLATES/webflyer.asp?docid=9051&intItemID=1528 &lang=1 (accessed Jan. 17, 2009).

Verburg, R. M., Drenth, P. J. D., Koopman, P. L., van Muijen, J. J. & Wang, Z. M. 1999. Managing human resources across cultures: A comparative analysis of practices in industrial enterprises in China and the Netherlands. *International Journal of Human Resource Management,* 10(3): 391–410.

Walder, A. G., Li, B. & Treiman, D. J. 2000. Politics and life chances in a state socialist regime: Dual career paths into the urban Chinese elite, 1949–1996. *American Sociological Review,* 65(2): 191–209.

Warner, M. 2004. Human resource management in China revisited: Introduction. *International Journal of Human Resource Management,* 15(4/5): 617–634.

Wei, L. & Lau, C. 2005. Market orientation, HRM importance and competency: Determinants of strategic HRM in Chinese firms. *International Journal of Human Resource Management,* 16: 1901–1918.

Wong, A. L. Y. & Slater, J. R. 2002. Executive development in China: Is there any in a Western sense? *International Journal of Human Resource Management,* 13(2): 338–360.

World Bank. 2009. *Gross Domestic Product 2009.* Available at: http://siteresources.worldbank.org/ DATASTATISTICS/Resources/GDP.pdf (accessed Jan. 17, 2009).

Xu, X. 2000. Changes in the Chinese social structure as seen from occupational prestige ratings and job preference. *Sociology Research* (in Chinese), 3: 67–85.

Zhang, W., Hu, X. & Pope, M. 2002. The evolution of career guidance and counseling in the People's Republic of China. *Career Development Quarterly,* 50(3): 226–236.

Zhao, W. & Zhou, X. 2004. Chinese organizations in transition: Changing promotion patterns in the reform era. *Organization Science,* 15(2): 186–199.

Zhu, C. J. & Dowling, P. J. 2002. Staffing practices in transition: Some empirical evidence from China. *International Journal of Human Resource Management,* 13(4): 569–597.

Zhu, Y. & Warner, M. 2004. Changing patterns of human resource management in contemporary China: WTO accession and enterprise response. *Industrial Relations Journal,* 35(4): 311–328.

12

Careers in Costa Rica

Enrique Ogliastri and Jorge-Vinicio Murillo

Introduction

This chapter summarizes the 5C findings for Costa Rica in two parts: the first synthesizes the country's context and environment, particularly its cultural context, economic and demographic trends, professional trends and practices, the education system, and employment. In the second part, research results and implications are presented: the study samples, meanings of career success, and career transitions.

Cultural Context

Cultural context influences individuals' behavior and social characteristics. Costa Rica's culture is peculiar within a global context; as Hofstede (2001) stated, we are faced with the "Costa Rican anomaly." Costa Rica is the only country in the world that does not have a large power distance (elitism) despite having high collectivism.

In Schwartz's (2008) model Costa Rica, like most Latin American countries, is located close to the global average in all seven dimensions. We found a clear congruence with the main global cultural studies that describe Latin American culture as collectivist (Hofstede, 2001; House, Hanges, Javidan, Dorfman & Gupta, 2004; Triandis, 1995). Collectivist cultures place great emphasis on groups and think more in terms of "us." In addition, they tend to avoid direct confrontation. Costa Ricans tend to use language to avoid all types of confrontations; they often use diminutives, and words and phrases that "soften" dialogue and provoke less direct communication.

If Hofstede's (2001) classification is used to explain differences among national cultures, Costa Rica is different from other Latin American countries in two aspects: it has lower power distance, which can be interpreted as less social inequality, and it is more egalitarian in terms of gender.

Catholicism has indisputably been present throughout the country's history, political power and cultural traditions, as in many parts of Latin America. However, some other religions represent a growing and important presence in religious affiliation (Helmuth, 2000: 43). In terms of religion, Costa Rica still lacked a clear separation between the state and the Catholic church in 2011. The country can be classified as a traditional authority society with a trend toward post-materialist values in the World Values Survey (Inglehart, 1997).

Economic and Demographic Trends

Costa Rica is characterized by its stable democracy and high quality of life, when compared to the rest of Central America. Costa Rica's GDP per capita is US$6,060, ranking it among middle- to high-income countries.[1] The country's economy is driven by services, and its main product is eco-tourism. During the last decade, the country has developed a high-technology sector, which has led to the creation of electronics, software and medical device companies. As indicated by the World Economic Forum (2009), Costa Rica has a good business climate, ranking fourth in Latin America after Chile, Puerto Rico and Barbados.

Costa Rica's recent economic history was first based on import substitution development strategies, and later on an export diversification model, mostly focused on agricultural production and the expansion of its service sector. Within this economic context, it is worth highlighting the government's extensive participation in economic and social activities and political stability.

Beginning in 1986, Costa Rica began following a new economic model centered around liberalizing trade policies (and, in particular, promoting its export sector), liberalizing its financial system and governmental reform. This model formed the basis for a series of trade negotiations that concluded with the signing of several trade agreements, including the Dominican Republic–Central American Free Trade Agreement (CAFTA–DR). In addition, the country has experienced stable economic growth during the last decade, which was mostly due to foreign direct investment.

According to the Programa Estado de la Nación (2009), benefits of this new development model are not distributed equally among all social classes. Mid-level businesspeople and experts often receive a better income under this model; however, the same is not true for other social classes. In addition, the public sector has been the best employ-ment option for many, including middle-income and working classes; this has not been true for experts (or "knowledge workers").

Costa Rica is an attractive destination in Central America thanks to its political stability and relatively high quality of life; as a result, it receives the highest number of immigrants in the region, mostly coming from Nicaragua and other neighboring countries (OECD, 2010).

In the last 20 years, Costa Rica's social class structure has evolved: in 2011, there are fewer workers and small business owners than in the past. The number of mid-level businesspeople, experts and the upper middle class has increased, contrary to what has happened to agricul-tural, industrial and service sector workers. Costa Rican society has become more urban, and its population is concentrated in the central part of the country. Beginning in 1950, Costa Rica's characteristically young population began to grow older. This population structure has resulted from low and stable mortality, a decrease in infant mortality and an increase in immigration during the last two decades (Programa Estado de la Nación, 2009).

Professional Trends and Patterns

Between 1990 and 2003 the total number of university degrees awarded annually practically tripled in Costa Rica (going from 7,250 to 25,740) (Programa Estado de la Nación, 2008). In 2006 a little more than 28,700 were awarded, showing the growth the country has had in its supply of college graduates each year.

The arrival of different international companies to the country has caused some important changes in the professional market. The most popular courses of study in 2006 were education, administration, com-puters, psychology and law (Programa Estado de la Nación, 2008). In some of these areas, there is an imbalance between the graduate supply and the demands of the labor market. According to Jofré (2009) the nurs-ing profession offers many employment possibilities in the health care field. In Costa Rica the quality of academic programs in this area is not a determining factor that influences hiring. In addition, there is a demand for people in this field in the United States, where nurses can receive attractive salaries. On the other hand, traditional engineering programs maintain a constant supply and demand, while graduates from non-traditional engineering programs continue to have good employment offers, including software engineering, ICT, industrial maintenance, medical technology and information technology, among others. These engineers are well paid, and in some cases the labor demand is greater than the supply. Systems or computer engineers continue to experience a strong market, but those who lack quality education have greater difficulties finding jobs (Jofré, 2009).

Graduates in the field of business administration are still quite in demand, but there is also a large supply. In 2006, of the total number of programs offered in private universities, 26.6 percent corresponded to administration and economics. In public universities, these fields represented 11.4 percent (Programa Estado de la Nación, 2008). For graduates in these fields, English has become an essential requirement for competing. In addition, specialties in finance and project administration offer value added.

The Educational System and Employment Context

Costa Rica's 4.5 million inhabitants demonstrate high levels of literacy, approximately 95.9 percent of the population (UNDP, 2009). However, the average number of years in school for school-age children is one of the indicators that places the country in the middle of the rankings when compared with other countries in the world. In the last few years, the country has improved this indicator, thanks to the implementation of different governmental strategies to provide incentives for students to continue studying (Programa Estado de la Nación, 2009).

In the last 20 years, the number of women in the workforce in Costa Rica has grown constantly; the participation of men has remained constant.

In general, during the last few years, households with children ages 12–18 have been able to keep their children in school. However, there are marked class differences, with the greatest gap corresponding to working-class agricultural households. In addition, the percentage of households whose adolescent children have education levels lower than the national average is quite high among the working class (Programa Estado de la Nación, 2009).

Findings From the 5C Study in Costa Rica

Before presenting the main findings of the study on Costa Rica, it is important to clarify the methodology that was used to achieve these results.

For this study in Costa Rica, we held 19 in-depth, semi-structured interviews with people in three careers: business executives, nurses and blue-collar workers (for example field workers, drivers, domestic service providers). In each category we looked for two different groups: young adults, ages 25 to 34, and older adults, ages 55 to 60.

We used a qualitative, semi-structured and in-depth interview questionnaire, common to all countries in the 5C study. The format focused on four issues: the concept or definition of "career," the meaning of "career success," career self-management and dealing with career changes or transitions. The interviews were held in different places, such as the interviewees' offices, houses or other areas. Table 12.1 shows the interviewees' profiles.

Meaning of Career Success

Based on the answers provided in all of the interviews, we created the following categories in descending order of what career success means to the interviewees:

- work–family balance;
- satisfaction;
- job stability;
- achievement/reaching goals;
- economic recognition;
- learning and professional development;
- social working environment.

The meaning of career success varied among the three populations who were interviewed in Costa Rica. For example, for business executives, both generations agreed that career success was associated with economic or non-economic recognition and reaching their goals. Nurses agreed that career success meant more personal job satisfaction and patient satisfaction. Finally, blue-collar workers indicated that career

Table 12.1 Costa Rica sample profile

| | Business executives | | Nurses | | Blue-collar workers | |
	Young adults	Older adults	Young adults	Older adults	Young adults	Older adults
Number	3	3	3	3	3	4
Gender	2 men, 1 woman	3 men	1 man, 2 women	3 women	3 men	2 men, 2 women
	N = 6		N = 6		N = 7	

Total N = 19.

success seemed to be related to stability and economic recognition, as well as good interpersonal relationships at work.

The meaning of career success also changed from one generation to the other in Costa Rica. For young adults it meant achieving their goals and improving their socio-economic status. For older adults career success related more to the satisfaction of having had a positive impact in their job and achieving and enjoying a better quality of life for their family (see Table 12.2 about meanings of career success).

Let us analyze each one of the main categories identified by the interviewees.

Balance between work and family life was mentioned by both older blue-collar workers and business executives. For these interviewees career success was more comprehensive and implied greater stability, including emotional stability. In societies like Costa Rica, where families represent the central nucleus, it is easy to understand why family well-being is part of career success for these groups. This finding seems to correspond with the classification done by GLOBE (House et al., 2004), Hofstede (2001) and Schwartz (2008) on Latin American countries: that they tend to be collectivist. However, it is worth mentioning that the younger generations, who do not have their own families yet and have a more independent vision, do not consider this aspect fundamental to their career success.

Satisfaction was mentioned by business executives and nurses, referring to several points of view. The first had to do with satisfaction with a job well done and subsequent recognition, and the second had to do with job satisfaction or enjoyment. Older adults mentioned satisfaction more than young adults, probably because older adults related to this desire for recognition, which seemed to dominate the older generation's feeling of success. In the case of nurses, they often felt a calling, and their answers indicated that they felt satisfaction from providing a service to their patients.

Table 12.2 Stated meanings for career success

Population	Young adults (30 years old)	Mature adults (60 years old)
Blue-collar workers	Success is economic stability.	Success is being sure of (and having no worries about) economic stability.
Nurses	Career success is to reach the established goals.	Success is satisfaction with the achievements of a meaningful and well-done job.
Business executives	Success is achieving goals, and social and economic status.	Success is contributing to society and getting recognition.

For the blue-collar interviewees there is no sense of "career" as a progression or a stable economic activity, but of having a "job" at the present time.

Another element of career success was job stability, which was synonymous with tranquility. This issue was mostly mentioned by older adult blue-collar workers. Older nurses also indicated that this element was important. Stability is understood as feeling secure about job conditions and continuation and when salaries allow people to meet their needs and those of their families.

For young adults one important element of career success was reaching goals (achievement). For example, in the case of young business executives, success was related to reaching challenging goals. Young nurses also differed from older ones in this area: while young adults based success on meeting their goals and objectives, older nurses based it on job satisfaction, probably because they have already achieved most of their proposed goals and reached their desired state of well-being, or do not have the same desire to try to reach it. It is worth mentioning that business executives indicated that achieving goals was important from the perspective of providing them with recognition, and therefore success. One interviewee stated:

> It's relative [career success]. You try to get recognized for what you have done
> to reach your goals, and that allows you to be self-satisfied.

Recognition was one of the aspects that was most repeated by interviewees in terms of monetary and non-monetary compensation. The young generation identified career success with monetary recognition and achieving higher socio-economic status more than the older generation, who were more likely to mention non-monetary recognition as part of their success. It is worth mentioning that, in the case of blue-collar workers, the greater their economic stability the more value they placed on recognition as part of career success. Recognition was mostly identified by business executives and blue-collar workers; nurses tended to incorporate more issues of having a calling in their definition of success. Young blue-collar workers in Costa Rica seemed to include fewer elements in their definition of success. Presumably because of their lower education levels and lesser work experience, they seemed to have a hard time defining their requirements.

Learning and professional development were also mentioned by the interviewees. However, this issue was considered more important by the older generation of nurses and blue-collar workers. This might have to do with the way those careers are scaled hierarchically, depending on years of experience. Both generations of business executives considered professional development to be part of their success. Young interviewees in this group seemed to have a longer-term and more planned-out vision for their career success.

Finally, the social working environment or good interpersonal relationships represented part of career success for blue-collar workers. This element seemed to accentuate the collectivist culture of Costa Ricans and their tendency to live in harmony, avoiding conflict as much as possible (Ogliastri, McMillen, Arias, de Bustamante, Dávila, Dorfman, Fimmen, Ickis & Martinez, 1999).

Another perspective on career success in this study focuses on the internal or subjective views about careers for individuals who are making decisions and handling in the best possible way their career paths. Individuals may have an internal focus of control, believing that their success depends basically on their own efforts. They may well be oriented to self-realization and not to serving society or the organization. However, the last two orientations may be different dimensions and in fact be independent. To what extent are these individuals oriented to altruistic goals? To what extent do they feel external control of their careers?

The blue-collars have an external focus of control: their careers develop according to external factors and are not the result of their own making but of chance (i.e. a job in their close neighborhood). They have no uncertainty avoidance and live life as it presents itself in every turn of events. Even if their work is objectively positive for society, it is hard to elaborate in these terms when people do not feel in control of their careers.

The nurses feel control of their career up to a glass ceiling, when political support becomes essential to climb the ladder. However, they see their career as a calling from the beginning to the end. Doing their job well results in doing good for society.

On the other side, executives believe their career depends on good planning and preparation. They rely on contacts, networking, training for new jobs and opportunities that may come up. The older generation are oriented to serving society and consider that a key element in job transitions. They tend to understand better the role of external factors in career success and do have a proactive view about their career. As Table 12. 3 shows, generational differences are large in the role given to external factors in career success. The younger generation seem to be more

Table 12.3 Influencing factors upon career success

Population	Young adults (30 years old)	Mature adults (60 years old)
Blue-collar workers	External factors (i.e. luck) account for career success and opportunities.	External factors (opportunities).
Nurses	Internal factors, internal focus of control.	Both internal and external factors.
Business executives	Internal factors.	Both internal and external factors.

self-reliant, while the older generation have a more balanced view on the weight of external factors on career development.

Career Transitions

Different categories existed, which can be grouped by the motivation that interviewees in Costa Rica had to make a transition in their careers. These categories include:

- satisfactory culmination of studies;
- improving socio-economic conditions;
- increasing responsibilities (new challenges);
- professional improvement (new knowledge);
- promotion because of capabilities;
- dropping out of school;
- moving home.

By observing the data generated by this study in Costa Rica (Table 12.4), it seems that many career transitions that interviewees mentioned were due to external causes rather than personal motivations, more so than in most countries of the 5C study. One external factor that is worth highlighting was the satisfactory culmination of educational studies, which made the interviewees transition into a career. For many, this was the start of their career. Despite this, career transitions marked by internal, self-inflicted motivations were also commonly noted by the interviewees as important. The ones that were most often cited were improving socio-economic conditions, increasing responsibilities (new challenges) and professional improvement (new knowledge).

These results seem to confirm Schwartz's (2008) model that Costa Rica is close to the global average in all seven cultural dimensions. There is a balance between career transitions that are self-motivated (autonomy values) and those that are passive responses to external factors (embeddedness with the context).

In terms of group results, business executives tended to make career transitions more as a result of their own internal motivations. On the other hand, nurses and blue-collar workers mostly transitioned owing to external factors. The business executives who were interviewed were individuals who had control over their careers and who considered planning and making an effort to reach their goals fundamental to their success. Despite the fact they had much flexibility, they did not improvise; on the contrary, they elaborated and implemented their plans very

Table 12.4 Costa Rica: motivation for career transitions

Total number of interviewees	Nurses	Blue-collar	Executives	Women	Men	Young	Older	Total
19	6	7	6	8	11	9	10	19
	Frequency with which the issue was mentioned out of the total listed:							
Frequency of external sources cited as a transition cause	14	14	12	19	21	15	25	40
Frequency of external causes/number of interviewees				2.38	1.91	1.67	2.50	
Frequency of internal sources cited as a transition cause	8	5	18	8	23	18	13	31
Frequency of internal causes/number of interviewees				1.00	2.09	2.00	1.30	

precisely. In the case of nurses, they had less control over their careers, and therefore their transitions had been based on taking advantage of opportunities or facing situations and adapting to take advantage of them. Finally, the case of blue-collar workers is noteworthy because their transitions mostly resulted from external factors, such as dropping out of school, moving home and family situations (such as deaths, divorces, births, etc.).

In terms of gender, the career transitions of women interviewed in Costa Rica tended to be due more to external factors, such as family situation, the satisfactory culmination of studies and promotion because of capabilities. For men, catalysts for career transitions had been more internal, including increasing responsibilities (new challenges) and improving socio-economic conditions. It is worth mentioning that this relation between internal and external factors, for almost all of the groups, was not very prominent, meaning that there was a balance between motivations for career transitions among the people interviewed in Costa Rica.

On the other hand, results showed that the younger generation have been more motivated to make career transitions owing to internal factors and as a result of self-determination. The older generation tended to make career transitions because of external factors. Professional improvement (new knowledge) and improving socio-economic conditions were the two factors most mentioned by young adults. This reaffirms the importance that the younger generation place on socio-economic conditions as a factor when making changes in their professional careers.

Summary and Conclusions

In summary, careers differences existed between age and occupational groups, implying that sharing a common culture was not enough to erase differences. Differences between the genders were obscured by the fact that predominantly female (nurses) and male (business executives) occupations were included; however, results showed that women were more likely to attribute career changes and success to external rather than internal (i.e. personal decisions) factors.

Blue-collar workers had little sense of "career" as a progression or a stable economic activity; to them it was more about having a "job" at the present time. For the younger generation "success" equaled economic stability, while for older adults "success" meant being sure of (and having no worries about) economic stability.

For young nurses "career success" was reaching their established goals. For older adults "success" was satisfaction from meaningful achievement and a job well done.

For young business executives "success" meant achieving objective goals, particularly social and economic status. For older executives it related to contributing to society and receiving recognition—a somewhat more "subjective" meaning.

In terms of factors that influenced career success, some differences existed among the occupational groups:

- Blue-collar workers, both young and older adults, indicated that external factors (i.e. luck, opportunities) accounted for career success and opportunities.
- For nurses, internal factors accounted for career success, meaning they focused more on internal controls. For the older generation, both internal and external factors influenced career success.
- The results for business executives were similar to those for nurses, meaning that they felt their success in life depended more on themselves than on external factors, contrary to blue-collar workers. The older generation focused more on the micro environment surrounding individuals.

In terms of the reasons provoking career transitions, the 5C study in Costa Rica found differences among the occupational groups and generations:

- Young blue-collar workers typically left school and found opportunities for work. For the older generation, opportunities came by sheer chance, or destiny.
- For nurses, having a vocational call was a key influence. Young adults were searching for professional improvement, while older adults took advantage of opportunities that came along.
- For young business executives, career transitions were attributable to the desire to invent their professional selves and improve their income, while older adults mentioned looking for new challenges and more independence.

Costa Rica has a stable political system and economy, rooted in traditional religious values and close-knit communities. Resulting career patterns were not surprising for such a society. Even if the country develops more to become part of advanced middle-income countries in the near future, mostly likely the values and way of living depicted in this study on careers will continue to be present, at least in the medium term.

Note

1 World Bank classification, http://datos.bancomundial.org/pais/costa-rica (accessed July 6, 2010).

References

Helmuth, C. 2000. *Culture and Customs of Costa Rica.* Westport, CT: Greenwood Press.

Hofstede, G. 2001. *Culture's Consequences: Comparing Values, Behaviors, Institutions, and Organizations Across Nations* (2nd ed.). Beverly Hills, CA: Sage.

House, R. J., Hanges, P. J., Javidan, M., Dorfman, P. W. & Gupta, V. (Eds.). 2004. *Culture, Leadership and Organizations: The GLOBE Study of 62 Societies.* Thousand Oaks, CA: Sage.

Inglehart, R. 1997. *Modernization and Postmodernization: Cultural, Economic and Political Change in 43 Societies.* Princeton, NJ: Princeton University Press.

Jofré, A. 2009. Profesiones con empleo. *La República,* Aug. 21. Available at: http://www.larepublica. net/app/cms/www/index.php?pk_articulo=28329 (accessed July 5, 2010).

OECD. 2010. *2010 Latin American Economic Outlook: Summary.* Available at: http://www.oecd. org/dataoecd/41/20/44305080.pdf (accessed July 6, 2010).

Ogliastri, E., McMillen, C., Arias, M. E., de Bustamante, C., Dávila, C., Dorfman, P., Fimmen, C., Ickis, J. & Martinez, S. 1999. Cultura y liderazgo organizacional en 10 países de América Latina: El estudio GLOBE. *Academia: Revista Latinoamericana de Administración,* 22, Bogotá.

Programa Estado de la Nación. 2008. *Segundo Informe del Estado de la Educación.* San José, Costa Rica: Programa Estado de la Nación.

Programa Estado de la Nación. 2009. *Decimoquinto Informe del Estado de la Nación.* San José, Costa Rica: Programa Estado de la Nación.

Schwartz, S. 2008. Cultural value orientations: Nature and implications of national differences. *Journal of Higher School of Economics,* 5(2): 37–67.

Triandis, H. 1995. *Individualism and Collectivism.* Boulder, CO: Westview.

UNDP. 2009. *2009 Human Development Report.* Available at: http://hdrstats.undp.org/es/countries/country_fact_sheets/cty_fs_CRI.html (accessed July 6, 2010).

World Economic Forum. 2009. *2009–2010 Global Competitiveness Index.* Available at: http://gcr. weforum.org/gcr09 (accessed July 6, 2010).

13

Careers in Israel

Asya Pazy and Dana Shefer

The Cultural Context

Over the last few decades, the core values of Israeli society have shifted from the emphasis on collectivism that was common in the initial years after the founding of the State to individualism and materialism, which focus less on ensuring the interests of smaller groups. These changes, which many see as indicators of "normalization" following the Holocaust and the establishment of a state with a renewed national identity, are manifested in almost every aspect of society, such as culture, forms of living, economy, the labor market and education.

A central characteristic that continues to shape Israeli society is its ethnic and cultural-religious diversity. Waves of Jewish immigration arrived in the area from the end of the nineteenth century with the rise of the Zionist movement. Ever since its establishment in 1948, the State of Israel has been encouraging and supporting the immigration of Jews from all over the world, granting them immediate citizenship under the Law of Return. Most recently, huge waves of immigration from the former Soviet Union and from Ethiopia have arrived in Israel. Despite considerable institutional and social efforts directed at creating a melting pot that would integrate all of these diverse groups, some of the lines that mark ethnic origin still constitute discernible sources of divisiveness in terms of social stratification, employment and economic power (Leon, 2008; Mazie, 2006; Swirski & Dagan-Buzaglo, 2009). Nevertheless, Israeli culture today is more integrated and varied than it used to be.

Jewish religious beliefs constitute another source of diversity, often manifested in conflicts between Orthodox and secular segments of Jewish society. This latter conflict has intensified owing to a considerable overlap between religious beliefs and political ideology, particularly with regard to the Israeli–Palestinian conflict. Strict religious affiliation is associated with lower participation in the workforce for both men and women. The protracted Israeli–Palestinian conflict that has prevailed in the area since the start of the twentieth century has had a strong influence on the problematic integration of Israeli Arabs and Jews, with its associated effects on Arab participation in the labor force (Ghanem, 2001; Khamaisi, 2009). The occupation of Palestinian areas since the Six Day War of 1967 continues to fuel the flames of the conflict, and it too affects almost every aspect of society life.

Israel's geo-political history, dominated by repeated military engagement and the ongoing Israeli–Palestinian conflict, has had a severe impact on societal and economic developments. The constant threat of war and political conflict has placed security matters at the center of the political agenda, sometimes at the expense of other social, cultural and economic issues. However, it might also be one of the reasons why certain collectivistic aspects of Israeli society have not changed over the years, primarily the prominence of the family, close-knit and rather intimate relationships among people, relative lack of distance even within hierarchical structures and a sense of in-group loyalty and common fate.

Economic and Demographic Trends

The total population in Israel is 7,509,000 (December 2009), of which three-quarters are Jewish (70 percent Israeli-born).

Israel has a technologically advanced market economy and has coped with limited natural resources by intensively developing first its agricultural and later its industrial sectors. The labor force is roughly divided into sectors as follows: agriculture: 2.6 percent; industry: 32 percent; services: 65.4 percent (2009 estimates; Israel Central Bureau of Statistics, 2010; Jewish Virtual Library, 2010).

After decades of relative isolation (being surrounded by enemy countries), tighter connections with the outside world and globalization have had an effect on Israel in recent decades. There is a shared feeling among Israelis that contemporary Israel is much more open to the world than it used to be, owing to current regulation, participation in international business, a relatively open border policy with regard to commerce, and various forms of electronic communication (television, the internet and even cinema). Israel sees itself as part of the (Western) world at large, as evidenced by the penetration of the English language, which is widely spoken in contemporary Israel.

The protracted military conflict has posed challenges for the Israeli economy. Nevertheless, one of its most valuable by-products has been the development of Israeli advanced technology, which has led to the establishment of prosperous companies that have earned Israel world renown for its high-tech industry (Bank of Israel, 2010). The high-tech industry symbolizes for many Israelis the idea of career progress and opportunity, and it constitutes for many a highly attractive route.

The global trend of outsourcing has penetrated Israeli business as well, to the point that many companies outsource work to other countries (Global Policy Network, 2007). This move has threatened a number of economic sectors in Israel, such as textiles and agriculture, which were the most adversely affected by globalization trends. Israeli textile factories are closing owing to high manufacturing costs, and the construction and agriculture sectors have become less attractive to Israeli employees owing to the low pay and low attractiveness of these occupations and the entrance of foreign employees (mainly from the Far East).

There has been an increasing tendency to privatize sectors that were formerly state-run and a concomitant weakening in the power of the labor unions (Hason, 2006). These tendencies have led to a growing number of persons employed under special contracts with less employment security. The idea of a career for life has been replaced for many by frequent change and instability. In line with that, the notion of personal responsibility for one's own career has become more pervasive.

In the past, educational advancement played a significant role in determining social status, whereas these days economic success is an important measure of a person's status. Education levels are still important, however, and are still mildly correlated with income, but this is mainly applicable to the upper-middle range. Likewise, humanities have become less attractive fields of study compared to business-related, engineering and other more practical fields.

As part of the growing emphasis on materialistic values, the gap between the affluent and the low-income population groups has widened over the years (Ben-David, 2010a, 2010b). In addition, despite the relatively small area of the country, most job opportunities are concentrated in the urban center of the country, so that peripheral areas tend to be neglected and lack true equality of opportunity.

Another important issue that must be referred to is the differences in birth patterns between different groups in the society: the birthrate in the Jewish ultra-Orthodox population is significantly higher than among the traditional and non-religious population; and similarly Israeli Arabs have a higher birthrate than Israeli traditional and non-religious Jews (Rebhun & Malach, 2009). The result of this is that the proportion of traditional and non-religious Israeli Jews in the population is somewhat shrinking. Furthermore, it is likely that the difference in fertility rates contributes to the widening economic gap between these sectors of the population.

Career Trends and Patterns

Several elements of the new psychological contract between individuals and their employers characterize the contemporary labor market in Israel as well, particularly instability, transactional short-term involvements and mutual recognition of the necessity of lifelong learning. As mentioned, there has been a trend towards privatization of previously state-operated sectors, with a weakening of labor unions. Occupational mobility is limited, but much more common among younger employees, and is apparently also more frequent in the central part of the country compared to the peripheral areas. On the other hand, there has been a rise in opportunities for entrepreneurial activities, most notably in the high-tech industry.

Military service continues to play a major role in preparing young people for their careers, as it offers numerous opportunities for professional training in a variety of fields that are subsequently of high demand in the labor market. Moreover, military service (particularly professional service beyond the compulsory period) provides access to networks that might be highly beneficial in the further stages of one's career. The high-tech industry, for example, has been based to a large extent on social networks that go back to military service in technological and intelligence units. Finally, in many occupations in contemporary Israel much more emphasis is being placed on professionalism, as a growing number of fields require prior professional training. As a result, institutes of professional training and academic or professional schools are proliferating.

The Educational System

In the last decade, there has been an upsurge in the number of academic institutes which are not funded by the state. This presages the end of the hegemony of the traditional research universities in Israel, which are all government funded, few in number and highly selective in terms of admission qualifications, thus preventing access to many people interested in acquiring higher education. The emergence of new non-profit, non-government-funded colleges has enabled many more people to acquire higher education.

A general cultural assumption is that further formal education results in higher earning power. As mentioned before, this assumption is valid for the higher mid-range employee. Similar to the case in the United States, a bachelor's degree (three- to four-year university degree) is seen simply as an entry requirement for a well-paid job in all professions and many trades. A college-level degree is likely to become mandatory for nurses, while it has not always been in the past. In business, on the other hand, anyone who can gather funds and be a successful entrepreneur can succeed without a college degree. However, a business degree and preferably an MBA are typically seen as entry requirements for established and more prestigious corporations. With blue-collar workers, there is still some informal apprentice-based training, but increasingly such workers require formal certification or choose to pursue a college degree.

Findings From the Study

Sampling

Our sample consisted of 19 participants, about equally divided between the three occupational groups (blue-collar, nursing and business) and two generations (the younger generation was around 30 years old and the older around 60 years old). Though a convenience sample, in some respects it is roughly representative of Israeli society, as the majority is Jewish (only a single Arab participant), one-sixth had recently immigrated from the former Soviet Union, and the gender composition reflected occupational segregation (female nurses, male blue-collar workers). Table 13.1 presents the Israeli sample profile.

Meanings of Career Success

A significant part of the interview was devoted to exploring the subjective notion of career success. Table 13.2 presents the major meaning categories and their frequencies.

Table 13.1 Israel sample profile

	Business graduates		Nurses		Blue-collar workers	
	Older	Younger	Older	Younger	Older	Younger
N =	3	3	3	3	4	3
Gender	2 males, 1 female	2 males, 1 female	3 females	3 females	4 males	3 males
	N = 6		N = 6		N = 7	

Total N = 19.

Table 13.2 Meanings of career success in Israel

Total number of interviewees N = 19	Occupation			Gender		Generation		Total number mentioning category
	Nurse	Blue-collar	Business	Female	Male	Younger	Older	
	6	7	6	8	11	9	10	
Person	6	7	6	8	11	9	10	19
Satisfaction	6	5	6	8	9	7	10	17
Achievement	4	6	6	6	10	9	7	16
Learning and development	4	3	6	6	7	5	8	13
Self-actualization	4	3	5	6	6	4	8	12
Job	6	7	6	8	11	9	10	19
Job security	1	3	1	2	3	4	1	5
Job/task characteristics	6	6	6	8	10	9	9	18
Job performance	3	3	3	4	5	4	5	9
Performing one's role	4	3	5	6	6	6	6	12
Interaction with the environment	6	7	6	8	11	9	10	19
Social working environment	5	5	5	6	9	7	8	15
Recognition	4	3	3	5	5	4	6	10
Work–life context/balance	4	1	4	5	4	6	3	9
Making a difference	4	1	4	6	3	3	6	9
Material output	3	5	2	4	6	7	3	10

The job-related meanings emphasized the nature of the job and the person's level of performance. Most noticeable were job/task characteristics, referring to the content of the job and the opportunities which it offers, as well as to challenge, autonomy and responsibility at work, and also to the meaning of effectively carrying out one's tasks (performing one's role and job performance).

Salient person-related meanings of career success were also relevant to work, as they consisted of enjoying work and experiencing growth through achievement, continuous development and self-actualization.

Learning and development was particularly prominent among business and/or older participants. As a business graduate commented:

> It's not about where you make more money today, but about where you learn more and have a chance to earn more money in the long run.

Education and training was perceived as a basis for success:

> Training in the organization helped a lot—the fact that I had an academic degree when I joined the bank, which was very rare in those days. I was then open to take every possible course in the bank. . . . I did everything I could in order to get an MBA; this degree carried great personal and organizational benefits.

For some nurses, academic education enhanced success through empowerment, narrowing the gap between them and physicians. It seems that the salient job- and person-related meanings of success echo Israeli society's preoccupation with growth and with becoming strong both on the level of the collective and in individual terms.

On the affective side, satisfaction was a consensual meaning of success across the various groups, though there were variations in emphasis; for blue-collar workers success was defined in terms of psychological success; for nurses satisfaction was derived from helping patients; and business graduates emphasized self-centered aspects related to career progress. Achievement was another prominent indicator of success across occupations and generations (a little less among nurses). This is consistent with the contemporary shift to individualistic goal-oriented values that are manifested in ambition and the desire to gain influence and reap the material and social benefits created. An older nurse said in this context:

> So far I have managed to achieve my goal. That's the greatest satisfaction. Not achieving a goal or a direction I set for myself would be the end of the world for me.

An older businessman combined the two meanings:

> [Success is] to reach the top in all that you do, to be in a decision-making position and to enjoy what you do. . . . Be satisfied, receive a high salary and be able to lead.

Success was less associated with self-actualization among blue-collar workers, perhaps reflecting their low occupational prestige and the view of blue-collar work as a means to earn a living rather than a career driven by aspirations of personal and professional growth. We note that self-actualization was more frequently mentioned by older participants who had apparently reached a mature phase in their career in which they were concerned about issues of goal fulfillment, self-expression and moral dimensions.

Among environment-related meanings, the majority stressed the importance of good working relationships with members of the organization (social working environment), for example:

> In the bank it's so important to be more than just professional. If you're not sensitive towards others, if you are aggressive, you ruin your image and this affects your career development.

Another important meaning of success in this category related to being appreciated at work (recognition). In one case:

> to be appreciated by others is more important for me than to earn a thousand dollars more.

Making a difference was also associated with career success (less by younger participants and by only one blue-collar respondent), reflecting again the pragmatic emphasis on career among younger people. On the other hand, nurses viewed their career as a calling, entailing devotion to patients, sometimes to the point of personal sacrifice.

Career success encompassed the home arena (work–life context or balance) for nurses (all women) and business graduates (and for only one blue-collar worker), and more so among the younger participants:

> In order to be successful, a person must put family and health before work. You can run the world, but if you do it by yourself you have failed in life.
> I paid a high family price for building my entire career. That's the only area where I didn't succeed.

As suggested by the latter statement, lack of work–life balance might even enhance the sense of failure regardless of the overall feeling of career success.

Finally, young and/or blue-collar participants were more likely to associate material output as well as job security with career success, reflecting the centrality of financial considerations at this age or in this occupational group. A preference for employers that guarantee secure work was often mentioned among these participants. Nurses' view of material benefits as defining success was quite complex. Only half of them mentioned material benefits, and they almost saw it as the opposite of professional satisfaction, as can be inferred from the words of a younger nurse:

> I still didn't get to a place that I would call success. I'm happy here, though it's difficult for me to live on my salary.

Career Transitions

Table 13.3 presents frequencies of responses in the various categories of career transitions. Career transitions are viewed as self-initiated, driven mostly by internal reasons such as a desire for novel experience, identification of opportunities or seeking further development. However,

Table 13.3 Career transitions in Israel

	Occupation			Gender		Generation		
Total number of interviewees	Nurse	Blue-collar	Business	Female	Male	Younger	Older	Total number mentioning category
N = 19	6	7	6	8	11	9	10	
Internally driven causes/triggers of career transitions:								
Own initiative (internal source)	5	6	5	6	10	8	8	16
Own initiative (external source/stimuli)	5	3	3	7	4	7	4	11
Externally driven causes/triggers of career transitions:								
Unsought opportunities	3	5	4	4	8	4	8	12
Organizationally driven	3	2	3	5	3	4	4	8
Family role	3	0	0	3	0	0	3	3
Individuals' management of career transitions:								
Job search	4	5	3	5	7	6	6	12
Planning/setting goals and priorities	2	0	4	3	3	4	2	6
Formal education, training, short courses	4	1	6	6	5	5	6	11
Informal training	4	4	5	5	8	5	8	13
Recreation	1	1	4	2	4	1	5	6

about half of our respondents were also aware of external reasons, thus attributing their transition to a mix of causes. Most participants reported initiating the transition completely on their own, for example:

> I didn't really want to leave but I left at the right time. I believe you have to leave when you feel that you aren't developing anymore in that place. . . . I personally didn't develop. I had walls around me that blocked me.

External causes consisted of unsought opportunities and organizational changes. In this context, externally driven transitions were responses to unexpected opportunities rather than a calculated, pre-planned process. An older blue-collar worker remarked:

> There was no future for me in antiques. . . . My partner worked for someone and got into trouble with him, so he suggested that I too should get into the business. I spontaneously decided to switch.

Interestingly, in spite of the central role attributed to family in Israeli society, family-related reasons were rather rare (coded only for three older nurses).

Blue-collar transitions appear more like job changes than goal-oriented career moves. Most of these changes were triggered by a combination of internal (e.g. need for change, dislike of previous job or its environmental conditions) and external (e.g. better position, layoffs, economic crisis in the field) causes:

> I was bored. There weren't that many exhibitions to set up, and there was nothing to do during the rest of the time; my body aches when I have nothing to do. Then they approached me for the current job.

On the other hand, business graduates attributed their transitions mainly to internal causes, such as a wish to advance in terms of company size and development opportunities or a need for change. External causes for business graduates were also unsought opportunities or organizational events.

Loyalty to the organization did not appear to be an important factor for younger business graduates when considering change, but the older generation did take it into consideration, though even for them the drive to progress and to break their routine was stronger than loyalty. Loyalty affected the transition process, however, as in the following account:

> I left first and then I started my search for my next "baby." I can't look for a new position as long as I'm in my old company. . . . I think it is unethical, though I have no fears of making the break.

Thus it seems that the dynamic nature of Israeli society and its movement from local to global considerations are reflected in how people view their own career transitions.

Managing Career Transitions

The typical ways of managing transitions were obtaining more formal or informal training and education and seeking new employment. Of secondary salience were goal setting, planning and prioritizing, or engagement in recreational activities.

External Influencing Factors of Career Transitions

Employer, supervisor and peers were all mentioned by more than half of the sample as external factors that influenced their transition (see Table 13.4). While the impact of peers was mostly supportive, primarily in a socio-emotional way, that of the organization and the supervisor was more complex, as both facilitating and hindering effects were reported.

Outside the organization, family and friends were significant factors influencing transitions, mostly in a positive direction ("My friends are knowledgeable and successful; they connected me to the right people and gave good advice"), though mixed in some cases. An older nurse described the impact of family:

> I could have advanced in my career 25 years ago, but would have had to neglect family, so I stayed a regular nurse in a hospital.
>
> The difficulty was the transition from being a housewife to working again as a nurse. For two years I worked part time, so that I could still take care of the children.

Most transitions of business graduates were triggered by recommendations and offers that were channeled through social and professional networks:

> It is crucial to create and maintain relations with the right people. Friendly relationships in the professional context are most important; otherwise the woman who recommended me wouldn't have remembered me.

This and other accounts demonstrate the strong emphasis in Israeli culture, particularly in business, on the benefits of friendships and social networking.

Table 13.4 External influencing factors of career transitions in Israel

Total number of interviewees	Occupation			Gender		Generation		Total number mentioning category
	Nurse	Blue-collar	Business	Female	Male	Younger	Older	
N=19	6	7	6	8	11	9	10	
Support	3	1	4	4	4	5	3	8
Barriers	3	1	2	4	2	4	2	6
Peers	5	5	2	5	7	6	6	12
Support	4	5	2	4	7	5	6	11
Barriers	1	0	0	1	0	1	0	1
Family	4	3	3	6	4	5	5	10
Support	3	1	3	5	2	3	4	7
Barriers	1	2	1	1	3	3	1	4
Friends	2	4	1	3	4	4	3	7
Support	1	4	1	2	4	3	3	6
Barriers	1	1	1	2	1	3	0	3
Organization	3	5	5	5	8	7	6	13
Support	2	3	4	4	5	4	5	9
Barriers	2	3	4	3	6	6	3	9
Network	4	3	3	5	5	5	5	10
Work	3	2	2	4	3	3	4	7
Personal	0	1	0	0	1	0	1	1
Professional	1	0	2	1	2	2	1	3
Education and training	1	2	4	2	5	4	3	7
Financial situation	0	0	1	1	0	1	0	1
Role of luck and contingencies	0	2	1	1	2	1	2	3

Interestingly, level of income was rarely mentioned as a factor in a person's transition. Only one business transition was driven by a pay increase, and none of the reported causes among nurses or blue-collar participants was directly related to pay, though stability and security did matter to them:

> In painting [the previous job], I earned much more than here. It's only the long-term security in this institution that convinced me.

Moreover, this person was even willing to leave the job he liked for a lower-paid position in a new field in order to achieve stable and secure employment. Accepting a lower pay offer, one younger nurse (who reported having financial difficulties) claimed that the increased responsibility and independence she would get through the transition were more valuable for her than pay.

Finally, according to their accounts, chance played a minimal part in respondents' accounts of their career transitions, indicating perhaps a sense of mastery which relates to viewing oneself as an active agent of one's career rather than as a pawn in the hand of fate.

Conclusion

In conclusion, a variety of career themes emerged out of the responses of this small but diverse sample. One is the salience of intrinsic components of how career success is experienced. The content of work, with its satisfaction and opportunities for growth, defines success more than financial attainment. This seems to contradict the materialistic shift in Israeli society, but perhaps it indicates that this shift is far from being complete. For a country under continuous threat, material security is existentially necessary, but it is not sufficient in defining success. Furthermore, the importance of the desire to achieve, to seek opportunities for professional development and thus to progress in one's career does constitute one aspect of the shift towards individualistic values. This individualistic pursuit, however, is still embedded in a collectivistic fabric, as evidenced by the relevance of social considerations to individuals' view of career development. Be it in the shape of the immediate social environments that influence career decisions through networking and recommendations, or in the shape of social relations in the working environment that increase satisfaction, all careers discussed were in some way or another affected by social relations. The combination of these two themes presents the Israeli sample as representing a culture in transition, moving away from one worldview to a new one without having completed the move.

The discussion of career transitions crystallized a common factor among the different professional groups and generations. Transitions are generally embraced. They are viewed in an optimistic way and are almost always perceived as smooth in nature, mostly resulting in favorable outcomes. Furthermore, they are frequently pursued (average among the young generation three times, and among the older generation six times). Taking into account a certain impact of social desirability, which might have illustrated the situation as more favorable than actually experienced, the optimistic and self-secure undertone concerning transitions speaks for itself. Furthermore, most career transitions are viewed (perhaps in retrospect) as initiated by the individual, suggesting that respondents prefer to think of themselves as active agents who shape their careers rather than as its victims. Though aware of external conditions, respondents seem to be able to master their situation to their own benefit.

In light of the above, an impression emerged of general optimism and self-satisfaction, of careers whose developments largely depend on intrinsic drives rather than extrinsic rewards. The importance of social relations, the frequency of transitions, and the centrality of subjective success and satisfaction seem to be a reflection of socio-cultural patterns typical of Israeli society. Formal and informal settings in Israel are characterized by social intimacy and a general sense of familiarity. This results from a combination of the country's small size and its difficult political and historical context, which despite the cultural and ethnic diversity fosters a strong sense of collective identity.

Moreover, Israeli society is highly dynamic, dominated by technological developments and political changes. Social, political and economic changes are part of everyday reality, occurring at an exceptionally fast pace. In other words, transitions in all spheres are normality, rather than an exception. The general embrace of transitions in this sample could thus be a result of society's familiarity with the latter. Transitions are an integral part of our respondents' reality and their self-understanding, and as such transitions are naturally accepted, possibly even desired, career patterns.

References

Bank of Israel. 2010. *Recent Economic Developments.* Available at: http://www.bankisrael.gov.il/publeng/publeslf.php?misg_id=8.

Ben-David, D. 2010a. *A Macro Perspective of Israel's Society and Economy.* Jerusalem: Taub Center for Social Policy Studies in Israel.

Ben-David, D. 2010b. *Israel's Labor Market Today, in the Past and in Comparison With the West.* Jerusalem: Taub Center for Social Policy Studies in Israel.

Ghanem, A. 2001. *The Palestinian-Arab Minority in Israel, 1948–2000.* New York: SUNY Press.

Global Policy Network. 2007. *Labor Market Conditions in Israel, 2006.* Tel Aviv: Adva Center.

Hason, Y. 2006. *Three Decades of Privatization* (in Hebrew). Tel Aviv: Adva Center.

Israel Central Bureau of Statistics. 2010. *Projections of Israel's Population Until 2025.* Available at: http://www.cbs.gov.il/publications/popul2005/popul2005_e.htm.

Jewish Virtual Library. 2010. *Latest Population Figures for Israel.* Available at: http://www.jewishvirtuallibrary.org/jsource/Society_&_Culture/newpop.html.

Khamaisi, R. 2009. *Arab Society in Israel: Population, Society, Economy.* Jerusalem: Van Leer Jerusalem Institute.

Leon, N. 2008. The secular origins of Mizrahi traditionalism. *Israel Studies,* 13(3): 22–42.

Mazie, S. V. 2006. *Israel's Higher Law: Religion and Liberal Democracy in the Jewish State.* Lanham, MD: Lexington Books.

Rebhun, U. & Malach, G. 2009. *Demographic Trends in Israel.* Jerusalem: Metzilah Center.

Swirski, S. & Dagan-Buzaglo, N. 2009. *Segregation, Inequality, and Lax Control: The Picture of Israeli Education* (in Hebrew). Tel Aviv: Adva Center.

14

Careers in Japan

Mami Taniguchi

The Cultural Context

Schwartz (2004) characterized Japan as a Confucian Asian country. Confucian Asia combines a strong stress on hierarchy (ascribed roles and obligations), embeddedness (independence and shared collectivism) and mastery (assertive actions to change the world). The region also accentuates collectivism.

According to Schwartz, Japan is very low on egalitarianism (versus hierarchy) but moderately high on self-expression (versus survival). For example, he emphasizes the idea that Japanese culture organizes relations of interdependency in role-based hierarchical terms. Hofstede (1980) explained Japan as the highest in masculinity out of the countries researched (based on more than 110,000 people from over 70 countries worldwide). According to Hofstede, masculinity describes a situation where success, monetarism and materialism are the predominant values in a society, whereas feminine dimensions represent cultures where considerateness and quality of life are predominant.

More recently, some value characteristics among Hofstede's findings have come into question after the collapse of the bubble economy in the 1990s. It has been said that psychological contracts have been broken in Japan, as exemplified by the restructuring of major companies. Collectivistic values began shifting into more individualistic values for Japanese careerists. More boundaryless, self-directed career concepts became consistent with the labor trend (a more detailed explanation is given below).

Another value that may be changing is uncertainty avoidance. Uncertainty avoidance measures frequency of making new rules and systems in order to avoid ambiguous situations. The Japanese tend to avoid uncertainty compared to American people. Lifetime employment systems and seniority-based pay and promotion practices symbolize the

Japanese attitude towards uncertainty. However, since the collapse of the bubble economy, the uncertainty avoidance value has been changing to some extent.

Economic and Demographic Trends

After the collapse of the bubble economy in the 1990s, Japan experienced a lasting recession. Since the beginning of the twenty-first century, the GDP annual rate of growth has been no more than 3 percent (a reduction from 4.4 percent in 1985).

In July 2009, the Japanese unemployment rate hit the highest point since World War II at 5.7 percent. Furthermore, the Japanese business environment has slowed down even faster since the repercussions of the recent global economic crisis.

In 2000, the deregulation of temporary workers in the labor market began a trend, spreading to major Japanese manufacturers as well.

As for demographic trends, Japan is experiencing a low birth rate and an aging society. The accentuation of Baby Boomer generation retirements in 2007 has been referred to as the "2007 Issue." This retirement of millions of Baby Boomers has been considered a serious issue. As of 2007, more than 5,000,000 Baby Boomer workers were between the ages 55 and 59. It has been estimated that up to 1,400,000 workers would retire every year, considering that the average retirement age of Japan is 60 years old.

Japanese companies, especially in manufacturing, are concerned about the problem of passing down their skilled workers' technologies to their unskilled workers, owing to the massive retirement of the Baby Boomer generation. The government has established a subsidy for career counseling and reduced tax for investing in skill development. In order for companies to solve this problem, they have extended the retirement age and have established reemployment systems.

Educational System/Occupational Background

According to a recent survey (Ministry of Education, Culture, Sports, Science and Technology, 2010) the percentage of students pursuing higher education reached 54.4 percent in 2010. However, the rate of MBA education in Japan is not as high as in Western countries. Under the lifetime employment system, Japanese companies tend to hire promising new graduates and develop them within their organizations. Japanese companies have considered talents developed with on-the-job training as more competent than those developed solely through MBA education. Practical business skills are not to be learned from formal training and outside companies. Consequently Japanese universities primarily place emphasis on undergraduate education instead of graduate studies.

However, the collapse of the bubble economy has altered Japanese mind-sets. Acquiring portable skills outside organizations can pay dividends in individuals' career changes. In early 2000, the government started an action plan for graduate schools and set up quotas on the number of graduate students. Since then, studying for an MBA has become popular in Japan. Also, because undergraduate education has been seen to lag behind that of leading countries, the Japanese government has taken measures to make it more comparable.

Japanese manufacturing companies hire new high school graduates and develop their craftsmanship within their organization. However, increasing university attendance rates have decreased the number of new high school graduates. This trend makes the problem of passing down their skilled workers' technologies twice as hard within Japanese manufacturing companies (as previously mentioned). In the case of nurses, students who have studied and graduated from nursing school are allowed to work in hospitals only after passing the national medical practitioners qualifying procedure. Following the governmental policy to increase the number of nurses, the number of nursing universities is increasing. This initiative keeps pace with the rising university advancement rate, and curbs the decline of nurse numbers. As medical technology improves, hospitals and regional nursing associations have begun supplying education systems, which helps the nurses to brush up their skills even after they are employed.

Career Trends and Patterns

The Japanese labor market and HR practices have witnessed many drastic changes in the turbulent decade since the collapse of the bubble economy. The lasting recession during the so-called lost decade forced a number of Japanese organizations to start restructuring their business, changing employment customs and laying off employees (Kawakita, 1997). For example, the lifetime employment system and seniority-based payment and promotion system are now in jeopardy and being abandoned to varying degrees. Many companies are becoming keen on hiring experienced, mid-career employees rather than relying heavily on recruiting "rookies" directly from schools and universities. They have shifted pay plans from the traditional seniority pay to the merit system in order to improve white-collar productivity and to survive in a global arena. These changes have brought about dilemmas and challenges to transform career perspectives among Japanese employees.

Under the seniority system, Japanese companies manage their employees' careers in a collective manner. Systematic training programs have been offered to employees according to their hierarchy from entry level to top management levels.

In the mid-twentieth century, career management was largely seen as an organizational responsibility (Baruch, 2003). However, in the mid-1990s, contemporary models of career emphasized a shift from the organization to the individual (Capelli, 1999; Parker, Arthur & Inkson, 2004). Organizations managed individual careers with a view to helping employees move up the organizational ladder (Thite, 2001) while developing organizationally specific skills (Baruch, 2004a; Hall & Mirvis, 1995).

Increasingly, employees are expected to "take care of their own employability" and "career" (Hiltrop, 1996) as a precondition to career success, not only in terms of their current job, but also in terms of their future employment (Baruch, 2004b; Garavan, Morley, Gunnigle & Collins, 2001). Especially since 2000, Japanese organizations have followed such trends. "Career autonomy" and "self-responsibility of the individual's career" have become buzzwords in Japan.

How have these changes in employment practices had an influence on career transition in Japan?

One impact is on the turnover ratio. Owing to cutbacks in personnel, a number of people changed their jobs, left their company in the early stages of their career and entered other companies as mid-career recruits.

The second impact has been on job transfers within an organization. Owing to the breakdown and rebuilding of organizations, a number of employees have been obliged to change their workplace.

The third impact has been on employees' profile and their relationship within a workplace. Owing to changes in lifetime employment, employees who have different backgrounds, such as non-regular workers or mid-career recruits, work together with "conventional" employees. Since supervisor–subordinate and peer relationships fluctuate, it is difficult to maintain long-term mentoring relationships and to have opportunities for on-the-job-training.

Even though career responsibilities were shifted from the organization to the individual, Japanese organizations did not completely renounce employees' career development and have added new initiatives for HR and HRD. First of all, organizations provide several supports in a different way, adjusting to diverse employees' needs and individual life designs to attract and retain human resources.

For example, companies offer "self-directed career seminars" to help individuals design their careers and position retirement or job transfers in their long-term career plans. Those seminars were targeted at people of about 58 or 60 (that is immediately before retirement). In addition, as a support for individual everyday life–career design, internal career advisors, coaches and mentors have been trained institutionally. Formerly, career advice was limited to the direct supervisor and HR staff.

Moreover, to encourage employees' self-determination before the transition period (such as early retirement), companies open up several career options. In-house staff recruitment systems, in-house free agents, and job posting give employees opportunities to make known job transfer desires by themselves. These efforts have functioned to improve employees' motivation.

Furthermore, Japanese companies provide a variety of different types of training to adjust to employees' diverse needs. By imparting a sense of self-determination to acquire skills and knowledge, companies prepare employees for a variety of in-house training or e-learning and encourage them to attend training outside the institution.

Another new strategic approach to organization-directed career development is managing the development for "high potentials." This management development is characterized by early selection of high potentials and the rotation cycle of select–train–assign in order to make the job developmentally "stretching" to support long-term succession planning. At the selection stages, some companies give employees a chance to identify themselves as candidates to be high potentials.

Findings From the Study

Sampling data has been taken from three different occupational groups. They are business graduates, nurses and blue-collar workers. A total of 20 people were interviewed, 7 females and 13 males, with 8 business graduates, 6 nurses and 6 blue-collars. The average age was 28.4 for the younger generation and 53.0 for the older generation. Table 14.1 outlines the Japan sampling profile.

Table 14.1 Japan sampling profile

Occupation	Business graduates		Nurses		Blue-collar workers	
Generation	Old	Young	Old	Young	Old	Young
Gender	0 females, 4 males	1 female, 3 males	3 females, 0 males	3 females, 0 males	0 females, 3 males	0 females, 3 males
Educational background	University or above	University or above	Nursing school	Nursing school	High school or vocational school	High school

Total N = 20.

Meanings of Career Success

Looking across the sample as a whole the following meanings of career success were coded by the research team for five or more of the 20 research participants:

Job/task characteristics	(11 people)
Recognition	(8 people)
Achievement	(7 people)
Performing one's role	(6 people)
Learning and development	(5 people)

Particularities Regarding Occupational and Generational Groups

In Japan, objective criteria of career success are largely emphasized. Recognition, achievement and performing one's role are consistent with an income or hierarchical advancement which is visible and "objectively" measurable (see, for example, Gattiker & Larwood, 1988; Judge & Bretz, 1994; Judge et al., 1995). This can also be endorsed by the Japanese culture of strong masculinity.

Job/task characteristics scored the highest among all the other factors answered by the 20 people, with the need for responsibility and challenges as the two most important sub-dimensions. Job/task characteristics were chosen by all of the blue-collar workers for both young and old.

As for nurses, four out of six answered that their meaning of career success was found in job/task characteristics. Job/task characteristics were chosen by only one out of the eight white-collar workers.

Their work centrality stems from their sequencing skill development process. Their current task is connected directly with each skill level and their technical skill acquirement measure. In other words, job/task characteristics is their skill identification measure.

Furthermore, it was interesting to see one female younger white-collar worker has answered that her meaning of career success is found in her job/task characteristics, while none of the male white-collar workers have mentioned anything concerning job/task characteristics. This may be because she is a female and minority within the Japanese manufacturing company. She feels valued when her prominent skill is acquired with her own experience, distinct from her male counterparts. Job/task characteristics is also her skill identification measure.

Recognition is considered as a meaning of career success for blue-collar workers and both young and old nurses. Out of six nurses who were interviewed, five of them answered that, for them, career success meant to be recognized.

> Evaluation from a patient can be a scale in measuring employees' career success.
>
> (Older female nurse)

> Earning a decent salary is important but, for me, I want to be acknowledged.
>
> (Younger blue-collar worker)

This tendency of leaning towards recognition can be explained by the Confucian culture of Japan. As Schwartz (2004) has mentioned, strong stress on hierarchy, embeddedness and mastery automatically gives authority to bosses within the workplace and for followers to respect them. This stems from their skill development process within manufacturing companies. Younger blue-collar workers acquire their manufacturing skill on-the-job instruction from a supervisor. Manufacturing skill level is developed in proportion to the length of one's service, and matches organizational hierarchy. Consequently, the younger generation naturally show respect for the elderly.

One older blue-collar worker said:

> The influence of the boss is big. Just after entering the company, I came to want to leave, but he persuaded me not to give up.

However nurses, unlike blue-collar workers, tend to find their meaning of career success by being recognized not only by their bosses but also by their patients.

It was surprising to see that none of the white-collar workers chose recognition as their meaning of career success. This shows a value change in collectivism versus individualism among white-collar workers after the collapse of the bubble economy. Occupation is capable of superseding culture.

Achievement was chosen by three out of four younger white-collar workers. It seems that the turbulent period after the collapse of the bubble economy has altered many of the younger white-collar workers' values in terms of career success.

This phenomenon has also had an impact on older white-collar workers, who have been supported by the seniority system:

> I had to survive, so I had to show results. . . . I had to be ambitious about my performance. I feel that the company has become more likely to appraise performance instead of seniority recently.
>
> (Older business graduate)

Achievement was chosen by only one blue-collar worker.

In Japan, in comparison to other countries, performing one's role had a significantly high score. Nurses chose this factor for "meeting requirements," and white-collar workers, especially older ones, chose this factor as a general meaning of career success.

This could be explained from the Japanese hierarchical culture (Schwartz, 2004) and high awareness towards uncertainty (Hofstede, 1980). First, hierarchical culture gives authority to superiors within the workplace. Second, a culture of high uncertainty avoidance keeps the workers conservative. Consequently, with the existence of these two cultures, Japanese workers became proficient at accomplishing the work given by their bosses rather than producing new and challenging work for themselves.

Learning and development is chosen as a fifth factor; however, there seems to be no obvious relationship between occupational and generational groups.

Findings can be summarized as follows. First, Japanese cultures and characteristics have strongly influenced popular meanings of career success amongst the Japanese interviewees. The interviewees focused on factors more in the objective category than in the subjective category, and this is one of the differences of Japan from other countries.

Second, gaps between success meanings seem to exist between the occupational groups. Meanings of career success for white-collars and blue-collars seem to vary. Nurses and blue-collar workers exhibit more similarities in their conceptualization of career, focusing on job/task characteristics for their career success, perhaps owing to team-based work and the skill development process.

Influencing Factors of Career Success

Influencing factors of career success can be differentiated into internal and external aspects. In Japan, externally influenced factors were more salient than internal factors.

Personal history	(9 people)
Ongoing learning and development	(5 people)
Context of work	(19 people)
Superiors	(9 people)
Company	(14 people)
Work network	(6 people)
Social environment (non-work)	(15 people)

As for internal factors, personal history was chosen by six out of seven white-collar workers. However, none of the blue-collar workers chose this factor. Ongoing learning and development was chosen by more than one person from each occupational group as well as generational groups.

As for external influences, context of work factors were coded for most interviewees and chosen by 19 out of 20 people.

Influence from superior(s) is chosen by more than two people from both blue- and white-collar workers. Both blue- and white-collar workers chose learning and developmental support as influencing factors.

Company influences are cited in some fashion by every occupational and generational group. It was interesting to see that seven out of eight (both younger and older) white-collar workers chose this category. This represents the importance of Japanese companies' "on-the-job training." As pointed out earlier, Japanese companies tend to educate employees after they are employed. This can be said for nurses and blue-collar workers as well. Japanese companies tend to treasure employees with concrete and tangible skills acquired on the job.

Work network influences were coded for exactly two people from every occupational group; however, when compared for generational groups, only older workers chose this criterion. In the sub-category, psychological support and learning developmental support were chosen the most. Considering that the average retirement age of Japan is around 60 years old, it seems to be important for older workers to maintain their network within their company before they retire.

Social environment (non-work) was mentioned by 15 out of the 20 people who were interviewed. When compared by occupational groups, white-collar workers and nurses were salient, with more than five people choosing this criterion. However, only two out of six blue-collar workers could be coded as citing this factor.

Career Transitions

Some of the typical Japanese work transition patterns were found to be the strong causal relationship that the organization itself played in the workers' decision to make a transition.

As an illustration of this, 12 out of all the interviewees replied that their transition was driven by the organization. The item "organizationally driven" includes promotion, routine job rotation, and change in leadership positions. When it came to inter-occupational comparison, nurses had the largest proportion of samples experiencing "organizationally driven" transitions. This item was also the most frequent cause both for blue-collar workers and for white-collar workers. Amongst nurses, the only person who did not mention this item was a young female. She had worked at the current workplace for only a few years and had not experienced any job rotation. Entering the hospital was the transition for her (own initiative). One of the nurses who mentioned "organizationally driven" perceived that her transition was also caused by the factor named "unsought opportunity from boss." Thus five out of the six interviewees were impacted by their organization. This might have resulted from the following: A nursing job is their calling and they do not intend to change their workplace by themselves. They are unaware about whether or not their career is organizationally directed or self-directed.

The number of blue-collar workers who had answered "organizationally driven" was three out of six, and all these people were young male individuals.

On the other hand, career transitions for many of the older workers were caused by the organization. Two of them utilized the early retirement program at their previous organization and worked as trainers at the global training center. The early retirement program has been embraced by many Japanese firms since the economic recession due to the burst of the bubble economy. Restructuring has taken place in many companies which have introduced an early retirement program as a countermeasure to cut their costs. All employees of a certain age are supposed to be equally targeted for the early retirement program. There are some differences among them. Some are forced to be self-directed, are advised to retire or stay and accept a lower salary contentedly. Others are advised to enjoy organizational careers, selecting options to obtain executive posts at affiliated companies or to be transferred to better positions within a company. The former case happens among white-collar workers, and the latter case happens among skilled workers such as blue-collars after the serious shortage of skilled labor in Japanese manufacturing companies. Following this inclination, although the two older blue-collar workers appeared to have moved to their current workplace on their own initiative, their intention might have been influenced by the organizational situation to some extent. Along with other major Japanese companies, their company, Nissan, has opened up several career options to encourage employees' self-determination before early retirement. As the two older blue-collar workers perceived their transitions as their own initiative, company efforts for self-determination were effective in improving employees' motivation.

It cannot be simply concluded that there are differences across the generations in terms of career transitions. The composition of career transitions of the blue-collar workers was made up by the younger workers who were directly rotated by the organization and the senior workers whose career transitions were not caused by the organization directly. However, the early retirement program and the increased proportion of temporary staff were types of situational factors around the organization. That is to say, those senior workers were affected indirectly by their organizational situation. It seems that there were some similarities across this occupation in that organizations have some influence on career transitions, though all senior workers' transitions were not directly caused by their organization as the opposite generational group's transitions were.

For white-collar workers, the "organizationally driven" influence was the most influential category, with it applying to five out of eight. Some were rotated to other functional divisions, and others were assigned to a new operational company. Two of the senior white-collar workers who were selected as candidates for high potential management development cited career influences that we coded as "organizationally driven" when their company, Nissan, initiated the first-track development program in early 2000. They experienced a new form of organizationally directed career development. Based on the fact that senior interviewees experienced job rotation within their organization, and given that job rotation is one of the characteristic systems of Japanese HR practice, it seems that Japanese characteristics of personnel practice have not been maintained and a new type of job rotation for high potentials has emerged.

Three out of four young white-collar male interviewees mentioned "their own initiative (internal source)." They had pursued an MBA on their own, and changed their jobs. The rest of the young interviewees were rotated to other functions.

Except for career changers, the strong organizationally directed career continues to be an important fact even in the post-bubble economy.

The results of the white-collar worker group showed more self-directed transitions emerging among younger white-collar employees, and some intergenerational differences were observed among this occupation. Changes in employment practices have had an impact on MBA holders, especially among the younger generation, and they change their job on their own initiative.

Themes and Implications

A few broad themes and implications can be found as follows.

Continuities Among Japanese Careerists

- Both career success and career transition are heavily affected by external factors. This is consistent with Schwartz (2004) in that Japan is high in hierarchy and mastery.
- Continuities exist for blue-collar workers and nurses. The finding that these two occupational groups put an emphasis on external factors may result from characteristics of their jobs: team-based work and an emphasis upon their skill development process.

Changes Among White-Collar Workers

- Although samples show strong "organizationally driven" characteristics in terms of both career success and career transition, white-collar workers show signs of change in values such as uncertainty avoidance and are starting to engage in self-directed careers.
- Occupation is capable of superseding culture. A value change in collectivism versus individualism among white-collar workers has been observed since the collapse of the bubble economy.

References

Baruch, Y. 2003. Career systems in transition: A normative model for organizational career practices. *Personnel Review*, 32(2): 231–251.

Baruch, Y. 2004a. The desert generation: Lessons and implications for the new era of people management. *Personnel Review*, 33(2): 241–256.

Baruch, Y. 2004b. Transforming careers: From linear to multidirectional career paths: Organizational and individual perspectives. *Career Development International*, 9(1): 58–73.

Capelli, P. 1999. Career jobs are dead. *California Management Review*, 42(1): 146–167.

Garavan, T., Morley, M., Gunnigle, P. & Collins, E. 2001. Human capital accumulation: The role of human resource development. *Journal of European Industrial Training*, 25(2/3/4): 48–68.

Gattiker, U. E. & Larwood, L. 1988. Predictors for managers' career mobility, success, and satisfaction. *Human Relations*, 41(8), 569–591.

Hall, D. T. & Mirvis, P. H. 1995. The new career contract: Developing the whole person at midlife and beyond. *Journal of Vocational Behavior*, 47: 269–289.

Hiltrop, J. M. 1996. Managing the changing psychological contract. *Employee Relations*, 18(1): 36–49.

Hofstede, G. 1980. *Culture's Consequences: International Differences in Work-Related Values*. Newbury Park, CA: Sage.

Judge, T. A. & Bretz, R. D., Jr. 1994. Political influence behavior and career success. *Journal of Management*, 20(1): 43–65.

Judge, T. A., Cable, D. M., Boudreau, J. W. & Bretz, R. D., Jr. 1995. An empirical investigation of the predictors of executive success. *Personnel Psychology*, 48(3): 485–519.

Kawakita, Takashi. 1997. Corporate strategy and human resource management. In M. Sako & H. Sato (Eds.), *Japanese Labour and Management in Transition*: 79–103. London: Routledge.

Ministry of Education, Culture, Sports, Science and Technology. 2010. *A School Basic Survey*. Tokyo: Ministry of Education, Culture, Sports, Science and Technology.

Parker, P., Arthur, M. B. & Inkson, K. 2004. Career communities: A preliminary exploration of member-defined career support structures. *Journal of Organizational Behavior*, 25: 489–514.

Schwartz, S. H. 2004. Mapping and interpreting cultural differences around the world. In H. Vinken, J. Soeters & P. Ester (Eds.), *Comparing Cultures: Dimensions of Culture in a Comparative Perspective*. Leiden: Brill.

Thite, M. 2001. Help us but help yourself: The paradox of contemporary career management. *Career Development International*, 6(6): 312–317.

15

Careers in Mexico

Ociel Colorado

The present chapter will let us explore the idiosyncrasy of Mexican employees belonging to three different occupational groups: blue-collar workers, nurses and businesspeople. The compilation of results and concluding thoughts will offer us a more precise idea about the meaning of career success and the nature of career transitions among Mexican individuals. International managers working in Mexico or those planning to start running operations in this country may take these outcomes as a reference for their own multinational companies. While just three kinds of occupations were investigated, this study may be taken as a first insight to better understand the way of thinking of Mexican individuals within the working context.

Country Profile

To better understand the environment where the people interviewed are working and living, we will go into a brief explanation about the cultural background of Mexico as well as its political, economic and demographic conditions. We will also explore the educational system and some of the career trends and patterns prevailing in this country.

Cultural Background

Mexico is diverse owing to the diversity of the people living there. The ancient history of Mexico, the mix of the pre-Hispanic cultures with the Spanish one, the adoption of Catholicism as a consequence of colonization, and its geographical proximity and strong interaction with the most powerful economy of the world, the U.S.A., are all examples of important factors influencing the idiosyncrasy of Mexican people and the way they conceive success in their personal and professional lives.

According to Schwartz's (2006) framework, Mexico lies away from the "autonomy" dimension, which means that the country's society is classified as collectivistic rather than individualistic, with family playing an important role. Mexican individuals normally belong to large families where not only parents and siblings are important members, but also cousins, uncles and aunts, as well as grandparents. These big communities are used to getting together to celebrate and enhance their national identity (the most important celebrations in Mexico are Independence Day, the Day of the Dead, Mother's Day and Christmas). Mexico is thus a country of traditions.

Religion is another crucial factor in describing the composition of Mexican society. With close to 90 percent of the population practicing Catholicism and its large population of 110 million people, Mexico is considered as one of the most emblematic places for Catholicism's practitioners in both Latin America and the world. As viewed in Schwartz's (2006) framework, this factor is represented through the dimension of embeddedness, where Mexico is placed closer to this side than the opposite one, the intellectual autonomy dimension. People in highly religiously attached societies like Mexico seem to feel more secure when their future is defined and protected by a spiritual force which is difficult to describe but easy to feel. This behavior is also described by Hofstede (1991) within his cultural framework through the dimension of uncertainty avoidance, where Mexico is ranked high on the dimension's score.

Even though family and religion are strong and important elements of Mexican society, they have recently been threatened by the influence of the globalized era. Young Mexican people are seemingly less interested in getting involved in religious rituals and also less interested in getting married. According to the Instituto Nacional de Estadística y Geografía (INEGI, the National Institute of Statistics and Geography) (2010), in 2008 there were 14 divorces per 100 civil unions, while the same ratio was 7.4 in 2000 and 3.2 in 1971. Women are also becoming more independent and looking for more professional opportunities and development. These phenomena may be consequences of the increasing linkage between Mexico and the U.S.A. (economically and culturally), where the behavioral patterns of an individualistic community like the U.S.A. are apparently overtaking some of the traditional values of Mexican collectivistic society.

Political, Economic and Demographic Conditions

In recent times, several events have been impacting the political history of Mexico and determining its current situation. In 1910, for instance, the country was the protagonist of the first major revolution of the twentieth century. As a result and based on the ideals of such an event, the Mexican Political Constitution was conceived in 1917, which is still the document governing the political life of the Mexican republic. Labor unions started in Mexico as well, as one of the results of this civil movement. Mexican workers achieved the opportunity to associate and claim their rights as a function of the political, social and economic changes of the country.

Another crucial event happened in 1929: the creation of the National Revolutionary Party (PNR). It was renamed in 1946 as the Institutional Revolutionary Party (PRI) and was the political organization leading the country until 2000, when Vicente Fox from the National Action Party (PAN) became the first president of the opposition after more than 70 years of PRI hegemony. The ideology of PRI at the beginning was mainly socialist but nowadays it is considered to be a neoliberal party. On the other hand, PAN is more aligned to a conservative ideology, with a political position of centre-right.

Concerning women in Mexican politics, even though they have recently started to be more active, they have not yet achieved the protagonist roles that men are accustomed to. This circumstance is derived in great part from their late incorporation into the public and political life of the country. They got the right to vote and to be elected about six decades ago, in 1953 to be precise, when President Adolfo Ruiz Cortines was leading the country. This circumstance has put women at a clear disadvantage to men in actively participating in the decision-taking processes of the country.

In terms of economic aspects, Mexico, the 13th largest world economy, is actually considered as one of the prominent emerging markets (O'Neill, Wilson, Purushothaman & Stupnytska, 2005). Its economic development has undoubtedly been impacted by some major events occurring in its recent past, for example in 1938 when President Lázaro Cardenas established the expropriation of the Mexican petroleum companies as they shifted from foreign to state management. The state oil company PEMEX was so created, removing foreign companies from controlling oil operations.

In the same tenor, President José López Portillo announced in 1982 the nationalization of bank corporations, being pressed in part by the world petroleum crisis. In the same year, the Mexican peso suffered one of its major devaluations along with the one registered in 1994, better known as "the December mistake," a term created by the outgoing President Salinas in reference to the new President Zedillo's decisions to devalue the Mexican peso. Both events affected the employment of many people owing to the contingency measures taken by several companies in the downsizing or reduction of working benefits.

In contrast to these difficult times, during the last two decades Mexico has achieved important modernization in several sectors of its economy like manufacturing and telecommunications. One of the triggers of this success has undoubtedly been the incorporation of the country into the North American Free Trade Agreement (NAFTA), a trilateral free trade agreement signed in 1994 in conjunction with Canada and the United States. Consequently, technological improvements have accompanied the development of Mexico, creating a set of conditions to better interact with two of the largest and strongest economies of the world.

In terms of demographics, Mexico is a country whose population has a majority of young people. As shown in INEGI statistics, in 2009 the population under the age of 30 was 56 percent. Furthermore, the economically active population older than 14 was reported as 45.2 million people. This large and relevant work labor force is one of the factors determining the status of Mexico as one of the promising emerging future economies (Prahalad, 2005).

Educational System and Career Trends/Patterns

The Mexican educational system is divided into three different groups: basic education (from 6 to 15 years old, including elementary and secondary school); middle education (from 15 to 18 years old, including high school or technical studies); and superior education (from 18 years onwards, including high-level studies and postgraduate studies). Basic education is mandatory and free, offered by the state. Nevertheless, there are many private organizations also offering this kind of education which can sometimes be considered better-quality.

Concerning our three groups of interviewees, blue-collar workers are normally perceived as people who had no chance to pursue their studies and thus their chances of progress are less. The nursing profession is generally conceived to be practiced by females and not always well remunerated, which is probably the result of the low recognition this kind of study has traditionally had. In reference to businesspeople, they are normally seen as privileged and influential individuals in society because of the better education and professional opportunities they generally have.

But, no matter which professional group we analyze, generally speaking we can say that young women in Mexico have started to clamor for a more egalitarian set of working opportunities. In a society where men have traditionally been playing the working role and women the family-caring role, this situation seems to be changing. Nowadays, it is more common to see young couples with females also performing a professional activity and thus contributing an important part of the household income. As a consequence, the available time for child-rearing is becoming less for these young couples, so the number of children they normally plan to have is fewer than in the past. According to INEGI, the growing population rate in 2009 was 0.86 percent compared with the 3.4 percent registered in the 1960s.

Finally, there are two important points to highlight regarding government support aimed at enhancing the development of the Mexican workforce. First, it is crucial to increase the quality of the public educational system as well as to ensure equal access to such education for all individuals. A more educated society is naturally stimulated to look for better opportunities of professional development. Another important action is to keep a permanent policy of creation of job positions. Thus most of the illegal immigration of Mexican workers going to the U.S.A. could be prevented. It is imperative that both policies are included in Mexico's long-term development planning.

Main Findings

This section is devoted to describing the characteristics of the Mexican interviewees as well as to discussing the facts discovered in relation to their way of defining career success and managing career transitions. The categories analyzed are shown in Tables 15.1 and 15.2, which represent the base material for this analysis.

Sample Details

The data collection for this study was focused on individuals living in the city of Monterrey, in northern Mexico. Being the third largest city in the country, Monterrey is a cosmopolitan and multi-faceted area suitable to finding individuals from different kinds of cultural and professional backgrounds. Considering that the three groups of individuals interviewed are naturally different, the strategies followed to invite them to participate in the study were different as well.

To invite blue-collar workers, people were recruited at the food services and cleaning services departments of one of the largest universities in town. Nurses were recruited at one of the biggest and most prestigious hospitals in the city of Monterrey. As for businesspeople, they were contacted through two initiatives: visiting the business incubator of the above-mentioned university and looking for people working in big corporations or running their own consultancy business. There is no special reason for not having included women as part of this group. It is simply that the number of available businessmen was considerably superior to that of the available businesswomen and so the final interviewees turned out to be all men.

The places where interviews were carried out varied. Businesspeople and nurses were interviewed at their working places, which definitely helped to achieve immersion in their own environments and day-to-day activities. Blue-collar workers were also targeted to be interviewed at their original working places, but the excess of noise and people passing by acted as adverse factors. Because of this, they were interviewed in a special room, which made them feel more relaxed and confident during the interview.

See Table 15.1 for the total number of interviewees, the number of interviewees in each occupational and generational group, the gender count of the sample, the educational level of the individuals, and the average age for the younger and older generations.

The group of people participating in this study constitute a heterogeneous sample in several respects. For example, there are blue-collar workers who belong to a low or medium socio-economic class as well as nurses or businesspeople who belong to a medium or high socio-economic class. Consequently, the background of the interviewees and their level of education are naturally different. Besides, there are some individuals working in companies in positions very different to those of others, while several of them are heading their own business. In addition, there are six different industries represented in the whole sample.

Table 15.1 Mexico sampling profile

	Blue-collar workers = 7		Nurses = 6		Businesspeople = 5	
Generation	Younger	Older	Younger	Older	Younger	Older
Gender	3 males	1 female, 3 males	3 females	2 females, 1 male	3 males	2 males
Educational level	Secondary or vocational school	Elementary, secondary or vocational school or none	University or nursing school	University or nursing school	University or master's in process	Master's or Ph.D. in process

Total N=18, with 6 females and 12 males. The average age was 26.5 for the younger generation and 52.4 for the older generation.

All these factors enriched the investigation and enabled us to get a set of better conclusions.

Career Success Patterns

A full profile of the career success data in Mexico is given in Table 15.2.

Table 15.2 Meanings of career success in Mexico

	Occupation			Gender		Generation		
Total number of interviewees	Nurse	Blue-collar	Business	Female	Male	Younger	Older	Total number mentioning category
18	6	7	5	6	12	9	9	
Person	6	6	5	6	11	8	9	17
Satisfaction	6	5	4	6	9	7	8	15
Achievement	4	7	5	4	12	7	9	16
Learning and development	3	4	3	4	6	5	5	10
Self-actualization	2	1	4	2	5	4	3	7
Job	6	5	5	6	10	8	8	16
Job security	0	1	0	0	1	0	1	1
Job/task characteristics	5	4	5	6	8	8	6	14
Job performance	2	1	0	2	1	2	1	3
Performing one's role	3	1	0	2	2	3	1	4
Contributing to organizational success	1	0	1	1	1	1	1	2
Interaction with the environment	5	5	5	5	10	7	8	15
Social working environment	4	3	2	4	5	5	4	9
Network	0	1	2	0	3	3	0	3
Recognition	4	4	1	4	5	4	5	9
Work–life context/balance	0	1	3	0	4	2	2	4
Making a difference	3	0	3	3	3	4	2	6
Material output	2	4	5	2	9	6	5	11
Basic survival	0	0	1	0	1	1	0	1
Financially supporting family	0	2	3	0	5	3	2	5
Affording material goods	0	1	0	0	1	1	0	1
Financial security	2	2	1	2	3	2	3	5

The meaning of career success for the 18 Mexican individuals was mostly defined in terms of the following categories:

Achievement	(16 people)
Satisfaction	(15 people)
Job/task characteristics	(14 people)
Learning and development	(10 people)
Social working environment	(9 people)
Recognition	(9 people)
Self-actualization	(7 people)
Making a difference	(6 people)

(Note: The categories considered were those mentioned for a third or more of the sample, which means six or more people.)

As we can see, the categories of satisfaction and achievement were the two most popular among Mexican interviewees. Both categories were equally represented in terms of occupational group, gender and generation. We may infer that the two-sidedness of the career concept proposed by Goffman (1961) is interpreted by these individuals in terms of satisfaction on the subjective side and achievement on the objective side.

The idea of knowing the "two-sidedness" of the career concept is not just to relate work with the objective career and non-work with the subjective career. The intention is to propose a broader vision of this concept, looking at it from both angles at the same time and not just from either the objective or the subjective one, which definitely offers a limited picture of reality. For Mexican employees this concept seems to be highly applicable.

Following are two quotes exemplifying satisfaction and achievement, the two sides of the coin:

> I think that a successful person is one who finds the job that really pleases him or her.
>
> (Older male Mexican blue-collar)

> I think that success is to do what you love and to achieve what you want. It is important to succeed in both the social and the economic aspects to consider it as a real success.
>
> (Younger Mexican businessman)

Another way to define success was in terms of job/task characteristics, another very popular category, more mentioned by the younger generation than the older one and by the totality of women interviewed. There is no obvious explanation to say why females are more focused on this category than men. Nevertheless, concerning the younger generation defining success in terms of the desired characteristics in their jobs, we may deduce that they are more concerned about constructing a solid and coherent career from the beginning than individuals belonging to the older generation, who normally have their careers already defined.

The learning and development aspect of the career success definition was equally mentioned by the younger and older generation participants, and no relevant difference among the occupational groups was detected. In contrast, women were more numerous in proportion to men in referring to this category. A possible explanation may be the new role of women in Mexican working society, who are gradually looking to be more participative than they were in the past.

Concerning the working environment aspect of the career success definition, the following quote brings us the opinion of one more individual:

> I perceive this hospital as a very professional institution with a very positive working environment. That's why I have decided to continue working here, even though I have received job proposals from other hospitals.
>
> (Older female Mexican nurse)

She refers to the importance of the social working environment when thinking about career success and personal/professional satisfaction. This category of career success was proportionally more mentioned by nurses and women. The nature of Mexican society as more collectivistic than individualistic is probably the reason why these people tend to consider the impact of coworkers in their perception of success. Nevertheless, there is no clear explanation from the interviews to justify the preference of women over men for the importance of the social working environment category. It is probably the nature of Mexican women to be traditionally more social-care oriented than men.

One more way to conceive career success is in terms of recognition. Nurses and blue-collar workers as well as females were the groups that most frequently mentioned this category, as indicated in the following quote:

> I work in the cleaning department of this university. When people who work in the areas I normally clean recognize my job, I feel really good. Sometimes they express their gratitude, giving me small presents.
>
> (Older female Mexican blue-collar)

In a society like Mexico where the distribution of power and material resources is quite unequal, people located at the bottom of the organizational hierarchy (as the blue-collar workers normally are) tend to feel compensated for the lack of such elements with certain kinds of recognition. That is why this individual and others in the same occupational group mentioned this category as an important part of their definition of success.

Finally, the self-actualization and making a difference categories were also amongst the most mentioned categories defining career success for Mexican individuals. This pair of subjective categories was more popular within the businesspeople group of interviewees than in the other two. The existing gap in terms of educational level of this group in comparison with nurses and blue-collar workers is the most tangible and evident reason for such difference in perceptions. In terms of generation and gender, there was no significant disparity reported, except regarding the making a difference category, which women were twice as likely to mention as their male counterparts.

Even though each of the three occupational groups expressed their definition of career success in their own terms, it is important to highlight the commonality apparent in mentioning that being dedicated to performing activities you really love and enjoy is an essential requisite to being considered a successful person. These ideas are included in the satisfaction category, which along with achievement was the most mentioned category within the whole Mexican sample.

Career Transition Patterns

Based upon the coding of the sample, two-thirds of the Mexican interview participants (12 people out of 18) were more likely to manage their career transitions in a self-driven way. Tables 15.3 and 15.4 give more information on career transitions in the Mexico data.

Patterns discovered with this population show that businesspeople, then nurses and then blue-collar workers are more likely to manage transitions based upon their own decisions. In terms of gender and generation, women and young interviewees showed a higher evidence of managing career transitions in an own-initiative way.

It is surprising how in Mexico, which is a collectivistic country, people show a tendency to manage their career transitions in a self-driven way, a characteristic more typically seen among people coming from individualistic countries like the U.S.A. One possible explanation is that the whole sample was constituted by people recruited in Monterrey, a northern industrialized city in Mexico, which has traditionally been conceived of as an entrepreneurial place highly influenced by the U.S. doing-business mentality.

Table 15.3 Career transition patterns in Mexico

	Occupation			Gender		Generation		Total number mentioning category
	Nurse	Blue-collar	Business	Female	Male	Younger	Older	
Total number of interviewees=18 N=	6	7	5	6	12	9	9	
Internally driven causes/triggers of career transitions:								
Own initiative (internal source)	4	3	5	5	7	7	5	12
Own initiative (external source/stimuli)	0	0	2	0	2	1	1	2
Externally driven causes/triggers of career transitions:								
Driven by graduation/certification	3	0	1	3	1	4	0	4
Driven by completion of obligation	0	0	0	0	0	0	0	0
Unsought opportunities	0	1	1	0	2	2	0	2
Counsel/encouragement	1	3	1	1	4	2	3	5
Organizationally driven	4	2	2	3	5	3	5	8
Health	0	0	0	0	0	0	0	0
Family role	0	1	0	1	0	0	1	1
Macro factors	0	0	0	0	0	0	0	0
Luck and contingencies	0	0	0	0	0	0	0	0
Individuals' management of career transitions:								
Job search	6	6	5	6	11	9	8	17
Planning/setting goals and priorities	5	1	4	6	4	5	5	10
Organization and time management	1	0	1	1	1	1	1	2
Formal education, training, short courses	0	0	2	0	2	2	0	2
Informal training	0	3	1	0	4	3	1	4
Making contingent/other plans	1	1	2	0	4	1	3	4
Recreation	0	0	0	0	0	0	0	0
Consequential thinking	1	1	3	2	5	1	4	5
Job experimentation	2	5	2	2	7	2	7	9
Financial planning	1	0	0	1	0	0	1	1

Table 15.4 External influencing factors upon career transition patterns in Mexico

Total number of interviewees = 18	Occupation			Gender		Generation		
	Nurse	Blue-collar	Business	Female	Male	Younger	Older	Total number mentioning category
N=	6	7	5	6	12	9	9	
Boss/superior	2	0	2	2	2	2	2	4
Support	2	0	0	2	0	1	1	2
Barrier	0	0	2	0	2	1	1	2
Peers	0	0	0	0	0	0	0	0
Support	0	0	0	0	0	0	0	0
Barriers	0	0	0	0	0	0	0	0
Family	0	1	2	1	2	2	1	3
Barriers	0	0	1	0	1	1	0	1
Friends	2	0	1	2	1	3	0	3
Support	2	0	1	2	1	3	0	3
Barriers	0	0	0	0	0	0	0	0
Organization	4	2	1	3	4	3	4	7
Support	4	1	1	3	3	2	4	6
Barriers	0	0	0	0	0	0	0	0
Network	4	4	2	4	6	4	6	10
Work	2	1	1	1	3	0	4	4
Personal	2	3	1	3	3	4	2	6
Professional	0	0	0	0	0	0	0	0
Education and training	4	0	4	3	5	5	3	8
Financial situation	1	2	0	1	2	1	2	3
Role of luck and contingencies	0	0	0	0	0	0	0	0

The following quote exemplifies the preferred way Mexican individuals manage their career transitions in a more self-driven way:

> My husband didn't allow me to work; he just wanted me to take care of our kids. But I have a sister working in this company as a secretary so she offered me a job. In that time my husband and I had some troubles in our relationship but everything was cleared later. I told him that I really wanted to work and thus contribute to our family expenses.
>
> (Older female Mexican blue-collar)

Apart from such evidence of internally driven causes/triggers of career transitions, there is an indicator related to the need of Mexican employees to constantly deal with an external factor completely out of their control. The non-stable economy of the country, more critical during the 1980s and 1990s, has recurrently led organizations to do some sort of downsizing and restructuring among their personnel. As shown in Table 15.3, this factor is mentioned by 8 out of the 18 interviewees through the organizationally driven category, indicating that it is the most common external trigger impacting their career transitions. The following quote exemplifies this issue:

> This was a very dramatic moment for me because I suddenly lost my job. Being in a very stable situation, the company started to face financial difficulties and some of the business units were closed, including the one I was working in. All this happened in 1982, when Mexico experienced one of the most severe economic crises in recent years.
>
> (Older Mexican businessman)

Concerning the individuals' management of career transitions, the three most mentioned categories were: job search, planning/setting goals and priorities, and job experimentation. The first reason was equally popular among the three occupational groups; the second was led by nurses and businesspeople; and the third was considerably more mentioned by blue-collar workers. In reference to the planning/setting goals and priorities category, the following quote tells us about the entrepreneurial characteristics of some Mexican young people:

> I was working while carrying out some projects as a freelance. After having the initial meeting of one of these projects I realized that it was too big and ambitious so I would need to be dedicated to it full time. As a consequence, I decided to resign my contract in the company and so founded my own graphic design business.
>
> (Younger Mexican businessman)

In Table 15.4 we can see the external influencing factors of career transitions listed. It is evident how the collectivistic side of Mexican society comes up again with the network category as the one most mentioned. Personal and work relationships, in that order, are important factors for the interviewees in supporting transitions in their respective careers. This phenomenon is very similar to the *guanxi* aspect of Chinese business culture, a collectivistic society too. This concept embraces the idea of using one's network of relationships in order to cooperate and support one another (Zhu & Zhang, 2007). In essence, it is related to the exchange of favors, which is expected to be carried out regularly and voluntarily. A similar ritual happens within Mexican business society.

Practical Implications

A better understanding of the Mexican working/business environment is important for international managers and others linked with Mexico's workforce. The way Mexicans conceive of their careers, and the factors influencing their perception of success are both important elements to address for these leaders. The following brief summary contains five relevant points related to the issue:

- Conception of career success. Mexican individuals seem to be highly influenced by emotional drivers. The satisfaction and identification they feel with their positions and companies are both important factors in being considered a successful person. Thus it is important to assign these individuals some sorts of activities they really love and enjoy.
- Components of success. In the Mexican working context employees tend to include more non-material things such as feelings, emotions and spirituality in their conception of success, most notably in the blue-collar sector. A proper understanding from superiors about this issue may enhance their interaction with employees, so increasing the individuals' organizational loyalty.
- Personal–working life linkage. One consequence of the collectivistic characteristic of Mexican society is seen at work. Mexican individuals normally don't separate their working lives from their personal lives, and it is quite normal to relate these two worlds in a close way. Thus any managerial decision impacting the employee's professional environment will have a direct impact on his or her personal life.
- Career planning. The concept of career planning is very well understood by businesspeople. They have a very good notion of the meaning of goals, stages and success; besides, they are normally focused on future events. As for nurses, they are used to guiding their careers in a less structured way, even though they have notions of what career planning is. In contrast, the blue-collar workers are not at all used to career planning. They live in the present, take decisions in the present and hope for the best from the future.
- Organizational hierarchies. The Mexican working environment is hierarchically structured. The way people take decisions is normally related to considering their superior's point of view. As a result, it is important to note that Mexican employees seem to expect some guidance or counseling when involved in a decision-taking process and thinking about making a transition in their careers.

This compilation of ideas represents a good starting point to better understand the Mexican business and working environment. Those with linkages to the Mexican workforce can take it as a reference when developing career plans, working policies and incentive programs, or simply to better understand the human resources they are working with. This better understanding should give them stronger tools to succeed in their daily managing activities.

References

Goffman, E. 1961. The moral career of the mental patient. In *Asylums*: 125–170. New York: Anchor.

Hofstede, G. 1991. *Cultures and Organizations: Software of the Mind*. London: McGraw-Hill.

Instituto Nacional de Estadística y Geografía (INEGI). 2009. *Día Mundial de la Población (11 de julio)*. Available at: http://www.inegi.org.mx/inegi/contenidos/espanol/prensa/aPropositom. asp?s=inegi&c=2734&ep=18 (accessed Nov. 11, 2009).

Instituto Nacional de Estadística y Geografía (INEGI). 2010. *Matrimonios y Divorcios en México (14 de febrero)*. Available at: http://www.inegi.org.mx/inegi/contenidos/espanol/prensa/contenidos/ estadisticas/2010/matrimonios10.asp?s=inegi&c=2751&ep=28 (accessed Feb. 15, 2010).

O'Neill, J., Wilson, D., Purushothaman, R. & Stupnytska, A. 2005. How solid are the BRICs? *Goldman Sachs Global Economics Paper*, 134: 1–23.

Prahalad, C. K. 2005. *The Fortune at the Bottom of the Pyramid*. Upper Saddle River, NJ: Wharton School Publishing.

Schwartz, S. H. 2006. *Value Dimensions of Culture and National Difference*. Available at: http://www. uib.no/psyfa/isp/diversity/content/reseach/multicultur/Workshop/Schwartz%20.pdf (accessed Feb. 15, 2010).

Zhu, Y. & Zhang, A. M. 2007. Understanding guanxi (connections) from business leaders' perspectives. *Business Communication Quarterly*, 70: 385–389.

16

Careers in Serbia

Biljana Bogićević Milikić and Jelena Zikic

The Cultural Context

Very few studies have investigated the characteristics of Serbian national culture. One study of the former Yugoslavia (Obradović, 1982) classified Serbian culture within the group of pre-industrial cultures, which is present mainly in agrarian countries. Such cultures are based on the implicit assumption about limited resources—everything that is valued (e.g. land and wealth, as well as power, position, friendship, love, health, honor and intelligence) is limited. Since the resources are limited, they cannot be increased but rather only redistributed among the members of the society. This assumption explains why egalitarianism, which assumes equality in distribution within any social group, is one of the major values of Serbian culture (Županov, 1985). Egalitarianism is also directly opposite to competition, which is not welcome, and in this way served as a strong base for the strengthening of communism in Serbia.

Interestingly, however, Serbian sociologists (e.g. Lazić, 1995) also emphasize the fact that numerous individuals in the former Yugoslavia simultaneously accepted liberal as well as traditional values. Traditionalism has deep roots in the (until recently prevailing) rural way of life, and some of its basic values—although in a somewhat transformed form—were also promoted in the socialist system (collectivism, solidarity, equality). At the same time, owing to the quasi-market nature of the system, which was opened to the West, Serbian society was penetrated by liberal values, which, however, retained a primarily promotional character.

Apart from egalitarianism, Serbian culture is also characterized by high collectivism (Hofstede, 2001), which assumes that the ties between individuals within one society are very tight. In Schwartz's (2006) framework Serbia would be considered part of Eastern Europe and thus lower in embeddedness compared with Africa, Asia and the Middle East, but higher in this dimension than Western Europe and the Americas. People are born into collectives or in-groups that may be their extended family, their tribe or their village. Everybody is supposed to look after the interest of his or her in-group and to have no opinions and beliefs other than those of their in-group; in exchange, the in-group will protect them when they are in trouble (Hofstede, 1983). Collectivism in Serbia is also strongly related to an external locus of control. For example, Serbian workers would stay with their companies even if they did not receive any salary for more than a year, and in this case they would ask the state to assist their employers instead of looking for a new job.

Another important cultural value in Serbia is high power distance (Hofstede, 2001; Hofstede & Hofstede, 2005), which assumes that Serbians accept and expect that power is distributed unequally in their society. This cultural value is deeply rooted in Serbian hierarchies of the state, political parties, companies and other types of organizations.

More recently, Schwartz (2006, 2008) has also addressed Serbian culture (as part of the former Yugoslavia) and classified it within the East European and Balkan region. The East European cultures, according to Schwartz, are low on embeddedness and hierarchy compared with Africa, the Middle East and Southeast Asia, but higher on these cultural orientations than Western Europe. According to Schwartz (2008: 8) cultures that emphasize embeddedness focus on social relationships, framing life in a collective context and maintaining the status quo. This value is contrasted with autonomy, whereby individuals are encouraged to pursue their own preferences and be unique. In hierarchical societies, on the other hand, unequal distribution of resources and power is legitimate and seen as important in guaranteeing productive behaviors; this is distinguishable from egalitarianism, which in Schwartz's terms views people as being on an equal footing, with concern for others' welfare and choosing to act for the benefit of others rather than pursuing selfish interests. Balkan states also seem to be somewhat lower on harmony than the East-Central European and Baltic states,[1] meaning that there is less emphasis on accepting, understanding and appreciating the world as it is, rather than trying to change it; protecting the environment and ensuring peace are important values in these cultures. Instead the Balkan and Eastern states, which would include Serbia, put more emphasis (according to Schwartz) on mastery, that is using active self-assertion to get ahead, changing the national and social environment in order to attain group or personal goals. One can only assume that, compared to East-Central and Baltic cultures which were also traditionally closer to Western Europe, more Eastern and Balkan regions, where Serbia is situated, have had a somewhat more turbulent history and significant political and economic struggles. In summary, according to Schwartz, the Balkan states (with the exception of Bosnia-Herzegovina) are towards the middle of the spectrum in most values when compared to other countries. The former Yugoslavia, that is Serbia today, tends to be more towards mastery than harmony and more towards hierarchy than egalitarianism and is near the middle of the spectrum between embeddedness and autonomy.

Christian Orthodox religious beliefs played a minor role among Serbs during times of communism, but have survived to some extent in their more intimate, familial circles rather than in public life. However, especially starting in the early 2000s, the Orthodox church has gained a more significant and explicit role within society, which is also confirmed by the introduction of the catechism in primary schools. Today Serbia has only 0.5 percent of the population who define themselves as atheists, and over 95 percent (95.5 percent)[2] of the country is theistic, with Christianity the leading religion (Orthodox 85 percent, Catholic 5.5 percent, Protestant 1.08 percent). Religious beliefs are also in accord with the external locus of control and egalitarian values, which are evident in the Serbian national culture.

Economic and Demographic Trends

For the last 19 years Serbia has been facing radical political, economic and social changes. During the 1990s Serbia witnessed the disintegration of the former Yugoslavia followed by civil wars in Croatia and Bosnia and Herzegovina, and extreme hyperinflation.[3] Further, Serbia experienced the loss of the former market, U.N. economic sanctions on foreign trade and FDI, maintenance of social ownership, NATO air strikes, spontaneous and tycoon privatization, strengthening of the informal sector (with a share of 34 percent in GDP) and considerable economic crisis. On October 5, 2000 Serbia managed to overthrow Milosevic's Socialist Party, and this event is often known as the Bulldozer Revolution. With the political changes, Serbia has again started the process of transition toward a market economy through much faster privatization, restructuring of enterprises, downsizing of public enterprises, macroeconomic stabilization and liberalization. These processes resulted in high GNP growth rates of 6 percent annually and significant growth of the SME sector, but also in a very high unemployment rate (above 30 percent during the 2000s and 22.5 percent in 2009), a significant role for the informal sector, still high levels of corruption, high political involvement in the economic sector and a fairly low standard of living (around 15 percent of the population is considered to be poor). The number of retirees is also very high (1.6 million), especially compared to the number of employed individuals. Thus pensions are often paid out from the Republic of Serbia national budget, as there is not enough in the pension funds, and the average pension is extremely low, only around 150 euros. The number of people living in poverty is increasing, and the middle class is slowly disappearing.

Earning power has gone down steadily to the point where many consider a two-income household not sufficient to make ends meet. The labor market has made explicit differences between the earnings of those with higher levels of education and the earnings of those with lower or no education. Thus higher education is becoming the basic requirement for finding a good job.

In analyzing these multiple transition processes in Serbia, Polovina (2007) indicated that under conditions of drastic economic crisis (and U.N. sanctions) the financial position of the majority of families had deteriorated dramatically, especially families with children, who are the most vulnerable ones. Many were faced with an inability to accumulate material goods which should have provided the coming generation with the basis for faster development. Massive impoverishment led to the additional employment of a great number of persons in Serbia since 1990 in the private sector, apart from their employment in socially owned companies. Sociological surveys have shown that all households reported additional jobs in irregular forms of work, without clearly defined working hours, often below their education level or skills, and in a manner of "daily opportunities" (Polovina, 2007). Social circumstances and crisis in value orientation of the population also brought a host of other problems, such as a lot of inconsistencies in moral norms and standards. Changes in the value system and the moral crisis have brought extremes and the unfortunate "normalization" of asocial and aggressive behavior (Lazić, 1995).

Educational System/Occupational Background

A general cultural assumption is that higher education results in higher earning power and a greater choice of higher-status jobs. A bachelor's degree (four-year university degree) is seen as a necessary entry requirement for a "good" job in all professions and many trades.

Nursing secondary school (a four-year program) has been the requirement for all nurses in Serbia. More recently, there have also been several universities across Serbia that offer "higher-level" nursing education, as well as recently formed master's programs in nursing studies. Despite these very recent developments, the majority of nurses and nursing assistants today have mostly attended a four-year nursing secondary school. However, in the near future there will be more and more demand for further education and higher and more academic degrees in this area.

In business, anyone who can gather funds and be a successful entrepreneur can succeed without a college degree. However, a business degree and preferably an internationally awarded MBA are typically seen as entry requirements for established corporations. About ten years ago, only public universities (departments of economics organizational studies) offered business economics programs, which stemmed from the 1950s. However, during the last decade there has been a springing up of multiple private business schools and universities (around 40) that offer a variety of courses and programs in the area of economics, business and management as well as master's-level studies in business. While the academic nature and quality of these programs is questionable, this situation attests to the recent popularity of and interest in business studies in general in Serbia. In the past, it was the case that general managers, executives and CEOs, as well as some engineers, were able to become business leaders without any particular business education. Now that seems to be changing, and business school education is looking more like that in the West.

With blue-collar workers, there is still some informal apprentice-based training, but increasingly such workers require formal certification or choose to pursue a secondary school degree (three or four years).

Career Trends and Patterns

Serbia presents a particularly interesting and unique context for studying careers. Given its recent turbulent history, its society is in transition, and some of the traditional views are being challenged by the arrival of the new economy, strong influences from the European Union and general forces of globalization. Following World War II, employees in Serbian companies enjoyed classic advancement through the organizational hierarchy, and a fairly stable employment contract was the norm for many individuals. Employees generally enjoyed very good living standards and had high loyalty to their (mostly state-owned) employers. Strong trade unions were also characteristic of the times, as well as secure employment. However, throughout the 1990s Serbians had to cope with many dramatic changes in the economic, political and socio-cultural contexts. At the beginning of the 2000s Serbia started the process of transition toward a market economy. The restructuring and privatization of companies have had a strong impact on the labor market, but also on the strengthening of existing vast regional differences in economic development and opportunities for employment.

The labor market in Serbia has the majority of characteristics which are commonly found in transition economies, such as an increase of unemployment in the early years of transition, long-term unemployment, a high unemployment rate among youth (the youth unemployment youth rate is 2.5 times higher than the unemployment rate among adults; Krstić & Sanfey, 2007), a higher percentage of people with lower education levels, big regional employment inequalities and large earning discrepancies between cities and other localities in favor of cities (Krsti, 2004; Litchfield, Reilly & Krstić, 2007). Currently, with a population of 7.5 million and an unemployment rate of 28 percent, Serbia is fighting against unemployment and for better living standards for its citizens. The informal sector (approximately 34 percent of GNP) facilitates workforce mobility in a way that absorbs surpluses, offers jobs to people who have lost them or are inactive, and also offers more flexible working practices (Krstić, 2004). The average monthly gross salary in 2009 was approximately 300 euros. Many individuals have been forced into various types of career transitions, from unemployment to dramatic career change, while others have been fortunate enough to apply their expertise in privately owned firms or to move to self-employment or the informal sector. All these trends have inevitably impacted the way Serbs define careers and their understanding of career success. Given this array of contextual peculiarities, it is also important to note that this recent history of Serbia has had a different effect across generations; thus it is likely that the current views of Serbs may vary significantly based on the age and gender of our respondents.

The "new careers" in Serbia are seen as much more independent of the organization. Society in general has seen an increase in wealth inequality, and much more value is placed on professionals, emotional independence from the organization, and affording material goods. Selection is now based more on market values and the abilities of candidates, with more emphasis placed on autonomy, variety of tasks and challenge at work. Younger people are much more aware of the importance of their career capital; many of those who can afford to will undertake international degrees and education abroad as well as locally. They are searching more proactively for higher-paid jobs, often within foreign companies settling in Serbia. Private owners are likely to lay off an employee with much more ease than before, since the role of trade unions is now very weak. As seen before, however, society still puts great emphasis on nepotism and political connections as important mechanisms for finding a job.

The family is no longer able to financially support children (the only exception is providing common housing), since the older generation suffered the most negative effects from organizational downsizing and restructuring. With these new conditions, the older generation are becoming almost completely unable to search for new jobs, to participate in training programs and to change their career path. Rather they are looking to fulfill the legal conditions to retire.

Traditionally in Serbia, only certain individuals were seen as having a "career"— these were army careers or medical careers, for example. The vast majority of individuals were considered to have "jobs" only, such as teacher, researcher or driver. It was also assumed that once people's education was completed (trade, apprenticeship or higher education) they would follow that same career or job path for the rest of their life. For the most part, that secure and very traditional career path was in fact realistic and achieved by the majority. Today, career and life uncertainty in Serbia is such that individuals are most likely to expect several career changes, and many of these will be driven by external triggers. In addition, individuals are much more likely to work in "survival" jobs and may have to exercise great career adaptability for the transition time that Serbs and Serbia are undergoing. In summary, careers in Serbia have moved from lifelong employment and exclusively organizationally driven careers to multiple career changes driven by individual initiatives and coping with all the characteristics of a society in transition.

Findings From the Study

To understand the findings, it is useful to understand where our research participants come from. Interviewees were gathered primarily from Belgrade, the capital of Serbia, with its population of 1.6 million and a share of 30 percent of the national GDP creation. The sample represents a relatively sophisticated, cosmopolitan and urban workforce. Table 16.1 shows the profile of the sample involved in the interviews.

Table 16.1 Serbia sample profile

	Business graduates		Nurses		Blue-collar workers	
	Older	Younger	Older	Younger	Older	Younger
N =	4	3	3	5	3	3
Gender	1 female, 3 males	3 females	3 females	3 females, 2 males	2 females, 1 male	2 females, 1 male
	N = 7		N = 8		N = 6	

Total N = 21.

As can be seen, the nurse sample is dominated by females. This is more or less representative of trends in this sector.

Meanings of Career Success

Looking across the sample as a whole the following meanings of career success were coded by the research team for the whole or almost the whole sample of 21 research participants. For more complete details, see Table 16.2.

Satisfaction	(21 people—whole sample)
Work–life context/balance	(21 people—whole sample)
Achievement	(20 people)
Social working environment	(20 people)
Network	(20 people)
Job/task characteristics	(20 people)
Learning and development	(19 people)
Self-actualization	(19 people)
Recognition	(19 people)
Job performance	(19 people)
Financially supporting family	(17 people)

Less frequent meanings of career success found in the Serbian sample were the following:

Basic survival	(3 people)
Contributing to organizational success	(4 people)
Job security	(7 people)
Making a difference	(10 people)

What Can Be Learned From This?

Small differences in how the meaning of career success was perceived among these occupational groups in Serbia point to a perhaps shared meaning by our population in general.

The results suggest that the definition of career success in Serbia consists of both subjective and objective meanings. Overall results show that a variety of subjective and objective meanings have been mentioned by Serbians. The results also indicate that Serbians perceive career success as rooted in personal satisfaction and provision of work–life

Table 16.2 Meanings of career success in Serbia

	Occupation			Gender		Generation		Total number mentioning category
Total number of interviewees 21	Nurse 8	Blue-collar 6	Business 7	Female 14	Male 7	Younger 11	Older 10	
Person	8	6	7	14	7	11	10	21
Satisfaction	8	6	7	14	7	11	10	21
Achievement	7	6	7	13	7	11	9	20
Learning and development	8	4	7	13	6	10	9	19
Self-actualization	8	4	7	13	6	10	9	19
Job	8	6	7	14	7	11	10	21
Job security	3	4	0	6	1	3	4	7
Job/task characteristics	8	5	7	14	6	11	9	20
Job performance	8	4	7	12	7	9	10	19
Performing one's role	7	4	5	12	4	8	8	16
Contributing to organizational success	0	1	3	3	1	2	2	4
Interaction with the environment	8	6	7	14	7	11	10	21
Social working environment	8	5	7	13	7	11	9	20
Network	8	5	7	14	6	11	9	20
Recognition	8	4	7	12	7	11	8	19
Work–life context/balance	8	6	7	14	7	11	10	21
Making a difference	7	1	2	8	2	6	4	10
Material output	8	6	7	14	7	11	10	21
Basic survival	0	3	0	2	1	0	3	3
Financially supporting family	7	4	6	10	7	7	10	17
Affording material goods	2	3	6	7	4	8	3	11
Financial security	6	5	2	10	3	6	7	13

balance as well as in objective indicators of success such as material output, achievement, recognition and financial achievement. This dualistic view of career success may in fact present some evidence of career interdependence. This is a long-standing tradition in career studies, and it assumes the duality of objective and subjective career dimensions, recognizing that objective and subjective careers do not exist in isolation from each other (Hughes, 1958). Recently, there has been a renewed interest in further understanding this interdependence (Arthur, Khapova & Wilderom, 2005; Khapova, Arthur & Wilderom, 2007).

Thus, on the one hand we did observe the overwhelming importance of subjective career success indicators in Serbia, which one may argue points in the direction of careers perhaps becoming more "boundary-less" in some ways, with changing career orientation and movement away from a strong emphasis on classic indicators of objective career success (Arthur et al., 2005; Schein, 1996). Yet Serbia also still relies heavily on objective definitions of career success and the importance of financially supporting one's family, for example. Given the amount of turbulence and instability in the society, objective definitions of career success quite understandably continue to play an important role. In fact, what we may be seeing here also is clear signs of a society in transition, where traditional values and reliance on more objective indicators are still very much present. At the same time, the society is undergoing significant changes, and there is also evidence of career success being defined by the individual and based on variety of subjective indicators. These findings contribute to making the study of career success across cultures and career theory a lot more inclusive (Heslin, 2005), especially by including countries such as Serbia, which have a unique history and therefore context in which careers develop.

Some of the most important meanings of career success in Serbia as mentioned above were satisfaction and work–life context/balance. Satisfaction or enjoying one's job/work was reported by a substantial number of participants, with no clear pattern as to subsamples.

> Even if someone succeeded in his career, if he did not have a family he would be an unsuccessful man.

In addition, respondents also talked a lot about their ability to have good networks, and this was clearly seen as one aspect of career success. This is also more typical of a society that is identified as fairly collectivistic and/ or more embedded according to Schwartz (2006) than, for example, Western Europe and the Americas. In addition, this also may be seen as a sign of high power distance in society and/or higher levels of mastery and hierarchy as compared with the Baltic and East-Central states.

> The sign of success is having more communication with as many important [right] people as possible.
>   If you want to find a good job in Serbia, you have to have good connections.
>
> (Younger person)

Achievement was also a popular meaning of career success across occupational, generational and gender subsamples in Serbia. The fact that achievement is such a popular meaning of career success is somewhat surprising, since in the collectivistic cultures personal achievement is not seen as perhaps the typical way to define career success. One possible explanation is that the achievement is understood by participants as someone's success in performing his or her job very well and being recognized by his or her environment as a good performer. On the other hand, this could also be the result of how Schwartz (2006) may classify Serbia as part of the Balkan and more Eastern states, which present lower levels of harmony, intellectual autonomy and egalitarianism and higher levels of mastery and hierarchy as compared with the Baltic and East-Central states. Recognition being important for our sample in Serbia, on the other hand, is quite expected given the somewhat collectivistic society that values its social surroundings, and thus being recognized and praised by one's social circle for achievements would be expected. Job/task characteristics for the majority of respondents were seen as part of that job satisfaction; that is, success in one's career is seen as satisfaction with the job and with the type of work done. Similarly, self-actualization and job performance are seen as stemming from the need for achievement and recognition described above. The majority of participants were likely to associate learning and development with career success. Learning and development represent an important mode in Serbian culture to achieve a career success.

Career Success Themes in Serbia

The most intriguing findings regarding occupational categories and career success indicate that business graduates put a lot of emphasis on subjective indicators of success such as learning environment, self-actualization and self-expression (Hall & Chandler, 2005), as well as other indicators such as recognition, autonomy and job performance. This may also be to some extent a function of their age and may be an indicator of Generation X and Y preferences. Blue-collar workers on the other hand were much more concerned with work–life balance, job security, basic survival and interestingly also having fun at their job. Nurses in Serbia are likely to view their career as a "calling," and thus their indicators of career success were more related to helping others, relationships with patients and making a difference to and having a positive impact on society.

The patterns of career success meanings reported here are consistent with the cultural values ascribed by Schwartz and others, and with the general independent career direction increasingly emphasized in Serbia. An emphasis upon achievement, recognition, job performance, making a difference, and learning and development reflects a group of career actors who believe they are finally gaining agency and even mastery over their career outcomes. This of course indicates that organizations have to be able to provide conditions that will lead to career success and provide opportunities that offer autonomy as well as a transparent path to desirable outcomes.

Career Transitions

The most striking outcome from looking at the data for the Serbian sample is the degree to which the reported career transitions were self-driven. See Tables 16.3 and 16.4 for more information on career transitions in our sample. The data show that 17 of the 21 research participants reported initiating the transition completely on their own. The data also indicate that, for initial stimuli from an outside influence, two people then exercised their agency to pursue a career transition. In contrast, only a few participants indicated that events (such as downsizing) really outside of their control drove their transition. This somewhat mixed view of transitions as being both individually and externally driven may also reflect, in Schwartz's terms, "mastery" as one of the dominant values.

This finding reflects the fact that career transitions may be understood as something that has traditionally been very rare in Serbia. Thus, if it happened, it was usually individually driven. Many people, especially in the nursing and blue-collar samples, are used to lifetime employment without changing their job ever. Thus, even if pushed out of their jobs, they would either remain passive or look for a similar job in a similar organization. The majority of career transitions in the Serbian samples are transitions within the same organization.

The older interviewees still had collectivistic values and an external locus of control and therefore took a passive role in managing their careers, and only if forced to do so by the influence of an external source such as organizational downsizing. Consequently, the older interviewees

Table 16.3 Career transition patterns in Serbia

Total number of interviewees=21	Occupation			Gender		Generation		
	Nurse	Blue-collar	Business	Female	Male	Younger	Older	Total number mentioning category
N=	8	6	7	14	7	11	10	
Internally driven causes/triggers of career transitions:								
Own initiative (internal source)	6	4	7	11	6	11	6	17
Own initiative (external source stimuli)	1	0	1	2	0	1	1	2
Externally driven causes/triggers of career transitions:								
Driven by graduation certification	3	0	2	4	1	5	0	5
Driven by completion of obligation	0	0	0	0	0	0	0	0
Unsought opportunities	1	3	3	4	3	5	2	7
Counsel, encouragement	0	0	1	1	0	1	0	1
Organizationally driven	4	3	5	7	5	4	8	12
Health	0	0	0	0	0	0	0	0
Family role	4	2	0	5	1	4	2	6
Macro factors	7	5	2	10	4	7	7	14
Luck and contingencies	1	4	1	4	2	3	3	6
Individuals' management of career transitions:								
Job search	7	5	3	12	3	11	4	15
Planning/setting goals and priorities	5	1	2	4	4	6	2	8
Organization and time management	1	0	0	0	1	1	0	1
Formal education, training, short courses	2	1	1	3	1	4	0	4
Informal training	2	1	0	1	2	3	0	3
Making contingent/other plans	3	2	3	2	6	5	3	8
Recreation	3	1	1	2	3	3	2	5
Consequential thinking	3	1	0	2	2	4	0	4
Job experimentation	1	1	2	4	0	4	0	4
Financial planning	2	3	1	1	5	4	2	6

Table 16.4 External influences upon career transitions in Serbia

Total number of interviewees=21	Occupation			Gender		Generation		Total number mentioning category
	Nurse	Blue-collar	Business	Female	Male	Younger	Older	
N=	8	6	7	14	7	11	10	
Boss/superior	2	5	6	9	4	8	5	13
Support	2	3	5	8	2	6	4	10
Barrier	0	3	1	2	2	3	1	4
Peers	6	4	5	12	3	7	8	15
Support	5	4	4	11	2	7	6	13
Barriers	1	0	1	1	1	0	2	2
Family	7	6	3	11	5	8	8	16
Support	7	5	2	9	5	7	7	14
Barriers	0	1	0	1	0	1	0	1
Friends	4	1	1	3	3	4	2	6
Support	4	1	0	3	2	4	1	5
Barriers	0	0	0	0	0	0	0	0
Organization	8	6	7	14	7	11	10	21
Support	6	5	7	13	5	10	8	18
Barriers	1	2	0	1	2	2	1	3
Network	8	5	5	13	5	11	7	18
Work	2	2	2	5	1	3	3	6
Personal	7	2	1	8	2	7	3	10
Professional	1	2	2	1	4	3	2	5
Education and training	4	3	3	8	2	8	2	10
Financial situation	3	4	0	4	3	6	1	7
Role of luck and contingencies	1	4	1	4	2	3	3	6

saw any kind of career change as a much more stressful and disruptive experience than the younger ones.

> First I was avoiding facing the fact that I needed to change my job. I am the type of person who does not like to make changes. In the end I realized I needed to move on.
>
> (Older businessperson)

> Before we did not have a lot of barriers and stresses. . . . I always advise young people to educate themselves—if you have the "know-how" you can be adequately paid.
>
> (Older blue-collar)

> Nowadays everything has changed—companies are smaller, problems are more complex but their solutions are much simpler, since there is no political committee which makes all decisions instead of you.
>
> (Older ex-general manager)

> I feel regret for the younger people today—they do not have any emotions for other people; they are exclusively financially driven.
>
> (Older nurse)

The younger interviewees were much more concerned with financial achievement and affording material goods, opportunities to become company owners, recognition and opportunities for learning, whereas the older interviewees were generally concerned with basic survival and how to financially support their families.

Triggers of career transitions for the younger interviewees were more internally based (e.g. seeking development, getting more money, missing creativity and challenge), so they took a more active role in managing their careers through additional education, training, making contingent plans and active job search.

Individual Management of Career Transitions

As the data indicate, the most common ways that individuals managed their career changes were through seeking new employment, making contingent/other plans and setting goals and priorities. This active career self-management applies much more to the younger generation than to the older generation.

External Influences Upon Career Transitions

The employing organization is cited by the whole sample as influencing their transitions, with the boss, networks (especially personal) and family discussed by the vast majority. In the majority of cases, these influencing factors were seen as positive. Additional education and training was also cited by almost half of the sample as an important influence on career transitions.

The boss was proportionately more likely than other groups to be perceived as having a negative impact upon career transitions, by being unsupportive or difficult in psychosocial or political ways. But, again, note that the boss was more often a positive influence. Organizations were seen as primarily positive influences. They provided the majority of opportunities and, while they could be perceived as inhibiting desired transitions, they did not seem to receive the negative attributions that sometimes were directed toward bosses. This finding may also point to the importance of social environment and relationships at work for Serbians, perhaps indicating some degree of embeddedness, as defined by Schwartz, as well as the importance of hierarchy.

In conclusion, what seems to define career transitions as well as success perceptions in Serbia is an extremely interdependent view of careers;

that is, the emphasis on subjective or individual factors in triggering career transitions is often intricately related to the external conditions and the more objective side of careers.

> There are various reasons for my transition. Serbia at that time was under NATO attack, and very few companies were in operation. The owner of the company was recruited, and it was not possible for me to do my job any longer. Also, the job was not engaging enough, and it did not allow me to further develop myself.
>
> (Younger business graduate)

> My financial situation has made me get a job at Company X. I see it as a temporary solution, as stagnation. I am not happy, especially given the times we are living in today, whereby one has to develop continually. You have to be ahead all the time.
>
> (Younger blue-collar)

This is very much in accord with what career scholars have long argued for, that is in favor of a more interdependent perspective, recognizing that the objective and subjective career do not exist in isolation from each other (Hughes, 1958). Recently, there has been a renewed interest in further understanding this interdependence (Arthur et al., 2005; Khapova et al., 2007).

> At the start I was bothered by several things: whether I would succeed at the new job, how the other owner would react to my change and whether I had made anybody mad.
>   The biggest help came from my husband and from my father, but people in my company were also fairly helpful. Both work and non-work life were affected by the transition. I had to work much longer hours, and that necessarily had an effect on my life outside of work. But after all I was happy.
>
> (Older businesswoman)

> I changed my job on my own initiative. The biggest fear that I had was whether I would be able to adjust and whether the people at the new job would be friendly with me or not. I am happy at the moment, but my work–life balance has been disrupted.
>
> (Younger nurse)

Themes and Implications

A few broad themes and implications are noted here for practitioners. These should *not* be interpreted as applying to all Serbians. Diverse approaches are exhibited by individuals and should be reflected by practitioners.

- Work–life balance and emphasis on family life are extremely important to both the younger and the older generation in Serbia.
- A positive social working environment and good interpersonal relations at work are very important factors in job satisfaction.
- Organizations should create conditions and a clear framework for career advancement, especially in transition economies.
- The younger generation are more individually driven, and organizations should provide pathways to allow for this.

Notes

1 These are Croatia, the Czech Republic, Estonia, Hungary, Latvia, Poland, Romania, Slovakia and Slovenia (Schwartz, 2008).
2 According to the 2002 Census of Population, and Dwellings Book, Statistical Office of the Republic of Serbia.
3 Ending at a monthly rate of 330 million percent at the beginning of 1994.

References

Arthur, M. B., Khapova, S. M. & Wilderom, C. P. M. 2005. Career success in a boundaryless career world. *Journal of Organizational Behaviour*, 26: 177–202.

Hall, D. T. & Chandler, D. 2005. Psychological success: When the career is calling. *Journal of Organizational Behaviour*, 26: 155–176.

Heslin, P. A. 2005. Conceptualizing and evaluating career success. *Journal of Organizational Behaviour*, 26(2): 113–136.

Hofstede, G. 1983. The cultural relativity of organizational practices and theories. *Journal of International Business Studies*, Fall: 75–89.

Hofstede, G. 2001. *Culture's Consequences*. Thousand Oaks, CA: Sage.

Hofstede, G. & Hofstede, G. J. 2005. *Cultures and Organizations: Software of the Mind* (revised and expanded 2nd ed.). London: McGraw-Hill.

Hughes, E. C. 1958. *Men and Their Work*. Glencoe, IL: Free Press.

Khapova, S. N., Arthur, M. B. & Wilderom, C. P. M. 2007. The subjective career in the knowledge economy. In H. Gunz and M. Peiperl (Eds.), *Handbook of Career Studies*: 114–130. Thousand Oaks, CA: Sage.

Krstić, G. 2004. *Labor Markets in Serbia and Montenegro: Republic of Serbia, an Agenda for Economic Growth and Employment*. Report No. 29258-YU: 91–113. Washington, DC: World Bank.

Krstić, G. & Sanfey, P. 2007. Mobility, poverty and well-being among the informally employed in Bosnia and Herzegovina. *Economic Systems*, 31: 311–335.

Lazić, M. 1995. Osobenosti globalne društvene transformacije Srbije [Specific characteristics of the global social transformation of Serbia]. In S. Bolčić (Ed.), *Društvene promene i svakodnevni život: Srbija pocetkom devedesetih* [Social changes and everyday life: Serbia in the early 1990s]. Belgrade: Institut za sociološka istraživanja Filozofskog fakulteta u Beogradu.

Litchfield, J., Reilly, B. & Krstić, G. 2007. An anatomy of male labor market earnings inequality in Serbia—1996 to 2003. *Economic Systems*, 31(1): 97–114.

Obradović, J. 1982. *Psihologija i sociologija organizacije*. Zagreb: Školska knjiga.

Polovina, N. 2007. Family–school cooperation in the context of traumatic transitions in Serbian society. *International Journal About Parents in Education*, 1: 230–236.

Schein, E. H. 1996. Kurt Lewin in the classroom, in the field and in change theory: Notes toward a model of managed learning. *Systemic Practice*, 9(1): 27–47.

Schwartz, S. H. 2006. A theory of cultural value orientations: Explication and applications. *Comparative Sociology*, 5(2–3): 136–182.

Schwartz, S. H. 2008. Cultural value orientations: Nature and implications of national differences. Unpublished manuscript, Hebrew University of Jerusalem.

Županov, J. 1985. *Samoupravljanje i društvena moć*. Zagreb: Globus.

17

Careers in South Africa
Julie Unite, Burger van Lill and Jon P. Briscoe

Historical and Cultural Context

It is difficult to understand South Africa's cultural context without understanding some of the historical background of the country. Much of South Africa's history is influenced by the apartheid era and the segregation of racial groups. Racial segregation started early with the abolishment of slavery in 1834 and then the formal regulation of relations between employers and workers with the Masters and Servants Act of 1841. This Act introduced "pass" laws for black (African) workers, regulated bilateral relations between "master" and "servant" and did not provide for representation of workers' issues. The pass laws in effect also regulated the migration of workers and, because they were applied along racial lines, also contributed to the polarization of race groups (Nel, 2002).

During the post-World War II slump in the late 1940s the National Party rose to power and won the elections in 1948. Many of their ideologies and policies were based on racial segregation and separate development for race groups ("apartheid"). All facilities were segregated, with separate facilities for "whites" and "non-whites," including schools, beaches, universities, government offices, toilets, sport clubs, residential areas, public transport, park benches and so on. Furthermore, the facilities for "non-whites" were usually vastly inferior to those for "whites." These policies also translated into separate institutions and laws for black and non-black workers.

One of these was the Industrial Conciliation Act of 1956, which became the new basis for labor legislation regarding collective bargaining. Its instigation had a number of effects; it caused further racial polarization by excluding all "Bantu" (including black African women), and it prohibited further registration of mixed race unions (except with ministerial permission). It also introduced a system of "job reservations" whereby a particular occupation could be legally reserved for a specific race group (contrary to popular belief, jobs were not necessarily reserved for whites only). The job reservation clause became one of the most notorious racially divisive elements of labor legislation (Bendix, 2004).

With the government situation as it was and the laws associated with it, there was obvious dissatisfaction and unrest among the disadvantaged racial groups. This culminated in 1990 to 1993 when there was unprecedented, revolutionary change in the political process, the structure of society, the economic environment and employment relations. Organizations such as the African National Congress (ANC) and the South African Communist Party (SACP) were un-banned, and they formed an alliance with the largest trade union confederation, the Congress of South African Trade Unions (COSATU), to participate in the political process.

In April 1994 the first democratic and non-racial elections were held, and the Government of National Unity (GNU) was formed with the ANC in power. New laws were passed, including the Constitution Act, which explicitly prohibits discrimination and guarantees fair labor practices for employers and employees. The Labor Relations Act (LRA) was also instituted and served to regulate employment relations and collective bargaining procedures. Associated with this, the Employment Equity Act specifies that affirmative action applies to "designated groups," i.e. "black people, women and people with disabilities" (sometimes called "previously disadvantaged groups/individuals"), where "'black people' is a generic term which means Africans, Colored and Indians." The Skills Development Act was also promulgated to regulate and to encourage organizations to initiate training and the development of their employees. These represent initiatives to improve the skills of employees.

Cultural Dimensions of South Africa

According to Schwartz (2006), South Africa falls into the Sub-Saharan Africa culture cluster. Schwartz characterizes countries in this cluster as being especially high in embeddedness and low in autonomy. This is reflected by an emphasis upon social relationships and group solidarity. Interestingly, Hofstede (1991) types South Africa as being slightly higher in individualism. Both Schwartz and Hofstede type South Africa as being hierarchical (or having a large power distance). In terms of mastery versus harmony, South Africa exhibits a slight inclination toward mastery in Schwartz's framework.

Economic and Demographic Trends

As a result of South Africa's racially discriminatory policies during the apartheid era and the accompanying legislation to support such policies, the international community turned against the government, and sanctions and boycotts were introduced. International companies left the country, and South Africa was increasingly isolated. After the democratic elections of 1994 and the economic sanctions were lifted, there were obvious changes and effects on many levels.

An open economy and an unstable currency have had a great effect on local companies (for example, cheap imports from China and India, including clothing, shoes, steel and cars). In the past, businesses could protect themselves from bankruptcy by retrenching workers. However, now with the more rigid labor laws and collective bargaining and the powerful unions it is virtually impossible to follow this route. The result is that businesses employ considerably fewer employees on a full-time basis, and a number of businesses in sectors such as agriculture, fisheries and retail employ casual workers on a short-term basis. Associated with this are low wages, no job security and no fringe benefits such as pensions and medical insurance. During the next two decades one can expect the number of informal sector contracts and casual opportunities to grow significantly and there to be little demand for permanent formal sector employees (Schreuder & Coetzee, 2006).

Larger organizations, depending on number of employees, turnover and business sector, have to submit an equity plan to the Department of Labour, indicating the distribution of the race groups. They also have to indicate how they would address a redistribution of their employees to reflect the population distribution in the region. Organizations that do not have a distribution that reflects the population usually find it difficult to get business from the government sector, and even large businesses are forced by government to consider the equity distribution of their suppliers before trading with them.

There have also been major changes to the composition of the labor force since 1994, with employment equity and affirmative action of previously disadvantaged groups now being ubiquitous. Nowadays the labor force consists of more women and more representatives of all races, and the number of dual-income families is increasing (Schreuder & Coetzee, 2006). Despite this, a number of the black employees are unskilled, and there are high levels of unemployment specifically among the previously disadvantaged groups. There are also a large number of skilled young people of all races leaving the country, with the allure of more jobs overseas. According to Statistics South Africa, the unemployment figure was 26.2 percent in September 2004; thus of 15 million economically active people in South Africa, 11.6 million were employed. Mid-year population estimates for 2005 for a population of 46.9 million were: Africans about 37.2 million (79 percent), white 4.4 million, colored 4.1 million and Asian 1.1 million (http://www.statssa.gov. za/news_archive/2jun2005_1.asp).

The AIDS epidemic also warrants consideration when thinking about the demographics of the country. The prediction for 2020 in the scenario of low AIDS infection is that, of the 29.7 million economically active, only 14.4 million will be employed in the formal sector. This means that in 2020 only 48 percent of the economically active population will have formal job opportunities, while more than 50 percent of all job opportunities will be casual, contract or franchise opportunities. In the worst case scenario, i.e. a high occurrence of AIDS and low fertility, there will be 19.4 million economically active, of which 9.3 million (48 percent) will have formal jobs (Schreuder and Coetzee, 2006).

Career Trends and Patterns

Apartheid and its consequences such as influx control, pass laws, job reservations and educational restrictions have undoubtedly had an effect on the career trends and patterns of those in South Africa in the past. Now, with a level playing field, South Africans are working to understand and develop applicable programs to help and to accommodate their new societal structure.

Some have criticized earlier career-related systems for supporting individuals. The first formal career guidance services in South Africa were introduced under the auspices of the National Institute of Career Guidance and catered exclusively for whites. Others have raised concerns about the applicability of models developed in other societies to the South African context (Akhurst & Mkhize, 1999). Theories and assessment instruments are to a large degree based on Western individualistic values and in some cases leave out contextual factors. These contextual factors have a bearing on career development and include such things as the importance of the relationship between self, family and community. In the context of South Africa (and with other cultures) it entails responsibilities towards family and community. The career is seen as a vehicle fulfilling such responsibilities. Similarly, parents are very important in career decision making (more so than guidance teachers). Parents, however, may be illiterate or unskilled in work and cannot advise their children. In such cases other community members, for example older peers, may play a role. The importance of community in the career choices of African students is demonstrated in their tendency to choose social types of occupations. Many career education programs also have little understanding of issues and limitations of choices experienced by people from disadvantaged backgrounds.

Educational System/Occupational Background

From as early as 1882 racial division was employed in education, and education was purposefully implemented to regulate career development. When the National Party came to power in 1948 racial segregation was firmly entrenched. At that stage white education was superior to black education, as more resources were channeled to the former.

Nowadays, the government has put into place systems regarding education and training, employment and career development. For example, in 1998 the National Skills Development Strategy and Employment Equity Act put legislative mechanisms in place to correct gender and race inequalities (Nicholas, Pretorius & Naidoo, 1999). In fact recent statistics in South Africa have shown that 71 percent of university students are now black, and black staff in universities has increased by 40 percent. Women, however, are still rated as having the lowest levels of skills and education.

Findings From the Study

Our sample was obtained predominantly in Cape Town, South Africa (one exception is a businessman from Johannesburg). The main population groups in the Cape are the whites, the blacks and a group called the "coloreds" which consist of people from Malay and/or Khoisan descent or a mixture of these groups and whites. Based on our region, a representative sample included interviews from these three racial groups: black, "colored" and white individuals. For a detailed picture of our sample see Table 17.1.

To obtain the sample, we contacted local factories and hospitals to gather nurses and blue-collar workers. Domestic staff were also included in the blue-collar sample, as they have made up a large proportion of unskilled labor in the past. Domestic workers are traditionally black or "colored" individuals who are employed by white families. Their role generally includes activities around the house such as cooking, cleaning and helping with the children. We mostly drew on personal contacts to obtain a sample of businesspeople.

Table 17.1 South Africa sample profile

	Business graduates		Nurses		Blue-collar workers	
	Older	*Younger*	*Older*	*Younger*	*Older*	*Younger*
Gender	2 males, 1 female	3 females, 3 males	6 females	1 female	2 males, 3 females	1 male, 2 females
Race	1 black, 1 colored, 1 white	1 black, 2 colored, 3 white	1 black, 4 colored, 1 white	0 black, 1 colored, 0 white	3 black, 1 colored, 1 white	1 black, 1 colored, 1 white
	N=9		N=7		N=8	

Total N=24 (16 females, 8 males), with 9 business graduates, 7 nurses and 8 blue-collar workers. The average age was 55 for the older generation and 29 for the younger generation.

Meanings of Career Success

The following meanings of career success were coded by the research team for 6 or more of the 24 research participants:

Achievement	(12 people)
Satisfaction	(8 people)
Making a difference	(8 people)
Learning and development	(7 people)
Self-actualization	(7 people)
Work–life balance	(7 people)
Social working environment	(6 people)
Material output	(6 people)

Achievement was one of the most popular meanings of career success across occupational, generational and gender subsamples in South Africa. The younger generation placed more emphasis on it than their older counterparts, and nurses placed the least emphasis on it. In most cases achievement was in a financial sense, but the interviewees also talked about it in terms of promotion and advancement. One individual describes both these aspects of achievement nicely here:

> Maybe I could be promoted to a level where people can see me as management and see that I am capable of doing this. That would be achievement for me. I suppose to be financially independent at some point in the future. Being able to retire early is something I would be able to say I've achieved some success in my life.
>
> (Younger businesswoman)

Satisfaction was the next most mentioned career success category for the South African sample. This was particularly so amongst the older generation and businesspeople. These results could be explained by simple maturation effects, with the older group having experienced all the other things needed and now happy to focus on achieving satisfaction in their careers. Interestingly the businesspeople had the greatest focus on satisfaction in their careers, which was perhaps a luxury they could indulge in, whereas the nurses and blue-collar workers had to focus on more menial things.

Linked with this, making a difference was emphasized by the older group and not mentioned at all by the younger generation. One older businessperson describes it:

> Yeah, I think maybe career success as well, it's the ability to—whether you're selling something to somebody, either a commodity or a service, the person appreciates it. I think for me that's the finest careers. Money is important, but I don't think it can buy that.
>
> (Older businessman)

For the nursing group and females in general, making a difference was the most important career meaning. This could be linked to their vocational calling and personality attributes, and as one nurse puts it:

> I suppose each phase I did I enjoyed doing it, but I think the personal interactions were valuable with the staff and most particularly the patients. It's funny, I don't really think about these things very much, but you get a lot of job satisfaction in nursing and you felt like you did—even what was quite mundane stuff you felt like it was valuable.
>
> (Older female nurse)

Learning and development was most mentioned by females and the nurses in our sample, which could be linked to the continuing education and skills training emphasized in this profession. Self-actualization was mentioned more by the females but also by the business group. One younger individual quotes:

> I think probably that I achieve the goals that I set out to achieve. I mean I made very specific—I set very specific goals when I was young, much younger, and then I achieved those goals.
>
> (Younger businesswoman)

Interestingly, work–life balance was only really mentioned by the businesspeople. For the blue-collar individuals and nurses it was not a feature. One white businessman talks about this:

> Well, none of these decisions are just mine without consulting my wife, for instance. She's always been very supportive with whatever I think is the right

thing to do, but we do discuss it and I ask for her input. And then it is important to me that a certain lifestyle—I need to be able to maintain a lifestyle, and
by that I don't mean money or procedures, something like that. It's just to
have enough time to do other things and maybe not being too stressed, have
a better quality of life.

(Younger businessman)

The above example shows work–life balance in more of the traditional
sense, but in the South African context we found that work–life balance
had a broader meaning. Implicit within the discussion around career
success for the black and "colored" interviewees was the importance of
family or their community. The family network was extensive and an
important part of their identity. With this, however, came a number of
responsibilities. Interviewees often talked about having to support other
members of the family who couldn't provide for themselves, and this
was both financially and in more practical ways. They often found themselves in conflicting positions, with their job and family both demanding their time. Consequently, many of them defined career success in
terms of how well they were able to juggle the two responsibilities. They
also placed more emphasis on working towards this in the future. In the
quote below, one woman talks about the importance of her family and
how her family define career success:

As black South Africans, we're very—your family unit is—for me, it's my
main source of support and identity. And I'm very close to my parents and
very close to my sister. And it's actually broader than that. It's not just my close
family. It's my cousins and my aunties and my grannies. We're all responsible
for each other. If somebody is sick, we look after them. If somebody's mother
is away, you look after their children. If your neighbor's kids are alone, you
take them in. That's just how we are.

My parents would like to see me married and having children [laughter]
and having a family. But then that goes back to the whole community family
thing. For them that is more—they feel it's great that I'm driven. And they
support me in everything. But they also feel you're successful if you can balance your work life with your family.

(Younger businesswoman)

Material output was another category that was mentioned by the
blue-collar workers and the older generation. It was fairly specific for
this group and context. On a general level, career success for this group
was predominantly focused on survival and meeting basic needs for supporting their families. Stanley, an older blue-collar worker, describes it
well:

> As I say, work is work. I can only speak for myself. To me whether you give me a job and tell me to sweep the floors all day, I'm happy as long as I've got a job. It is very important to be successful for whatever you do, no matter what you do. Whether it's management or whether it's just being a laborer or no matter what the duty, it is very important, because if you can't work you can't eat. And if you can't eat you're going to go hungry. It's not about money. It's just about survival.
>
> (Older male blue-collar worker)

A domestic worker puts it more simply:

> I am happy in my job and I am happy when they pay me.
>
> (Older female blue-collar worker)

Finally, the social working environment was mentioned by the blue-collar workers, and more by the older people than the younger groups. In the case of South Africa, this was mentioned particularly by the domestic workers in the sample, because their role is so intertwined with the daily living of the families they work for. They talked a lot about establishing a good relationship with their employers, and if this relationship was not established then it made their jobs very difficult. An older domestic worker describes this here:

> The people at my job are all like my family. I feel very nice. My madam, she's like my mother and like my sister.
>
> (Older female blue-collar worker)

Career Success Themes in South Africa

The context of the country plays a big role in shaping how individuals define career success. The stories from the older generation and more so the previously disadvantaged individuals (blacks and "coloreds") were often quite dramatic and provide evidence of a massive shift underway in their careers and lives. For them the emphasis on career success was in many cases on survival and material output to support their families. Our results also reflect career stage and maturation effects in that certain career success factors were more important purely because of the age of the interviewees (e.g. satisfaction for the older interviewees). Similarly, some of our results also reflect the characteristics of the occupation. This was seen for the nurses and business workers in particular.

Career Transitions

The most striking outcome from looking at the data for the South African sample is the degree to which the reported career transitions were self-driven. The data show that 13 of the 24 research participants reported initiating the transition completely on their own. Outside influences driving a career transition were mostly organizationally driven or due to the requirements of the family. One example of this is from a nurse who talks about how her role as a mother initiated many of her job transitions:

> I sort of worked more part time with my children. I carried on working for a little while, and after my children were born I didn't actually work until my second son was about four. Then I just used to work part time on the night shift, 'cause night shift seemed to fit in with the family situation better, and then I worked there quite a long time until my daughter was born.
>
> (Older female nurse)

In terms of patterns amongst subgroups, businesspeople, then blue-collars and then nurses were most likely to drive their own career transitions. Amongst gender and generational categories, females and older workers were similar in their drive for career transitions. Interestingly, there were also some stories from the older previously disadvantaged individuals about how their earlier career transitions were driven, mostly by the government policies in place during the apartheid era. Two older blue-collar workers describe this here:

> I didn't have the choice to go to varsity [university] or studying a particular area I wanted. So that's why I took whatever I could.
>
> (Older male blue-collar worker)

> I am not educated because where I grew up school was not important.
>
> (Older female blue-collar worker)

Individual Management of Career Transitions

As the data indicate, the most common way that individuals managed their career changes was through seeking more formal and informal education.

External Influences Upon Career Transitions

Family support was cited by more than half of the sample as influencing their transitions. This is highly reflective of the embeddedness Schwartz characterizes South Africa with. Family was not only the most commonly mentioned influence amongst our research participants, but also cited as a positive influence in the majority of cases. Many interviewees talked about a mentor of some sort and their parents as being models or offering knowledge, advice, financial assistance and encouragement. One younger black individual talked about the unique learning orientation in her household as a child, which provided a foundation for many of her career choices and transitions:

> My dad has forever been studying. So has my mom. My mom is doing her third career. My parents felt they don't have so much money for me to inherit. So the best they could do was to educate me so at least I can fend for myself. When growing up, my parents were always exposing us to certain things. Like they would take me for courses at the museum, things that other kids in the township were like, "What is that?" Some kids have never been to the museum.
>
> (Younger businesswoman)

Other team members and colleagues were also important sources of support, and often normalized many of the initial fears associated with a change or transition. One older blue-collar worker describes this:

> The people around you, your colleagues wherever, that is very important, how you get along with each other.
>
> (Older male blue-collar worker)

He then goes on to talk about how his peers are also a source of informal trainers and provided support when he was first learning his job:

> I mean, working with the other guys, you just learn from them. They will always guide you. Not this, you must pack this, you do this or do that, or this has got to go to that particular place. There is someone who knows, after you get to know your way around.
>
> (Older male blue-collar worker)

Themes and Implications

Equal Access to Education and Career Opportunities

Education and career choice is now an equal right for all the races in South Africa. Many of the previously disadvantaged individuals we interviewed showed evidence of being the first generation in their family to have a professional career or orientation.

- Many of the new professionals do not have familial or peer examples to rely upon. Effective formal and informal mentoring systems need to be fostered and developed so these first-generation professionals can learn skills for how to interact in professional environments and how to develop career skills. In many cases, life and career skills are more in need than the technical and working skills.

Consequential Thinking and Active Career Management

"Consequential thinking" describes the simple idea of being able to think ahead and project out how current behaviors and strategies might result in certain outcomes and consequences. This very basic skill was found lacking in the blue-collar workers. While most business and nurse interviewees *could* engage in consequential thinking, not all of them did it or did it well.

Alongside this, the most successful people in all of the occupations *actively* managed their career. For the blue-collars, this meant working hard on the psychological contract with a single employer. For the nurses it meant being aware of promotional opportunities within the hospital or higher level and even out of the country. For the businesspeople, it was manifest by being proactive and assertive in terms of identifying and pursuing opportunities that would improve them and their careers.

- Consequential thinking and skilled career behavior related to it could be taught early on to schoolchildren, college students and early career employees in order for them to find success in today's career environment. This is at a very basic level for those new to this environment.
- For those more established in the professions, of all races, they could be trained to engage in more holistic career development. This means learning to consider their values and their career management tactics intelligently and effectively.

Generations and Communities

Our interviews highlighted a strong contrast in terms of older and younger generations amongst colored and black individuals, although not so much with the white interviewees. Community and "each other" were among the few things that disadvantaged groups enjoyed and relied upon in the more difficult past years, particularly for the older generation. Now, the new career opportunities may threaten to make people in these communities more independent and isolate the younger individuals from the traditional ways they relied upon before.

- How can newer career orientations and the collective sense of community coexist? Are there ways that traditional boundaries of community and newer "boundaryless" careers can inform each other?
- How can corporations acknowledge these communities and their unique bonds in ways that allow them and the corporations to thrive?
- Corporations and other employers need to work with human resources in a way that addresses work–life flexibility.
- Employees new to large employers may need to be trained in work–life balance skills and how to address competing demands from work and home.

References

Akhurst, J. & Mkhize, N. J. 1999. Career education in South Africa. In G. B. Stead & M. B. Watson (Eds.), *Career Psychology in the South African Context*: 163–179. Pretoria: J. L. van Schaik Academic.

Bendix, S. 2004. *Industrial Relations in South Africa* (4th ed., 5th impression, revised). Cape Town: Juta.

Hofstede, G. 1991. *Cultures and Organizations: Software of the Mind*. London: McGraw-Hill.

Nel, P. S. (Ed.). 2002. *South African Employment Relations: Theory and Practice* (4th ed.). Pretoria: Van Schaik.

Nicholas, L., Pretorius, T. & Naidoo, A. V. 1999. Historical perspective of career psychology in South Africa. In G. B. Stead & M. B. Watson (Eds.), *Career Psychology in the South African Context*: 1–12. Pretoria: J. L. van Schaik Academic.

Schreuder, A. M. G. & Coetzee, M. 2006. *Careers: An Organisational Perspective* (3rd ed.). Lansdowne, Cape Town: Juta.

Schwartz, S. H. 2006. A theory of cultural value orientations: Explication and applications. *Comparative Sociology*, 5(2–3): 136–182.

18

Careers in Spain

Mireia Las Heras

Cultural Background

According to Schwartz's framework of cultural orientations, Spain is a decidedly egalitarian culture, which means that people value others' welfare, social justice and traditions. This is reflected in Spain, like most countries in Western Europe, having a universal and free public health care system and a generous public pension system in which workers may receive up to 100 percent of their taxable income. In the past, however, equal opportunities for men and women have not always been granted. An example of such lack of equality is the 57th article of the Civil Code, which was known as *permiso marital*, which forbade women from employment, owning property and traveling without the consent of their husband. The law was revoked in 1975 and, although this was not so long ago, Spain has been proactive in broadening equal opportunities for men and women. In 2007, the Spanish parliament passed the Law of Equality (*Ley de Igualdad*), legislation that requires at least 40 percent of political candidates to be women, encourages major companies to promote females in management and decision-making roles, implements the right for women to reduce their working hours to care for children, and introduced a paternity leave policy for fathers of up to ten paid working days, which will be augmented to four weeks in 2011 (El País, 2009).

Spain is also low in mastery and high in harmony. This means that, on average, Spaniards do not emphasize the importance of getting ahead, success and competence, but rather focus on fitting in with the environment. These values are demonstrated by the fact that, as in many southern European countries, the family network is an important aspect in Spanish society (Bover, 2008). Family is a core feature in both social and business life. The close family unit often involves not just immediate family members but extended family as well. It is not unusual for more than two generations to live within one household, and grandparents are often childcare providers. Families most often eat together, as it is an opportunity to strengthen relationships between family members, to exchange impressions and to socialize.

Taking time to eat and enjoy a meal is also another significant aspect of Spanish life. Many students and employees go home for their lunch break. Small stores, typically in suburbs or in small towns, close down between 1 and 4 in the afternoon and resume until 9 or 10 in the evening. To most foreigners, lunchtime is often recognized as *siesta* time, or the time to nap. However, it is not necessarily the time for napping in the middle of the afternoon, but more of a time to enjoy lunch, relax and break up the morning and afternoon to evade the hottest part of the day. Dining is a social event, even within the workplace, as business and negotiations are often conducted over lunch.

Business transactions in Spain are often based on trust and personal relationships, and Spaniards place great importance on the character of those they do business with. Businesses are often run by family members, both immediate and extended, and control is often passed from one generation to the next. A few examples of major global corporations that began as family-owned operations and continue to be managed by members of the family include: Grupo Santander, a major financial services company in Spain and Latin America that is run by the Botin family; Inditex, the parent company of Zara, which is under management by the Ortega family; and the two largest wineries that produce cava in the country, Codorniu and Freixenet, which are owned by the Raventos and the Ferrer-Sala families respectively and have remained within their respective families for at least two centuries.

Economic and Demographic Trends

Spain and Portugal became the 11th and 12th countries to join the European Economic Community in 1986, and after a wave of high unemployment in the early 1990s Spain began a prosperous economic cycle. Membership of the European Union and the euro has been advantageous for the economic well-being of the country. The median net household income rose by more than 56 percent from 2000 until 2008 (Eurostat, 2010a). Low interest rates coupled with a surge of immigration attracted a lot of national and foreign investment, particularly in the real estate sector. The real estate bubble imploded during the global economic crisis of 2008, and unemployment became a national crisis. By the end of 2009, the unemployment rate was over 18 percent and climbing; the European Union average was less than 9 percent (Eurostat, 2009).

The most significant change in the past few decades, however, has been the role of women in the workforce since the 1970s. Only about one out of five women were present in the workforce at the end of the 1970s (Solsten & Meditz, 1988). Within the last three decades, however, the rate of women in the workforce has steadily increased to almost the rate of men. About half of the employed women, however, work only part time, which is in contrast to Spanish males, of whom only one out of 20 work part time (Eurostat, 2010b).

Educational System/Occupational Background

Although the educational system is currently in the process of transformation owing to the Bologna process, which is planned to be completed in Spain by 2011,[1] the traditional Spanish university education structure is quite different from the Anglo-Saxon model. Three-year university degrees, called *Diplomaturas*, are comparable to a four-year bachelor's degree (BA/B.Sc.) in English speaking countries. Five- or six-year university degrees, called *Licenciaturas*, are equivalent to a six-year master's degree (MA/M.Sc.) or degrees from professional schools, such as medicine, business or law.

The most popular field of study for students enrolled in a *Diplomatura* is teaching, followed by business administration, nursing and tourism (INE, 2008). For students enrolled in *Licenciaturas*, law is the most popular field of study followed by MBA students, and graduate students in psychology, philology, and economics (INE, 2008).

The greatest change in education has been the integration of women into university education. Only a few decades ago, university education was socially unacceptable for Spanish women. By the mid-1980s, the enrollment rates between the sexes had evened out, and now the enrolled figures of females enrolled for *Diplomaturas* and *Licenciaturas* are much higher than for males. The pace at which Spanish females have graduated from tertiary education has currently outstripped that of males and, by 2007, for every one Spanish male graduate in tertiary education there were 1.4 females (Eurostat, 2010c).

Career Trends and Patterns

The Spanish Labor Market

The generation of people who are now in their 60s started their careers in a country dominated by state-owned (or subsidized) companies or low-cost manufacturers, which were typically small or medium-sized, family-owned businesses. The employment market was very inflexible, with strict laws protecting employees from being laid off or fired. There was almost no outside competition because few multinational companies could establish a presence in Spain. Goods produced within the borders used to be protected by imposing high taxes on imports. Thus companies and jobs were very stable. As a consequence of all these features, Spaniards had the opportunity to, and did, spend their whole career in one organization. Mobility was regarded with suspicion, and compensation systems were based on tenure to reward "fidelity."

Employment laws have changed in recent years, and the cost of laying off an employee is now cheaper than it used to be. However, Spain still has one of the most inflexible labor markets in Europe. In terms of layoffs, Spain is considered the third most expensive country in Europe, after only Germany and Greece. The average cost of a layoff is 56 weeks of the employee's salary—an entire year's salary. Therefore it is economical for companies to hire employees temporarily: the duration of a temporary contract can be anywhere between a few months and a few years; after that, companies must either offer a permanent position or terminate the contractual relationship. Since 2005, temporary contracts have added over 2 million workers to the workforce and account for over 30 percent of the labor force, which is double the European Union average (Johnson, Carreyrou & Walker, 2005). Many Spanish employers use short-term contracts with few or no benefits that they can terminate when they no longer want or need an employee.

The Changing Labor Market

Spanish youth who are now entering their professional careers have been developing a sense of responsibility for their own career trajectory that previous generations used to transfer to the organization. Organizations were once perceived as lifelong employers; however, the younger generation no longer consider staying in the same company for their entire career. The perception of a lifelong employer has changed for several reasons.

First, because it is more economical and perhaps perceived as less risky for organizations to first hire employees as temporary contractors, many in the younger generation often begin their careers with one or several temporary positions before receiving a permanent offer. Moreover, careerists no longer regard permanent contracts as valuable. Permanent jobs are no longer considered reliable, as many of the younger generation have witnessed massive layoffs of prior generations owing to jobs moving abroad.

Second, the cost of changing companies or jobs in the first few years of a career has become much lower. Employers no longer penalize employees as they once did when they viewed these changes with suspicion. Having experience at more than one company or job is now regarded as an added value to the organization.

Third, salaries of entry positions are very low. Therefore people do not lose much when they change jobs or companies early in their careers. Additionally, organizations do not reward fidelity with a salary increase.

Fourth, many in the younger generation are living with their parents[2] for longer, and therefore the need to stabilize a job early in a career is delayed. People before used to marry in their early to mid-20s, and by that time they wanted to have a stable job in one organization. Now people continue to live with their parents until their late 20s or early 30s; thus they are not as interested in having a stable job so early in their career.

And Why Some Career Patterns Have Not Changed . . .

Other actors in the job market arena, such as the universities and governmental agencies, have changed little of their modus operandi. Universities do not have careers services to offer advice and assistance. The workload during college years, coupled with class schedules, makes it difficult to obtain competitive experience before graduation.[3] Moreover, most university students live with their parents. Therefore most students still depend on their parents for extra expenses and do not have much pressure to earn extra money during their studies. Nine out of ten students attend publicly funded universities, where tuition fees are not a major lifetime expense. Therefore most students do not need to search for sufficient financing or loan options for their studies.

Even more importantly, most disciplines in universities are fundamentally theoretical. This is particularly true in operational fields such as engineering and architecture. As a result, students finish their years in college having no real work experience and, therefore, have never experienced the tedious task of a job search or prepared for a job interview. Most students graduate without developing any skills or knowing which tasks they excel at or which specific areas in their fields they wish to pursue or avoid. And, most importantly, they graduate without having built up a "real-world" network of colleagues or peers who can orient them or refer them to other people.

Findings From the Study

Sample: Details

Interviews have purposefully been chosen in both rural and urban locations (12 in rural areas and 9 in urban areas). Rural areas in Spain are very well developed, and people have access to education, health care, good transportation infrastructures and other services. However, the perceptions and culture with respect to career development might be different in rural areas than in urban locations, and if so we wanted all to be represented and captured in our research.

Spanish people tend to remain in the place where they were born and raised. Most of the interviews in Spain were carried out in the Northeast area (15 in the Catalan region), even though other regions are also represented (3 Central, 1 North-Central and 2 South). The Northeastern area is more affluent, even though living standards in the whole country are high, ranking 15th in the Human Development Index[4] among countries worldwide. The sample also included people in three occupational categories: business professionals (6), nurses (6) and blue-collar workers (9). The people in those occupations belong to two different generations: Generation Y (13) (those in their mid-20s and early 30s) and Baby Boomers (8), who are in their 50s (the oldest person in the sample was 65, which is the mandatory retirement age in Spain). We have used theoretical sampling because it facilitates discovering categories and their properties, and allows the uncovering of relationships to develop a theory (Glaser & Strauss, 1967). Each additional case included in the sample has served specific purposes: to fill theoretical categories; to extend the emerging theory; to replicate previous case(s) to test the emerging theory; or to illustrate a polar opposite to extend the emerging theory. See Table 18.1 for the sample profile.

Career success in Spain is a multi-faceted concept which usually overlaps with family and personal well-being. Our data suggests that there are four relevant types of elements that trigger the feeling of success:

Satisfaction   (17 people)
Job/task characteristics   (13 people)
Work–life balance   (7 people)
Achievement   (7 people)

Table 18.1 Spain sample profile

Occupation	Business professionals		Nurses		Blue-collar		
Generation	Older	Younger	Older	Younger	Older	Younger	
Gender	2 males	4 females	2 females	4 females	4 females	3 females, 2 males	
Educational background	University	University or above	University	University	Some high school	Some high school/high school/some college	
Geographical areas	2 Northeast 1 rural, 1 urban	3 Northeast, 1 Central 1 rural, 3 urban	1 Northeast, 1 Central 1 rural, 1 urban	3 Northeast, 1 South 3 rural, 1 urban	4 Northeast 2 rural, 2 urban	2 Northeast, 1 North-Central, 1 Central, 1 South 4 rural, 1 urban	

Total N=21 (17 females and 4 males), with 6 business professionals, 6 nurses and 9 blue-collar workers; 12 people living in rural areas and 9 in urban areas; 15 living in the Northeast, 3 in Central, 1 in North-Central and 2 in the South. The average age is 24.8 for the younger generation and 56.7 for the older generation.

What Can Be Learned From This?

Satisfaction was the foremost important characteristic across occupational, generational and gender subsamples in Spain. Satisfaction for Spanish people has to do with enjoying the task at hand and feeling that the job fits one's personal characteristics. The following quote illustrates how people define their success in terms of satisfaction:

> For me to feel successful will mean that my work has always felt interesting, so that I'm not always looking forward to going home, but that I like staying at work. I think that that is really crucial, and it's not easy to have it! And to feel successful you need to do something that you feel you are good at, and that allows you to have a family, and also so that you can provide for them. So, basically, you need to do something you really enjoy doing.
>
> (Younger businesswoman)

It is interesting to note that, although satisfaction is important for people in most countries, it was the most salient feature (17 out of the 21 people in the sample mentioned it) in Spain. There may be several reasons for this. First, the market is very inflexible, and people regard changing careers or jobs as something very complex. If you are in a position that is satisfying, that by itself is an achievement. Second, salaries in Spain are very different for people at different company levels. Therefore, if you make less than you would in a similar position at another organization, satisfaction is often considered sufficient compensation.

The second most important dimension of career success in the Spanish sample is job/task characteristics. Working in the same field that you have studied or trained in is considered very important to young adults. Thus, if the job does not have the characteristics that allow a person to do what he or she had expected, the person might feel rather frustrated or unsuccessful. For Spanish people the fit between what one has been trained to do and what one does is crucial to the feeling of success.

For nurses it is also very important to make a difference in their patients' lives. The claim of a senior nurse summarized both the young and senior nurses' perceptions of what makes them feel successful in what they do:

> You work a lot with people and help them. That makes you feel good because of the service you render, not as a charity thing, but as your professional work, with which you are useful and efficient. It is a hands-on type of work in which you can see the result of your daily tasks and it ends up being very rewarding.
>
> (Senior nurse)

Making a difference in patients' lives was such a crucial element for nurses in Spain that our interviews revealed that nurses who have different conceptions of success are likely to change occupations.

Work–life balance was also a central element of their success. Work days entail very long hours in Spain, which, coupled with double-income families and a family-centered culture, make work–life balance very difficult yet desirable. People feel the need to make decisions that facilitate that balance, and so they felt it was a success if they achieved it. The quote from an older businessman illustrates the desire for such balance:

> It gets to a point where more responsibility would have conflicted with enjoying my spouse, my children and other people. If I had wanted to go higher I should have had to trade off either more hours at work or more hours with my family. A little more satisfaction in my work would have meant much less satisfaction in my family life.
>
> (Older businessman)

Achievement is also an essential part of career success for many Spaniards. Achievement for Spanish people refers to promotions. It also refers to being able to deliver good results within one's position, or to create one's own business. According to a young Spanish man who had studied for an MBA:

> For me to feel very successful I should be able to attain the goals I set for myself when I was studying for my MBA: to create my own business, with which I can provide for my family, and I can serve society by giving good jobs to people . . . that would make me feel successful!
>
> (Younger businessman)

Career Success Themes in Spain

The most important themes that define career success in Spain are consistent with the cultural values of the country, and especially with the preference for egalitarian and harmonious relationships and situations. See Table 18.2 for more detailed information on career success. Satisfaction, job/task characteristics, work–life balance and achievement are goals that when achieved can advance one's harmonious relationships. It is interesting to note that Spain is one of the only countries in our sample of 11 countries for which achievement is neither the first nor the second most important meaning of career success. This is consistent with a low value for mastery. Mastery emphasizes getting ahead and ambition, and the lack of such values leads Spanish people not to define

Table 18.2 Meanings of career success in Spain

Total number of interviewees N = 21	Occupation			Total number mentioning category
	Nurses 6	*Blue-collar* 9	*Business* 6	
Person	5	7	6	18
Satisfaction	5	7	5	17
Achievement	2	1	4	7
Learning and development	3	1	2	6
Self-actualization	2	1	0	3
Job	4	6	5	15
Job security	2	0	1	3
Job/task characteristics	2	6	5	13
Job performance	4	1	0	5
Performing one's role	0	0	0	0
Contributing to organizational success	0	0	1	1
Interaction with the environment	3	5	2	10
Social working environment	2	2	1	5
Network	0	0	0	0
Recognition	3	0	1	4
Work–life context/balance	1	5	1	7
Making a difference	3	0	1	4
Material output	2	1	3	6
Basic survival	0	0	1	1
Financially supporting family	2	1	0	3
Affording material goods	0	1	1	2
Financial security	0	0	1	1

their career success in terms of the number of promotions they have had or the money they have made.

Career Transitions

The most surprising result in the Spanish sample is that most people report that career transitions have been internally driven and not driven by external circumstances. See Table 18.3 for transitions data. Seventeen of the 20 interviewees reported initiating the transition on their own, and three reported that they did it after an external stimulus triggered their intention to move to a new situation. Only a few people in the sample attributed some of the transitions in their career to external situations, such as change in family roles, for example becoming a mother, or a change in the organization, for example downsizing. However, these interviews were conducted in 2007. Responses might be different if the interviews were conducted today, considering the economic crisis

Table 18.3 Career transition patterns in Spain

	Occupation			Gender		Generation		Total number mentioning category
Total number of interviewees N = 21	Nurse 6	Blue-collar 9	Business 6	Female 16	Male 5	Younger 13	Older 8	
Internally driven causes/triggers of career transitions:								
Own initiative (internal source)	5	7	5	13	4	13	4	17
Own initiative (external source/stimuli)	1	2	0	2	1	3	0	3
Externally driven causes/triggers of career transitions:								
Driven by graduation/certification	3	0	1	4	0	4	0	4
Driven by completion of obligation	0	0	0	0	0	0	0	0
Unsought opportunities	0	4	0	3	1	2	2	4
Counsel/encouragement	0	1	0	1	0	0	1	1
Organizationally driven	1	2	1	3	1	2	2	4
Health	0	0	0	0	0	0	0	0
Family role	0	4	2	5	1	4	2	6
Macro factors	2	2	1	4	1	2	3	5

of 2008 and the ever-increasing unemployment rate in Spain (currently at 18 percent).

Individuals talked about transitions continuously and in different contexts. The most evident examples were related to major life events that triggered transitions, for example having children, moving to a new area or obtaining a very different job (going from part-time to a permanent contract was also often considered a transition). Many Spaniards put a lot of emphasis on work–life balance and often engaged in dramatic changes or career transitions for better balance and the good of their immediate family. For example, some people would quit a job in an organization in order to help the family business; others would search for a job that would fit their family life and specifically childcare responsibilities. Interestingly enough, however, when these situations occur, most of the time the focal persons still see themselves as agentic, so they appear as the ones deciding on the change even though the circumstances might play a role in the decision process.

The younger generation often talked about family planning and were clearly aware of possible transitions that may have been driven by their future family needs. Work-related transitions were also dominant, as they often were brought up in relation to external influences such as work role change, transition between organizations or industries, or moving into self-employment. Most of the time these transitions were voluntary; however, many of the blue-collar workers, for example, often talked about more involuntary transitions such as closure or reduction in the workforce, project completion and similar.

Even though most people reported that triggers were personally initiated, their explanations show that they actually wanted to conform to some external norms or to what other people were doing. Yet others talked about how conforming to a family tradition was something important. Therefore they were heavily influenced by what others in their close reference group were expecting of them:

> I'm working at my dad's company. They had a little problem there. My oldest sister is pregnant, and she is the one in charge of all kind of clients. . . . I had always been against working in my dad's company, especially because I have not had enough experience in other types of businesses. However, I felt that I really had to do it; it is some kind of moral obligation, because they are my family.
>
> (Younger businesswoman)

Even though the interviewees reported internal locus of control, and personal reasons for decisions, they also reported a willingness to stay in a company for a long time once they found a position that they enjoyed.

This reflects strongly the egalitarian and harmonious values of the country. For instance, one younger nurse reported:

> I am 29 now, and they would need to offer a lot for me to move from here. Here I find good colleagues at work, I like the work and I learn a lot, so I plan to stay here until I retire.
>
> (Younger nurse)

Early Career Decisions

In the Spanish sample it is interesting to take a close look at early career decisions. For many of the interviewees in Spain, career choice was often guided by clear external triggers, such as family tradition and pressures. In these cases there was very little exploration or reflection before engaging in that choice or pursuing studies in a different domain. In our sample, family seems to influence career choice through three different mechanisms. First, it provides young decision makers with possible selves and possible identities:

> I studied business, basically because my father is in business, and he has inculcated into me what it means to be in business. I guess because I was somehow interested in it, too, and I was also attracted by the challenge it would entail.
>
> (Younger businesswoman)

Second, it passes on a tradition that is supposed to be followed. Third, it transmits a sense of duty to be fulfilled. This is especially relevant when the older generation has created or worked in a family business, even if it is small, such as a workshop or a bar. Felipe explains how he decided his studies and his career:

> My family has owned a textile business for over 150 years. When I finished high school I studied textile engineering and specialized in knitted products. . . . I'm the oldest in the family, so my father wanted me to be in the family business. However, my brother studied law. He did not even think about working in the family business, because I was already there.
>
> (Senior businessman)

Themes and Implications for Spain

Many other sources of competitive advantage have disappeared in Spain. Salaries are no longer low compared to other European Union countries or even the United States. More than ever before sources of competitive advantage are springing from people's skills and abilities. Recognizing that the basis for competitive advantage has changed is crucial for the organization in designing its human resources strategies, policies and practices accordingly.

It is important to realize that the same accomplishments and rewards do not necessarily lead to the same feelings of career success for every individual. People have different needs, goals and preferences. Those with technical backgrounds, such as engineers or scientists, tend to differ from people in staff positions, such as accounting or human resources. Similarly, young people in their first years of career development differ notably from people in more advanced stages of their careers and their lives. To end this chapter we review some key themes related to success, and how to account for those preferences that tend to depend on the age of the employee.

At an early career stage, career success means:

- To learn, to be exposed to different things and to improve in self-knowledge, in terms of discovering what one is good at and what one doesn't like.
- To overcome challenges and to acquire practical knowledge. Employees push the boundaries of what they can do and what they are capable of doing.

What can help, at an early stage, achieve such success is:

- Clear evaluation processes that establish processes to set specific goals for each employee. In doing so the company transmits to the person what is important to the company and the way to achieve those results. For instance, the evaluation process can, and should, include elements regarding the culture and values of the company, leadership style and practices, and teamwork.
- Mentoring programs, in which the employee is assigned to one or more senior employees who do not participate in his or her evaluation process but who help the employee to navigate the company, to assimilate and analyze failures and successes, and to set personal goals for competency, leadership development and learning.

At a later stage, career success means:

- To be satisfied with one's job, to learn, and to progress within the hierarchical structure of the company.

- To develop commitments in meaningful aspects of one's life, namely in the family domain. Thus the person is more aware of the opportunity cost of working long hours and of job inflexibility, and feels that any extra hour of work beyond the threshold (which is usually over 40 hours) is time that he or she is not devoting to other meaningful tasks or endeavors.
- Using one's skills and accumulated experience.

What can help at a later stage to achieve such success is:

- Policies and practices that are related to work–life balance.
- Policies and practices that facilitate people in this cohort to have an impact on the long-term results of the company.

Notes

1 The resolutions may be viewed at http://www.boe.es/boe/dias/2007/10/30/pdfs/A44037-44048. pdf (in Spanish; accessed Sept. 15, 2009).
2 In 1990 only 25 percent of youth between 26 and 29 lived at home with their parents. The latest Youth Reports indicate that, in 1996, 46 percent of the population between 26 and 29 still lived at the home of origin, and in 2000 this figure was 50 percent (Moreno Mínguez, 2003).
3 Most universities do not offer on-campus work (or they may offer on-campus jobs to no more than 0.5 percent of the students).
4 The Human Development Index (HDI) of the Human Development Report (UNDP) is a composite index measuring average achievement in three basic dimensions of human development—a long and healthy life, knowledge, and a decent standard of living. Performance in each dimension is expressed as a value between 0 and 1 and the higher the number the better the result. This data corresponds to 2002: http://globalis.gvu.unu.edu/indicator_detail.cfm?Country=ES&IndicatorID=19

References

Bover, O. 2008. Wealth inequality and household structure: US vs. Spain. *Documentos de Trabajo*. Madrid: Banco de España.

El País. 2009. El permiso de paternidad será de cuatro semanas desde 2011. In ELPAÍS.com (Ed.), *El País*. Madrid: El País.

Eurostat. 2009. *Unemployment Rate by Gender*. Brussels: European Commission.

Eurostat. 2010a. *Mean and Median Income by Household Type*. Brussels: European Commission.

Eurostat. 2010b. *Persons Employed Part-Time (Percentage of Total Employment)*. Brussels: European Commission.

Eurostat. 2010c. *Tertiary Education Graduates*. Brussels: European Commission.

Glaser, B. G. & Strauss, A. 1967. *The Discovery of Grounded Theory*. Chicago, IL: Aldine.

INE. 2008. *Las Mujeres en Cifras 1983–2008*. Madrid: Instituto de la Mujer (Ministerio de Igualdad).

Johnson, K., Carreyrou, J. & Walker, M. 2005. Amid Europe's gloom, Spain blossoms with short-term jobs. *Wall Street Journal—Eastern Edition*, 246(64): A1–A13.

Moreno Mínguez, A. 2003. The late emancipation of Spanish youth: Keys for understanding. *Electronic Journal of Sociology*. Available at: http://www.sociology.org/content/vol7.1/minguez.html (accessed Apr. 5, 2011).

Solsten, E. & Meditz, S. W. 1988. Spain: Social values and attitudes. In *Country Studies*, Vol. 2010. Washington, DC: U.S. Library of Congress.

19

Careers in the United Kingdom
Emma Parry and Michael Dickmann

The United Kingdom (U.K.) is an entity that consists of England, Wales, Scotland and Northern Ireland. It is a constitutional monarchy governed by a parliament situated in London, its capital. The total area of the United Kingdom is approximately 243,610 square kilometers, and it had 58.8 million inhabitants at the last official census in 2001, rising to an estimated 61.8 million in 2009 (ONS, 2010). This makes the U.K. the third most populous country in the European Union, of which it has been a member since 1973.

The Cultural Context

In Schwartz's (1992) framework, the U.K. is one of the English speaking cluster, as is the U.S.A. The countries in this cluster score highly on two main cultural dimensions. First, English speaking clusters are high on "autonomy," which is defined as the freedom and independence to pursue one's own ideas, as opposed to "embeddedness" and shared collectivism (Schwartz, 1992). This support's Hofstede's (1991) finding that the U.K. scores highly (89) on individualism. Second, English speaking countries score highly on "mastery," which is the use of assertive actions to change the world, as opposed to "harmony," which is described as fitting into the world as it is. High mastery can be seen in the U.K. through the country's historically relatively dominant role in world events.

While Hofstede sees culture through an attitudinal lens (programming of the mind; Hofstede, 2001), Tayeb (2003: 10) integrates both attitudes and behaviors in a definition of culture as "historically evolved values, attitudes, and meanings that are learned and shared by the members of a community and which influence their material and non-material way of life." Using the (organizational) culture framework of Edgar Schein (1992), French (2010) distinguishes between artifacts, norms and values as well as basic assumptions in outlining overlapping national and organizational culture levels. Concentrating on English culture, Fox (2005) has used a range of descriptors. The anthropologist observes high levels of social inhibition, discomfort in social situations and interactions, embarrassment, awkwardness and fear of intimacy and calls this a "social dis-ease" of the English. One can imagine the career impact in terms of social networking that might result. Moreover, Fox identifies reserve and inhibition, expressed through the importance of politeness, as further cultural artifacts. Next, she argues that humor is more pervasive in English society and more highly valued as a capability. In other cultures there may be a time and place for humor, but in England it is a constant, expressed through irony, wit, banter, teasing, mockery, wordplay, satire, understatement, humorous self-depreciation, sarcasm and silliness. Humor is the "default mode" of English conversation (Fox, 2005: 402).

Key values and norms in England relate to fair play (demonstrated for instance through the importance of queuing), modesty (at least the appearance of modesty, as the author states that the English are not naturally modest; Fox, 2005: 408) and courtesy (saying "sorry" when bumped into). Other descriptors used include stoicism and a high acceptance of eccentricity. Deeper assumptions in English society are seen to relate to pragmatism and empiricism and a certain class-consciousness (Marr, 2007). There are many class indicators for a person familiar with the culture, including speech, manner, taste and lifestyle choice. Many of these values, norms and patterns of behavior have an impact on one's identity and pursuit of careers as well as on the social capital one can resort to.

Economic and Demographic Trends

The U.K.'s economy is highly geared to services, and its gross domestic product (GDP) is amongst the top ten in the world. The service sector has over the last few decades grown substantially, and it constituted more than two-thirds of GDP in 2009. The City of London, the financial district of the capital, is dominated by banks, insurance companies and other financial firms and is one of the key financial centers of the world. Other important industries include tourism, creative services, the automotive and pharmaceutical sectors and other professional services such as legal or consulting.

The U.K.'s economy is highly international. For instance, there are intensive flows of goods and services in terms of imports and exports. Moreover, many major MNCs headquartered in Britain—such as BP,

PricewaterhouseCoopers, GlaxoSmithKline—are highly global and occupy high ranks on the OECD's list of transnational firms. This opens a range of opportunities for managers, technical experts and others to pursue an international career.

The U.K. is unlike many countries in the European Union in that it has experienced population growth rates of about 0.5 percent in the last decade. Recently, natural population growth—in 2008 the average total fertility rate per woman was 1.96 babies—has overtaken net immigration as the main contributor of this growth.

Living abroad is a widespread phenomenon. The United Nations (U.N.) estimated that there were 191 million migrants in 2005 (U.N., 2006), representing 3 percent of the global population. The reasons to leave one's country to live and work in another can be linked to political instability, poverty, climate changes, persecution and high levels of insecurity. Other important reasons for migration include conflict, public health situations, gender policies and their implications, the openness of borders and diverse levels of economic development.

Germany, France, the U.K. and Spain (in descending order) are home to some of the world's largest immigrant populations (U.N., 2006). Britain is often regarded as relatively open to immigration, with approximately 8 percent of the population having moved to the UK from abroad. In the last official census, more than 1 million people identified themselves as black, more than 1 million as Indian and more than 0.5 million as mixed race or Pakistani. This ethnic diversity varies substantially by region and city. For instance, London and Leicester are estimated to have more than 30 percent non-white citizens. This encourages multiculturalism and diversity in the world of work, with effects as to the tolerance and culture-sensitive policies, practices and behaviors needed.

Educational System and Occupational Background

As in some other countries, educational matters are devolved from the centre to the level of the country. Thus the educational systems of Scotland and Wales differ from that of England. Universal state education has been compulsory in the U.K. for more than a century now. The majority of children are educated in the state sector, while the U.K. has a large number of independent schools, some of these "public schools" (such as Eton, Harrow and Rugby) being well known outside the U.K. England also has some famous and highly ranked universities such as the University of Cambridge, University of Oxford, Imperial College London and University College London. For MBA students, institutions such as London Business School or Cranfield School of Management are regularly ranked highly in publications such as the *Financial Times* or *The Economist.*

The creativity and impact of British inventors can be seen from a number of notable deeds. For instance, the steam locomotive (Richard Trevithick and Andrew Vivian), the jet engine (Frank Whittle) and the hovercraft (Christopher Cockerell) were invented by Britons. The electric motor by Michael Faraday, the first practical telephone by Alexander Graham Bell and the internet by Tim Berners-Lee are further examples. Moreover, some notable advances in science were achieved by Britons, such as the laws of motion and gravity (Isaac Newton), the theory of evolution (Charles Darwin) and the structure of DNA (Francis Crick and others), as well as the discovery of penicillin (Alexander Fleming).

For almost three decades now it has been the aim of various governments to increase the percentage of U.K. school students who proceed to university. In fact, the assumption is that a university degree will have many beneficial effects throughout life. For instance, the chances of becoming unemployed are lower and the time to find a new job is shorter for university graduates compared to non-university-educated persons. With respect to the three occupational groups that the 5C research analyzed, it has become the norm that managers and nurses have gone to university, while it is an exception if a blue-collar worker has attended tertiary education. While there are certainly many self-made managers in the U.K., a bachelor's degree (normally three years) has nowadays become an entry requirement for a "good" job. With respect to vocational training for blue-collar workers, the old apprenticeship approach has withered and been replaced by a system of national vocational qualifications (NVQs).

Career Trends and Patterns

As described in other country chapters, career trends and patterns have undergone substantial change in recent years. Based on ideas developed mostly in North America, new career theories stressing individualistic career patterns and drivers have become accepted into the mainstream. The book outlines these in more detail elsewhere. While individuals have gradually become seen to be the masters of their own careers, the role of the organization has mutated over time. However, it is probably wrong to say that at any time in the last three decades a majority of career academics or observers attributed no or only a marginal role to organizations to manage their staff's careers. Instead, the role of career management—providing coaching, mentoring, career systems and so on—has shifted.

In the 1990s the psychological contract between organizations and individuals became radically different in the wake of several rounds of downsizing, streamlining and reorganizations driven by the corporate strive for efficiency, quality and innovation (Conway and Briner, 2005). The new psychological contract stressed employability rather than security and focused on equipping professionals and other staff with usable skills, insights and knowledge. In Britain as in the U.S.A., this was the gradual birth of the career capitalist who would seek to maximize knowing how, knowing why and knowing whom. While this approach to careering was not new, it became more propagated, and individuals became more conscious of the need to invest in their own careers (Inkson and Arthur, 2001).

Increasingly, overseas work experience is seen as highly important to progress to the higher echelons in major MNCs. Thus global corporations have major leadership development programs that entail talent moving abroad to work and live (Dickmann and Baruch, 2011). The implications for their future career patterns and for corporate learning, coordination across borders and knowledge exploitation are immense (Dickmann, Brewster & Sparrow, 2008).

Findings From the Study

We will first describe where our research participants came from. Next, we will describe the main characteristics of our data on career success and career transitions.

Sampling

Interviewees were gathered through convenience sampling within the three occupational groups—nurses, businesspersons and blue-collar workers—and within the two age groups. The nurses interviewed were employed at a single NHS foundation trust hospital, situated in a large countryside town in the southeast of England. Businesspersons were identified via the alumni database of a single business school in the east of the U.K., although the interviewees themselves were located in the east, southeast and London. Blue-collar workers were identified through personal contacts. These interviewees resided in the east and southeast of the U.K.

Table 19.1 shows the profile of the sample involved in the interviews. It can be noted that the nurse sample is all female and the blue-collar sample all male. This is because of the general trends in these industries. Unfortunately, only one younger nurse was available for interview, as the nursing population in the hospitals used for the U.K. research tended to be older. It should also be noted that the all-white sample does not reflect the multicultural nature of the U.K. population and therefore may bias the results.

Meanings of Career Success

Career Success Themes in the U.K.

Across the sample as a whole, the following four meanings of career success were coded for five or more of the 17 research participants:

Job/task characteristics	(8 people)
Achievement	(8 people)
Work–life balance	(6 people)
Satisfaction	(6 people)

Details can be found in Table 19.2.

What Can Be Learned From This?

Job/task characteristics was endorsed as a meaning of career success across occupational, generational and gender subsamples in the U.K. Most of the responses in this area (five people) fell into the sub-category

Table 19.1 U.K. sample profile

	Business graduates		Nurses		Blue-collar workers	
	Older	Younger	Older	Younger	Older	Younger
N =	3	4	4	1	3	2
Gender	1 female, 2 males	4 males	4 females	1 female	3 males	2 males
Race	All white	All white	All white	All white	All white	All white
	7		5		5	

Total N = 17.

Table 19.2 Meanings of career success in the United Kingdom

	Occupation			Gender		Generation		Total number mentioning category
Total number of interviewees = 17	Nurse 5	Blue-collar 5	Business 7	Female 6	Male 11	Younger 7	Older 10	
Person								
Satisfaction	3	2	1	4	2	2	4	6
Achievement	1	2	5	2	6	3	5	8
Learning and development	0	1	2	0	3	2	1	3
Self-actualization	1	0	1	1	1	2	0	2
Job								
Job security	0	0	1	0	1	1	0	1
Job/task characteristics	3	1	4	4	4	2	6	8
Job performance	0	0	0	0	0	0	0	0
Performing one's role	0	0	0	0	0	0	0	0
Contributing to organizational success	0	0	0	0	0	0	0	0
Interaction with the environment								
Social working environment	0	0	1	0	1	1	0	1
Network	0	0	0	0	0	0	0	0
Recognition	1	0	1	1	1	1	1	2
Work–life context/balance	2	2	2	2	4	3	3	6
Making a difference	0	0	0	0	0	0	0	0
Material output								
Basic survival	0	0	0	0	0	0	0	0
Financially supporting family	1	0	1	1	1	1	1	2
Affording material goods	0	0	0	0	0	0	0	0
Financial security	0	0	1	0	1	1	0	1

of seeing results. The responses in this category were given by both nurses (3) and business graduates (2). The following quote is from a younger male business graduate:

> Some people like to get the money in the door and then worry about the rest of it. But I'm much more focused on making sure that the jobs we've got, that we do well. You know, we look at the detail of the work and develop the people in the process . . . improve the systems that we have to work with, to work with a commercial team on bringing new work in.

For other people, job/task characteristics referred to the scope and variety of tasks (one person), autonomy or participation (one person), having a reasonable workload (one person) and responsibility (one person).

Achievement was also seen as important as a meaning of career success, with eight participants suggesting meanings related to achievement. In this case five of the eight individuals citing achievement as a meaning of career success were business graduates, two were blue-collar workers and one was a nurse. Six out of the eight were female (although this reflects the makeup of the business graduate and blue-collar sample). Achievement was a popular meaning of career success across both generations. Four of the eight participants saw achievement as relating to financial rewards. For example, one younger male business graduate explained:

> What I saw as success at that point onwards was I wanted to earn more money.

Other participants saw achievement as promotions or advancement (two people), outperforming others (one person), a leadership position (one person) or improved job performance (one person). Like the U.S.A., the U.K has a highly individualistic culture; therefore it is not surprising that achievement has arisen as an important meaning of career success.

Work–life balance was another meaning of career success, cited by six of our interviewees. The perception of work–life balance as important occurred across all occupational groups, both generations and both genders. Four of the six participants citing work–life balance as a meaning of career success discussed the importance of combining personal life with work. The other two participants suggested that career success was being able to address others' (such as family's) needs. One older female nurse explained:

> For me it's, it's being happy in what I do and, probably more importantly, fitting in with home life, is what I would say would be my priority for career success.

Satisfaction was also seen as a meaning of career success for six inter-viewees. Interviewees from all three occupations and both genders and generations endorsed satisfaction as a meaning of career success. Four of the six interviewees discussed satisfaction with their work or job, two discussed life quality and one also talked about enjoyment and fun.

Career Themes in the U.K.

The findings for meanings of career success in the U.K. are consistent with the cultural values suggested by Schwartz (1992), as the focus on achievement, work–life balance, satisfaction and even seeing results (job/task characteristics) indicates that these individuals feel in control of their own career outcomes and appreciate the autonomy to manage their own work and careers as they see fit.

Career Transitions

The vast majority of career transitions discussed by our interviewees were self-driven. See Tables 19.3 and 19.4. In fact 16 of the 17 inter-viewees reported that their career transition was driven by their own initiative owing to some internal source, while six interviewees also cited external stimuli for a career transition. These six suggested that orga-nizational factors had initially driven their career transition, although they had then made the move through their own initiative. One younger male business graduate described how he regularly moves jobs in order to carry on developing himself:

> I'm also determined to get as much as I can out of it in terms of training and experience because I'm not naive enough to believe that, you know, it may last two years, it may last three years, at some point it may not be lasting at all, and so I want to get as much out of it as I possibly can to move on to something else.

This finding is consistent with the characteristics of the English speaking cultural cluster, according to Schwartz (1992), and with the notion of the individualistic culture found in the U.K. These findings are also con-sistent with the findings in the other country from Schwartz's English speaking cluster in our data—the United States.

Table 19.3 Career transition patterns in the United Kingdom

Total number of interviewees = 17 N =	Occupation			Gender		Generation		Total number mentioning category
	Nurse 5	Blue-collar 5	Business 7	Female 6	Male 11	Younger 7	Older 10	
Internally driven causes/triggers of career transitions:								
Own initiative (internal source)	4	5	7	5	11	7	9	16
Own initiative (external source/stimuli)	1	3	2	1	5	3	3	6
Externally driven causes/triggers of career transitions:								
Driven by graduation/certification	0	0	0	0	0	0	0	0
Driven by completion of obligation	0	0	0	0	0	0	0	0
Unsought opportunities	0	0	0	0	0	0	0	0
Counsel/encouragement	1	0	0	1	0	0	1	1
Organizationally driven	2	0	4	3	3	4	2	6
Health	0	0	0	0	0	0	0	0
Family role	0	0	0	0	0	0	0	0
Macro factors	0	1	1	0	2	1	1	2
Luck and contingencies	0	0	0	0	0	0	0	0
Individuals' management of career transitions:								
Job search	0	1	0	0	1	0	1	1
Planning/setting goals and priorities	0	0	0	0	0	0	0	0
Organization and time management	0	0	0	0	0	0	0	0
Formal education, training, short courses	1	0	2	1	2	2	1	3
Informal training	2	0	0	2	0	0	2	2

Table 19.4 External influences upon career transitions in the United Kingdom

Total number of interviewees = 17 N =	Occupation			Gender		Generation		Total number mentioning category
	Nurse 5	Blue-collar 5	Business 7	Female 6	Male 11	Younger 7	Older 10	
Boss/superior								
Support	1	1	2	1	3	3	1	4
Barrier	0	0	1	0	1	1	0	1
Peers								
Support	3	0	1	3	1	2	2	4
Barriers	1	0	1	1	1	1	1	2
Family								
Support	1	3	0	1	3	3	1	4
Barriers	1	0	1	1	1	1	1	2
Friends								
Support	1	1	0	1	1	1	1	2
Barriers	0	0	0	0	0	0	0	0
Organization								
Support	1	0	2	1	2	3	0	3
Barriers	0	0	0	0	0	0	0	0
Network								
Work	0	0	1	0	1	1	0	1
Personal	0	0	0	0	0	0	0	0
Professional	0	0	0	0	0	0	0	0
Education and training	1	0	0	1	0	0	1	1
Financial situation	0	0	0	0	0	0	0	0
Role of luck and contingencies	0	0	2	1	1	1	1	2

Individual Management of Career Transitions

The most common way that our interviewees had sought new career transitions was through formal education (three people), informal training (two people) and job search activities. Both of the interviewees who had used informal training were older nurses. This may be a reflection of the tradition of nurses historically "learning on the job" (younger nurses now undertake formal undergraduate degree training). Interestingly, most interviewees found it difficult to think of strategies by which they had managed the career transition, suggesting that, while career transitions are self-initiated, our interviewees did not take any conscious steps to manage them.

External Influences on Career Transitions

Interviewees obtained the support that they needed during career transitions from their family, peers and boss or superior (four people for each). Nurses appeared more likely to rely on their peers, whereas blue-collar workers were more likely to obtain support from their families. A small number of interviewees also suggested that family (two people), peers (two people) and their boss or superior (one person) could act as a barrier to a career transition. Friends (two people) and organizational support (three people) were also cited as external influencing factors of career transitions.

Generally, family support took the form of social support. For example, one younger male blue-collar worker described how his girlfriend had supported him when he started his own business:

> She is very encouraging. She's always sort of getting me to do something. And she keeps nagging me about things.

Peer support tended to take the form of more practical task support, whereas support from a boss or superior could be social, task or career support.

Themes and Implications

A number of themes can be identified through our examination of the U.K. interview findings. However, it should be noted that, as only a small number of interviews were conducted, these should not be taken as being generalizable to the U.K. population as a whole.

Autonomy and Individualization

- The nature of the U.K. as universalistic is apparent in our interviewees' career experiences. Individuals appear to like to use their own initiative when managing their careers.
- This suggests that career management schemes should allow employees' careers to be self-directed, permitting individuals to have some control over their own career outcomes and to make career choices for themselves.

Age and Generations

- There is some evidence either that individuals' aspirations for their careers change as they get older, or that the older generation (Baby Boomers) have different needs to the younger generation. For example, older individuals were more likely to define career success as being about satisfaction, achievement and job/task characteristics, whereas younger individuals were more likely to focus on learning and development.

Career Success as a Multi-Dimensional Construct

- Interviewees endorsed a range of factors as constituents of career success, most notably job/task characteristics, achievement, satisfaction and work–life balance.
- Interestingly, most interviewees identified a number of different factors as dimensions of career success, indicating that, while financial and hierarchical achievement is still important for individuals, it might not be sufficient. Employers should also look at job content and work–life balance in order to stratify their employees.

Conclusions

In summary, therefore, conceptualizations of career success within the U.K. sample are similar to those in the other English speaking country in our research, the U.S.A. Career success was generally viewed as being about job/task characteristics, achievement, work–life balance and satisfaction. This is consistent with the cultural values suggested by Schwartz

(1992) for the English speaking cultural cluster. Most career transitions experienced by our interviewees were self-driven, supporting the notion that individuals in today's organizations take responsibility for their own careers. Interviewees most commonly managed their career transitions through formal education or informal training and obtained support from family, peers or their line manager. Taken as a whole the data support the idea of the U.K. as an individualistic culture and of careers as being self-directed.

References

Conway, N. & Briner, R. (Eds.). 2005. *Understanding Psychological Contracts at Work: A Critical Evaluation of Theory and Research.* Oxford, U.K.: Oxford University Press.

Dickmann, M. & Baruch, Y. (Eds.). 2011. *Global Careers.* London: Routledge.

Dickmann, M., Brewster, C. & Sparrow, P. (Eds.). 2008. *International Human Resource Management: A European Perspective* (2nd ed.). London: Routledge.

Fox, K. 2005. Watching the English: The hidden rules of English behaviour. In E. Schein (Ed.), *Organizational Behaviour.* London: Hodder & Stoughton.

French, R. 2010. *Cross-Cultural Management in Work Organisations.* London: CIPD.

Hofstede, G. 1991. *Cultures and Organisations.* London: McGraw-Hill.

Hofstede, G. 2001. *Culture's Consequences* (2nd ed.). Thousand Oaks, CA: Sage.

Inkson, K. & Arthur, M. 2001. How to be a successful career capitalist. *Organizational Dynamics,* 30(1): 48–60.

Marr, A. 2007. *A History of Modern Britain.* London: Macmillan.

ONS. 2010. *Fertility: Rise in UK Fertility Continues.* London: Office for National Statistics.

Schein, E. H. 1992. *Organizational Culture and Leadership.* San Francisco, CA: Jossey-Bass.

Schwartz, S. H. 1992. Universals in the structure and content of values: Theoretical advances and empirical tests in 20 countries. In M. P. Zanna (Ed.), *Advances in Experimental Social-Psychology:* 1–65. Orlando, FL: Academic.

Tayeb, M. H. (ed.). 2003. *International Management: Theories and Practices.* London: Pearson Education.

United Nations (U.N.). 2006. *International Migration 2006.* Population Division, Department of Economic and Social Affairs, United Nations. Available at: http://un.org/esa/population/publications/2006Migration_Chart/Migration2006.pdf (accessed July 9, 2009).

20

Careers in the United States

*Jon P. Briscoe, Douglas T. Hall, Mireia Las Heras
and Julie Unite*

The Cultural Context

Perhaps more than any other feature, U.S. culture can be characterized by its individualistic values. From its colonial origins U.S. culture was driven by a desire to pursue religious and political freedom and to live life according to the "beat of one's own drummer," as Henry David Thoreau proclaimed in his 1854 book *Walden.*

In Schwartz's (2006) framework, the U.S.A. is decidedly represented by the cultural dimensions of "autonomy" and "mastery." Autonomy is easily seen. According to Hofstede's (1991) research, the U.S.A. is the most individualistic country in the world, and individual freedom and perception of choice are of paramount importance.

Mastery is also not hard to observe. It is the belief that things can be controlled. Americans (we refer to U.S. career actors in this chapter as "American," while recognizing that other countries can accurately be labeled "American" as well) are dominant in an attitude of *internal* locus of control, believing they direct events and are not directed by them.

An archetypal model of "the American Dream" is that anyone can become anything. This is illustrated dramatically by the election of Barack Obama, who rose from very humble beginnings to the highest office in the land. Such perceived opportunity and potential, however, may also create cognitive dissonance for people when they feel as though their dreams and "possible selves" (Markus and Wurf, 1987) are not in fact realized.

This is a significant factor with career issues. In our experience it is often difficult for people in the U.S.A. to understand losing their jobs through "downsizing" without attributing some responsibility to themselves, which discourages them. In our view they often attribute more to themselves than may be merited, while underestimating the power of social institutions and economic mechanisms to influence careers.

Surprisingly for some, the U.S.A. emphasizes "hierarchy" more than "egalitarianism" in Schwartz's framework. The U.S.A. perceives itself as "the land of opportunity," and in that sense it seems that the opportunities might be distributed to all. But in fact the emphasis on mastery and autonomy makes Americans quite tolerant of great disparity in power. The working logic may be that successful people "earned" it so they deserve it. One example is that CEO pay in proportion to that of the lowest-paid worker is significantly higher in the U.S.A. than in any other country.

Beyond Schwartz's framework, Americans have a "doing" versus "being" (Kluckhohn & Strodbeck, 1961) attitude toward life. They are thus oriented to the future and its potential. This is in part an instrumental attitude that implies we can control our culture. It also seems to result in a culture that does not value the wisdom of the old, but the strength, potency and potential of youth. Relatedly, Americans have a short-term time orientation and are not as likely to look at the long-term ramifications of their actions or at the long-term lessons of the past.

Religious life plays a prominent role in the U.S.A. It has the highest level of religiosity of any country in the world, and over 90 percent of the country is theistic, with Christianity the leading religion. This has overtones for everything from politics to career choice and career success. It also plays out in interesting ways that counter other dominant cultural features. For example, many students who believe that God directs their lives have a hard time reconciling this with their simultaneous attitude of an internal locus of control.

Economic and Demographic Trends

Globalization and modernization have hit the U.S.A. dramatically, just as they have every other country. Many jobs, starting with manufacturing, have been outsourced to other countries, with even professional jobs and services being increasingly outsourced. This is especially threatening to blue-collar workers who work for large corporations. They once could count on high-paying work, and now they cannot even count on a job.

Earning power has gone down steadily to the point where many consider a two-income household necessary not to excel but simply to make ends meet. There seems to be a widening gap between the rich and the poor and working poor, with the middle class shrinking in size.

The U.S.A. is aging rapidly, approaching a time when two-thirds of the population will be of retirement age or older. One interesting aspect of this for career scholars is how the older generation will be utilized in the workforce, especially when, as this book is written, retirement accounts were wiped out for many in the 2008–09 recession.

Era portends interesting differences. The "greatest generation" (as opined by one popular newsman), who matured through World War II, were traditional in their views of authority and success and honored authority and had heroes (Bennis & Thomas, 2002). The "Baby Boomers" (those born to the World War II era parents up until 1964) came of age in a more complicated time and are more ambivalent about authority and trusting organizations, a factor certainly relevant for careers. The children of the Boomers, Generation X, grew up as "latchkey" children (meaning they returned from school to an empty home) who experienced two parents working and a higher rate of divorce than was the norm in prior years. The newest generation (Y) is savvy in technology. Growing up playing computer games, they have a more calculated and sophisticated sense of, and willingness to take, risk. They want work–life balance. They are much more interested in being recognized and being given opportunities *now* versus waiting, and they are not likely to honor authority for its own sake—quite the opposite.

Ever increasing diversity within the U.S. population is a major issue, recently highlighted by tensions around immigration reform, mostly focused upon Latinos. Recently in Chicago, Latinos displaced African Americans (blacks) as the largest minority group in the city. Even in small towns, Latinos have a decided presence. However, as expected, most diversity is concentrated in large cities. There is anxiety on the part of some over losing a cultural identity if English is compromised as some sort of working standard.

While the U.S.A. is diverse, unlike the case in other countries overseas experiences are not a common rite of passage for youth or a requirement for business executives (although for the latter group this is starting to change). In this sense, the U.S. population is neither broadly cosmopolitan nor sophisticated in cross-cultural knowledge. This is likely the result of being a very large cultural (and almost geographic) island. It would take 50–60 hours to drive from the East Coast to the West Coast, and it may be that the country is large enough, powerful enough, prosperous enough and so on for youth not to feel the need to wander beyond its borders.

Career Trends and Patterns

Careers in the United States have undergone significant change in the last few decades. In 1976 Hall chronicled the emerging individualistic career with the label "protean" in a book titled *Careers in Organizations*. At this time, the organizational career was still assumed to be the norm.

While many people did not in fact have lifetime employment for most of the twentieth century (since the popularization of the modern bureaucracy), the psychological contract most people were operating under was "relational" (Rousseau, 1995). This meant that a posture of reciprocity and loyalty was the default assumption of employers and employees alike.

The new career environment is dominated by a transactional psychological contract, with terms like "free agent nation" (Pink, 2001) and the "war for talent" characterizing the employment situation. In the academic realm the "boundaryless" career (Arthur, 1994), in which the career actor crosses organizational, vocational, temporal and other boundaries, is the major gestalt employed by career theorists in addition to the protean career (Hall 1976, 2002).

However, while assumptions about employment have changed, it is very important to understand that most Americans do not necessarily prefer constant change; they just accept it as inevitable. While many understand the nature of the new deal, only a portion of them have learned the skills to handle these new careers effectively. The old mental models are firmly in place, even as external conditions warrant a more modern approach to the career. The psychology governing U.S. individuals, like most humans, does not tolerate a huge amount of ambiguity and appreciates supportive work environments.

Companies also are rethinking the new performance-based contract. Briscoe and DeMuth (2003) found that out of more than 30 major U.S. corporations the majority were migrating toward a performance-based contract or had one in place, but a few excellent companies we consider progressive and with a long history of effective leadership development were rethinking this approach and emphasizing common values with employees in almost a "covenant" of sorts.

The terrorist attacks of September 11, 2001 should not be underestimated in their impact upon U.S. careers. Many people re-assessed their values and realized some of their long-term values such as family and shifted careers to be more congruent with such values (for example, they moved closer to home). This may have hastened a trend that was underway already—that of bringing the "whole person" to work more. It is much more popular and visible to bring personal values to work (family, religion and so on) or to bound work in a way that allows one to honor outside values. For example, articles about spirituality at work regularly appear in newspapers. In separate research from this we have heard anecdotes of executives refusing training or promotion for family reasons. This is dramatically different from the past and represents a real shift in work and identity.

Thus, while the new career may be more firmly in place in the U.S.A. than elsewhere, the details of this new arrangement are still being "negotiated" both within individuals and companies and between them.

Educational System/Occupational Background

A general cultural assumption is that further formal education results in higher earning power. The percentage of two-income households has increased dramatically, while earning power has shrunk. In this changing trajectory, a bachelor's degree (four-year university degree) is seen as simply an entry requirement for a "good" job in all professions and many trades.

A college-level degree has become a requirement for nurses, which it has not always been in the past, and many are now pursuing master's degrees, with some pursuing quasi-physician-level careers as practitioners. In business, anyone who can gather funds and be a successful entrepreneur can succeed without a college degree, including the celebrated CEO of Apple Computer, Steve Jobs. However, a business degree and preferably an MBA are typically seen as entry requirements for established corporations. With blue-collar workers, there is still some informal apprentice-based training, but increasingly such workers require formal certification or choose to pursue a college degree.

Findings From the Study

To understand our findings, it is useful to understand where our research participants come from.

Sampling

Interviewees were gathered primarily through convenience sampling in three geographical areas: Boston, MA, Northern Illinois and Madison, WI. The sample in Boston represents a relatively sophisticated, cosmopolitan, highly educated and urban workforce. The Northern Illinois sample includes a few Chicago "suburbanites" but mostly people from smaller towns in semi-rural Illinois. Finally, most of the nurse sample

Table 20.1 U.S. sample profile

	Business graduates		Nurses		Blue-collar workers	
	Older	*Younger*	*Older*	*Younger*	*Older*	*Younger*
N =	3	5	3	3	3	3
Gender	2 males, 1 female	4 females, 1 male	3 females	2 females, 1 male	2 males, 1 female	3 males
Race	All white	1 African American, 1 Asian American, 3 white	All white	All white	2 white, 1 Latina	2 white, 1 Latino
	N = 8		N = 6		N = 6	

Total N = 20.

was interviewed in Madison. Madison has some sophistication as a college town (home to the University of Wisconsin) but also represents a traditional "Midwest" community in many senses. While Madison is more liberal than most Midwest cities, the Midwest as a rule is much more conservative than areas in the Northeast or the West Coast. See Table 20.1 for a full profile of the U.S. sample.

It can be noted that the nurse sample is dominated by females and the blue-collar sample is dominated by males. This is more or less representative of trends in those industries.

Meanings of Career Success

Looking across the sample as a whole the following meanings of career success were coded by the research team for 5 or more of the 20 research participants:

Achievement	(8 people)
Recognition	(7 people)
Job performance	(7 people)
Making a difference	(7 people)
Job/task characteristics	(7 people)
Satisfaction	(6 people)
Learning and development	(5 people)

For details, see Table 20.2.

Table 20.2 Meanings of career success in the United States

Total number of interviewees N = 20	Occupation			Gender		Generation		Total number mentioning category
	Nurse 6	Blue-collar 6	Business 8	Female 11	Male 9	Younger 11	Older 9	9
Person	5	6	6	10	7	10	7	17
Satisfaction	2	1	3	4	2	3	3	6
Achievement	3	2	3	4	4	5	3	8
Learning and development	2	1	2	4	1	4	1	5
Self-actualization	2	1	1	2	2	3	1	4
Job	1	3	4	3	5	2	6	8
Job security	0	0	0	0	0	0	0	0
Job/task characteristics	2	2	3	2	5	2	5	7
Job performance	2	2	3	3	4	2	5	7
Performing one's role	1	2	1	1	3	1	3	4
Contributing to organizational success	1	1	1	2	1	0	3	3
Interaction with the environment	4	2	5	6	5	4	7	11
Social working environment	2	0	0	2	0	1	1	2
Network	0	0	0	0	0	0	0	0
Recognition	3	1	3	3	4	2	5	7
Work–life context/balance	0	1	3	2	2	2	2	4
Making a difference	5	1	1	5	2	4	3	7
Material output	1	3	1	3	2	1	4	5
Basic survival	0	0	0	0	0	0	0	0
Financially supporting family	0	4	0	1	3	1	3	4
Affording material goods	1	1	1	2	1	1	2	3
Financial security	0	2	0	0	2	1	1	2

What Can Be Learned From These?

Achievement was a popular meaning of career success across occupational, generational and gender subsamples in the U.S.A. It was most popular amongst nurses, males and the younger generation. The following quote represents achievement for one older businessman:

> But, in the bigger picture, I guess people gauge how successful you are as how and where you are in the food chain and how you fit into the organization— that's what it comes down to.
>
> (Older businessman)

For many people achievement is represented by formal promotion or position in the hierarchy, in a similar way to that indicated in the quote above. The fact that achievement is such a popular meaning of career success is not surprising, since the individualistic culture and belief that one can master the environment logically result in such an orientation.

It was a bit surprising that nurses were even more likely than businesspeople to emphasize achievement.

When it comes to recognition, it is a little less surprising that nurses were at the top in terms of the proportion of the sample indicating it was an important aspect of career success. Nurses are often not in power as compared to doctors and administrators but certainly are in a reciprocal role that appreciates recognition. Older people in our sample were also much more likely to define career success in terms of recognition. As an older male blue-collar worker remarked:

> For me career success is making a lot of money and being recognized for doing a good job.

In contrast the younger generation is somewhat more focused upon achievement versus recognition.

For many people effective job performance is how they define career success. This was more evident amongst blue-collar employees, males and older employees, with the difference most pronounced between young and old employees. There seemed to be a certain pride amongst older workers in doing a good job and, as the above quote reflects, being recognized for such.

While the distribution was equal across occupations, a greater proportion of males and older workers associated career success with desirable job/task characteristics. Reflecting upon the interviews does not offer a ready explanation of why males and older workers value these conditions so much more. It could be they were focused more on conditions than self-expression for some reason.

Making a difference was important predominantly for nurses. As one younger nurse said, for her career success was:

> being able to see what you've done, how you've helped in the long run.

This is not surprising, although it is important to note that this was *not* universally true across each culture represented in the study. The fact that nurses focus upon making a difference, achievement and recognition indicates that they have infused the career with meaning beyond its mere functional value.

For equal proportions of nurses, blue-collar workers and businesspeople, desirable job/task characteristics represented career success. However, males and older workers were much more likely to indicate this than females and younger workers. Why? For older workers it is not clear if this is a developed preference that younger workers will eventually develop or whether it is a difference belonging to an era. It is not immediately clear why males would report this more than females.

Basic career satisfaction and enjoying one's job/work were reported by a substantial number of research participants, with no clear pattern as to subsamples other than the fact that the blue-collars were half as likely as their nursing and business counterparts to report it.

Opposite to job/task characteristics females and younger employees are more likely to associate learning and development with career success. Learning and development represent a striving and changing mode. Consider how a younger blue-collar worker put it:

> Let's say if a situation, like in my situation, I think I've developed myself extremely well for what I've done. Am I wealthy? No. But still, I'm rich in what I've learned. . . . I would say, if I had to pinpoint what was most important, whether monetary or just my experience, I would definitely base it on my experience, just because I am younger and I still got a whole life ahead of me.
> (Younger male blue-collar worker)

Could it be that such a learning and development mode represents a trajectory more focused on "becoming," whereas job/task characteristics are more preferred by those who measure career success factors in a more "static" or ongoing fashion? Note that, while self-actualization was not coded for five or more research participants, those for whom it was coded were also more likely to be young and female.

Also, it should be recognized that career success is a changing target. For businesspeople especially, their values and definitions of career success seem to shift as they mature and gain experience. Consider this older businesswoman's explanation for how her career success had evolved:

> Well, at first, happiness meant to me making money. Then happiness meant having more power. And then happiness meant having the certain amount of recognized prestige. And then happiness meant being part of something really terrific. So it kind of—and then it would always be learning.
>
> (Older businesswoman)

Career Success Themes in the U.S.A.

The patterns of career success meanings reported here are consistent with the cultural values ascribed by Schwartz and others, and with the general independent career direction increasingly emphasized in the country. An emphasis upon achievement, recognition, job performance, making a difference, and learning and development all reflect a group of career actors who believe they have agency and even mastery over their career outcomes. This of course indicates that, to shape job and career conditions that lead to career success, leaders and organizations need to provide opportunities that offer autonomy and a transparent path to desirable outcomes.

Career Transitions

The most striking outcome from looking at the data for the U.S. sample (see Tables 20.3 and 20.4) is the degree to which the reported career transitions were self-driven. The data show that 12 of the 20 research participants reported initiating the transition completely on their own. Alongside this, while for some the initial stimulus was an outside condition, three people then exercised their agency to pursue a career transition. In contrast only a few participants indicated that events (such as downsizing) really outside of their control drove their transition.

This finding reflects again the theme of an individualistic culture and a self-directed career mentality. It is possible that these represent attribution more than reality—meaning that outside events are simply neither perceived nor acknowledged to any great extent by our U.S. sample—but many of the stories seemed to demonstrate otherwise. For example, an older businesswoman recalled a time when she purposefully removed herself from a successful senior role in a regional bank that she had worked hard to achieve. As she describes it she was worried

Table 20.3 Career transition patterns in the United States

	Occupation			Gender		Generation		Total number mentioning category
Total number of interviewees = 20 N =	Nurse 6	Blue-collar 6	Business 8	Female 11	Male 9	Younger 11	Older 9	
Internally driven causes/triggers of career transitions:								
Own initiative (internal source)	4	2	6	7	5	7	5	12
Own initiative (external source/stimuli)	0	1	2	1	2	2	1	3
Externally driven causes/triggers of career transitions:								
Driven by graduation/certification	1	0	1	0	2	2	0	2
Driven by completion of obligation	0	0	0	0	0	0	0	0
Unsought opportunities	0	1	2	2	1	2	1	3
Counsel/encouragement	0	2	2	3	1	2	2	4
Organizationally driven	2	1	1	2	2	0	4	4
Health	0	1	1	1	1	2	0	2
Family role	0	1	1	0	2	0	2	2
Macro factors	0	1	2	2	1	2	1	3
Luck and contingencies	0	0	2	1	1	1	1	2
Individuals' management of career transitions:								
Job search	2	1	3	4	2	5	1	6
Planning/setting goals and priorities	1	1	1	1	2	2	1	3
Organization and time management	0	0	3	2	1	3	0	3
Formal education, training, short courses	3	2	1	4	2	5	1	6
Informal training	2	1	1	2	2	2	2	4

Table 20.4 External influences upon career transitions in the United States

	Occupation			Gender		Generation		Total number mentioning category
Total number of interviewees = 20 N =	*Nurse* 6	*Blue-collar* 6	*Business* 8	*Female* 11	*Male* 9	*Younger* 11	*Older* 9	9
Boss/superior	1	3	4	4	4	3	5	8
Support	0	3	2	2	3	2	3	5
Barrier	0	0	2	1	1	1	1	2
Peers	5	2	5	10	2	7	5	12
Support	3	0	4	6	1	4	3	7
Barriers	2	2	1	4	1	3	2	5
Family	3	4	6	6	7	10	3	13
Barriers	0	0	0	0	0	0	0	0
Friends	0	3	2	1	4	4	1	5
Support	0	2	2	1	3	3	1	4
Barriers	0	1	0	0	1	1	0	1
Organization	4	2	5	7	4	6	5	11
Support	4	1	4	6	3	5	4	9
Barriers	0	1	2	2	1	1	2	3
Network	1	2	2	2	3	3	2	5
Work	0	1	1	1	1	0	2	2
Personal	1	2	0	0	3	2	1	3
Professional	0	1	0	0	1	0	1	1
Education and training	1	3	5	4	5	6	3	9
Financial situation	0	0	2	2	0	1	1	2
Role of luck and contingencies	0	0	2	1	1	1	1	2

about being put into a "box" and decided to look for a new learning opportunity:

> So I said, "I'm limiting myself." You know being a—I guess somebody one time introduced me as a nationally recognized expert in the business. And I kind of looked at myself and I said, "Oh no." . . . I wanted to move on from this industry.
>
> (Older businesswoman)

This sort of desire for learning and variety can be seen in an example related from an older blue-collar male as well:

> I worked there [a manufacturing facility] about five years and I got pretty bored so, like, meanwhile I built another house. Then I decided I was getting a little bored with that so I sold everything, packed my tools, and went out to California for a while.
>
> (Older male blue-collar worker)

While there was a definite independent streak in evidence amongst much of the sample, this is not to say that everyone has this sort of independence. One older nurse reported how, in a series of career transitions in her hospital, the new jobs were given to her but not sought:

> When I was doing clinical support, I was working that job plus working on the unit, also on the floor. And then when they took that job away, they put me in the, what we call the clinical development coordinator position.
>
> (Older female nurse)

In terms of patterns amongst subgroups, businesspeople, then nurses and then blue-collars were most likely to drive their own career transitions. Amongst gender and generational categories, females and younger workers were moderately more likely to drive career transitions than were their counterparts.

Individual Management of Career Transitions

The data indicate that the most common ways individuals managed their career changes were through seeking new employment and through obtaining more education and training. "Consequential thinking" (anticipating and planning for outcomes in a cause-and-effect way) and experimenting with possible alternatives were also ways of managing the transition.

External Influences Upon Career Transition

Family, peers and one's employing organization were all cited by more than half of the sample as influencing their transitions, with one's boss and education/training discussed by almost half. In the majority of cases, these influencing factors were seen as positive.

Family was not only the most commonly mentioned influence amongst our research participants but also cited as a positive influence in every case. For example, one young businesswoman discussed the critical factors in helping her explore a career change and leave a job that troubled her without a new one:

> Probably husband support. You know, just that you know it's like, we will be fine working on one income and we'll just make it, and you know our main goal now is to start our family and move on with him.

As a proportion of responses, boss and peers were more likely than other groups to be perceived as having a negative impact upon career transitions. Sometimes they inspired them by being unsupportive or difficult in psychosocial or political ways. But, again, note that they were more often a positive influence. Organizations were seen as primarily positive influences. After all, they provided the majority of opportunities and, while they could be perceived as inhibiting desired transitions, they did not seem to receive the negative attributions that sometimes were directed toward peers and bosses.

Themes and Implications

A few broad themes and implications are noted here that are designed for practitioners. The reader is cautioned *not* to interpret these as applying to all Americans and to realize that diverse approaches are exhibited by individuals and should be reflected by practitioners.

A Need for Being Self-Directed and Autonomous

- Employees like to understand how they can directly impact the outcomes of their work and career, and most people do not like simply fulfilling roles.
- Work design, motivational techniques, career development and so on should allow some participative role for the employee, and transparency. If this is perceived as contrived, it will backfire.

- In career development and leadership development, employees may need to be made more aware of the external factors (people, resources and so on) that can influence their actions and outcomes, in order to make more effective decisions.
- Recognition is appreciated and even expected to validate one's contributions.

Marching to the Beat of One's Own Drummers: Myriad Forms of Career Success

- Achievement and recognition are high on many people's list, but diverse definitions of career success are the norm. Leadership, motivation, retention, career development, recognition, compensation and so on should be flexible enough to recognize many different needs and not assume that "one size fits all."

The Psychological Contract Has Changed, or Has It?

- While we see that people are managing their careers more than in the past, we also see that they recognize the organization as a key source of career opportunities. In our view people want to be independent, but this does not mean constant mobility or preclude a desire for community at work.

The Whole Person Has Arrived

- Whereas in the past people were more likely to give up a lot of themselves for work, this is much less so now, and they want work and career to meet many of their needs.
- Work–family balance is one way that people are seeking to honor their whole selves and the people important to those selves. Virtually every major company is looking at efforts to improve work–family balance.

Age Is Not What It Used to Be

- Increasing life spans, shifting assumptions about retirement, shrinking retirement accounts and an aging society all add up to a reexamination of what work means for older Americans. Companies would be wise not to make assumptions about older generations' desires and abilities.

- The youngest generation in the workforce is rewriting age rules as well. They desire more work–life balance and meaning than was typical of other generations at their career stage.

References

Arthur, M. B. 1994. The boundaryless career: A new perspective for organizational inquiry. *Journal of Organizational Behavior*, 15: 295–306.

Bennis, W. G. & Thomas, R. J. 2002. *Geeks and Geezers: How Era, Values, and Defining Moments Shape Leaders*. Boston, MA: Harvard Business School Press.

Briscoe, J. P. & DeMuth, Rachel F. 2003. The impact of the protean career on executive development practice: Evidence from 32 North American companies. Society for Industrial and Organizational Psychology annual conference, Orlando, FL, Apr. 12.

Hall, D. T. 1976. *Careers in Organizations*. Glenview, IL: Scott, Foresman.

Hall, D. T. 2002. *Careers In and Out of Organizations*. London: Sage.

Hofstede, G. 1991. *Cultures and Organizations: Software of the Mind*. London: McGraw-Hill.

Kluckhohn, F. & Strodbeck, F. L. 1961. *Variations in Value Orientations*. Evanston, IL: Row, Peterson.

Markus, H. & Wurf, E. 1987. The dynamic self-concept: A social psychological perspective. *Annual Review of Psychology*, 38: 299–337.

Pink, D. H. 2001. *Free Agent Nation: How America's New Independent Workers Are Transforming the Way We Live*. New York: Warner.

Rousseau, D. M. 1995. *Psychological Contracts in Organizations*. Thousand Oaks, CA: Sage.

Schwartz, S. H. 2006. A theory of cultural value orientations: Explication and applications. *Comparative Sociology*, 5(2–3): 136–182.

Index

Note: References are to page numbers: *f* and *t* indicate figures and tables, and 'n' refers to a note.